COMPUTER AWARENESS

Highly Useful for
SSC, Railway, Banking, DSSSB, CPCT, State PCS & Other One Day Exams

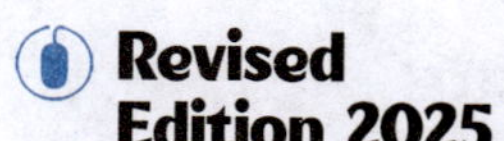

COMPUTER AWARENESS

Highly Useful for

SSC, Railway, Banking, DSSSB, CPCT, State PCS & Other One Day Exams

Author

Shaifali Saini

ARIHANT PUBLICATIONS (INDIA) LIMITED

Administrative & Production Offices

Regd. Office

'Ramchhaya' 4577/15, Agarwal Road, Darya Ganj, New Delhi -110002
Tele: 011- 47630600, 43518550

Head Office

Kalindi, TP Nagar, Meerut (UP) - 250002
Tel: 0121-7156203, 7156204

Sales & Support Offices

Agra, Ahmedabad, Bengaluru, Bareilly, Chennai, Delhi, Guwahati, Hyderabad, Jaipur, Jhansi, Kolkata, Lucknow, Nagpur & Pune.

PRICE ₹ 185.00

PO No. : TXT-59-T070914-5-26

Published by Arihant Publications (India) Ltd.

For further information about the books published by Arihant, log on to www.arihantbooks.com or e-mail at info@arihantbooks.com

CONTENTS

01 Introduction to Computer

- The word computer is derived from the Latin word **computare**, which means **to calculate** or **to count**.
- Computer is an automatic electronic device that accepts data as **input**, processes this data and produces information as **output**.
- It can store, retrieve and manipulate data to perform a wide range of tasks, from simple calculations to complex simulations and communications.
- **Charles Babbage** is known as the father of Computer and **Edward Roberts** is known as the father of Personal Computer.
- Computer Literacy Day is celebrated on **2nd December** every year.

In this Chapter

- Components of Computer
- Basic Functions of Computer
- History of Computers
- Generations of Computer
- Classification of Computer
- Characteristics of Computer
- Limitations of Computer
- Applications of Computer

"Computers have lots of memory but no imagination.

~ Bill Gates"

Components of Computer

A computer is a system made up of several interconnected parts, each playing a specific role in the overall functioning of the device. The primary components include:

1. Input Unit

- The input unit allows users to enter **data** and **instructions** into the computer. It converts the data into a form that the computer can process.
- Some of the common input devices are keyboard, mouse, joystick, scanner, floppy disk, barcode reader, etc.

2. Central Processing Unit (CPU)

- CPU is the main component of computer, responsible for processing instructions and performing calculations. It is known as the **brain of computer**.
- It has three main components
  - (i) **Arithmetic Logic Unit** (ALU) performs arithmetic and logical operations.
  - (ii) **Control Unit** (CU) directs the flow of data and instructions, coordinating the activities of all other components.
  - (iii) **Memory Unit** (MU) is responsible for storing data and instructions temporarily while the CPU processes them.

3. Output Unit

- The output unit displays or presents the processed data as result to the user. It converts data from **machine-readable** form into a **human-readable** format.
- Some common output devices are monitor, printer, speaker, etc.

Basic Functions of Computer

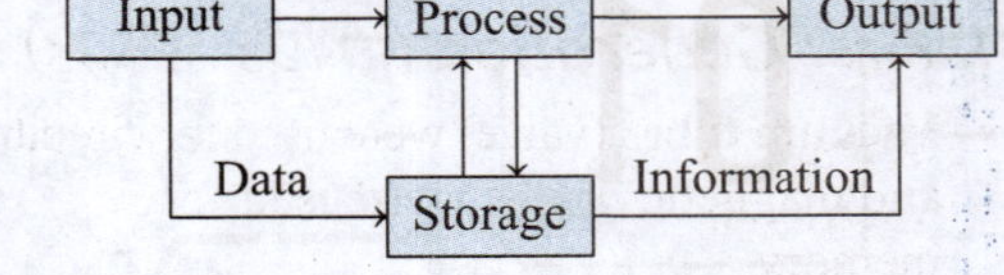

1. **Input** The process of giving instructions to the computer using various input devices like keyboard, mouse, scanner and microphone etc., is called input.
2. **Process** The computer processes the input data according to the given instructions. This is primarily done by the CPU.
3. **Storage** Computer saves the information for later use. This involves both **temporary storage** (like RAM) and **permanent storage** (like hard drives).
4. **Output** After processing the input data, computer produces result as output.

History of Computers

Invention	Inventor	Description
Abacus (1602)	Tim Cranmer	▪ Abacus was the first calculating device, invented in **Babylon** around 2400 BCE. ▪ Beads are used on rods to perform arithmetic operations.
Napier's Bones (1617)	John Napier	▪ An early calculating tool used for multiplication and division. ▪ First calculating device that uses the decimal point.
Pascaline (1642)	Blaise Pascal	▪ A mechanical calculator, performed addition and subtraction using gears and dials. ▪ It is also called **adding machine**.
Leibniz's Calculator (1673)	Gottfried Wilhelm Leibniz	▪ Improved on Pascal's design to perform multiplication and division. ▪ It was known as **Stepped Reckoner**.
Difference Engine (1822)	Charles Babbage	▪ It was powered by turning a hand crank calculating machine to compute and print mathematical tables.
Analytical Engine (1837)	Charles Babbage	▪ It was a general-purpose mechanical computer with components like an arithmetic logic unit, control flow and memory. ▪ It is considered the first automatic mechanical computer.
Tabulating Machine (1884)	Herman Hollerith	▪ A mechanical device used for processing data. ▪ Used **punched cards** to automatically collect and tabulate data.
ABC (1939)	John Atanasoff and Clifford Berry	▪ The ABC (Atanasoff-Berry Computer) was the first automatic electronic digital computer.
Mark-1 (1944)	Howard H. Aiken	▪ One of the earliest fully automated electromechanical computer. ▪ Also known as the **ASCC** (Automated Sequence Controlled Calculator).
ENIAC (1945)	John Mauchly and J.P. Eckert	▪ It was the first programmable, general-purpose electronic digital computer.
EDVAC (1947)	John Mauchly and J.P. Eckert	▪ EDVAC, was one of the first computer to use **stored-program concept**. ▪ One of the first computer to use binary instead of decimal.
EDSAC (1949)	Maurice Wilkes	▪ It was the second stored program computer, developed at the **University of Cambridge**.
UNIVAC-1 (1951)	J.P. Eckert and John Mauchly	▪ First commercially available computer. ▪ Used magnetic tape for storage, unlike punch cards in earlier machines.
Microprocessor (1971)	Ted Hoff	▪ The introduction of the **Intel 4004** (first microprocessor) marked the beginning of microcomputers (PCs). ▪ Integrated thousands of transistors into a single chip.
CRAY-1 (1976)	Seymour Cray	▪ First commercially successful supercomputer, designed by **Seymour Cray** (known as the **father of supercomputer**).
Apple II (1977)	Steve Wozniak	▪ The Apple II was one of the first highly successful microcomputer (PC), introduced by Apple Inc.

Generations of Computer

1. First Generation (1940s-1950s)

- **Vacuum tubes** (valve) were used for circuitry and magnetic drums were used for memory.
- **Punch card** and **paper tape** were used for storage of data and software.
- Speed of computer was measured in **milliseconds**.
- **Low Level Language** (Machine language) was used for preparing software.
- They were bulky in size and consumed lot of electricity and generated significant heat.

Example ENIAC, EDVAL, UNIVAC, IBM 701, Mark I

2. Second Generation (1950s-1960s)

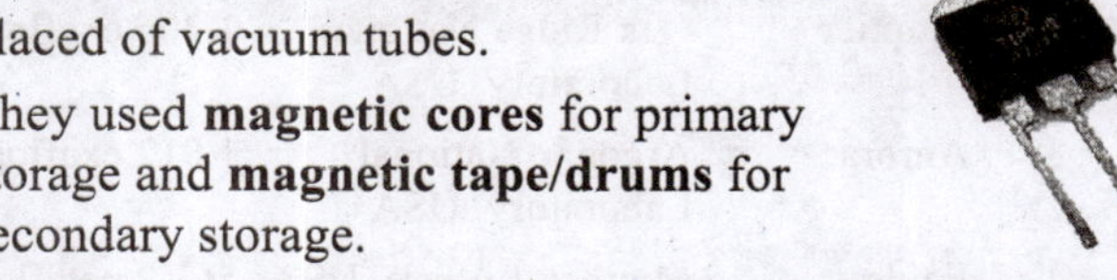

- **Semiconductor transistors** were used in placed of vacuum tubes.
- They used **magnetic cores** for primary storage and **magnetic tape/drums** for secondary storage.
- Their speed was slightly higher than the first generation, measured in **microseconds**.
- They used assembly language (which uses mnemonics code).
- Size was smaller, more energy-efficient, more reliable and less expensive than first-generation of computers.

Example IBM 7090, UNIVAC 1107, CDC 1604.

3. Third Generation (1960s-1970s)

- They used **Integrated Circuits** (ICs), which combined multiple transistors into a single chip. The first IC chip was designed by the **Jack Kelby**.
- They improved magnetic disk storage (hard drives) and magnetic tapes for secondary storage.
- Speed was measured in **nanoseconds**.
- They introduced **high-level programming languages** like FORTRAN, COBOL, BASIC and operating systems for multitasking.
- They were dramatically smaller, faster and more affordable.
- Supported time-sharing and multiprocessing capabilities.

Example IBM System/360, PDP-8, Honeywell 6000

4. Fourth Generation (1970s-1980s)

- Modern technology of IC chip called **microprocessor** with **VLSI circuits** is used in fourth generation.
- They introduced floppy disks, CDs and hard drives, later evolved to Solid State Drives (SSD).

- Speed is measured in picoseconds, modern processors operate in **gigahertz** (billions of instructions per second).
- Rise of **Graphical User Interfaces** (GUIs) and widespread use of operating systems like Windows, Linux and Mac OS.
- Computers became personal and portable, widely accessible and capable of complex tasks like gaming, video editing and internet browsing.

Example Apple II, IBM PC, modern laptops and desktops

5. Fifth Generation (1990s-Present)

- They focus on AI-driven hardware, quantum computing, nanotechnology and parallel processing.
- They use **ULSI** to further enhance processing power.
- They utilize cloud storage and high-capacity SSDs.
- Focused on parallel processing, AI-enhanced computing and quantum speed (still under research).
- Driven by machine learning, AI algorithms, natural language processing and cloud-based applications.
- Aimed at solving complex problems using artificial intelligence, supercomputing and natural language interaction.
- Still under active research with innovations in fields like AI, robotics and quantum computing.

Example Quantum computers, AI-powered systems, Google's DeepMind, IBM Watson

Facts Drive

- The first computer in the world is often considered to be the **ENIAC**.
- First computer installed in India was the **HEC-2M**, which was set-up at the **Indian Statistical Institute** (ISI) in Kolkata in 1955.
- **Alan Turing** is referred as the **father of computer science** and is recognized for his foundational contributions to the field of computing and artificial intelligence.
- **Spacewar** is credited as the first widely available and influential computer game.
- Ada Lovelace/Ada Augusta Known as the **first computer programmer**. She wrote the first program for **analytical engine**.

Classification of Computer

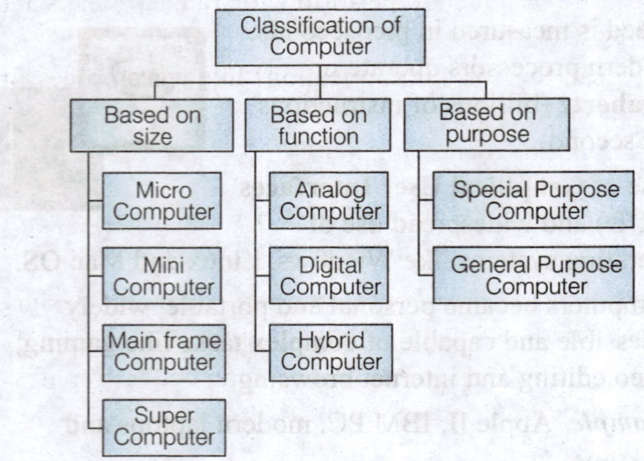

Based on Size

1. Micro Computer

- Microcomputers commonly referred to as personal computer (PCs), are designed for individual use.
- Typically consists of single microprocessor (CPU).
- They are the smallest in terms of size and processing power and also cost-effective.
- They are mainly used for general computing tasks such as internet browsing, general computing and gaming, etc.

Example Desktops, laptops, tablets and smartphones

2. Mini Computer

- Mini computers also known as **mid-range computers**, they fall between mainframe and micro computers in terms of size and power.
- They are typically used by small organizations for tasks like database management or serving multiple users in a networked environment.

Example PDP-11, IBM AS/400

3. Mainframe Computer

- Mainframes are large and powerful systems as compare to micro and mini computers.
- They are also referred as **big iron** or **big machine**.
- Designed for handling and processing very large amounts of data quickly.
- They are often used by large organisations like banks, insurance companies and government agencies to manage large-scale transactions and data processing.
- Mainframes support multiple users simultaneously and are known for their **reliability** and **security**.

4. Super Computer

- Super computers, also called **multi-user computers** are capable of processing trillions of instructions per second.
- They are the fastest and most powerful computers in the world.
- Supercomputers are measured in **FLOPS** (floating-point operations per second).
- They are used for complex calculations like climate research, nuclear simulations and large-scale data processing.
- They have thousands of processors working together in parallel to solve large-scale problems.

Top 10 Super Computers in the World

Rank	Name	Location	Performance
1.	El Capitan	Lawrence Livermore National Laboratory, USA	1.742 exaflops
2.	Frontier	Oak Ridge National Laboratory, USA	1.206 exaflops
3.	Aurora	Argonne National Laboratory, USA	1.012 exaflops
4.	Eagle	Microsoft Azure, USA	561.2 petaflops
5.	Fugaku	RIKEN Center for Computational Science, Japan	442.01 petaflops
6.	LUMI	CSC, Finland	379.70 petaflops
7.	Alps	CSCS, Switzerland	270 petaflops
8.	Leonardo	CINECA, Italy	241.20 petaflops
9.	MareNostrum 5 ACC	BSC, Spain	175.30 petaflops
10.	Summit	Oak Ridge National Laboratory, USA	148.60 petaflops

Super Computers in India

- In 1980s, development of the first Indian supercomputer, **PARAM 8000** was initiated by the Centre for Development of Advanced Computing (C-DAC), Pune.
- **Dr. Vijay Bhatkar** founder and executive director of C-DAC also known as the **father of super computer in India**, has played an important role in the development of supercomputers in India. He led the development of the PARAM series of supercomputers.
- **National Supercomputing Mission (NSM)** was launched in 2015 to enhance the country's supercomputing capacity. It aims to develop a network of supercomputers for research and development across various fields.

3 NEW Super computers

- The three supercomputers were launched by PM Narendra Modi.
  - **PARAM RUDRA** supports advanced research in physics, earth sciences and astronomy.
  - **Arka** and **Arunika** are high-performance computing systems focused on enhancing weather and climate forecasting capabilities.
- These three supercomputers have been deployed in **Pune, Delhi** and **Kolkata**.

Some other Indian Supercomputers

Name	Company/Year
Pratyush	IITM, Pune/2018
Mihir	IITM,Pune/2018
PARAM Siddhi -AI	C-DAC/2022
PARAM Brahma	C-DAC/ 2019
PARAM Yuva II	C-DAC/2013
SAGA-220	ISRO/2011
PARAM Ganga	IIT, Roorkee/2022

Based on Function

1. Analog Computer

- Analog computers handle continuous data and work on physical quantities like voltage, temperature and pressure.

Example Flight simulator, slide rule, voltmeter

2. Digital Computer

- They are used for wide range of tasks from simple calculations to running complex simulations.
- They process data in **binary form** (0 and 1).

Example Personal computers, smartphones, tablets

3. Hybrid Computer

- Hybrid computers combine the features of both **analog** and **digital** computers.
- They are basically used for applications that need real-time processing of both continuous (analog) and discrete (digital) data.

Example CT Scan machines

Based on Purpose

1. Special Purpose Computer

- These computers are made to perform specific tasks.
- They have limited capabilities and are optimized for specific tasks like controlling an engine or a smart home device.

Example Embedded systems

2. General Purpose Computer

- These are designed to perform wide range of tasks and can be used in many fields.
- They can run various applications like word processors, games and database.

Example Personal computers

Other Types of Computers

Workstations

- Workstations are high-performance computers designed for technical or scientific applications.
- They have more powerful processors, better graphics capabilities and larger storage than typical PCs.

Servers

- Servers are the computers that provide services to other computers in a network called **clients**.
- They can manage, store and deliver resources such as files, database and emails, etc.

Embedded Computers

- Specialised computing systems designed to be integrated into other devices like washing machines, digital watches, etc., to perform dedicated functions.

Quantum Computers

- Utilise principles of quantum physics to process information in ways classical computers cannot.
- Use **qubits** (quantum bits) instead of classical bits.

Nano computers

- Computers that operate at the nanoscale (1 to 100 nanometers) using nanoscale components for processing and storage.

Facts Drive

- Punch Card was developed by **Herman Hollerith**.
- Transistors were invented by **John Bardeen, Walter Brattain and William Shockley** at Bell Labs in 1947.
- Bengaluru is known as the **Silicon Valley of India** due to its status as a major IT hub, housing numerous tech companies and startups.
- The first microprocessor, the **Intel 4004** (released in 1971), was developed by Intel engineers Ted Hoff, Federico Faggin and Masatoshi Shima.
- IBM developed the supercomputer named **Deep Blue** that defeated world chess champion Garry Kasparov in 1997.
- As of 2024, **El Capitan** is the fastest supercomputer, capable of performing over 1.7 exaflop.
- The first mobile phone in the world is **Motorola DynaTAC 8000X,** introduced in 1983 by Martin Cooper, an engineer at Motorola.
- India's first analog computer was designed by **Samarendra Kumar Mitra** in the early 1950s.

Characteristics of Computer

The characteristics of computers can be broadly classified into serveral key features:

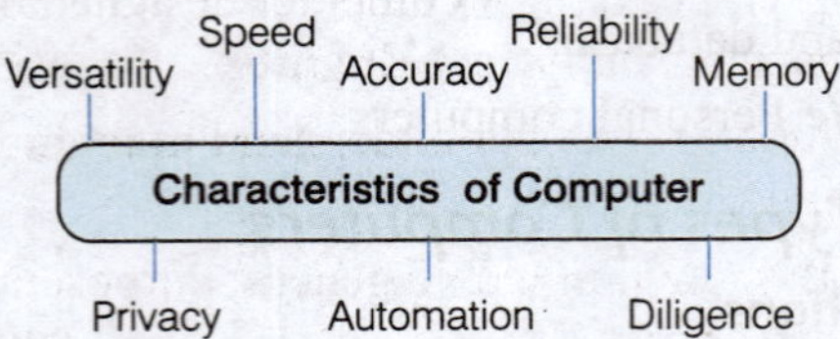

1. **Speed** Computers can process data and perform calculations at incredible speed, often in milliseconds.
2. **Accuracy** Computers give precise result minimal errors, as long as the input data and instructions are correct.
3. **Reliability** A computer is reliable as it gives consistent results for similar sets of data, if we give same input at any time we will get the same output.
4. **Memory** Computer can store large amount of data and information in its memory.
5. **Diligence** A computer will never fail to perform its task due to distraction or laziness.
6. **Automation** Once the instructions are fed into computer it performs tasks automatically without human intervention.
7. **Privacy** Computers are equipped with various security features to protect data from unauthorized access and cyber threats.
8. **Versatility** Computers can perform wide range of tasks, from simple calculations to complex simulations and multimedia processing.

Limitations of Computer

1. **No intelligence** Computer have zero IQ; they cannot act on situations that are not programmed into them.
2. **Human dependency** A computer is fully automated once switched ON but it cannot switch itself ON. Some human assistance is always required.
3. **Electricity Dependent** Computers require constant power supply, they cannot work without electricity.
4. **Virus Threat** Computers are vulnerable to virus and hacking attacks, which can compromise the security of sensitive data.

Applications of Computer

Today we cannot imagine growing our technology without computers.

The various field where the computer is very essential are:

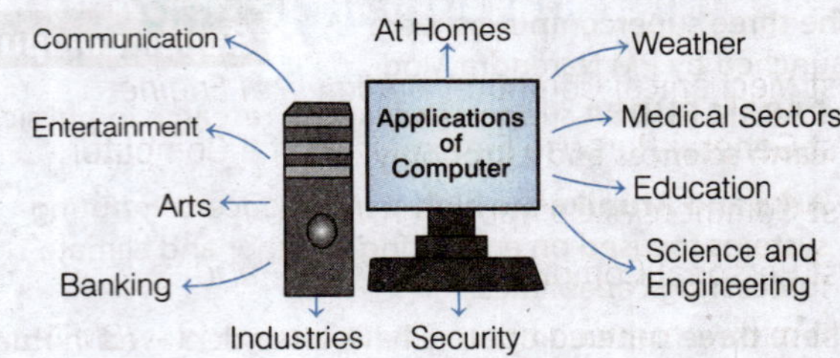

1. **At Homes** Computers at home are used for various tasks like online learning, entertainment (watching movies, gaming) and online bill pay. They also help with communication *via* emails or social media.
2. **Medical Sectors** Computer-based AI diagnostics and robotic surgeries are revolutionising healthcare. Telemedicine and e-health apps have made healthcare services accessible in remote areas.
3. **Science and Engineering** Computers play a vital role in genetic research, space science and climate change modeling. Technologies like quantum computing have accelerated the pace of research.
4. **Industries** Computers are used for automating manufacturing processes, managing inventory and controlling machinery in industries. They also assist in data analysis and communication within the industry.
5. **Banking** In the banking sector, computers are used for managing transactions, maintaining customer accounts and processing loans. They also help in online banking, ATMs and fraud detection.
6. **Arts** In the arts sector, computers are used for digital painting, graphic design and animation. They also aid in creating 3D models, virtual exhibitions, etc.
7. **Entertainment** Computers support video games, digital media production and streaming services, providing various entertainment options.
8. **Education** Along with computers, AI now helps deliver personalized learning experiences, such as through adaptive learning platforms. Virtual classrooms, AR/VR-based learning, and 3D simulations have made education more interactive.
9. **Security** Modern defense systems include AI-powered drones, cyber defense mechanisms and automatic threat detection. In cyber security, computers help protect against hacking, data breaches and digital warfare.
10. **Weather Forecasting** Computers can analyse vast amounts of data to predict weather patterns and natural disasters accurately.

Note **Pratyush** and **Mihir** supercomputers are used in the fields of weather forecasting and climate monitoring in India.

11. **Communication** They enable email, instant messaging, video conferencing and social media, to connect people globally.

First in Computer Field

- First Mechanical Computer – *Analytical Engine*
- First General-Purpose Electronic Digital Computer – *ENIAC*
- First Commercial Computer – *UNIVAC I*
- First Personal Computer(PC) – *Altair 8800*
- First mass-produced computer in the world – *IBM 650*
- First Graphical User Interface(GUI) – *Xerox Alto*
- First Microprocessor – *Intel 4004*
- First Computer Programming Language – *FORTRAN (Formula Translation)*
- First Supercomputer in the World – *CDC 6600*
- First Supercomputer in India – *PARAM 8000*
- First Minicomputer – *PDP 1*
- First Laptop Computer – *Epson*
- First commercially successful portable (Laptop) computer – Osborne 1
- First computer developed in India – *Siddharth*
- First Microprocessor developed in India – *SHAKTI Microprocessor*
- First operating system made in India – *BharOS (Bharat Operating System Solutions)*
- First use of computer in India – *HEC-2M 1955 (In Kolkata)*
- First fully computerized post office of India – *New Delhi*

Important Abbreviations

ENIAC Electronic Numerical Integrator and Computer
UNIVAC Universal Automatic Computer
EDVAC Electronic Discrete Variable Automatic Computer
EDSAC Electronic Delay Storage Automatic Calculator
IBM International Business Machine
VLSI Very Large Scale Integration
ULSI Ultra Large Scale Integration
SLSI Super Large Scale Integration

PYQs Oneliner

1. The first mechanical computer designed by Charles Babbage is **Analytical Engine**. *SSC CHSL 2024*
2. A computer can only understand **machine language** directly. *CPCT 2024*
3. The first programmable general purpose computer in the world is **ENIAC**. *SSC CHSL 2024*
4. The first mechanical calculator was called **Pascaline**. *UPSSSC 2023*
5. **Charles Babbage** is the father of computer. *BPSC PGT 2023*
6. First generation of computer is based on **Vacuum Tubes**. *CPCT 2023*
7. **Transistor** was used in second generation of computers. *MPPSC 2023*
8. In fifth generation computers, **Technological advancement** is the difference from other generation computers. *BPSC TGT 2023*
9. **Blaise Pascal** invented mechanical calculator for adding numbers. *CPCT 2022*
10. **Param 8000** is considered to be the first supercomputer developed by C-DAC in India. *CPCT 2022*
11. **University of Pennsylvania** designed and developed the first electronic computer (ENIAC). *RRB NTPC 2021*
12. ENIAC was first computer without mechanical parts built by **J W Mauchly** and **J Presper Eckert**. *RRB NTPC 2021*
13. **Alan Turing** is considered the father of modern computers. *RRB NTPC 2021*
14. **Vijay Bhatkar** is considered the father of Indian supercomputers. *RRB NTPC 2021*
15. **Super computer** is used for climate research and weather forecasting. *SSC CHSL 2021*

Practice Exercise

Introduction to Computer

1. A computer can only understand .... directly. *CPCT 2024*
(a) machine language (b) algorithms
(c) high-level language (d) middle-level language

2. The data sent to the computer is called
(a) process (b) output
(c) input (d) algorithm

3. Which of the following statements about computers is correct? *RRB NTPC 2021*
(a) Computer can organize all the information itself.
(b) Computer cable is made of software.
(c) Computer is made up of hardware only.
(d) It is an electronic device that stores, retrieves and processes data.

Components of Computer

4. Which of the following cycles includes its components as input, processing, output and storage?
(a) Processing (b) Output
(c) Data (d) Storage

5. .... provides the raw facts while .... makes the data meaningful.
(a) Information, reporting
(b) Data, information
(c) Information, bits
(d) records, bytes

6. The data or information used to run a computer is called
(a) hardware (b) peripheral
(c) CPU (d) None of these

7. When information is fed into the computer, which of the following is created?
(a) Data (b) Ideas
(c) Objects (d) Facts

8. Which of the following is an example of non-numeric data?
(a) Name of the employee (b) Test score
(c) Bank account number (d) All of these

9. It is data that has been organized and presented in a meaningful fashion.
(a) Process (b) Software
(c) Storage (d) Information

Basic Functions of Computer

10. Computer has four main functions
(a) Input, processing, output and storage
(b) Learning, thinking, output and intelligence
(c) Data, information, bits and bytes
(d) Hardware, software, modeling and operations

11. Which of the following functions does a computer not perform?
(a) Processing (b) Understanding
(c) Controlling (d) Inputting

12. Information that comes from an external source and is fed into the computer software is called
(a) output (b) throughput
(c) input (d) report

13. Using data for preparing information is called
(a) feedback (b) programming
(c) processing (d) analysis

14. Output is
(a) received from the user
(b) provided to the user
(c) provided to processor by user
(d) All of the above

History of Computers

15. The first calculating machine is
(a) difference engine (b) pascal
(c) calculator (d) abacus

16. In which country was the abacus invented?
(a) India (b) China (c) America (d) Greece

17. The name of the first electronic digital computer of the world is *RRB NTPC 2021*
(a) Param (b) Prolog (c) UNIVAC (d) ENAIC

18. The first mechanical calculator was called *UPSSSC 2023*
(a) Calculator (b) OPT
(c) Galileo (d) Pascaline

19. The analytical engine built by Charles Babbage is
(a) electronic (b) electrical
(c) mechanical (d) technical

20. Which of the following is considered the first mechanical computer designed by Charles Babbage? *SSC CHSL 2024*
(a) UNIVAC (b) Abacus
(c) Analytical Engine (d) ENIAC

21. .... invented mechanical calculator for adding numbers. *CPCT 2022*
(a) Charles Babbage (b) Newton
(c) Blaise Pascal (d) Piano

22. What is the full form of ENIAC in the field of computing? *SSC CHSL 2020*
(a) Electronic Numerical Integrated Advanced Computer
(b) Electronic Nerves Integration and Computer
(c) Electronic Numerical Integrator and Computer
(d) Electronic Numerical Integration and Computing

23. Which of the following universities designed and developed the first electronic computer ENIAC? *RRB NTPC 2021*
(a) Howard University
(b) University of Pennsylvania
(c) Stanford University
(d) Oxford University

24. What was the name of the first computer without mechanical parts built by J W Mauchly and J Presper Eckert? *RRB NTPC 2021*
(a) EDVAC (b) ENIAC
(c) Mark II (d) Mark I

25. Who among the following created the Electronic Discrete Variable Automatic Computer (EDVAC) with memory that stores programs as well as data? *SSC CGL 2018*
(a) Thomas H Floor (b) Arthur Samuel
(c) Bletchley Park (d) John von Neumann

26. Who invented EDSAC?
(a) Howard H. Aiken (b) John von Neumann
(c) Maurice Wilkes (d) Herman Hollerith

27. Who is the father of computer? *BPSC PGT 2023*
(a) James Gosling (b) Charles Babbage
(c) Dennis Ritchie (d) More than one of the above

28. Who is considered the father of modern computers? *RRB NTPC 2021*
(a) Gordon E. Moore (b) Alan Turing
(c) Charles Babbage (d) James Gosling

29. Which was the first programmable general purpose computer in the world? *SSC CHSL 2024*
(a) Pascaline (b) Napier's bones
(c) ENIAC (d) Mark I

Generations of Computer

30. In which generation were computers bulky, vacuum based and costly? *RRB NTPC 2021*
(a) Fourth generation (b) Third generation
(c) First generation (d) Fifth generation

31. Assembly language is an example of.... generation programming language. *RRB NTPC 2021*
(a) First (b) Fourth
(c) Second (d) Third

32. Which generation of computers used machine code as the programming language? *SSC CHSL 2023*
(a) Second (b) First
(c) Third (d) Fourth

33. Which of the following was used as a storage device in the first generation of computers? *DSSSB Patwari 2020*
(a) Optical disc (b) Magnetic drum
(c) Magnetic core (d) Transistor

34. Which electronic components was used in second generation of computers? *MPPSC 2023, SSC Selection Post 2023*
(a) Vacuum tubes (b) VLSI
(c) Transistor (d) None of these

35. Which of the following is a second generation system? *SSC CHSL 2023*
(a) IBM notebooks (b) Sun workstations
(c) Honeywell 400 (d) Apple II

36. What was the working life of second generation of computers? *UPSSSC 2018*
(a) 1940-1956 (b) 1963-1972
(c) 1956-1964 (d) 1973-present

37. Which among the following generations of computers used vacuum tubes? *SSC CHSL 2023*
(a) First generation (b) Third generation
(c) Fourth generation (d) Second generation

38. Which of these generations for the first time in computers use of integrated circuits in their CPU to be done? *Rajasthan Police Constable 2020, IBPS RRB Office Assistant 2022, 2021*
(a) First generation (b) Third generation
(c) Fourth generation (d) Second generation

39. Which operating system is used in third generation computers? *IBPS RRB Office Scale 2021*
(a) Batch (b) Time sharing system
(c) Real time system (d) GUI interface
(e) None of these

40. IBM 360 was developed in which of the following generations of computers? *SSC CHSL 2023*
(a) Second generation (b) First generation
(c) Third generation (d) Fourth generation

41. Cobol is an example of.... generation programming language. *RRB NTPC 2021*
(a) First (b) Fourth
(c) Second (d) Third

42. Chips are made from thousands of .... switches.
(a) electrons (b) charges
(c) transistors (d) etches

43. IC is made of
(a) transistor (b) microprocessor
(c) vacuum tube (d) Both (a) and (b)

44. Which of the following is required for the production of IC chips for computers?
(a) Chromium (b) Copper
(c) Platinum (d) Silicon

45. Who has developed the integrated circuit chip?
(a) S V Raman (b) Robert Nayak
(c) JS Kilby (d) Charles Babbage

46. The full form of IC in electronics is
(a) Internal circuit (b) Independent circuit
(c) Integrated circuit (d) In-built circuit

47. Apple II is an example of Generation of computer. *SSC CHSL 2023*
(a) Third (b) Second
(c) First (d) Fourth

48. In which generation did microcomputers start?
(a) First generation
(b) Second generation
(c) Third generation
(d) Fourth generation

49. Which of the following generation of computers are used microprocessors? *RRB Office Assistant 2021*
(a) Fourth generation computers
(b) Third generation computers
(c) First generation computers
(d) Second generation computers

50. Advanced technologies, such as artificial intelligence, quantum computing, etc. were mainly for ..... generation computers. *UPPCL TG 2019*
(a) third (b) fourth
(c) fifth (d) second

51. In fifth generation computers, what is the difference from other generation computers? *BPSC TGT 2023*
(a) Technological advancement
(b) Object-oriented programming
(c) Scientific code
(d) more than one of the above
(e) None of the above

52. The specialty of the fifth generation computer is
(a) artificial intelligence
(b) microprocessor
(c) very low price
(d) household use

53. Fifth generation computers do not have
(a) speech recognition
(b) artificial intelligence
(c) very large scale integration
(d) vacuum tube

54. Notebook computer belongs to which generation of computers? *CPCT 2024*
(a) First (b) Second
(c) Fourth (d) Fifth

55. Which of the following statements is not valid about the magnetic tape? *CPCT 2024*
(a) It is a plastic ribbon.
(b) It is coated on both sides with iron oxide.
(c) It can be erased and reused.
(d) It cannot be used as a storage medium.

56. Honeywell 6000 was developed in which of the following generation of computer? *SSC CHSL 2023*
(a) First (b) Third
(c) Second (d) Fourth

57. Which of the following is not a second generation system?
(a) IBM notebooks (b) Sun workstations
(c) Mark I (d) All of these

58. PARAM supercomputer belongs to which generation of computers? *SSC CHSL 2023*
(a) Second (b) First
(c) Fifth (d) Third

59. Graphical User Interface (GUI) was developed during which of the following generations of computer? *SSC CHSL 2023*
(a) Fourth generation (b) Second generation
(c) First generation (d) Third generation

Classification of Computer

60. Which among the following type of computer is also known as a notebook? *SSC CGL 2023*
(a) Micro computer
(b) Multi core
(c) Work station
(d) Laptop computer

61. A personal computer is designed to meet the computing needs of
(a) any person (b) any department
(c) company (d) city

62. Which of the following is a small microprocessor based computer, which can be used by one person at a time?
(a) Notebook (b) Super computer
(c) Mini computer (d) Personal computer

63. Micro computer is also known as
(a) computer on heel
(b) computer on a chip
(c) computer on a ship
(d) All of the above

64. Computers that are portable and convenient for traveling users
(a) super computer (b) laptop
(c) mini computer (d) file servers

65. Which of the following can be considered a portable computer?
(a) Mini computer (b) Mainframe computer
(c) PDA (d) Workstation

66. What is a laptop? *CPCT 2021*
(a) Desktop computers used in clinical laboratories
(b) Portable, light weight and can fit in briefcase
(c) Hearing noise recognition system
(d) Desktop

67. .... are highly portable devices that support the use of a stylus or pen to input commands and data. *CPCT 2021*
(a) Notebook (b) Laptop
(c) Desktop (d) Tablet

68. What type of small and inexpensive computers are used in many houses?
(a) Mainframe (b) Mini computer
(c) Microcomputer (d) None of these

69. What types of computers are desktop computers, laptop computers, tablets and smartphones? *SSC CGL 2018*
(a) Supercomputers
(b) Mainframe computers
(c) Microcomputers
(d) Mini computers

70. Which of the following types of computer is found in digital clock?
(a) Mainframe computer
(b) Embedded computer
(c) Super computer
(d) Notebook computer

71. Which of the following is the fastest and smallest computer, which works like a brain?
(a) Super computer (b) Quantum computer
(c) Param 10000 (d) IBM chips

72. Consider the use of nanostructures to fabricate devices at extremely microscopic levels.
(a) Nanotechnology
(b) Micro technology
(c) Computer forensics
(d) Artificial intelligence

73. What types of computers are client computers in client server system?
(a) Mainframe (b) Mini computer
(c) Microcomputer (d) PDA

74. The first minicomputer was
(a) PDP-8 (b) ENIAC
(c) UNISAC (d) EDVAC

75. Which of the following computers is large and expensive and can process the data of thousands of users simultaneously?
(a) Handheld computer (b) Mainframe computer
(c) Personal computer (d) Tablet computer

76. Which of the following computers is used by large institutions and government agencies like banks, railways etc. to handle very large amounts of data? *CPCT 2023*
(a) Workstation (b) Mainframe
(c) Microcomputer (d) Mini computer

77. World's first supercomputer was created in
(a) 1942 (b) 1964
(c) 1980 (d) 1978

78. Super computer
(a) are smaller in size and processing capacity compared to mainframe computers
(b) contains thousands of microprocessors
(c) common in most homes
(d) are of the same size as a laptop

79. Which of the following is the largest, fastest and most expensive computer?
(a) Personal computer (b) Super computer
(c) Laptop (d) Notebook

80. To access a mainframe or supercomputer, users often use
(a) Terminal (b) Node
(c) Desktop (d) Handheld

81. Which of the following computers is used in weather forecasting?
(a) Super computer (b) Mainframe computer
(c) Mini computer (d) Microcomputer

82. Which of the following computers was used in military agencies and scientific research laboratories? *DSSSB Patwari 2020*
(a) Mainframe computer (b) Mini computer
(c) Super computer (d) Analog computer

83. Which of the following types of computers is used for climate research and weather forecasting? *SSC CHSL 2021*
(a) Super computer (b) Microcomputer
(c) Minicomputer (d) Mainframe computer

84. Who among the following is known as the father of supercomputing? *SSC CGL 2018*
(a) Ken Thompson (b) Seymour Cray
(c) Alan Parlis (d) Vint Cerf

85. Who among the following is considered the father of Indian supercomputers? *RRB NTPC 2021*
(a) RA Mashelkar
(b) Vijay Bhatkar
(c) Jayant Narlikar
(d) Nandan Nilekani

86. An example of a supercomputer is
(a) Cray 2 (b) Cray XMP 24
(c) Tianhe 2 (d) All of these

87. In 1991, India's first supercomputer .... was developed by Vijay Bhatkar. *SSC CGL 2018*
(a) Prayas 3000 (b) Prayog 2000
(c) Param 8000 (d) Pragati 5000

88. Which of the following is a supercomputer manufactured by India? *SSC CGL 2018*
(a) Param Yuva 2 (b) Onshape
(c) Venngage (d) Pixir

89. Where was the first computer installed in India?
(a) Tata Institute of Fundamental Research (TIFR), Mumbai
(b) Indian Statistical Institute (ISI), Kolkata
(c) Computational Research Laboratory (CRL), Pune
(d) Indian Railways, New Delhi

90. Which of the following is the PARAM series of supercomputers developed by Indian scientists? *RRB NTPC 2021*
(a) Param Mitra (b) Param 8000
(c) Param Bhrama (d) Param 8600

91. Which of the following is considered to be the first supercomputer developed by C-DAC in India? *CPCT 2022*
(a) Mihir (b) Param 8000
(c) Pratyush (d) EKA

92. Param Siddhi implies *RRB NTPC 2021*
(a) a nuclear reactor
(b) an artificial intelligence supercomputer
(c) industrial piercing
(d) agricultural equipment

93. .... is India's first multi-petaflop supercomputer that has been set up at the Indian Institute of Tropical Meteorology (IIMT) Pune. Developed at a cost of Rs. 450 crore. The super computer is used for weather and climate predictions. *RRB NTPC 2021*
(a) Pratyaksh (b) Param
(c) Pratyush (d) Aaditya

94. Those computers, which measure physical quantities and express their results in numbers, are called
(a) digital computers
(b) hybrid computers
(c) analog computers
(d) mainframe computers

95. India's first analog computer was designed by *SSC CHSL 2020*
(a) Samarendra Kumar Mitra
(b) Deb Kumar Bose
(c) Subodh Chandra Das Gupta
(d) Bimal Kumar Bhattacharya

96. PARAM supercomputer belongs to which generation of computers? *SSC CHSL 2023*
(a) Second (b) First
(c) Fifth (d) Third

97. Which category of computers are being used today?
(a) Digital (c) Analog
(b) Mechanical (d) Manual

98. The principle of working of digital computer is
(a) calculation and logic (b) operating
(c) measurement (d) software

99. Calculator works on which type of working method of computer?
(a) Hybrid computer (b) Analog computer
(c) Digital computer (d) None of these

100. Which of the following is related to converting computer analog output into digital form?
(a) Digital computer
(b) Analog computer
(c) Analog-to-digital (ADC) computer
(d) Mainframe computer

101. .... computer is the most common type of computer. It is commonly used in binary number system to process information with quantities. *UPSSSC 2018*
(a) Hybrid (b) Digital
(c) Analog (d) Complex

102. Which are the computers designed to do specialized work?
(a) Mainframe computer
(b) Special purpose computer
(c) Portable computer
(d) Super computer

103. Which of the following types of computer is used in climate research and weather forecasting?
(a) Mainframe computers
(b) Microcomputers
(c) Minicomputers
(d) None of the above

104. Which of the following does not belong to the category of microcomputers? *CPCT 2024*
(a) Desktop computers (b) Cray-1
(c) Palmtop computers (d) Workstations

105. Which of the following is not a portable computer? *CPCT 2024*
(a) Laptop (b) PDAs
(c) Desktop (d) Tablet

106. PDP-11 is an example of .... *CPCT 2024*
(a) minicomputers
(b) microcomputers
(c) supercomputers
(d) mainframe computers

Characteristics/ Limitations of Computer

107. Which of these is not a computer characteristic? *RRB NTPC 2021*
(a) Intelligence quotient (b) Data storage
(c) Speed (d) Accuracy

108. Which of the following is a specialty of a computer?
(a) Fast speed (b) Error free work
(c) Secrecy (d) All of these

109. Modern computers are very reliable, but they are not .... *CPCT 2023*
(a) precise (b) cheap
(c) accurate (d) infallible

110. Some of the characteristics of computers include being free from dullness, fatigue and lack of concentration. These characteristics are called .... *DSSSB Patwari 2022*
(a) automation (b) accuracy
(c) diligence (d) versatility

111. Match the following with reference to computer features *DSSSB Patwari 2020*

(i) Versatility	(A)	Provide consistent results for the same set of data
(ii) Accuracy	(B)	Ability to perform a variety of tasks
(iii) Diligence	(C)	make error free calculations
(iv) Reliability	(D)	Performing millions of tasks or calculations

(a) (i) → (B), (ii) → (C), (iii) → (A), (iv) → (D)
(b) (i) → (B), (ii) → (C), (iii) → (D), (iv) → (A)
(c) (i) → (B), (ii) → (A), (iii) → (D), (iv) → (C)
(d) (i) → (C), (ii) → (B), (iii) → (D), (iv) → (A)

112. Which of the following is not a characteristic of a computer? *DSSSB Patwari 2022*
(a) Power to remember (b) Accuracy
(c) Emotions (d) Speed

Applications of Computer

113. Which of these is an application of computers in healthcare?
(a) Online shopping
(b) Medical diagnosis using AI
(c) Social networking
(d) Photo editing

114. Which of the following is an example of a computer application in the entertainment industry?
(a) CAD software
(b) Music composition
(c) Stock market analysis
(d) Supply chain management

Answers

1. (a)	2. (c)	3. (d)	4. (a)	5. (b)	6. (d)	7. (a)	8. (a)	9. (d)	10. (a)
11. (b)	12. (c)	13. (c)	14. (b)	15. (d)	16. (b)	17. (d)	18. (d)	19. (c)	20. (c)
21. (c)	22. (c)	23. (b)	24. (b)	25. (d)	26. (c)	27. (b)	28. (b)	29. (c)	30. (c)
31. (c)	32. (b)	33. (b)	34. (c)	35. (c)	36. (c)	37. (a)	38. (b)	39. (b)	40. (c)
41. (d)	42. (c)	43. (a)	44. (d)	45. (c)	46. (c)	47. (d)	48. (d)	49. (a)	50. (c)
51. (a)	52. (a)	53. (d)	54. (c)	55. (d)	56. (b)	57. (d)	58. (c)	59. (a)	60. (d)
61. (a)	62. (d)	63. (b)	64. (b)	65. (c)	66. (b)	67. (d)	68. (c)	69. (c)	70. (b)
71. (b)	72. (a)	73. (c)	74. (a)	75. (b)	76. (b)	77. (b)	78. (b)	79. (b)	80. (a)
81. (a)	82. (c)	83. (a)	84. (b)	85. (b)	86. (d)	87. (c)	88. (a)	89. (b)	90. (b)
91. (b)	92. (b)	93. (c)	94. (c)	95. (a)	96. (c)	97. (a)	98. (a)	99. (c)	100. (c)
101. (b)	102. (b)	103. (d)	104. (b)	105. (c)	106. (a)	107. (a)	108. (d)	109. (b)	110. (c)
111. (b)	112. (c)	113. (b)	114. (b)						

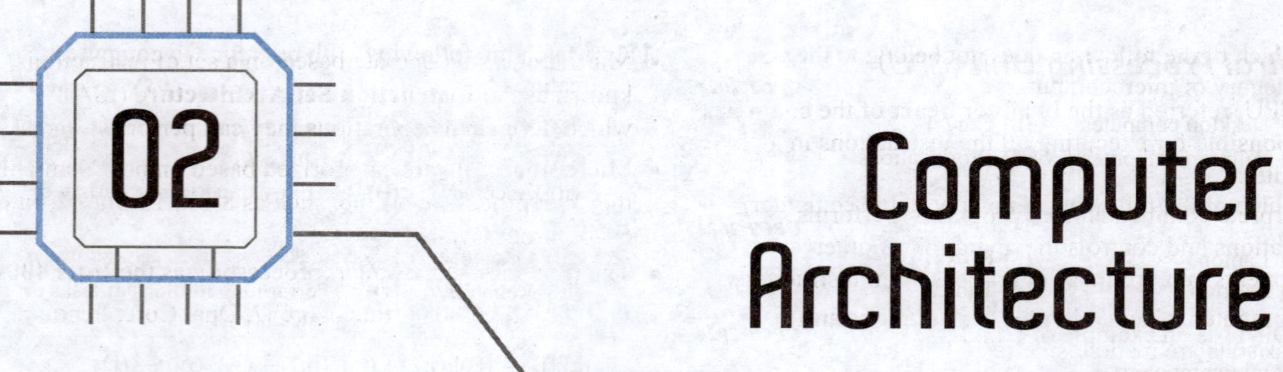

Computer Architecture

- Computer architecture refers to the **conceptual design** and **fundamental operational** structure of a computer system.
- It includes the hardware components (CPU, memory, Input/output devices) and their interconnections.
- The first computer architecture, **Von Neumann architecture**, was introduced by **John von Neumann** in 1945.

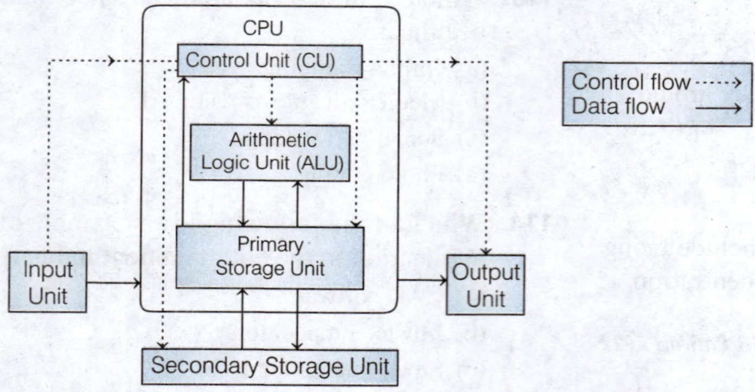

In this Chapter

- Components of Computer Architecture
- Microprocessor
- Motherboard
- Interconnection of Units *Via* Buses
- Instruction Cycle
- Computer Ports
- Factors Affecting CPU Performance

> "The computer was born to solve problems that did not exist before."
>
> ~ **Bill Gates**

Components of Computer Architecture

Computer architecture is divided into following key components

1. Input Unit

- The input unit is responsible for receiving data and instructions from external sources and converting them into a format that the CPU can process.
- Functions performed by an input unit
  - It accepts the instructions from the user.
  - It converts these instructions.
  - It supplies the converted instructions to computer system for further use.

2. Output Unit

- The output unit is responsible for delivering processed data from the CPU to the user or external devices.
- Functions performed by an output unit
  - It accepts the results produced by the computer which are in coded form.
  - It converts these coded results to readable form and shows the converted results to the user.

3. Central Processing Unit (CPU)

- The CPU, referred as the **brain** or **heart** of the computer, is responsible for executing all the instructions in a computer.
- It interprets commands from programs, performs calculations and controls the operation of other components and produces output based on instructions.
- In a computer system, all major calculations and comparisons are made inside the CPU.

CPU can be divided into following parts:

Arithmetic Logic Unit (ALU)

- The ALU is responsible for performing all the **mathematical** and **logical** operations.
- It handles operations like addition, subtraction, multiplication, division and comparisons (like greater than, less than or equal to).

Control Unit (CU)

- The control unit directs the operations of the CPU.
- It fetches instructions from memory, decodes them and then sends signals to execute them.
- It acts like a traffic controller, coordinating how data moves between the CPU and other components (like memory and input/output devices).

4. Memory Unit

- The memory (storage) stores data and instructions needed by the CPU for processing.
- It includes **primary memory** (RAM and ROM) and **secondary memory** (HDDs, SSDs etc.),
- Primary memory is used for short-term, fast data access and is essential for active **program executions** whereas secondary memory provides **data storage**.
- It also includes **cache memory** for storing frequently accessed data and employs memory management techniques like virtual memory to optimize resource usage.
- **Registers** are a type of computer memory used to quickly accept, store and transfer data and instructions that are being used by the CPU immediately.

Microprocessor

- A microprocessor is the **central unit** of a computer system which performs all the important computational tasks.
- It is a single **Integrated Circuit** (IC) that contains the CPU of a computer.
- Microprocessors operate based on a set of instructions known as the **Instruction Set Architecture** (ISA), which defines the operations they can perform.
- Microprocessors are categorized based on how many bits they can process at a time, such as 8-bit, 16-bit, 32-bit or 64-bit processors.
- The first commercial microprocessor was the **Intel 4004**.

Example Intel 8086, Intel Core i7, Dual Core, Pentium.

Motherboard

- The motherboard is the main **Printed Circuit Board** (PCB) of a computer, which acts as the backbone that connects and allows communication between all other components and peripherals.
- It holds crucial parts such as the processor (CPU), memory (RAM) and expansion slots and manages power distribution and data flow.
- **Peripheral Components Interconnect** (PCI) slot resides on motherboard.
- Key parts of a motherboard include CPU socket, memory slots, chipset, expansion slot, power connectors, BIOS/UEFI chip, CMOS battery, input/output ports and heat sink/fan headers etc.

Interconnection of Units via Buses

- The interconnection of units refers to how various components of a computer system are connected to communicate and transfer data.
- CPU sends data, instructions and information to the components inside the computer as well as to the peripheral devices attached to it.

Bus Architecture

- A bus is a common communication pathway that allows multiple components to connect and transfer data.

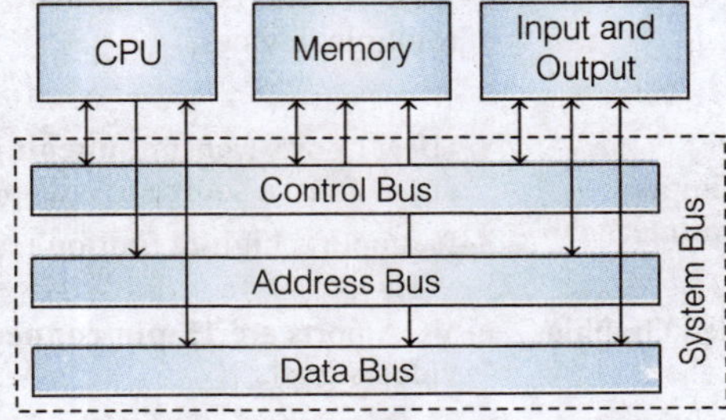

- It consists of a set of **parallel wires** that allows multiple components to communicate over a single channel.
- Hardware components are linked to the bus, allowing them to interact and collaborate effortlessly and these all together are called **bus architecture**.

Types of Buses

Internal Buses

- Internal buses are communication pathways that connect components within the computer's main system, primarily inside the CPU and the motherboard. Internal buses are also called **system buses**.
- Internal buses are of three types
  1. **Data Bus** carries the actual **data** being transferred between components. It is **bidirectional**, allows data to flow in both directions.
  2. **Address Bus** carries the **addresses** of the data that the CPU wants to access. It is **unidirectional**, sends address information from the CPU to memory or I/O devices.
  3. **Control Bus** carries **control signals** from the CPU to other components. These signals manage operations such as read/write commands, interrupts and clock signals.

External Buses

- External buses also referred as **expansion buses**, are communication pathways that connect the computer to external devices, such as peripherals and storage devices.
- External buses include PCI (Peripheral Component Interconnect), Universal Serial Bus, Thunderbolt etc.

Facts Drive

- The world's first microprocessor, the **Intel 4004**, had only 2,300 transistors. Compare that to today's processors, which have billions of transistors packed into the same space.
- A **UPS (Uninterruptible Power Supply)** is a device that provides backup power during outages and protects against surges, allows you to save work and shut down safely.

Instruction Cycle

The instruction cycle is a **sequence of steps** that the CPU follows to execute an instruction. This is also known as **machine cycle**.

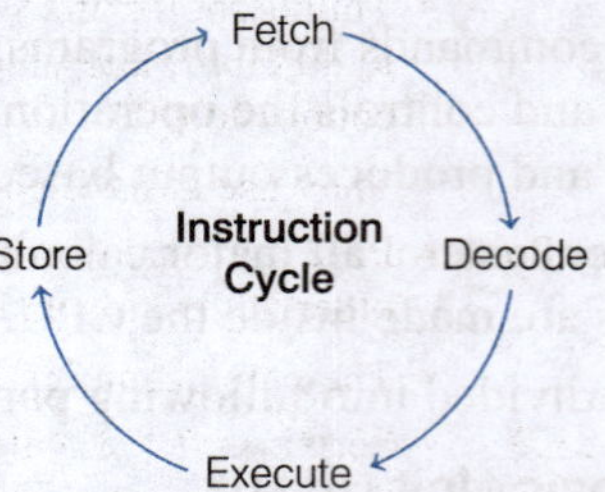

It typically consists of four main stages i.e.

1. **Fetching** The CPU retrieves the next instruction from memory and prepares it for processing.
2. **Decoding** This process allows the CPU to determine what instruction is to be performed.
3. **Executing** The CPU carries out the specified operation, which may involve performing calculations or manipulating data.
4. **Storing** The result of the execution is saved back to memory, ensuring any changes made during the operation are retained.

Computer Ports

- Computer ports are physical or virtual **connection points** that allow a computer to communicate with external devices.
- They provide the interface through which data is sent and received between the computer and peripheral devices such as printers, keyboards, monitors and external storage devices.

Some common types of computer ports

Port	Description	Uses
USB (Universal Serial Bus)	▪ USB ports come in various types, includes, Micro-USB, USB 3.0 and USB-C and are designed for connecting multiple devices.	▪ Connects **peripherals** like keyboards, mouse, printers, external hard drives and smartphones. ▪ It also provides power for charging devices and transferring data.
HDMI (High-Definition Multimedia Interface)	▪ HDMI ports transmit **uncompressed** digital video and audio from a source to a display. ▪ It supports high-definition resolutions.	▪ Connects computers to monitors and TVs for high-quality video and audio output. ▪ It supports various formats, including 4K, 3D and multi-channel audio.
VGA (Video Graphics Array)	▪ VGA ports are **15-pin connectors** that transmit analog video signals. ▪ They are often used with older monitors and projectors.	▪ Connects older displays and projectors to computers. ▪ VGA is less common today due to its lower quality compared to digital connections.
DVI (Digital Visual Interface)	▪ DVI ports come in several configurations (DVI-D for digital, DVI-A for analog, DVI-I for both). ▪ They can transmit digital video signals without compression.	▪ Connect monitors to computers, especially in professional settings where high video quality is required. ▪ DVI is commonly used in older graphics cards.

Port	Description	Uses
Ethernet Port (RJ-45)	▪ Ethernet ports use an **8P8C** connector and are used for wired network connections. ▪ They support various speeds, including 10/100/1000 Mbps.	▪ Connects computers to Local Area Networks (LAN) for internet access. ▪ Ethernet is preferred for stable and fast connections, especially in office environments.
Thunderbolt	▪ Thunderbolt ports support high-speed data transfer (up to 40 Gbps) and video output through a single connection. ▪ They use USB-C connectors in recent versions.	▪ Thunderbolt is especially useful in professional **video editing** and **gaming setups**.
PS/2 Port (Mouse Port)	▪ PS/2 ports are **6-pin connectors** used for connecting older keyboards and mouse. ▪ They are becoming less common in modern systems.	▪ Connects legacy keyboards and mouse to computers. ▪ PS/2 ports can be useful in scenarios where USB ports are limited.
Serial Port (RS-232)	▪ Serial ports are typically **9-pin** or **25-pin connectors** that transmit data one bit at a time over long distances.	▪ Serial ports are still used in specific fields such as manufacturing and telecommunications. ▪ They are often used in **industrial applications.**
Parallel Port (Printer Port)	▪ Parallel ports use a **25-pin connector** and can transmit multiple bits of data simultaneously.	▪ Connects printers and other parallel devices to computers.
FireWire (IEEE 1394)	▪ FireWire ports can connect devices at speeds of up to 800 Mbps. ▪ They support both data transfer and power delivery, allowing devices to operate without an external power source.	▪ Connects external hard drives, camcorders and audio interfaces, particularly in video editing and professional audio production. ▪ FireWire is less common today due to the development of USB and Thunderbolt.

Factors Affecting CPU Performance

Several factors affect the speed of the CPU and its overall performance.

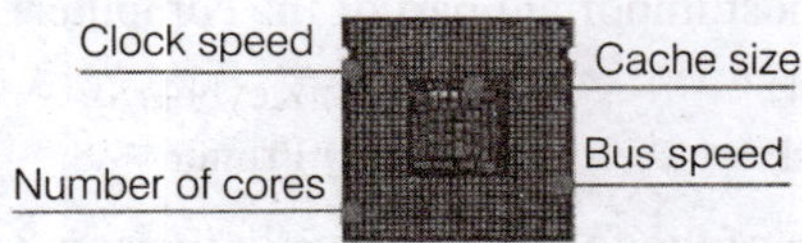

Here are the key factors

- **Clock Speed** The clock speed, measured in **GHz** (gigahertz), determines how many cycles per second the CPU can execute. Higher clock speeds generally mean faster processing.
- **Number of Cores** Modern CPUs have multiple cores (dual-core, quad-core, etc.), which allow them to perform multiple tasks simultaneously. More cores improve multitasking and parallel processing.
- **Cache Size** The CPU cache is a small, high-speed memory that stores frequently used data. A larger cache allows the CPU to retrieve data faster, reducing the need to access slower RAM.
- **Bus Speed** The speed of the system bus affects how quickly data is transferred to and from the CPU. A faster bus speed improves overall CPU performance.
- **Power Supply** The quality and stability of power supply can also affect CPU speed and performance.

These factors combined influence how efficiently and quickly the CPU can execute tasks.

Important Abbreviations

CPU Central Processing Unit
ALU Arithmetic Logic Unit
CU Control Unit
IC Integrated Circuit
ISA Instruction Set Architecture
PCB Printed Circuit Board
PCI Peripheral Components Interconnect
USB Universal Serial Bus
HDMI High Definition Multimedia Interface
VGA Video Graphics Array
DVI Digital Visual interface

PYQs Oneliner

1. To listen to songs from computer, you need to install **sound card**. *CPCT 2024*
2. The three main parts of CPU are **ALU**, **control unit** and **memory**. *DSSSB TGT 2023*
3. **Parallel port** is also known as line printer port. *SSC CGL 2023*
4. **Single core** is the oldest type of Central Processing Unit. *SSC CGL 2023*
5. **PS/2 port** is also called as mouse port. *SSC CGL 2023*
6. **Parallel port** is used for connecting 8 or more data wires to provide high speed data transmission. *DSSSB Patwari 2022*

Practice Exercise

Introduction to Computer Architecture

1. .... forms the backbone for building successful computer system.
(a) Computer architecture (b) Computer model
(c) Computer instructions (d) None of these

2. The first computer architecture was introduced in
(a) 1970 (b) 1945 (c) 1971 (d) 1973

3. Which of the following is a way in which the components of a computer are connected to each other?
(a) Computer architecture (b) Computer parts
(c) Computer hardware (d) None of these

Components of Computer Architecture

4. The three main parts of central processing unit (CPU processor) are *DSSSB TGT 2023*
(a) Cache, ALU and RAM
(b) Control unit, RAM and cache
(c) ALU, control unit and registers
(d) ALU, control unit and RAM

5. Which of the following statements is/are false?
(i) The Central Processing Unit (CPU)is fabricated as a single Integrated Circuit (IC) chip and is also referred to as microprocessor.
(ii) Arithmetic and logic unit holds the CPU's instruction set, which is a list of all operations that the CPU can perform. *DSSSB Patwari 2022*
(a) Only (ii) (b) Both (i) and (ii)
(c) Only (i) (d) Neither (i) nor (ii)

6. ....is the oldest type of Central Processing Unit (CPU). *SSC CGL 2023*
(a)Triple core (b) Single core
(c)Dual core (d) Quad core

7. Which among the following statements is incorrect about Central Processing Unit? *SSC CGL 2023*
(a) Control Unit controls the order in which instructions enter and leave the processor and how the instructions are executed.
(b) Arithmetic Logic Unit is responsible for taking the input, converting it into a signal and storing it for further processing
(c) Arithmetic Logic Unit is also known as the mathematical brain of a computer.
(d) Control Unit directs and manages operation sequences.

8. ……is a high-speed device used in CPU that is utilized to store data temporarily during processing. *SSC CGL 2023*
(a) Arithmetic and Logic Unit (ALU)
(b) Auxiliary Memory
(c) Control Unit
(d) Registers

9. The speed of a CPU can be measured in .... *RRB NTPC 2021, SSC Selection Post 2023*
(a) megahertz (MHz) (b) bits per second (Bps)
(c) lux (d) horsepower

10. ………… unit performs the arithmetic and logical operations on the data made available to it. *HSSC 2021*
(a) Input unit (b) Storage unit
(c) Output unit (d) ALU

11. Which of the following controls memory, input and output devices?
(a) CPU (b) ALU
(c) CU (d) Memory

12. The most important part of the computer. *RRB NTPC 2020*
(a) CPU (b) Keyboard
(c) Disk (d) Printer

13. Which of the following units in the computer is responsible for data processing and is also known as the electronic brain of the computer? *SSC CHSL 2020*
(a) Central Processing Unit (CPU)
(b) Keyboard
(c) Hard Disk
(d) RAM

14. Which of the following statements is not correct? *UP RO/ARO Pre 2021*
(a) E-mail refers to Electronic mail.
(b) WWW refers to World Wide Web.
(c) CPU refers to Control Processing Unit.
(d) ALU refers to Arithmetic Logic Unit.

15. In the context of computer, ALU stands for *RRB NTPC 2020*
(a) Algebraic Logic Unit
(b) Arithmetic Logic Unit
(c) Algebraic Local Unit
(d) Arithmetic Local Unit

16. .... unit is the part of the CPU that controls or directs the actions of the processor. *SSC CGL 2023*
(a) Control (b) Memory
(c) Arithmetic logic (d) Data

17. Which of the following is the function of control unit in CPU? *UKPSC (Pre) 2021*
(a) Decode program instruction
(b) Performing logical work
(c) Storing programs
(d) None of the above

18. The process of writing new data in the register *SSC CHSL 2018*
(a) Erases the first contents of the register
(b) Does not destroy the existing content
(c) Possible only if the register is operator
(d) None of the above

19. The speed of the microprocessor is known as .... *RRB NTPC 2021*
(a) clock speed (b) mega speed
(c) bit speed (d) rotation

20. Critical system components such as Central Processing Unit (CPU) and Random Access Memory (RAM) modules directly linked to .... *SSC CHSL 2023*
(a) magnetic tape (b) motherboard
(c) optical disc (d) flash memory

21. The system unit
(a) coordinates input and output devices
(b) is the container that houses electronic components
(c) is a combination of hardware and software
(d) controls and manipulates data

22. A(n) .... device is any device that provides information, which is sent to the CPU.
(a) input (b) output (c) CPU (d) memory

23. Which of the following includes as a type of input?
(a) Data (b) Programs
(c) Commands (d) All of these

24. Input unit converts data in computer in .... form.
(a) suitable (b) acceptable
(c) understandable (d) rejectable

25. This unit sends the processed results to the user.
(a) Input (b) Output (c) Memory (d) CPU

26. Output unit includes
(a) plotter (b) printer (c) monitor (d) All of these

27. This component is required to process data into information and consists of integrated circuits.
(a) Hard disk (b) RAM
(c) CPU (d) ROM

28. Which of the following statements about the Central Processing Unit (CPU) is/are correct? *SSC CGL (T-II) 20.01.2025*
1. The CPU is often referred to as the 'brain' of the computer.
2. The CPU consists of three main units: the control unit (CU), arithmetic logic unit (ALU) and cache memory.
(a) Neither 1 nor 2 (b) Only 2
(c) Only 1 (d) Both 1 and 2

29. Where does computer add and compare data?
(a) Hard disk (b) Floppy disk
(c) CPU (d) Memory chip

30. In computer, which of the following unit is responsible for processing and also known as brain of computer? *SSC CGL 2019*
(a) CPU (b) Keyboard
(c) Hard disk (d) RAM

31. The main job of a CPU is to
(a) carry out program instructions
(b) store data/information for further use
(c) process data and information
(d) Both (a) and (c)

32. The main purpose of time-sharing techniques used in computers is to make the best use of the
(a) CPU (b) peripherals
(c) secondary storage (d) floppy disk

33. What is the purpose of the Arithmetic Logic Unit (ALU) in a Central Processing Unit (CPU)? *SSC CHSL 2024*
(a) It executes program instructions by performing calculations and logical comparisons.
(b) It manages the data flow between the CPU fan.
(c) It controls the speed of the CPU fan.
(d) It connects the CPU to peripheral devices.

34. The CPU comprises of control, memory and ..... units.
(a) microprocessor (b) arithmetic/logic
(c) output (d) ROM

35. Select which of the given statement(s) is/are True or False for the Central Processing Unit (CPU) of the Computer Systems. *SSC CGL (T-II) 18.01.2025*
(i) The CPU's clock speed controls the timing and execution speed of instructions.
(ii) The CPU's cache memory provides high-speed access to frequently used instructions and data.
(a) (i) True, (ii) True (b) (i) False, (ii) True
(c) (i) False, (ii) False (d) (i) True, (ii) False

36. Which unit of computer helps in communication between the memory and the arithmetic logical unit?
(a) CMU (b) CCU (c) UPS (d) CPU

37. Which part of the computer is used for calculating and comparing?
(a) ALU (b) Control unit
(c) Disc unit (d) Modem

38. Pick the odd one out in the Central Processing Unit (CPU) of a computer. *SSC CHSL 2023*
(a) ALU and control unit both
(b) Control unit
(c) ALU (Arithmetic Logic Unit)
(d) Output unit

39. It is responsible for all numerical and logical calculations
(a) CPU (b) CU (c) MU (d) ALU

40. The … unit is that part of the CPU which controls or directs the operations of the processor. *SSC CHSL (T-II) 2023*
(a) memory (b) arithmetic logic
(c) control (d) data

41. Processors contain a control unit and a/an
(a) control unit (b) primary storage unit
(c) input unit (d) arithmetic logic unit

42. Which of the following executes the computer commands?
(a) Arithmetic unit (b) Logic unit
(c) Both (a) and (b) (d) Control unit

43. Which unit is a combinational digital electronic circuit that performs arithmetic and bitwise operations on integer binary numbers?
(a) BOU (b) AEU (c) CPU (d) ALU

44. Internal memory in a CPU is nothing but
(a) a set of registers (b) a set of ALU
(c) microprocessor (d) bus

45. Which among the following is a small set of data holding place that is a part of the computer processor and may hold an instruction, a storage address or any kind of data?
(a) Register (b) WAN (c) Bus (d) Address

46. The portion of the CPU that coordinates the activities of all the other computer components is the
(a) motherboard (b) coordination board
(c) control unit (d) arithmetic logic unit

47. Which among the following is an important circuitry in a computer system that directs the operation of the processor?
(a) Memory (b) Address Bus
(c) Accumulator (d) Control unit

48. The part of a computer that coordinates all its functions, is called
(a) ROM program (b) system board
(c) arithmetic logic unit (d) control unit

49. The control unit controls other units by generating
(a) control signal (b) timing signal
(c) transfer signal (d) command signal

50. Control unit of a digital computer is often called the
(a) clock (b) nerve centre
(c) Both (a) and (b) (d) IC

51. Memory unit that communicates directly with the CPU is called the
(a) main memory (b) secondary memory
(c) auxiliary memory (d) register

52. CPU retrieves its data and instructions from
(a) secondary memory (b) auxiliary memory
(c) main memory (d) All of these

53. Which computer memory is used for storing programs and data currently being processed by the CPU?
(a) Mass memory (b) Internal memory
(c) Non-volatile memory (d) PROM

54. The I/O processor has a direct access to …… and contains a number of independent data channels.
(a) main memory (b) secondary memory
(c) cache (d) flash memory

55. The word computer usually refers to the central processing unit plus
(a) external memory (b) internal memory
(c) input devices (d) output devices

56. Which is not an integral part of computer?
(a) CPU (b) Mouse
(c) Monitor (d) UPS

Microprocessor

57. Who invented the first microprocessor?
(a) Vint Cerf (b) Terence Percival
(c) John Mauchly (d) Ted Hoff

58. A microprocessor is the brain of the computer and is also called a
(a) microchip (b) macrochip
(c) macroprocessor (d) calculator

59. Microprocessors can be used to make
(a) computer (b) digital system
(c) calculators (d) All of these

60. High power microprocessor is *UPSSSC 2019*
(a) Pentium, Pentium pro
(b) Pentium II and III
(c) Pentium II
(d) All of these

61. The microprocessor of a computer
(a) does not understand machine language
(b) understands machine language and high level language
(c) understands only machine language
(d) understands only high level languages

Motherboard

62. Which of the following option can be used to describe a sound card? *DSSSB Patwari 2022*
(a) Supports adjacent vertical lines of different sound that are machine readable
(b) Used to detect sound on a card device
(c) Used to detect sound directly on computer screen.
(d) Translates analog audio signals from microphone into digital codes and vice-versa, so that the computer can store and process

63. To listen to the songs from your computer, you need to install a ………… on your computer. *CPCT 2024*
(a) sound card
(b) network interface card
(c) memory card
(d) PC card

64. The main Printed Circuit Board (PCB) in a computer is …… . *SSC CGL 2018*
(a) ROM (Read Only Memory)
(b) CPU (Central Processing Unit)
(c) RAM (Random Access Memory)
(d) Motherboard

65. Personal computers use a number of chips mounted on a main circuit board. What is the common name for such boards?
(a) Daughterboard (b) Motherboard
(c) Broadboard (d) None of these

66. Which of the following are the components that reside on motherboard?
(a) CMOS battery (b) Fan
(c) PCI slot (d) All of these

67. What is the main function of a motherboard?
(a) To store data
(b) To connect and communicate between computer component
(c) To provide power to the CPU
(d) To execute instructions

68. …. is the key circuit board holding the essential processing parts of a computer. *SSC CHSL 2023*
(a) Firmware
(b) Central processing unit
(c) Random access memory
(d) Motherboard

Interconnection of Units *Via* Buses

69. In computer memory, ….. bus is used to transfer addresses between CPU and the main memory. *SSC CHSL 2023*
(a) address (b) data
(c) status (d) control

70. ….are a set of wires, which carries a group of bits in parallel and has an associated control scheme. It provides a communication path between two or more devices of a computer system. *SSC CGL 2023*
(a) Buses (b) Control unit
(c) Register (d) Cache

71. ………… is a set of connections between two or more components/devices, which are designed to transfer several/all bits of a word from the source of the destination. *HSSC 2021*
(a) Memory (b) Bus
(c) Processor (d) None of these

72. ………… connects the different external devices, peripherals, expansion slots, I/O ports and drive connections to the rest of the computer. *HSSC 2021*
(a) Internal bus (b) System bus
(c) External bus (d) Data bus

73. ………… provides a path to transfer data between CPU and memory. *HSSC 2021*
(a) Control bus (b) Address bus
(c) Data bus (d) None of these

74. Which of the following best describe the system bus? *SSC CGL 2023*
(a) A single bus that handles all operations
(b) A combination of address, data and control buses
(c) A bus used only for input/output devices
(d) A bus dedicated to graphics data transfer

75. A physical connection between the microprocessor memory and other parts of the micro computer is known as
(a) path (b) bus
(c) route (d) All of these

76. The read/write line belongs to
(a) the data bus (b) the control bus
(c) the address bus (d) CPU bus

77. The name of the location of a particular piece of data is its
(a) address (b) memory name
(c) storage (d) data location

78. Which of the following is used to connect the different external devices?
(a) Address bus (b) Data bus
(c) Control bus (d) External bus

79. A device that not only provides surge protection, but also furnishes the computer with battery backup power during a power outage is
(a) battery strip (b) UPS
(c) surge strip (d) USB

80. What is a power strip? *UPSSSC 2019*

(a) It is an electrical device that is used to expand the capacity of a wall outlet which can accommodate the devices.
(b) It plugs multiple components into one power outlet.
(c) It provides power supply for electronic devices.
(d) It is used to increase the magnitude of voltage/ current/power of an input signal.

Instruction Cycle

81. What is the purpose of the decode phase in the instruction cycle?

(a) To retrieve the instruction from memory
(b) To determine the instruction to be performed by the CPU
(c) To perform the actual operation
(d) To write the result back to memory

82. Which of the following phases is responsible for carrying out the operation specified by the instruction?

(a) Fetch
(b) Decode
(c) Execute
(d) Store

83. What happens during the store phase of the instruction cycle?

(a) The instruction is retrieved from memory
(b) The result of execution is written back to memory
(c) The instruction is decoded
(d) The next instruction is fetched

Computer Ports

84. Which of the following port is used for connecting eight or more data wires to provide high speed data transmission? *DSSSB Patwari 2022*

(a) Parallel
(b) Serial
(c) USB
(d) Firewire

85. Which among the following ports is also known as Line Printer Port? *SSC CGL 2023*

(a) Parallel
(b) Video Graphic Array
(c) High Definition Media Interface
(d) Display

86. A ….. port transmits one bit of a byte at a time as a single stream of bits.It is meant for transmitting slow data over long distances. *SSC CGL 2023*

(a) parallel (b) universal serial bus
(c) serial (d) display

87. Which among the following ports is also called as mouse port? *SSC CGL 2023*

(a) Video Graphic Array
(b) High Definition Media Interface
(c) Firewire
(d) PS/2

Factors Affecting CPU Performance

88. Which of the following factors directly affects the speed of a computer's CPU?

(a) Clock speed (b) Screen resolution
(c) Operating system (d) Number of USB ports

89. How does an increase in RAM improve computer performance?

(a) By increasing processing power
(b) By allowing more data to be stored temporarily
(c) By improving graphic resolution
(d) By speeding up the hard drive

90. How does a higher cache memory in the CPU affect computer performance?

(a) It improves the quality of audio output
(b) It reduces the amount of data stored on the hard drive
(c) It speeds up the retrieval of frequently used data
(d) It increases the size of the monitor display

Answers

1.	(a)	2.	(b)	3.	(a)	4.	(c)	5.	(a)	6.	(b)	7.	(b)	8.	(d)	9.	(a)	10.	(d)
11.	(c)	12.	(a)	13.	(a)	14.	(c)	15.	(b)	16.	(a)	17.	(a)	18.	(a)	19.	(a)	20.	(b)
21.	(a)	22.	(a)	23.	(d)	24.	(c)	25.	(b)	26.	(d)	27.	(c)	28.	(c)	29.	(c)	30.	(a)
31.	(d)	32.	(a)	33.	(a)	34.	(b)	35.	(a)	36.	(d)	37.	(a)	38.	(d)	39.	(d)	40.	(c)
41.	(d)	42.	(d)	43.	(d)	44.	(a)	45.	(a)	46.	(c)	47.	(d)	48.	(d)	49.	(a)	50.	(b)
51.	(a)	52.	(c)	53.	(b)	54.	(a)	55.	(b)	56.	(d)	57.	(d)	58.	(a)	59.	(d)	60.	(d)
61.	(c)	62.	(d)	63.	(a)	64.	(d)	65.	(b)	66.	(d)	67.	(b)	68.	(d)	69.	(a)	70.	(a)
71.	(b)	72.	(c)	73.	(c)	74.	(b)	75.	(b)	76.	(b)	77.	(a)	78.	(d)	79.	(b)	80.	(b)
81.	(b)	82.	(c)	83.	(b)	84.	(a)	85.	(a)	86.	(c)	87.	(d)	88.	(a)	89.	(b)	90.	(c)

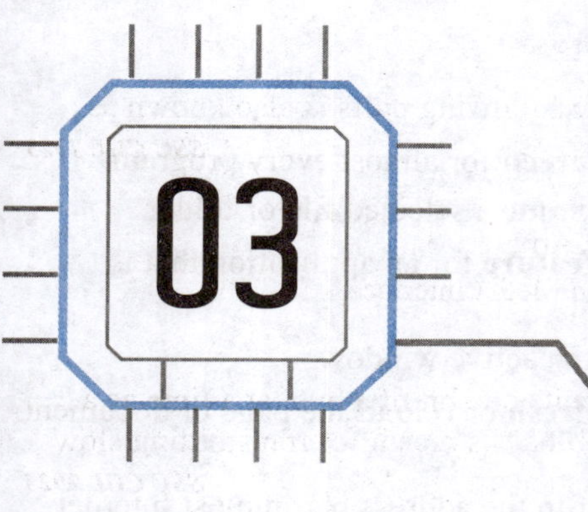

Input and Output Devices

- Input and output devices are the medium to **establish connection** between the user and the computer.
- **Input devices** allow users to provide data and instructions to the computer, whereas **output devices** display or convey the processed data from the computer to the user.
- Input devices act as the communication channel from the user to the computer.
- Output devices act as the communication channel from the computer back to the user.

In this Chapter

- Input Devices
  - Manual Data Entry Devices
  - Direct Data Entry Devices
- Output Devices
  - Hard Copy Output
  - Soft Copy Output
- Devices that Serve Both Input and Output Functions

> "Computers are good at following instructions, but not at reading your mind.
>
> ~ **Bill Gates**"

Input Devices

- The devices which are used to give instructions and provide data to the computer are known as **input devices**.
- They act as the **bridge** between the user and the computer's internal systems.
- Input device includes keyboards, mouse, scanners and microphones, etc.

Classification of Input Devices

- Manual Data Entry Devices
  - Keyboard
  - Mouse
  - Joystick
  - Light Pen
  - Track Ball
- Direct Data Entry Devices
  - Scanner
  - Digitizer
  - Bar Code Reader
  - OCR/OMR
  - MICR
  - Smart Card Reader
  - QR code Reader
  - Biometric
  - Microphone
  - Webcam
  - Digital Camera
  - Voice Recognition System

Manual Data Entry Devices

Keyboard

- Keyboard is also known as the **primary/standard input device.**

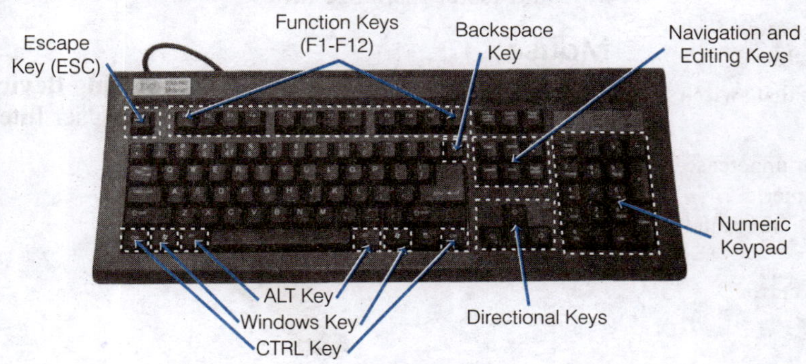

- Keyboard was invented by **Christopher Latham Sholes** in 19th century.
- Keyboard is used to enter **alphanumeric data** into the computer.
- A standard keyboard typically has **104 keys** whereas multimedia keyboard can have upto 110 keys.

Types of Keys on a Keyboard

Name	Description
Alphanumeric Keys	▪ Includes **letters** (A-Z) and **numbers** (0-9) for typing text and numbers.
Function Keys	▪ Located at the top (F1 to F12), these keys perform special functions.
Control Keys	▪ Includes keys like Ctrl, Alt, Shift and the Windows/Command key. ▪ Used for **shortcuts** or **combined** with other keys to perform actions.
Navigation Keys	▪ Arrow keys, Home, End, Page Up and Page Down are used for moving the **cursor** or **scrolling**.
Numeric Keypad	▪ A set of **numbers** and **mathematical symbols** located on the right side for quick numerical input. ▪ Numeric keys are also present on main keyboard and both have same result.
Special Character Key	▪ These keys include **special character** (!, @, #, $, %, ^, &, *, ( )) and **punctuation** (comma (,), period (.), question mark (?), etc.)
Escape Key	▪ A key located at the top-left corner of the keyboard. ▪ Used to **cancel operations**, **close dialogs** or **exit full-screen mode**.
Enter Key	▪ A key typically located on the right side of the main section of the keyboard. ▪ Used to execute commands, input data or create a new line in text applications.
Backspace Key	▪ Deletes the character to the **left of the cursor**.
Delete Key	▪ Deletes the character to the **right of the cursor**.
Spacebar	▪ Used to insert **spaces** between words and characters. ▪ This is the **longest** key on the keyboard.
Tab Key	▪ Used to create **indentation** in text or move the cursor to the next field in forms or tables.
Toggle Keys	▪ Toggle keys on a keyboard are keys that **switch functions** ON or OFF. ▪ Toggle keys include **Caps Lock** (for uppercase letters), **Num Lock** (controls the numeric keypad) and **Insert** (toggles between insert and overwrite modes).
Print Screen (PrtScn)	▪ A key that captures an image of the current screen.

Function Keys

- **F1** opens the **help screen** for almost every program.
- **F2** allows you to **rename** a selected file or folder.
- **F3** opens a **search feature** for an application that is active at the moment.
- **F4** Alt + F4 **closes** the active window.
- **F5** allows you to **refresh** or **reload** the page or document window.
- **F6** moves the cursor to the address bar in most Internet browsers.
- **F7** used to check **spelling** and **grammar** in microsoft apps.
- **F8** used to access the **boot menu** in Windows when turning on the computer.
- **F9** refreshes a document in Microsoft Word and sends and receives emails in Outlook.
- **F10** Opens the menu bar of an open application. Shift + F10 is the same as right clicking.
- **F11** enters and exits **full screen mode** in Internet browsers.
- **F12** opens the **Save As** dialog box in Microsoft Word.

Types of Keyboard

1. **QWERTY Keyboard** The most common keyboard layout, named after the first six letters on the top row of letters.
2. **Ergonomic Keyboard** Designed to reduce strain on the hands and wrists, often featuring a split layout.
3. **Virtual Keyboard** An on-screen keyboard used on touchscreens (e.g., tablets, smartphones).
4. **Mechanical Keyboard** Uses individual mechanical switches for each key, preferred by typists and gamers for tactile feedback.
5. **Membrane Keyboard** Common in most modern computers, with a pressure pad beneath the keys.
6. **Gaming Keyboard** Comes with additional features like customizable RGB lighting, programmable keys and faster response times.

Mouse

- A computer mouse is a **handheld pointing device** used to interact with a computer's Graphical User Interface.

- Mouse stands for **Manually Operated User Selection Equipment.**
- It allows users to move the cursor on the screen, select objects and execute commands by clicking.
- It was invented by **Douglas Engelbart** in 1964. The first prototype was made of wood and had two metal wheels to detect movement.
- The first commercially available mouse was produced by **Xerox** for its **Alto computer** in the 1970s.

Mouse Pointer/Cursor

A visual indicator on the screen that shows the current position where the mouse is pointing or where text will be entered. The cursor changes shape based on the context.

Pointer Shapes

Normal Select	↖	Vertical Resize	↕
Help Select	↖?	Horizontal Resize	↔
Working in Background	↖⌛	Diagonal Resize 1	↖↘
Busy	⌛	Diagonal Resize 2	↙↗
Precision Select	+	Move	✥
Text Select	I	Alternate Select	↑
Handwriting	✎	Drag-make copy	↖⊞
Unavailable	⊘	Drag-make shortcut	↖⧉

Functions of a Mouse

1. **Single Click**
   - Pressing and quickly releasing the left mouse button once is called **single click.**
   - It selects an item (like files, folders or icons) and opens an application or file when clicked on its icon.
2. **Double Click**
   - Rapidly pressing and releasing the left mouse button twice is called **double click.**
   - It opens files or applications (e.g., double-clicking a document icon).
3. **Right Click**
   - Pressing and releasing the right mouse button opens a context menu with options related to the selected item.
4. **Dragging and Dropping**
   - Users can click and hold the left mouse button on an item, move the mouse to a new location and then release the button to drag the item to a different position or folder.
5. **Scrolling**
   - Most mouse have a scroll wheel that enables vertical scrolling through documents, web pages and lists.
   - This function allows users to move up and down without using scroll bars.
6. **Pointing**
   - A mouse is used to point or mark any object on the monitor.

Types of Computer Mouse

1. **Mechanical Mouse** uses a **rubber** or **metal ball** to detect movement.
2. **Optical Mouse** uses a **Light-Emitting Diode (LED)** and a **sensor** to detect movement on surfaces.
3. **Laser Mouse** uses **laser technology** for high precision on various surfaces.
4. **Wireless Mouse** connects *via* Bluetooth or RF, eliminating the need for cables.

Joystick

- A joystick is an input device used to control **video games** or **computer applications** by moving a stick in different directions.

- It can be **analog** (smooth, continuous movement) or **digital** (fixed directional inputs).
- Joystick is used in gaming, flight simulators and robotics for precise control.

Light Pen

- A light pen is an input device that allows users to interact with a computer screen by **pointing** and **drawing** directly on it.

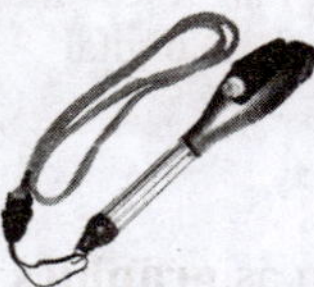

- This is commonly used in graphic design, CAD applications and for educational purposes, especially for drawing and annotations.

Track Ball

- A trackball is an input device that consists of a **stationary ball** housed in a socket, allowing users to control the cursor by rolling the ball with their fingers or palm.

- Track ball was developed by **Ralph Benjamin** in 1946.

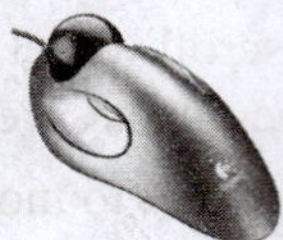

- This is used in graphic design, CAD applications and for users with limited mobility, as it requires less arm movement compared to traditional mouse.

Direct Data Entry Devices

Scanner

- A scanner is an input device that converts physical documents, images or objects into digital format for storage and manipulation on a computer.

- It uses a **light source** and **sensors** to capture the details of the document, creating a digital image that can be saved in various file formats (e.g., JPEG, PDF).
- Used in various fields for digitizing documents.

Types of Scanner and their Use

Scanner	Description	Use
Flatbed Scanner	▪ Features a flat glass surface where documents or images are placed for scanning.	▪ Ideal for scanning books, magazines, photos and documents.
Handheld Scanner	▪ A portable scanner that can be moved over the document or image being scanned.	▪ Great for on-the-go scanning or for items that cannot be placed on a flatbed.
Drum Scanner	▪ Uses a cylindrical drum to hold the document and scan with high precision.	▪ Primarily used in professional printing and high-resolution imaging.
3D Scanner	▪ Captures the physical shape of an object and creates a 3D digital model.	▪ Commonly used in engineering, design and gaming industries.

Digitizer

- A digitizer also known as **graphics tablet**, is an input device that allows users to create digital drawings by drawing directly onto a flat surface with a **stylus** or **light pen**.

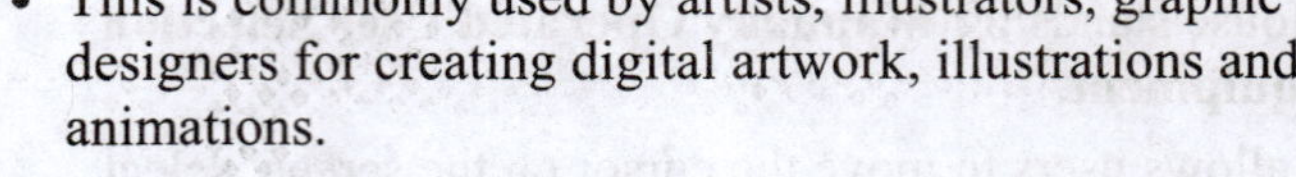

- This is commonly used by artists, illustrators, graphic designers for creating digital artwork, illustrations and animations.

Barcode Reader

- A barcode reader is a **hand held** input device that captures and interprets barcode data, converting it into a digital format that can be processed by computers.

- It uses a **laser** or **camera** to scan the barcode, which consists of parallel lines and spaces that represent data (like product information).
- It is used in retail, inventory management, shipping and receiving and healthcare for tracking products.

OCR (Optical Character Reader/ Recognition)

- OCR is an input technology that converts different types of documents, such as scanned paper documents, PDFs or images, into editable and searchable data.

- It analysis the shapes of characters in the scanned images and translates them into machine-encoded text. This process involves recognising letters, numbers and symbols.

OMR (Optical Mark Reader/Recognition)

- OMR is an input technology used to capture and read human-marked data from specially printed paper.

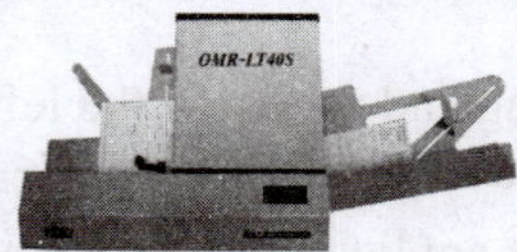

- OMR is used in standardized testing (e.g., multiple-choice exams), surveys and voting systems, where quick and accurate data collection is essential.

MICR (Magnetic Ink Character Reader/Recognition)

- MICR is an input technology used to read and process documents printed with special **magnetic ink**, primarily for **financial transactions**.

- MICR is used in banking for processing cheques and other financial documents.

Smart Card Reader

- A smart card reader is an input device that reads data from smart cards, which are embedded with **microchips** that can store and process information.

- It used in banking, access control, identification and mobile payments.
- It provides secure authentication and data transfer.

QR Code Reader

- A QR code reader is a device that scans and interprets QR codes, which are **two-dimensional barcodes** that can store various types of information, such as URLs, text or contact details.

- It uses a camera or scanner to capture the QR code image, then processes the pattern of black and white squares to extract the encoded information and display it on the screen.

Biometric

- Biometric input devices are technology systems that identify and verify individuals based on unique **physiological characteristics**, such as fingerprints, facial recognition, voice recognition or iris patterns.

- It is used in security systems, access control, mobile devices (like smartphones) and border control to enhance security and streamline identity verification processes.

Microphone

- A microphone is an input device that converts **sound waves** into **electrical signals** and allows audio to be captured for **recording** or **amplification**.

- It is used in music production, broadcasting, public speaking and communication technologies, enabling clear audio capture and transmission.

Webcam

- Webcam is a small camera connected to a computer or integrated into a laptop that captures video and images, typically used for video communication.

Web camera

Digital Camera

- A digital camera captures and digitizes images and videos, converting them into electronic data that can be stored and processed by computers.

Voice Recognition System

- A voice recognition system is an input device that converts **spoken language** into **text** or **commands**, allow users to interact with devices using their voice.
- It captures audio through a microphone, processes the sound waves and uses algorithms to analyse and recognise the spoken words or phrases, translating them into actionable data or commands.

Facts Drive

- Any external devices that connect to the computer to expand its capabilities, including both input and output devices are called **peripheral devices**.
- **Ralph H. Baer** is known as the **Father of Video Games** and played a significant role in the development of joysticks for gaming.
- **Space bar** is the longest key on keyboard.

Output Devices

- A device that converts information into human understandable form and presents it to the user is called an **output device**.
- Some output devices are monitor, printer, projector, etc.

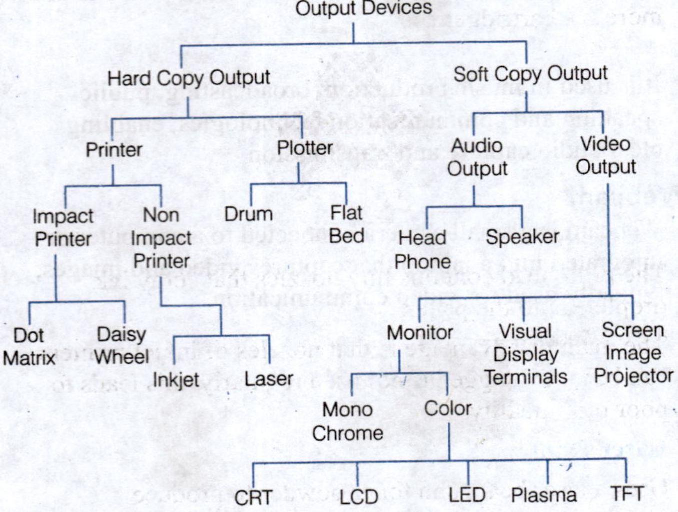

Hardcopy Output Devices

Printer

- A printer is an output device that prints the information received from the computer on paper.
- Printers can produce either **monochrome** or **color** prints.
- They are widely used for printing text documents, photos and other graphics.
- Printer quality is measured by **resolution** (DPI- Dots per Inch) for sharpness, **print speed** (PPM- Page per Minute) for efficiency.

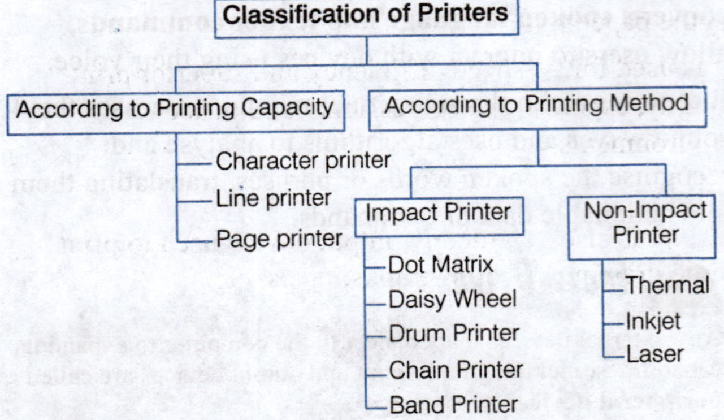

A. According to Printing Capacity

1. Character Printers

- Character printers are a type of printer that print **one character** at a time.
- Its printing quality is measured in **Character Per Second** (CPS).
- These printers use mechanical methods to create text by **striking** an **inked ribbon** against paper.
- Its ability to print only one character at a time, makes it slower compared to page or line printers.

Example Daisy wheel printer, dot matrix printer

2. Line Printer

- Line printers print **one entire line** of text at a time, rather than one character.
- Its printing quality is measured in **Line Per Minute** (LPM).
- These printers are designed for high-speed, bulk printing of large volumes of text, typically in environments that require continuous, large-scale printing.

Example Drum printer, chain printer and band printer.

3. Page Printer

- Page printers are a type of printer that can print an entire page of text or graphics in a single pass.
- Its printing quality is measured in **Page Per Minute** (PPM).
- Page printers are much faster and more efficient, makes them ideal for high-volume, high-quality printing.

Example Laser printer and inkjet printer.

B. According to Printing Method

Impact Printer

- Impact printers are a type of printer that uses mechanical force to strike an ink ribbon against the paper.
- This method of printing is similar to the typewriter method.

There are many types of impact printers

1. Dot Matrix Printer

- Creates text and images by striking pins against an ink ribbon to form dots on the paper.
- The combination of these dots creates characters and graphical images.

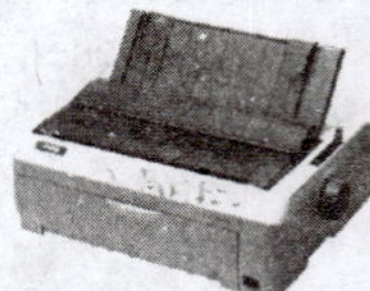

- The print head of dot matrix printer consists of a matrix of tiny pins (usually 9 or 24 pins) arranged in a vertical row. The pins move back and forth to strike the ink ribbon.
- Dot matrix printer is also called **bidirectional printer** as it can print in both directions- left to right and right to left.

2. Daisy Wheel Printer

- Prints text by striking a wheel with pre-formed characters against an inked ribbon, transferring ink onto the paper.
- The core component of a daisy wheel printer is a daisy-shaped wheel.
- Each petal of the daisy contains a different character (like letters, numbers or punctuation).
- Although not as fast as dot matrix printers, it is known for producing high-quality text compared to dot matrix printers.

3. Drum Printer

- Uses a rotating drum with pre-formed characters or symbols to print text on paper.
- The drum contains a series of characters engraved on its surface and as it rotates, the appropriate characters strike the paper through an inked ribbon, transfers ink and creates the printed text.

4. Chain Printer

- Prints text by using a rotating chain with characters or symbols attached to it.
- The chain moves continuously and the appropriate character strikes against the paper *via* a hammer, transfers ink from the ribbon to the paper.

5. Band Printer

- Uses a continuous band (often metal or plastic) with pre-formed characters to print text onto paper.
- The band rotates and positions the appropriate character in front of an impact hammer or print head, which strikes the ribbon and transfers the character onto the paper.

Non-Impact Printer

- A non-impact printer is a type of printer that does not rely on mechanical impact or striking to transfer ink or toner onto paper.
- Instead, non-impact printers use different technologies like heat, lasers or inkjets to print text or images on paper, resulting in a quieter and faster printing experience.

There are three types of non-impact printers

1. Thermal Printer

- Uses **heat** to transfer ink or create an image directly on paper.
- Thermal printers use special heat-sensitive paper called **thermal paper**.
- Thermal printers are fast, quiet and low-maintenance, makes them ideal for applications like receipt printing, barcode labeling and ticketing.

2. Inkjet Printer

- Creates images and text by **spraying liquid ink** onto paper.
- Inkjet printers use liquid ink, which is stored in one or more ink cartridges.

- The print head contains tiny nozzles that spray ink droplets onto the paper.
- The main disadvantage is that nozzles of inkjet printers can become clogged if not used regularly, this leads to poor print quality.

3. Laser Printer

- Uses a laser beam and toner powder to produce high-quality text and graphics on paper.

- In a laser printer, the process begins with the drum being electrically charged and a laser discharges specific areas to form the image.
- Toner powder is then applied to the drum, sticking to the discharged areas. The toner is transferred onto paper and heat from the fuser unit melts and permanently bonds it to the paper.
- It is used for its speed, efficiency and superior print quality, especially in professional and office environments.

Plotter

- Plotter is also a hardcopy output device used to print large drawings, charts, graphs, maps, etc.

- It is also used in 3D printing.

There are two types of plotter

1. Flatbed Plotter

- Flatbed plotters are ideal for creating detailed graphics, as they can handle large-sized papers or sheets.
- They are commonly used in engineering, architecture and graphic design.

2. Drum Plotter

- A drum plotter works by rolling a cylindrical drum with paper wrapped around it while the pen moves across the paper's surface to draw the image.
- Drum plotters were widely used for creating technical drawings and maps, but are now less common due to the rise of inkjet and laser printers.

Soft Copy Output Devices

Monitor (VDU- Visual Display Unit)

- Monitors are an essential part of computer output devices, provide visual displays of data, images and graphics generated by a computer.
- It serves as the **primary interface** through which users interact with the computer's software and data.
- It creates images by arranging microscopic dots in a rectangular pattern, called **pixels**.
- The quality of an image is determined by the number of pixels.

There are two types of monitors

Monochrome Monitor

- A monochrome monitor displays images and text in a single color on a contrasting background, typically **black** and **white**.

Color Monitor

- A color monitor can display a **full range of colors**, allows for more complex and visually detailed graphics, videos and images.

1. CRT (Cathode Ray Tube) **Monitor**

- CRT monitors were the standard type of monitors used in computers and televisions before the widespread of LCD, LED and other modern display technologies.
- It contains a large **vacuum tube** in which display is obtained by controlling the electron beam.

2. LCD Monitor

- In this, **liquid crystal** is filled between two layers, due to which display is created by voltage.
- They rely on backlighting (typically fluorescent lights) to produce a visible image.

3. LED Monitor

- A type of LCD monitor that uses LED lights for backlighting instead of traditional fluorescent lights.
- In LED monitors, display is created with the help of **light emission**.
- It produces **white light** as well as **RGB** (Red, Green, Blue) light.

4. Plasma Monitor

- Plasma monitors use **ionized gases** (plasma) that glow when electrically charged.
- Each pixel in a plasma screen is a small gas-filled cell. Larger and bulkier than LCD or LED monitors.
- Plasma displays were more commonly used in large-screen televisions.

5. TFT-Monitor

- TFT stands for Thin Film Transistors-Monitors.
- Its display is made with the help of active matrix technology.

Quality of Monitor

The quality of a monitor depends on various factors, which influence its overall performance and suitability for specific tasks.

Here's a breakdown of the key aspects that define the quality of a monitor.

1. Pixel

- Each image shown on the monitor is made up of tiny bright dots called **pixel.**
- It is the smallest unit of a digital image or display.
- It is measured in **Dots Per Inch** (DPI).

2. Resolution

- Resolution refers to the **number of pixels** displayed on the screen, typically given as width × height (e.g., 1920 × 1080).
- Higher resolution provides sharper and more detailed images.

3. DPI (Dots Per Inch)

- DPI is a measurement used to express the resolution of a display or printing device.
- It indicates how many dots or pixels can fit in one inch of space.

4. Refresh Rate

- Refresh rate refers to the number of times the screen refreshes the image per second.
- It is measured in Hertz (Hz).
- A higher refresh rate leads to smoother, more realistic on-screen visuals.

5. Response Time

- The time a monitor takes for a pixel to change from one color to another is called **response time**. It is measured in **milliseconds** (ms).

Projector

- A projector is an electronic device used to display an image or video on a large surface.
- It works by shining light through a lens onto a reflective surface to magnify and project the content to a bigger size.
- These are used for presentations, entertainment, education and business purposes.

Headphone

- Headphones (or earphones) are small personal audio devices worn over or in the ears.
- They provide a private listening experience by delivering sound directly to the user's ears.
- These are used for listening music, video calls, gaming and general media consumption.

Speaker

- A speaker is an output device that converts **electrical signals** (audio signals) into **sound waves**.
- These sound waves are heard by the listener in a room or space.
- Speakers are typically used for listening to music, watching videos, gaming or during presentations.

Devices that Serve Both Input and Output Functions

1. Touch Screen

- A touch screen is a versatile device that combines the functions of input and output.
- It allows users to interact with digital devices by touching the screen. It enables actions such as selecting items, typing or zooming (input).
- Simultaneously, it displays visual content like text, images, videos and apps (output).

2. Modem

- A modem is an Input/Output device that converts digital data into analog signals for transmission (output) and analog signals back into digital data for processing (input).
- It enables two-way communication, like sending requests and receiving data over the internet.

3. Network Interface Card (NIC)

- A NIC, enables a computer or device to connect to a network, such as the internet or a Local Area Network (LAN).
- It facilitates both receiving and sending data packets over the network.

4. Headset (with Microphone)

- A headset that includes both headphones and a microphone serves as both an input and output device.
- The microphone captures audio, such as voice during phone calls or video conferences, while the headphones output sound, allows the user to listen to music, calls or other audio content.

5. Facsimile (Fax) Machine

- A fax machine sends and receives documents through telephone lines. It scans a physical document, converts it into a digital signal and transmits it over the phone line.
- The fax machine acts as an input device when sends the documents and as an output device when receives them.

6. External Hard Drive

- An external hard drive functions as both an input and output device by allowing users to store and retrieve data.

Facts Drive

- The first touchscreen was invented in 1972 by **Dr. Samuel Hurst** at the **University of Kentucky**.
- The HP Page Wide Web Press holds the record for the fastest printer, printing 1,000 ft per minute.
- **Resolution** and **color depth** are key factors when considering output devices, especially monitors and printers.

Important Abbreviations

OCR Optical Character Reader
OMR Optical Mark Reader
MICR Magnetic Ink Character Reader/Recognition
DPI Dots Per Inch
PPI Pixels Per Inch
PCI Peripheral Component Interconnect
DVI Digital Visual Interface
LCD Liquid Crystal Display
VDU Visual Display Unit
TFT Thin Film Transistor
LED Light Emitting Diode
HD High Definition

PYQs Oneliner

1. A **trackball** is a stationary pointing device with a ball mechanism on its top. *CPCT 2024*
2. **Joystick** is generally used to play fast computer games. *CPCT 2024*
3. The bank's code number and cheque number printed on the cheques can be detected by a/an **MICR** reader. *CPCT 2024*
4. On the computer keyboard, function keys are labelled **F1 to F12**. *DSSSB 2024*
5. **Enter** is the command key on the keyboard. *DSSSB 2024*
6. The Cathode Ray Tube (CRT) display consists of small picture elements known as **pixel**. *CPCT 2024*
7. **Pointing device** is used to communicate with the computer by pointing to locations on the monitor screen. *HSSC 2021*
8. A **daisy wheel** printer cannot print more than one character at a time. *SSC CHSL 2021*
9. **OMR** is capable of recognising a pre-specified type of mark by pencil or pen. *SBI Clerk 2021*
10. Typically, a QWERTY keyboard contains **104** keys. *RRB NTPC 2021*
11. **Function keys** are present on the top row of the keyboard. *RRB-JE 2019*

Practice Exercise

Input Devices

1. After a picture has been taken with a digital camera and processed appropriately, the actual print of the picture is considered as
(a) data (b) output
(c) input (d) the process

2. OCR stands for *CPCT 2024*
(a) Optical Character Recognition
(b) Optical CPU Recognition
(c) Optimal Character Rendering
(d) Optical Computer Record

3. Which of the following is not a pointing device? *CPCT 2024*
(a) Joystick (b) Mouse
(c) Keyboard (d) Touch screen

4. A ………… is a stationary pointing device with a ball mechanism on its top. *CPCT 2024*
(a) trackball (b) mouse
(c) touchpad (d) touchscreen

5. The black and white elements of a barcode is scanned by illumination of the code with the …… , which is then converted into matching text. *CPCT 2024*
(a) yellow light (b) green light
(c) red light (d) blue light

6. Which of the following devices scans a particular document by recognising its individual characters and converting it into editable form? *CPCT 2024*
(a) Optical Mark Reader
(b) Optical Character Recognition
(c) Magnetic Ink Character Recognition
(d) Bar Code Reader

7. Which of the following devices consists of one or more buttons and a stick to control the movement of the cursor on the screen by pointing in all directions? *CPCT 2024*
(a) Mouse (b) Keyboard
(c) Joystick (d) Light pen

8. ………… is generally used to play fast computer games. *CPCT 2024*
(a) Track ball
(b) Joystick
(c) Touch surface
(d) Touch screen

9. Which of the following may not be a solution if the keyboard types the wrong letters? *CPCT 2024*
(a) Must have a settings issue and that's easy to fix.
(b) Need to set the correct keyboard layout.
(c) Make sure Num Lock isn't ON
(d) Having spacebar key replaced

10. Neeti wants to use an input device that works by sensing the user's finger movement and downward pressure. Which among the following should she use? *SSC CHSL 2023*
(a) Scanner (b) Touchpad
(c) Light pen (d) Keyboard

11. Which of the following is an input device? *SSC CHSL 2021*
(a) Speaker (b) Scanner
(c) Projector (d) Monitor

12. Which of the following is frequently used to ensure that data is correctly entered into a computer? *DSSSB TGT 2023*
(a) Keyboards (b) Speakers
(c) Input controls (d) Digitizers

13. .... is a reading device that reads printed text by scanning it character by character. *SSC CGL 2023*
(a) Track Ball
(b) Digitizer
(c) Magnetic Ink Card Reader (MICR)
(d) Optical Character Reader (OCR)

14. Which among the following statements is incorrect for input devices? *SSC CGL 2023*
(a) Input devices are not called as peripheral device.
(b) Input devices accepts user data.
(c) Input devices helps computer in receiving data.
(d) Optical Mark Reader is an input device.

15. Which of the following input devices works with a CRT monitor but not compatible with an LCD monitor? *CPCT 2024*
(a) Light pen (b) Mouse
(c) Keyboard (d) Webcam

16. The barcode scanner consists of a light source, a lens and a light sensor that .... *CPCT 2024*
(a) converts analog signal to digital signal
(b) translates optical impulses into electrical impulses
(c) converts digital signal to analog signal
(d) converts electronic wave to magnetic wave

17. In MICR, C stands for *CPCT 2024*
(a) Code (b) Colours
(c) Computer (d) Character

18. Which of the following devices is used to capture an image (drawing or photo) so that it can be stored on a computer? *CPCT 2024*
(a) Modem (b) Software
(c) Scanner (d) Keyboard

19. The bank's code number and cheque number printed on the cheques can be detected by a/an .... reader. *CPCT 2024*
(a) OCR (b) smart card
(c) MICR (d) barcode

20. .... is the scanning of paper to detect the presence or absence of a mark in a predetermined position. *CPCT 2023*
(a) OMR (b) OCR
(c) MICR (d) PICR

21. ...... is used to communicate with the computer by pointing to locations on the monitor screen. *HSSC 2021*
(a) Pointing device (b) Wireless device
(c) Network device (d) None of these

22. What are keys from F1 to F12 called? *HSSC 2021*
(a) Modifier (b) Function
(c) Number (d) None of these

23. How many alphabet keys are there on keyboard of computer?
(a) 24 (b) 25 (c) 26 (d) 27

24. Which of the following is an input device which can sense light and is used to point at spots on a video screen? *RRB JE CBT 2019*
(a) Joystick (b) Mouse
(c) Plotter (d) Light pen

25. .... keys are present on the top row of the keyboard. *RRB-JE 2019*
(a) Function (b) Navigation
(c) Arrow (d) Numeric

26. Mouse and .... are also examples of input devices. *RRB NTPC 2021*
(a) monitor (b) scanner
(c) printer (d) speakers

27. A device used for video games, flight simulators, training simulators and for controlling industrial robots. *IBPS Clerk 2020*
(a) Mouse (b) Light pen
(c) Joystick (d) Keyboard

28. Which of the following is capable of recognising a pre-specified type of mark by pencil or pen? *SBI Clerk 2021*
(a) OMR (b) Winchester
(c) Bar code reader (d) Image scanner

29. Which of the following is not a point-and-draw device? *IBPS Clerk 2020*
(a) Keypad (b) Trackball
(c) Touch screen (d) Mouse

30. What is the name given to a device like typewriter, which is used to send or command data in computers? *RRB NTPC 2021*
(a) Mouse
(b) Optical Character Reader (OCR)
(c) Joystick
(d) Keyboard

31. Typically, a QWERTY keyboard contains ...... keys. *RRB NTPC 2021*
(a) 120 (b) 98 (c) 104 (d) 100

32. What are you calling the key on the computer keyboard which is used to move the point (cursor) on the screen? *SSC CHSL 2021*
(a) Navigation key (b) Numerical key
(c) Function key (d) Control key

33. What is the tab key used for? *SBI Clerk 2020*
(a) To move the cursor on the screen
(b) To indent paragraphs
(c) To move the cursor down on the screen
(d) Both (a) and (b)

34. Which of the following is command key on the keyboard? *DSSSB 2024*
(a) Backspace (b) Insert
(c) Enter (d) Delete

35. On the computer keyboard, function keys are labelled .... to......... . *DSSSB 2024*
(a) F1, F12 (b) F7, F14 (c) F1, F9 (d) F10, F11

36. Depending on what you are working on, ... changes the form. *RBI Grade-B 2018*
(a) Active tab (b) Insertion point
(c) Mouse pointer (d) Ribbon

37. Which of the following input devices is used to enter motion data into computers or other electronic devices? *SSC CHSL 2019*
(a) Plotter (b) Printer
(c) Monitor (d) Joystick

38. Which of the following converts analog information into digital form? *SSC CHSL 2019*
(a) Barcode reader (b) Optical mark reading
(c) Digitizer (d) Game pad

39. Which one of the following is a lever which can be rotated in many directions to control the speed of a shape on a computer monitor or a similar display screen? *SSC CHSL 2019, 2020*
(a) MIDI equipment (b) Optical mark reader
(c) Joystick (d) Visual display unit

40. Which of the following is an input device? *SSC CHSL 2024*
(a) Speaker (b) Monitor
(c) Printer (d) Keyboard

41. .... is a reading device, which reads the printed key by scanning it character by character. *SSC CGL 2023*
(a) Trackball
(b) Digitizer
(c) Magnetic Ink Character Reader (MICR)
(d) Optical Character Reader (OCR)

42. Which key is used to use the selected command in Windows keyboard?
(a) Tab (b) Enter (c) And (d) Space

43. OMR is used in Recognition Technology, what is the full form of 'M' in it? *RRB NTPC 2021*
(a) Manipulator (b) Mirroring
(c) Magnetic (d) Mark

44. Microphone converts .... *RRB NTPC 2021*
(a) mechanical energy into sound energy
(b) sound energy into mechanical energy
(c) electrical energy into sound energy
(d) sound energy into electrical energy

45. The first barcode system was developed by whom? *SSC CHSL 2021*
(a) Norman Joseph Woodland
(b) John McCarthy
(c) John Bargar
(d) David Bradley

46. Which of the following is not a hardware?
(a) Processor chip (b) Printer
(c) Mouse (d) Java

47. What is the primary function of a scanner? *SSC Selection Post 2023*
(a) To input graphical images and text into a computer.
(b) To project images on a screen.
(c) To produce audio output.
(d) To create printed copies of documents.

48. A device is used to input handwritten text or drawings into a computer is called a
(a) graphics tablet (b) light pen
(c) joystick (d) trackpad

49. What is the primary function of a barcode reader?
(a) Translates physical text into computer readable data
(b) Capture images for video conferencing
(c) Convert paper documents into digital format
(d) Read and interpret barcodes into digital data

50. Which of the following consists of an electronic writing area and a special pen that works with it?
(a) Trackball (b) Plotters *SSC CHSL 2019*
(c) Abacus (d) Graphics tablet

51. A light pen is primarily used for *RRB NTPC 2021*
(a) inputting text (b) drawing on the screen
(c) scanning documents (d) printing graphics

Output Devices

52. Which type of computer peripheral is dot-matrix, deskjet, inkjet and laser? *CPCT 2024*
(a) Keyboard (b) Software
(b) Monitor (d) Printer

53. Which of the following plotter draw on negatively charged paper with positively charged toner? ***CPCT 2024***

(a) Drum (b) Flatbed
(c) Electrostatic (d) Inkjet

54. Which of the following printers does not require ink, toner and other supplies? ***CPCT 2024***

(a) Laser jet printer only
(b) Inkjet printer only
(c) Thermal printer
(d) Both inkjet printer and laser printer

55. Which of the following is used to connect to a computer to generate sound, which is, one of the most common output devices? ***CPCT 2024***

(a) Speaker (b) Printer
(c) Microphone (d) Plotter

56. .... is used to draw complex design and graphs, charts. ***CPCT 2024***

(a) Flatbed plotter
(b) Flatbed scanner
(c) Drum plotter
(d) Inkjet printer

57. There are .... types of plotters. ***CPCT 2024***

(a) one (b) five
(c) two (d) six

58. The Cathode Ray Tube (CRT) display consists of small picture elements known as .... ***CPCT 2024***

(a) parameters (b) pixels
(c) icons (d) pictures

59. Which of the following is a non-impact printer? ***CPCT 2024***

(a) Daisy wheel printer (b) Dot matrix printer
(c) Thermal printer (d) Drum printer

60. Which of the following is a solid font printer? ***CPCT 2024***

(a) Inkjet printer (b) Laser printer
(c) LED printer (d) Band printer

61. In color inkjet cartridge, the ink is in primary pigments ......, ... and .... ***CPCT 2024***

(a) cyan, magenta and yellow
(b) green, red and yellow
(c) green, magenta and yellow
(d) cyan, red and yellow

62. Which of the following is not an output device? ***CPCT 2024***

(a) Plotter (b) Monitor
(c) Joystick (d) Printer

63. Which of the following is not a printer type? ***CPCT 2024***

(a) Dot matrix printer (b) Line printer
(c) Chain printer (d) Brand printer

64. Which of the following is an example of an output device? ***SSC CHSL2024***

(a) Printer (b) Microphone
(c) Scanner (d) Mouse

65. A device used for vector graphics output to draw graphs, maps, blueprints of buildings and ships, is called ....

(a) designer (b) plotter
(c) trackball (d) digitizing tablet

66. Which of the following printer uses electrostatic chemicals inkjet technologies for producing high quality output?

(a) Daisy wheel printers
(b) Dot matrix printers
(c) Drum printers
(d) Non-impact printers

67. Select the option that represents the correct matching of the below lists.

	List-I	List-II
I.	The number of pixels in horizontal and vertical direction	A. Dot pitch
II.	The distance between pixels on a computer display	B. Refresh rate
III.	High resolution, flat screen and panel	C. Resolution of screen
IV.	The number of times per second the pixels are recharged	D. Liquid Crystal Display

(a) I-C, II-A, III-B, IV-D (b) I-C, II-A, III-D, IV-B
(c) I-B, II-C, III-D, IV-A (d) I-D, II-C, III-A, IV-B

68. Which among the following devices is also known as Visual Display Unit (VDU)?

(a) Printer (b) Scanner
(c) Track Ball (d) Monitor

69. Which among the following is incorrect about Laser printers?

(a) Uses laser lights for producing dots to form characters on a page
(b) Can print multiple copies at a time
(c) Fast speed
(d) Supports multiple fonts and sizes

70. Which of the following is not an output device?

(a) Plotter (b) Monitor
(c) Mouse (d) Printer

71. Speed of .... printer is measured in Characters Per Second (CPS). ***SSC CHSL 2023***

(a) dot matrix (b) line
(c) inkjet (d) laser

72. When do you need a printer?
(a) When you wish to scan a document.
(b) When you want a hard copy of a document.
(c) When you want to access your document from any device.
(d) When you wish to send a document over the internet.

73. Which printer prints data or images by spraying small droplets of ink at high speed onto the surface of the paper?
(a) Ink jet printer (b) Laser printer
(c) Drum printer (d) Dot matrix printer

74. Which of the following units is not used to measure the speed of a printer?
(a) CPM (b) LPM
(c) PPM (d) BIT

75. Which output device is used for presentations?
(a) Printer (b) Speaker
(c) Projector (d) Mouse

76. A system that automates the drafting process with interactive computer graphics is called
(a) Computer Aided Engineering (CAE)
(b) Computer Aided Design (CAD)
(c) Computer Aided Manufacturing (CAM)
(d) Computer Aided Instruction (CAI)

77. A pixel is ....
(a) a computer program
(b) the smaller resolvable part of a picture
(c) a picture stored in secondary memory
(d) a programming language

78. Which among the following units is used to count the speed of modern printers?
(a) CPM (b) PPM
(c) LPM (d) BIT

79. What is the full form of DPI with regard to digital images?
(a) Decimal per inch (b) Dots per inch
(c) Digits per inch (d) Data per inch

80. Which of the following options represents the number of pixels per inch printed on a page?
(a) Print margin (b) Resolution
(c) Filter (d) Colour mode

81. A printer that prints one line at a time and has a predefined set of characters is called ....
(a) laser (b) drum
(c) inkjet (d) impact

82. Which of the following is a temporary output?
(a) Hard copy (b) Soft copy
(c) Duplicate copy (d) On paper

83. The devices that are used to give single or multiple large colored images and drawings are ....
(a) monitors (b) printers
(c) plotters (d) VDUS

84. A .... monitor looks like a television and are normally used with non-portable computer systems.
(a) CRT (b) LCD
(c) LED (d) Flat panel

85. Which of the following is an example of an output device? *SSC CHSL 2024*
(a) Mouse (b) Scanner
(c) Microphone (d) Printer

86. Which of the following groups has only output devices? *MPPSC (Pre) 2019*
(a) Scanner, printer, monitor
(b) Keyboard, printer, monitor
(c) Mouse, printer, monitor
(d) Plotter, printer, monitor

87. In which part of the computer are the functions performed by the operator visible? *SSC MTS 2022*
(a) CPU (b) VDU
(c) ALU (d) IBM

88. Neil wants to use a character printer. Which of the following should he choose? *SSC CHSL 2023*
(a) Chain printer (b) Laser printer
(c) Drum printer (d) Dot matrix printer

89. A.........printer cannot print more than one character at a time. *SSC CHSL 2021*
(a) line (b) daisy wheel
(c) laser (d) dot matrix

90. Which of the following devices is used for applications such as Computer Aided Design (CAD)? *RRB NTPC 2021*
(a) Speaker (b) Pantograph
(c) Scanner (d) Plotter

91. Results are obtained from computer through its
(a) input unit (b) ALU unit
(c) CU unit (d) output unit

92. The higher the resolution of a monitor, the
(a) larger the pixels
(b) less clear the screen is
(c) further apart the pixels
(d) closer together the pixels

93. The rate at which refreshing is repeated in a CRT is called
(a) refresh rate (b) resolution
(c) pitch (d) bandwidth

94. An example of peripheral equipment is
(a) printer
(b) CPU
(c) spreadsheet
(d) microcomputer

95. Dot matrix printer is
(a) unidirectional (b) bi-directional
(c) sequential (d) random

96. The impact printers are
(a) dot matrix (b) drum
(c) inkjet (d) Both (a) and (b)

97. Drum printer is an example of
(a) input (b) output
(c) processing (d) storage

98. Which of the following printers, are you sure, will not to use if your objective is to print on multi carbon forms?
(a) Daisy wheel (b) Dot matrix
(c) Laser (d) Thermal

99. Laser printers belong to
(a) line printer
(b) page printer
(c) band printer
(d) dot matrix printer

100. Which of the following is not an output device of computer? *RSMSSB LDC 2025*
(a) Webcam
(b) Monitor
(c) Plotter
(d) Printer

Devices that Serve Both Input and Output Functions

101. Which of the following is an example of a device that serves both input and output functions?
(a) Keyboard (b) Monitor
(c) Touchscreen (d) Scanner

102. Which device allows the user to both send information to and receive information from the computer?
(a) Light pen (b) Projector
(c) Webcam (d) Headset

103. A modem is considered an input-output device because
(a) it only sends data.
(b) it only receives data.
(c) it sends and receives data.
(d) it processes data internally.

104. Identify the device that serves as the both input and output among the following.
(a) light pen (b) fax machine
(c) NIC (d) Both (b) and (c)

105. A digital camera acts as both input and output because it can
(a) only capture images (b) only stores images
(c) only transmit images (d) capture and display images

106. Which device is used in video gaming serves as both input and output?
(a) Monitor (b) VR headset
(c) Gamepad (d) Keyboard

Answers

1. (b)	2. (a)	3. (c)	4. (a)	5. (c)	6. (b)	7. (c)	8. (b)	9. (d)	10. (b)
11. (b)	12. (c)	13. (d)	14. (a)	15. (a)	16. (b)	17. (d)	18. (c)	19. (c)	20. (a)
21. (a)	22. (b)	23. (c)	24. (d)	25. (a)	26. (b)	27. (c)	28. (a)	29. (a)	30. (d)
31. (c)	32. (a)	33. (d)	34. (c)	35. (a)	36. (c)	37. (d)	38. (c)	39. (c)	40. (d)
41. (d)	42. (b)	43. (d)	44. (d)	45. (a)	46. (d)	47. (a)	48. (a)	49. (d)	50. (d)
51. (b)	52. (d)	53. (c)	54. (c)	55. (a)	56. (a)	57. (c)	58. (b)	59. (c)	60. (d)
61. (a)	62. (c)	63. (d)	64. (a)	65. (b)	66. (d)	67. (b)	68. (d)	69. (b)	70. (c)
71. (a)	72. (b)	73. (a)	74. (d)	75. (c)	76. (b)	77. (b)	78. (b)	79. (b)	80. (b)
81. (b)	82. (b)	83. (c)	84. (a)	85. (d)	86. (d)	87. (b)	88. (d)	89. (b)	90. (d)
91. (d)	92. (d)	93. (a)	94. (a)	95. (b)	96. (d)	97. (b)	98. (c)	99. (b)	100. (a)
101. (c)	102. (d)	103. (c)	104. (d)	105. (d)	106. (b)				

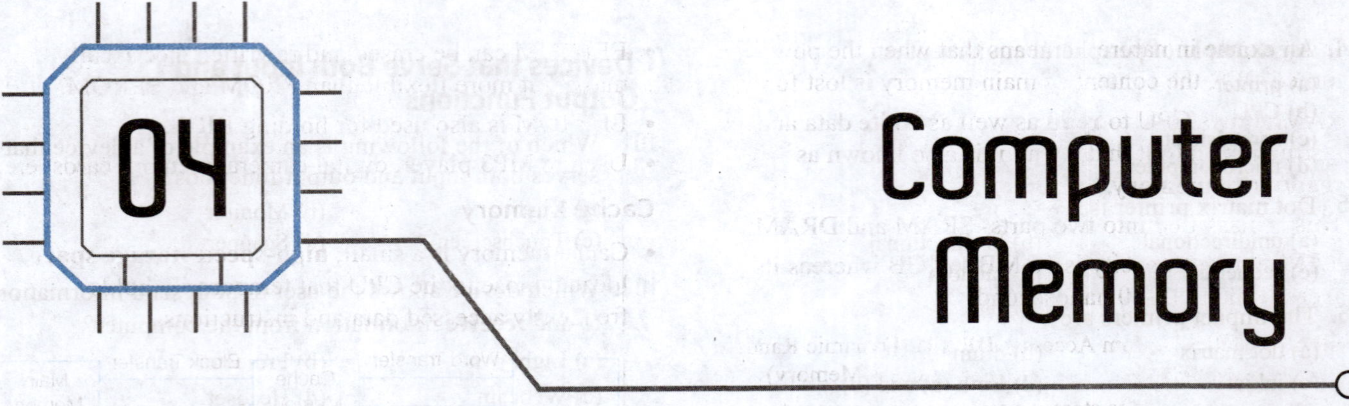

04 Computer Memory

- Computer memory is the **storage space** where data, information, programs are stored **permanently** or **temporarily**.
- It enables the computer to quickly **access, retrieve** and **store information**, needed for running applications.
- It works like a **human brain.**

In this Chapter

- Classification of Computer Memory
  - Primary Memory
  - Secondary Memory
- Memory Hierarchy

> “Computers are like a bicycle for our minds.
>
> **~ Steve Jobs**”

Classification of Computer Memory

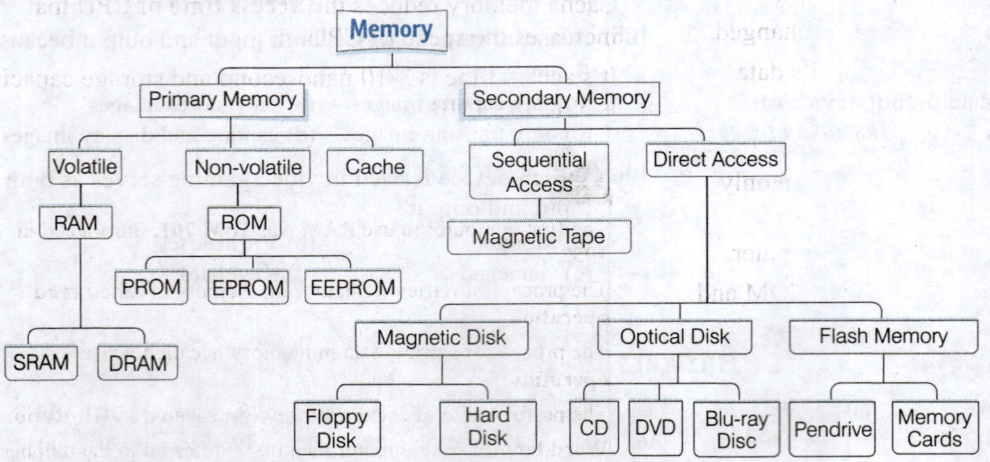

1. Primary Memory

- The memory unit that communicates directly with the CPU is called **primary memory**.
- It is also known as **main memory** or **internal memory**.
- Primary memory allows fast access to data, ensuring the smooth execution of tasks.
- It is classified into two parts – RAM and ROM

Characteristics of primary memory

- These are semiconductor memories.
- Faster than secondary memory.
- A computer cannot run without primary memory.

RAM (Random Access Memory)

- The primary memory that processes all the tasks to run a computer is called **RAM**.
- It stores data for some time that's why it is also known as **temporary memory**.

- It is **volatile** in nature, it means that when the power is turned OFF, the content of main memory is lost forever.
- RAM allows CPU to **read** as well as **write** data and instructions into it that's why it is also known as **read/write memory**.
- This is classified into two parts- SRAM and DRAM.
- RAM storage capacity is 16 MB to 4GB whereas its access time is 11-60 nanosecond.

SRAM (Static Random Access Memory)	**DRAM** (Dynamic Random Access Memory)
Transistors are used to store information.	Capacitors are used to store information.
It has less storage capacity.	It has large storage capacity.
These are used in cache memories.	These are used in main memory.
SRAM is expensive.	DRAM is cheaper.
It is faster than DRAM.	It is slower than SRAM.
Used in computers that control stock markets and air traffic.	Used in personal computers, laptops, tablets, etc.

ROM (Read Only Memory)

- ROM is a type of computer memory which stores permanent data and instruction that cannot be changed.
- It is **non-volatile** in nature it means it retains its data even when the computer is turned OFF.
- It is also known as **permanent memory**.
- As its name refers to read-only memory, user can only read the programs and data stored in it.
- It is also called the **built in memory** of the computer.
- ROM is classified into three parts- PROM, EPROM and EEPROM

1. PROM (Programmable ROM)

- Once the data is written to PROM using a special programming device, it cannot be **altered** or **erased**.
- It is used to store data that does not need to be changed often, such as **firmware** or **software** that is rarely updated.
- Used in microcontrollers and medical devices.

2. EPROM (Erasable PROM)

- EPROM can be erased using **ultraviolet (UV) light** and reprogrammed.
- It is suitable for applications where data needs to be updated occasionally.
- It is also called the **ultra violet EPROM**.
- Used in TV tuner card, BIOS storage.

3. EEPROM (Electrically EPROM)

- The data written in EEPROM can be delete within a short time through electrical signals.
- EEPROM can be erased and rewritten **electrically**, making it more flexible than PROM and EPROM.
- EEPROM is also used for holding BIOS.
- Used in MP3 player, digital camera, memory cards, etc.

Cache Memory

- Cache memory is a small, **high-speed storage space** located close to the CPU that temporarily holds frequently accessed data and instructions.

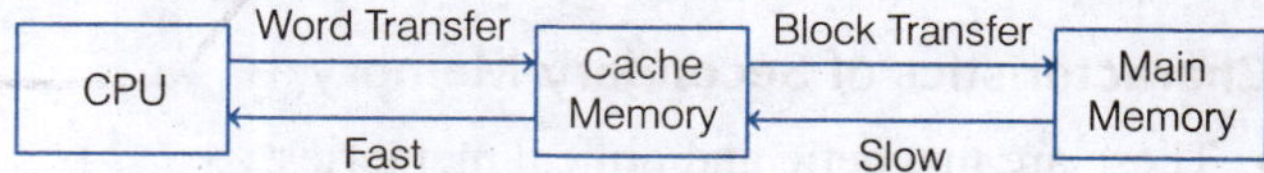

- It acts as a **buffer** between the CPU and the main memory.
- Cache memory operates on the **principle of locality of reference**, which means it stores data that the CPU is likely to use again and again.
- It is also known as **CPU's memory**.
- It is small in size but much faster than the main memory of the CPU.
- Cache memory reduces the **access time** of CPU that increases the speed of CPU.
- It's access time is 3-10 nanosecond and storage capacity is 32KB to 4MB.

Facts Drive

- The first computer to use RAM was **IBM 701**, introduced in 1952.
- The process of retrieving data from memory is called **read operation**.
- The process of storing data in memory is called **write operation**.
- The performance of cache memory is measured in **Hit Ratio**.
- **Word length** in a computer memory is referred to the number of bits a computer processor can process at once.
- **Buffer memory** is a temporary storage area used to hold data while it is being transferred from one place to another in a computer system.
- There's a built-in main memory (sometimes called internal memory), made up of **silicon** chip.

2. Secondary Memory

- A memory that cannot be accessed by CPU directly is called **secondary memory**.
- It is also known as **external memory, auxiliary memory** or **backup memory**.
- It includes various forms of storage, such as hard disk drives (HDDs), solid-state drives (SSDs), optical discs (like CDs and DVDs) and USB flash drives.

- Secondary memory provides much larger storage capacity than primary memory but is generally slower in data access speed.
- It is essential for storing files, applications and backups, ensuring that important data is preserved for long-term use.

Example DVD, Hard Disk, CD-ROM

- It is classified into two parts- sequential access memory and direct access memory.

Characteristics of Secondary Memory

- These are magnetic and optical memories.
- Slower than primary memory.
- Data is permanently stored even if power is switched OFF.
- It is a non-volatile memory.
- A computer can run without secondary memory.

Sequential Access Memory

- Sequential Access Memory is a memory in which data is accessed in the same order in which the data is stored.
- It is used in video player and tape cassette.

Magnetic Tape

- Magnetic tape contains a thin plastic ribbon coated by magnetic material (iron oxides).
- Its data read/write speed is slow because of sequential access.
- It is used to store digital and analog data.

Direct Access Memory

- Direct or non-sequential access memory allows for immediate and random retrieval of data from any location.

Example CD, DVD, pen drive, hard disk, floppy disk.

Magnetic Disk

- A magnetic disk is a storage device that uses magnetic storage technology to read and write data.
- It consists of a flat, circular platter coated with a magnetic material, allows data to be stored in the form of tiny magnetic charges.
- It comes in two main forms i.e., hard disk drives (HDDs) and floppy disks.

Floppy Disk

- The core of the floppy disk is a thin, flexible magnetic disk made of a plastic substrate coated with a magnetic material and enclosed in a square plastic case.

- The floppy disk drive contains a **read/write head** that moves across the surface of the disk to access or write data.
- When the disk spins, the head can read the magnetic patterns or change them to store new data.
- It is used to store less data or small programs.
- Presently it is replaced by **pen drive**.

Floppy disks and their storage capacity

Size	Storage Capacity
8 inch	Up to 1 MB
5.25 inch	1.22 MB
3.5 inch	1.44 MB

Hard Disk

- A hard disk is a device used to store digital data on a computer or other electronic device.
- It is also known as a **hard drive** or **hard disk drive** or **fixed disk**.

- Its **storage capacity** is 160 GB- 16 TB and its **access time** is 10-50 nanosecond.
- A hard disk uses **rotating magnetic disks** (platters) to read and write data.
- HDDs are usually installed inside desktop computers, mobile devices, consumer electronics and enterprise storage arrays in data centers.
- The speed of hard disk is measured in **RPM** (Revolution Per Minute).

- In windows operating system, the hard drive is known as the **C drive** whereas in Mac, it is simply called as the **hard drive**.
- Modern computer contains a hard drive of **1 terabyte**.

Components of Hard Disk

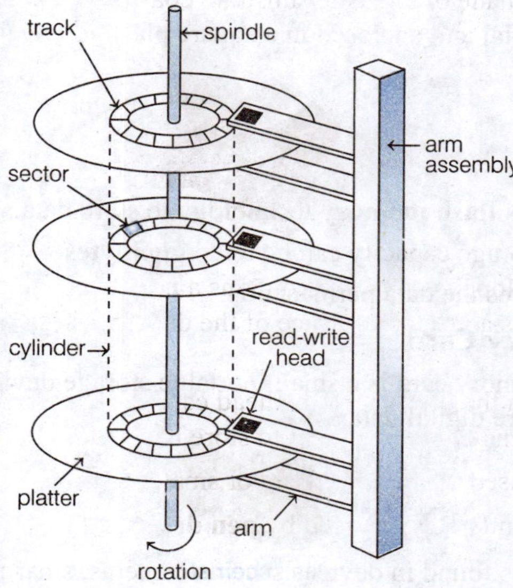

1. **Platters**
   - Circular disks coated with a magnetic material where data is stored.
   - In hard disk, data is first fetched on the platter.
2. **Spindle**
   - The motor that holds and spins the platters at high speeds.
   - It allows the read/write heads to access data by rotating the platters.
3. **Read/Write Heads**
   - Tiny components that float just above the platter surfaces.
   - These heads move across the platters on an arm.
4. **Tracks**
   - Circular paths on the platter where data is recorded.
   - The read/write heads access data by following these tracks.
5. **Sectors**
   - The smallest unit of data storage on a hard disk.
   - Sectors are the **subdivisions of tracks**.
   - Each sector holds a specific amount of data and is addressed individually by the file system.
6. **Clusters**
   - Group of sectors that the file system treats as a single unit for storing files.
   - Clusters help organise data on the hard disk.

Types of Hard Disk

Types	Description	Uses
SATA (Serial ATA)	▪ Modern interface for connecting hard drives with higher speed than PATA. ▪ Its data transfer rate is up to 600 MB/s.	▪ Desktop and laptop computers, SSDs.
PATA (Parallel ATA)	▪ Older interface (also known as IDE) used for connecting hard drives, slower than SATA. ▪ Its data transfer rate is upto 133 MB/s	▪ Older desktop and laptop computers.
SCSI (Small Computer System Interface)	▪ Older technology for connecting hard drives and other peripherals; often used in servers. ▪ Its data transfer rate is up to 640 MB/s.	▪ Workstations and servers.
SSD (Solid State Drive)	▪ Storage device that uses flash memory to store data.	▪ Personal computers, laptops, gaming.

Memory Partitioning

- In a computer, memory partitioning (disk partitioning) divides a single physical storage device into separate sections called **partitions**.
- Each partition acts as a separate drive even though they all exist on one physical disk.

Here's a quick breakdown of common drive letters

1. **C: Drive** The primary drive where the operating system (like Windows) is installed, along with system files and programs.
2. **D: Drive** A secondary drive or partition, used for data storage or recovery.
3. **E: F: G: Drives** Assigned to additional storage, such as external hard drives, USB drives or network drives.

Optical Disks

- Optical disks are storage media that use **laser technology** to read and write data.
- The data in optical disk is arranged in a continuous **spiral track**, starting from the inner edge to the outer edge of the disk.

Types of optical disk are as follows

1. Compact Discs (CDs)

- CDs are used to store small programs and audio/video files.

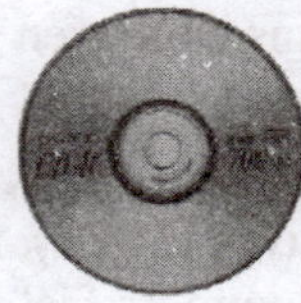

- Standard CDs can hold about 700 MB of data or around 80 minutes of audio.
- They come in different types, such as CD-ROM, CD-R and CD-RW, each serves specific purposes.
  (i) **CD-ROM** is used to store data that can only read but cannot be modified and write.
  This is used for software applications and games.
  (ii) **CD-R** allows users to write data onto the disc only once.
  After recording, the data cannot be erased.
  It is also called **WORM** (Write Once, Read Many).
  (iii) **CD-RW** allows users to write, erase and rewrite data multiple times.
  CD-RWs are commonly used for backing up important files, allows users to update the backup as needed.

2. Digital Versatile Discs (DVDs)

- It is also known as Digital Video Disc.
- DVDs have a different data encoding technology than CDs, allows them to store more information in the same physical space.
- They can have one or two layers and each layer can store data on both sides of the disc.
- Single-layer DVDs can hold about 4.7 GB of data whereas dual-layer DVDs can store up to 8.5 GB.
- **Red laser beam** is used to read the data in DVDs.

3. Blu-ray Discs (BRD)

- Introduced in the early 2000s, Blu-ray discs were designed for high-definition video storage.
- This is also called **BD**.
- They offer significantly higher storage capacity compared to CDs and DVDs, making them suitable for modern multimedia applications.
- It uses a **blue-violet laser** that's why these are known as **Blue Ray Disc**.
- Single-layer Blu-ray discs hold about 25 GB, while dual-layer discs can hold up to 50 GB.

Flash Memory

- Flash memory was invented by Japanese engineer **Masuoka Fujio** in the early 1980s.
- Flash memory is a type of non-volatile storage technology that retains data even when the power is turned OFF.
- It is widely used in various applications, including USB drives, solid-state drives (SSDs), memory cards and embedded systems due to its fast read and write speeds, durability and compact size.
- This is classified into two parts

Pen Drive

- A pen drive, also known as a **USB flash drive,** is a portable data storage device that connects to a computer or other devices via a USB port.

- It uses **flash memory** technology to store data.
- Its storage capacity can be up to **gigabytes**.
- It stores the data permanently.

Memory Card

- A memory card is a small, portable storage device used to store digital data.

- This is found in devices such as cameras, smartphones, tablets and gaming consoles.
- It is also called **multimedia card.**

Secondary memory devices, their capacity and storage method

Secondary Memory Device	Storage Method	Capacity
Hard Disk	Magnetic	Upto 16 TB
Floppy Disk	Magnetic	1.44 MB
Magnetic Tape	Magnetic	Upto 1TB
CD-ROM	Optical	640MB- 680 MB
DVD-ROM	Optical	4.7GB- 17 GB
Pen Drive	Solid State	1GB – 512 GB

Virtual Memory

- It is a technique that allows the execution of processes that are not completely in main memory.
- The main advantage of this is that programs can be larger than physical memory.
- This technique enables systems to run larger applications or multiple applications simultaneously, even if the physical RAM is limited.

Important Points Related to Memory

Registers

- Computer registers are small storage areas inside the CPU. They hold data temporarily while the CPU processes instructions.

- These are not a part of main memory but considered as the fastest memory of computer.
- The size of a register maybe 8, 16, 32 or 64 bits.
- Its access time is 1-2 nanosecond and storage capacity is upto 8 bytes.

Basic Units of Memory Measurements

1 Bit	Binary Digit (0 or 1)
4 Bits	1 Nibble
8 Bits	1 Byte = 2 Nibble
1024 Bytes	1 KB (KiloByte)
1024 KB	1 MB (MegaByte)
1024 MB	1 GB(GigaByte)
1024 GB	1 TB(TeraByte)
1024 TB	1 PB(PetaByte)
1024 PB	1 EB(ExaByte)
1024 EB	1 ZB(ZettaByte)
1024 ZB	1 YB(YottaByte)
1024 YB	1 (BrontoByte)
1024 BB	1 (GeopByte)

Note Bit is the smallest memory measurement unit whereas GeopByte is the largest memory measurement unit.

Memory Hierarchy

- The memory hierarchy is a structured arrangement of storage systems that provides different levels of speed, size and cost.
- It organizes memory components from the fastest and most expensive types to the slowest and least expensive, optimizing performance and cost-effectiveness.

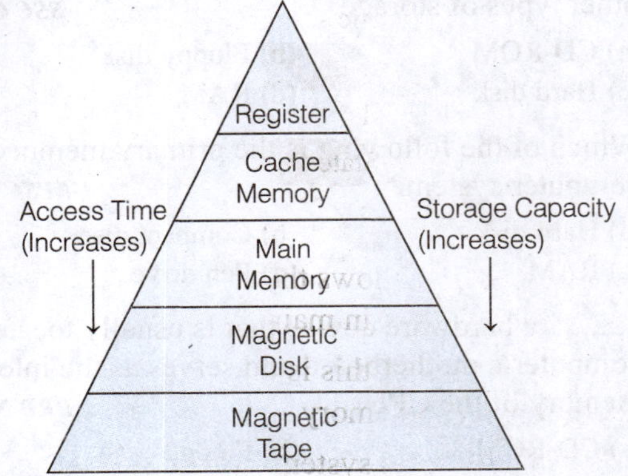

Memory Storage Capacity

Register< Cache< Primary Memory < Secondary Memory

Speed of Memory

Register> Cache> Primary Memory > Secondary Memory

Important Abbreviations

RAM Random Access Memory
SRAM Static Random Access Memory
DRAM Dynamic Random Access Memory
ROM Read Only Memory
PROM Programmable Read Only Memory
EPROM Erasable Programmable Read Only Memory
EEPROM Electrically Erasable Programmable Read Only Memory
CD Compact Disk
CD-ROM Compact Disk Read Only Memory
CD-R Compact Disk Recordable
CD-RW Compact Disc Rewritable
DVD Digital Versatile Disc/ Digital Video Disc
BRD Blu Ray Disc
SSD Solid State Drive
HDD Hard Disk Drive
SATA Serial Advanced Technology Attachment
PATA Parallel Advanced Technology Attachment
SCSI Small Computer System Interface
MMU Memory Management Unit
MBPS MegaByte Per Second
MbPS MegaBit Per second

PYQs Oneliner

1. **EEPROM** is an example of a type of ROM that can be electronically erased and reprogrammed multiple times. *SSC CGL (T-II) 18.01.2025*
2. **Primary and secondary** is the valid categorisation of computer memory. *CPCT 2024*
3. RAM is a **volatile** memory. *CPCT 2024*
4. The most frequently used instructions of a computer program are fetched from **cache memory**. *CPCT 2024*
5. There are **1024 kilobyte** in megabyte (MB). *SSC CHSL 2023*
6. **120mm** is the diameter of a Blu-ray disk. *SSC CHSL 2023*
7. **Solid state drive** is also known as electronic disk. *SSC CGL 2023*
8. **Cache memory** is used to increase the processing speed by making current programs and data available to the CPU at a faster pace. *SSC CGL 2023*
9. **1.44 MB** is the storage capacity of a 3.5-inch floppy disk. *RRB NTPC 2021*
10. **RAM** in computers is faster to read and write than other types of storage. *SSC CHSL 2020*

Practice Exercise

Introduction to Computer Memory

1. …… stores data and instructions required during the processing of data and output results.
(a) Memory (b) Architecture
(c) Input (d) Output

2. Where is data saved permanently?
(a) Memory (b) ALU
(c) CPU (d) Printer

3. How many types of memory does a computer have?
(a) Four (b) Eight
(c) One (d) Two

4. The term ……… refers to data storage systems that make it possible for a computer or electronic device to store and retrieve data.
(a) retrieval technology (b) input technology
(c) output technology (d) storage technology

5. Which of the following is valid categorization of computer memory? *CPCT 2024*
(a) Primary and secondary (b) Permanent and secondary
(c) Secondary and tertiary (d) CD and DVD

Primary Memory

6. ….is a high-speed device used in CPU that is utilised to store data temporarily during processing.
(a) Arithmetic and Logic Unit (ALU) *SSC CGL 2023*
(b) Auxiliary memory
(c) Control unit
(d) Registers

7. Which of the following is an essential role of ROM in a computer system? *SSC CHSL 2024*
(a) Storing data temporarily
(b) Storing data permanently for boot-up processes
(c) Performing calculations
(d) Storing files created by the user

8. Identify the memory that is used between central processing unit and the main memory.
(a) Read only memory (b) Random access memory
(c) Cache memory (d) Virtual memory

9. ……….. memory is sometime used to increase the speed of processing by making current programs and data available to the CPU at a rapid rate.
(a) Backup (b) Auxiliary
(c) Main (d) Cache

10. The memory unit that communicates directly with the CPU is called ……… memory. *SSC CGL 2023*
(a) cache (b) backup (c) main (d) auxiliary

11. If a memory chip is volatile, it ………
(a) stores data permanently.
(b) lose its contents if the power is turned OFF.
(c) is used for data storage only.
(d) is referred to as ROM.

12. Virtual memory is ……………
(a) a memory that the CPU uses as an extended RAM
(b) a ROM
(c) only necessary if you do not have any RAM in your computer
(d) a backup device for floppy disks

13. The ……… acts as a buffer between the CPU and the main memory.
(a) primary memory (b) cache memory
(c) secondary memory (d) RAM

14. ROM is primarily used for which of the following purposes? *SSC CGL (T-II) 20.01.2025*
(a) Random data access
(b) Temporary data storage
(c) Storing files for permanent access
(d) Storing the BIOS or firmware

15. ……… in a computers are faster to read and write than other types of storage. *SSC CHSL 2020*
(a) CD-ROM (b) Floppy disk
(c) Hard disk (d) RAM

16. Which of the following is the primary memory in a computer system? *UKPSC (Pre) 2021*
(a) Hard disk (b) Compact disc
(c) RAM (d) Pen drive

17. ...., a hardware device that is usually located on a computer's motherboard and serves as the internal memory of the CPU. *RRB NTPC 2021*
(a) CD-ROM (b) Floppy
(c) RAM (d) DVD-ROM

18. Which of the following statements is true? *RRB NTPC 2022*
(a) SRAM requires periodic refreshing
(b) DRAM is faster than SRAM
(c) SRAM is non-volatile memory
(d) SRAM and DRAM, both are random access memory

19. When the processor uses the CPU, where are the data and programs kept? *SSC CHSL 2021*

(a) Main Memory (b) Secondary Memory
(c) Disk Memory (d) Program Memory

20. What is used to operate program instructions, which can never be changed in a computer? *SSC CHSL 2023*

(a) ROM (b) Register
(c) RAM (d) Cache

21. Which of the following is an example of a type of ROM that can be electronically erased and reprogrammed multiple times? *SSC CGL (T-II) 18.01.2025*

(a) EEPROM (b) PROM
(c) EPROM (d) Mask ROM

22. Which of the following is not a property of ROM (Read Only Memory)? *RRB NTPC 2021*

(a) It holds system software such as boot loader
(b) Information is not lost even when the computer is turned OFF
(c) It is known as volatile memory
(d) It stores information permanently

23. What is the full form of WORM? *RRB NTPC 2021*

(a) World Open, Receive Many
(b) Wireless Once, Receive Man
(c) Write Others, Read Me
(d) Write Once, Read Many

24. Which of the following types of Read Only Memory can be erased and reprogrammed by exposing it to an electrical charge? *RRB NTPC 2022*

(a) EEPROM (b) EPROM
(c) PROM (d) ROM

25. In the field of information and communication technology, what is the full form of EEPROM? *SSC CGL 2018*

(a) Electrically Erasable Programmable Read Only Memory
(b) Electrically Efficient Portable Read Only Memory
(c) Electrically Efficient Programmable Read Only Memory
(d) Enhanced Electrical Portable Read Only Memory

26. Which of the following statements is/are correct? *UPPCL 2019*

1. The access time of primary memory is maximum than the access time of secondary memory.
2. For the same storage capacity, DRAM is cheaper than SRAM.

Codes

(a) Only 1 (b) Only 2
(c) Both 1 and 2 (d) Neither 1 nor 2

27. .... memory is sometimes used to increase the processing speed by making current programs and data available to the CPU at a faster pace. *SSC CGL 2023*

(a) Cache (b) Main
(c) Back up (d) Auxiliary

28. Which of the following works as a buffer between CPU and the main memory, which saves the processor from waiting to receive programs and data from the main memory? *RRB NTPC 2022*

(a) Cache Memory (b) Tertiary Memory
(c) Auxiliary Memory (d) Optical Memory

29. Which of the following statements is incorrect? *SSC CGL 2023*

(a) Cache memory holds those programs which can be run in a short time
(b) Cache memory stores data in permanent use
(c) Cache memory is faster than main memory.
(d) Cache size is usually small

30. Which of the following is mainly used for cache memory?

(a) SRAM (b) DRAM
(c) Blu-ray disk (d) DVD

31. The performance of cache memory often is measured in................ *RRB JE 2019*

(a) Set-associate mapping
(b) Register
(c) Collaborative mapping
(d) Hit ratio

32. Cache memory is located in the middle of the .... *UPSSSC PET 2018*

(a) CPU and RAM (b) RAM and ROM
(c) CPU and Hard Disk (d) All of these

33. What is the term used for temporarily stored data? *UPSSSC PET 2019*

(a) Method Data (b) Cache Data
(c) Pick Data (d) Tempo Data

34. Non-volatile memory is a type of computer memory, which can also retrieve stored information. *RRB NTPC 2021*

(a) Without processing (b) Intermittent walking
(c) On walking (d) Not operational

35. Primary storage is .... as compared to secondary storage.

(a) slow and inexpensive (b) fast and inexpensive
(c) fast and expensive (d) slow and expensive

36. What is the primary reason DRAM needs to be refreshed periodically? *SSC CGL (T-II) 18.01.2025*

(a) To prevent data corruption caused by magnetic fields
(b) To recharge the capacitors storing data bits
(c) To clear unused data
(d) To allow the CPU to access new data

37. The two kinds of main memory are
(a) ROM and RAM
(b) primary and secondary
(c) floppy disk and hard disk
(d) direct and sequential

38. Which of the following statements about computer memory is/are correct? *SSC CGL (T-II) 18.01.2025*
1. RAM is volatile memory, meaning it loses data when power is turned off.
2. ROM is used to store essential instructions required for the computer to boot.

(a) Neither 1 nor 2 (b) Only 1
(c) Both 1 and 2 (d) Only 2

39. Cache and main memory will not be able to hold their contents when the power is OFF. They are
(a) dynamic (b) static
(c) volatile (d) non-volatile

40. In computer terminology, what is the full form of RAM? *SSC CGL 2018*
(a) Random Access Memory
(b) Repeated Access Memory
(c) Rapid Access Memory
(d) Regular Access Memory

41. The advantage of DRAM is
(a) it is cheaper than SRAM
(b) it can store data more than that of SRAM
(c) it is faster than SRAM
(d) data can be erased easily from it as compared to SRAM

42. What is the full form of PROM? *SSC CHSL 2019*
(a) Programmable Read Only Memory
(b) Program Read Output Memory
(c) Program Read Only Memory
(d) Primary Read Only Memory

43. Which of the following is a very high speed semiconductor memory which can speed up the CPU? *SSC CHSL 2019*
(a) Secondary memory
(b) Main memory
(c) Primary memory
(d) Cache memory

44. What data is stored in ROM?
(a) Temporary data
(b) Operating system data
(c) Permanent instructions like BIOS
(d) User files

45. Random Access Memory (RAM) is a .... type of memory. *CPCT 2024*
(a) short-term (b) permanent
(c) flash (d) smart

46. .... is used for storing programs and data currently being processed by the CPU. *CPCT 2024*
(a) Mass memory (b) RAM
(c) ROM (d) PROM

47. Which of the following is not a type of RAM? *CPCT 2024*
(a) SRAM (Static RAM)
(b) Prime RAM
(c) DDR RAM (Double Data Rate RAM)
(d) SDRAM (Synchronous Dynamic RAM)

48. .... is a volatile memory. *CPCT 2024*
(a) RAM (b) ROM (c) EEPROM (d) EPROM

49. Which of the following is the hardware in a computing device where the operating system, application programs and data in current use are kept so they can be quickly reached by the device's processor? *CPCT 2024*
(a) RAM (b) CD-ROM
(c) Flash Drive (d) Hard Disk

50. Which of the following memories must be refreshed many times per second? *CPCT 2024*
(a) EPROM (b) ROM
(c) Static RAM (d) Dynamic RAM

51. The most frequently used instructions of a computer program are fetched from .... *CPCT 2024*
(a) register (b) main memory
(c) cache memory (d) hard disk

52. Which of the following is a fast and expensive memory that stores copies of data from the main memory that needs to be frequently accessed by the CPU? *CPCT 2024*
(a) Primary memory (b) Cache memory
(c) Secondary memory (d) Registers

Secondary Memory

53. Which of the following is a storage allocation scheme in which secondary memory can be addressed as though it were part of the main memory?
(a) Secondary memory
(b) CPU buffer memory
(c) CPU register memory
(d) Virtual memory

54. Which storage media supports only sequential access?
(a) Hard disk (b) CD
(c) Magnetic tape (d) DVD

55. Which of the following is an illusion of an extremely large main memory?
(a) Cache memory (b) Virtual memory
(c) Hard Disk (d) Associative memory

56. Select the option that represents the correct matching of the below lists.

	List-1		List-2
I.	Backup for data and instructions	A.	Secondary memory
II.	Central Processing Unit	B.	Cache memory
III.	Random Access memory	C.	Brain of computer
IV.	A very high speed memory	D.	Primary memory

(a) I-A, II-C, III-D, IV-B (b) I-D, II-A, III-C, IV-B
(c) I-C, II-A, III-B, IV-D (d) I-D, II-C, III-B, IV-A

57. Which of the following statements is/are true?
(i) The surface of magnetic disk is divided into concentric circles known as sectors.
(ii) In magnetic disk, the time taken to move the read/write head to the desired sector is called the seek time.
(a) Neither (i) nor (ii) (b) Only (i)
(c) Both (i) and (ii) (d) Only (ii)

58. Which among the following statements is correct about secondary memory?
(a) It is known as the backup memory.
(b) Data is permanently stored even if power is switched OFF.
(c) Computer may run without the secondary memory.
(d) All of the above

59. Which of the following is also known as a flash drive?
(a) Disk Array (b) HDD (c) SSD (d) Pen drive

60. Which among the following is a magnetic storage?
(a) Winchester disk (b) Floppy drive
(c) Magnetic tape (d) All of these

61. ……… refers to a secondary data storage unit of the computer.
(a) Registers
(b) Hard disk
(c) Read Only Memory
(d) Random Access Memory

62. Which of the following uses a method similar to that of the VCR for storing data?
(a) Magnetic tape (b) Video disk
(c) Digital tape (d) Audio disk

63. Which of the following is not secondary memory? ***MPPSC (Pre) 2020***
(a) Solid state drive
(b) Hard disk
(c) Random access memory
(d) USB pen drive

64. Which of the following memory is not auxiliary memory in a computer? ***RRB NTPC 2020***
(a) Magnetic tape (b) PROM
(c) CD-ROM (d) Floppy

65. ……… is a small portable flash memory card plugged into a computer's USB port and acts as a portable hard drive. ***SSC CHSL 2020***
(a) CD-ROM (b) Flash drive
(c) DVD-ROM (d) CD-RW

66. Which of the following does not use data and programs and provides long-term storage for current use? ***UPPCL 2019***
(a) DRAM
(b) Primary memory
(c) Secondary memory
(d) SRAM

67. Which of the following is incorrect about secondary memory? ***SSC CGL 2023***
(a) Data is stored permanently even when there is no electricity
(b) It is an unstable memory
(c) Computer can run without secondary memory
(d) It is known as backup memory

68. ………. is also known as electronic disk. ***SSC CGL 2023***
(a) USB stick
(b) Network storage server
(c) Solid state drive
(d) USB hard drive

69. What is the storage capacity of a 3.5 inch floppy disk? ***RRB NTPC 2021***
(a) 1.40 MB (b) 1.44 MB
(c) 2.44 MB (d) 1 GB

70. What is the diameter of a Blu-ray disk? ***SSC CHSL 2023***
(a) 115 mm (b) 100 mm
(c) 110 mm (d) 120 mm

71. Which of the following is not magnetic storage? ***SSC CGL 2023***
(a) Winchester disk
(b) Floppy drive
(c) Memory card
(d) Magnetic tape

72. The typical acronym of reusable optical storage will be ***SSC CHSL 2019***
(a) CD (b) CD-RW
(c) ROM (d) DVD

73. What is the difference between a CD-ROM and a CD-RW?
(a) Both are same–There are only two different terms which are used by different manufacturers
(b) CD-ROM can be written to and a CD-RW cannot
(c) Any other than the given options
(d) CD-ROM can be written to and CD-RW can only be read

74. Which of the following statements is/are incorrect? *UPPCL 2019*
1. CD-R is a rewrite disc that allows erasing previously recorded data and writing new data on it.
2. The meaning of the letters RW in CD-RW is Read and Write.
(a) Only 1 (b) Neither 1 Nor 2
(c) Only 2 (d) Both 1 and 2

75. ……… is the ability of a device to jump directly to the requested data.
(a) Sequential access (b) Random access
(c) Quick access (d) All of these

76. The ……… is the amount of data that a storage device can move from the storage to the computer per second.
(a) data migration rate
(b) data digitizing rate
(c) data transfer rate
(d) data access rate

77. The secondary storage devices can only store data but they cannot perform
(a) arithmetic operations (b) logic operations
(c) fetch operations (d) All of these

78. Where do you save the data that, your data will remain intact even when the computer is turned OFF?
(a) RAM
(b) Motherboard
(c) Secondary storage device
(d) Primary storage device

79. The storage device used to compensate for the difference in rates of flow of data from one device to another is termed as
(a) chip (b) channel
(c) floppy (d) buffer

80. Which of the following is not a magnetic storage device?
(a) Hard disk (b) Compact disc
(c) Audio tapes (d) All of these

81. In hard disk, which part is a pie-shaped wedge on the track? *SSC Selection Post 2023*
(a) Sectors (b) Platter
(c) Spindle (d) Sensor

82. Which of the following is/are example(s) of magnetic storage media?
(a) Zip disk (b) CD-ROM
(c) Floppy disk (d) Both (a) and (c)

83. Floppy disks are organized as
(a) files (b) heads and folders
(c) tracks and sectors (d) All of these

84. Magnetic tape is not practical for applications where data must be quickly recalled because tape is *CPCT 2024*
(a) a random access medium
(b) a sequential access medium
(c) a read only medium
(d) fragile and easily damaged

85. Which of the following can hold maximum data?
(a) Optical disc
(b) Floppy disk
(c) Hard disk
(d) Magnetic tape

86. Which of the following computer disk allows the user to write data permanently on to the disk and it cannot be erased? *SSC Selection Post 2023*
(a) CD - recordable (b) CD - rewritable
(c) DVD - RW (d) Magneto - optical disk

87. A flat metallic disk that contains a large amount of permanently stored information read optically, is called a
(a) monitor (b) ALU
(c) CD-ROM (d) RAM

88. DVD stands for ………… *CPCT 2024*
(a) Digital Vertical Disc
(b) Digital Versatile Disc
(c) Data Varying Disc
(d) Digital Vertical Data

89. Three types of compact disks include CD, CD-R and ………… *CPCT 2024*
(a) CD-W (b) CD-RAM
(c) CD-DVD (d) CD-RW

90. Which of the following device performs the same basic function as a hard drive, but data is instead stored on interconnected flash memory chips that retain the data even when there is no power flowing through them? *CPCT 2024*
(a) Cache memory chip (b) Dynamic RAM
(c) Static RAM (d) Solid state drive

91. A typical CD consists of reflective layer coated with *CPCT 2024*
(a) brass (b) zinc
(c) mercury (d) aluminium

92. Which of the following represents secondary memory? *CPCT 2024*
(a) RAM (b) ROM
(c) Cache memory (d) HDD

93. The storage capacity of a CD-ROM is approximately
(a) 700MB (b) 4.7MB
(c) 50 GB (d) 1 TB

94. What type of storage device is used to store data permanently and is non-volatile?
(a) DRAM (b) SSD
(c) Cache memory (d) Registers

95. Identify the secondary memory device from the list below.
(a) Magnetic drum (b) Magnetic disk
(c) Floppy disk (d) All of these

96. Secondary storages are primarily used for *SSC CHSL 2024*
(a) Temporary data storage
(b) Long term data retention
(c) Speeding up processing
(d) Running applications

Memory Measurement Units

97. Arrange the following units of measurement for digital information into correct order, starting with the smallest unit first and going to the largest unit:
(1) Kilobyte (2) Byte
(3) Megabyte (4) Terabyte
(5) Gigabyte (6) Bit
(a) 2 6 1 4 3 5 (b) 6 2 1 3 5 4
(c) 6 2 1 4 5 3 (d) 2 6 1 3 4 5

98. A unit equaling approximately, on thousand bytes (1024, to be exact) is called a
(a) Megabyte (b) Terabyte
(c) Gigabyte (d) Kilobyte

99. Which of the following has the maximum storage capacity in computer system?
(a) Kilobyte (b) Gigabyte
(c) Terabyte (d) Megabyte

100. Each cell of a memory device is capable of storing one bit of information in the form of binary numbers. What does the word 'bit' mean? *RRB NTPC 2022*
(a) Binary divisor
(b) Binary digit
(c) Bidirectional divisor
(d) Bidirectional digit

101. Computer memory is made up of many cells. Each cell capable of storing .... information as binary numbers. *RRB NTPC 2022*
(a) one byte
(b) one bit
(c) two bit
(d) a nibble

102. Which of the following relations is not correct? *UP RO/ARO (Pre) 2021*
(a) 1 byte = 8 Bits
(b) 1 Kilobyte = 1024 Bytes
(c) 1 Gigabyte = 1024 Kilobytes
(d) 1 Terabyte = 1024 Gigabytes

103. 1 Terabyte per second= .... bytes per second *SSC CHSL 2023*
(a) 2^{40} (b) 2^{10}
(c) 2^{20} (d) 2^{30}

104. There are 1024 .... in megabyte (MB). *SSC CHSL 2023*
(a) gigabyte (b) kilobyte
(c) terabyte (d) byte

105. ...... is the smallest unit of data in a computer. *SSC CGL 2018*
(a) Gigabyte (b) Bit
(c) Byte (d) Terabyte

Answers

1.	(a)	2.	(a)	3.	(d)	4.	(d)	5.	(a)	6.	(d)	7.	(b)	8.	(c)	9.	(d)	10.	(c)
11.	(b)	12.	(a)	13.	(b)	14.	(d)	15.	(d)	16.	(c)	17.	(c)	18.	(d)	19.	(a)	20.	(a)
21.	(a)	22.	(c)	23.	(d)	24.	(a)	25.	(a)	26.	(b)	27.	(a)	28.	(a)	29.	(b)	30.	(a)
31.	(d)	32.	(a)	33.	(b)	34.	(a)	35.	(c)	36.	(b)	37.	(a)	38.	(c)	39.	(c)	40.	(a)
41.	(a)	42.	(a)	43.	(d)	44.	(c)	45.	(a)	46.	(b)	47.	(b)	48.	(a)	49.	(a)	50.	(d)
51.	(c)	52.	(b)	53.	(d)	54.	(c)	55.	(b)	56.	(a)	57.	(d)	58.	(d)	59.	(d)	60.	(d)
61.	(b)	62.	(a)	63.	(c)	64.	(b)	65.	(b)	66.	(c)	67.	(b)	68.	(c)	69.	(b)	70.	(d)
71.	(c)	72.	(b)	73.	(c)	74.	(d)	75.	(b)	76.	(d)	77.	(d)	78.	(c)	79.	(d)	80.	(b)
81.	(a)	82.	(d)	83.	(c)	84.	(b)	85.	(c)	86.	(a)	87.	(c)	88.	(b)	89.	(d)	90.	(d)
91.	(d)	92.	(d)	93.	(a)	94.	(b)	95.	(d)	96.	(b)	97.	(b)	98.	(d)	99.	(c)	100.	(b)
101.	(b)	102.	(c)	103.	(a)	104.	(b)	105.	(b)										

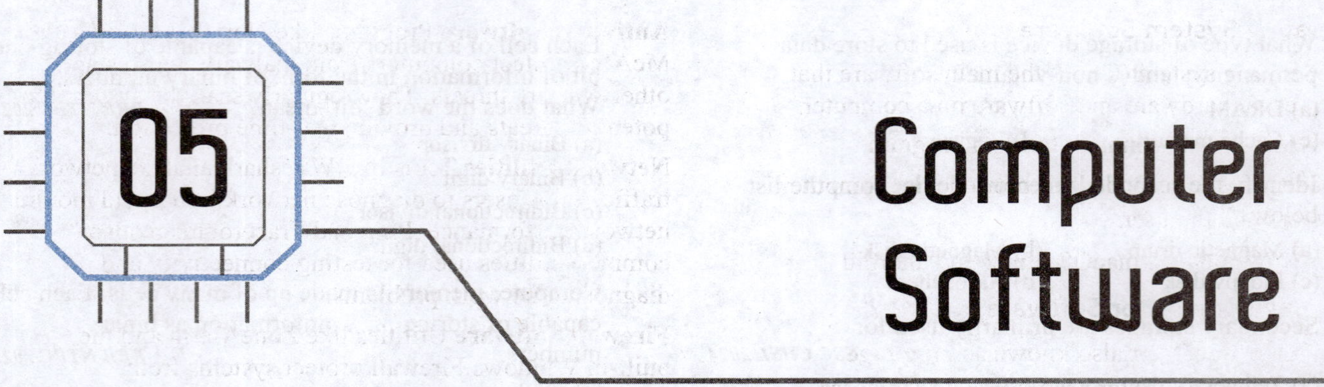

05 Computer Software

- Computer software refers to the **set of instructions** or **programs** that tell a computer how to perform specific tasks.
- This is a part of computer which can only be **seen** but cannot be **touched.**
- It acts as the **interface** between the hardware and the end users.
- It controls all the tasks of computer.

Example Tally, MySQL, QuickBooks, MS access, MS-Dos, Linux, PowerPoint.

In this Chapter

- Types of Software
  - System Software
  - Application Software
- Other Categories of Software
- Terms Related to Software

"People who are really serious about software should make their own hardware.
~ Alan Kay"

Types of Software

Computer software are mainly divided into two parts

1. System Software
2. Application Software

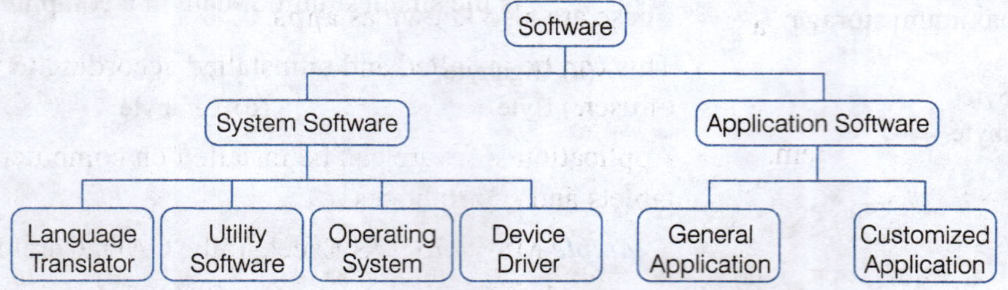

System Software

- System software is a computer program that manage the computer's hardware and operate application software.
- It acts as a **mediator** between users and the hardware.

Example Operating systems (Windows, Linux), firmware (software embedded in hardware) and utility programs (antivirus software, disk management tools).

System software is mainly divided into four categories

1. Operating System Software
2. Language Translator Software
3. Utility Software
4. Device Driver

1. Operating System Software

- An operating system (OS) is the main software that manages all hardware and software on a computer.
- It provides an environment to run a program.
- Its function is to provide **link** between the computer hardware and the user.

Example Windows, macOS, linux and android

2. Language Translator Software

- A language translator also known as **language processor** is a computer program that **translates source code** from one programming language to another.
- Computer understand only **machine language** (0 and 1) and it is difficult to write code in machine language that's why translator software is used.

There are three main types of language translators

1. **Assembler** is a program that converts assembly language code into machine code (0 or 1)
2. **Compiler** is a translator that translate code written in high level language into machine readable language.
3. **Interpreter** is a translator that translates higher-level code into machine language line by line.

3. Utility Software

- Utility software is also a system software that helps to maintain the proper and smooth functioning of a computer system
- Utility software serves as a tool to enhance the functionality and performance of the operating system.
- This is also known as **service program software**.
- It keeps bug away from the computer and provides security.

Example CCleaner, Defraggler, Norton, McAfee, CleanmyPC, Wireshark, Net Protector

Functions of Utility Software

- **Disk Clean Up** Applications such as CCleaner help users free up disk space by removing temporary files, system caches and other unnecessary data.
- **Disk Defragmenters** Applications like Defraggler reorganize fragmented data on a hard drive to improve access speed and overall system performance.
- **Backup Program** Programs like Acronis True Image and Windows Backup allow users to create backups of their data, ensures that important files are preserved in case of system failure or data loss.
- **Antivirus Software** Programs like Norton Antivirus and McAfee protect computers from malware, viruses and other security threats. They regularly scan the system for potential threats and provide real-time protection.
- **Network Utilities** Tools like Wireshark analyze network traffic, helps users to diagnose network issues and monitor network performance. Ping and Traceroute are also common utilities used for testing connectivity and diagnosing network problems.
- **Firewall Software** Utilities like ZoneAlarm and the built-in Windows Firewall protect systems from unauthorized access and cyber threats by monitoring incoming and outgoing network traffic.

4. Device Driver

- A device driver connects the operating system with hardware devices, allowing them to communicate.
- It enables proper working of devices like printers, keyboards and monitors by translating system commands into device-specific instructions.
- Each hardware device requires its own specific driver to function correctly with the computer system.

Example Graphics Card Driver, Sound Card Driver.

Application Software

- When a user interacts directly with a piece of software, it is called **application software**.
- It performs a specific function for a user.
- These are also known as **apps**.
- This can be installed and uninstalled according to the need of user.
- Application software can be installed on computers, tablets and smartphones.

Example MS Word, MS Excel, Tally, CAD, Corel Draw

These are classified into two parts- General Application Software and Customized Application Software

General Application Software

- These types of software are used for general purpose.
- They allow people to do simple computer tasks.

Example Microsoft Word, Excel, PowerPoint, Outlook, Adobe Photoshop, Corel Draw, Quick Books, CAD, etc.

Customized Application Software

- These softwares are designed to perform specific tasks.
- These type of application softwares generally have one purpose to execute.
- These are also known as **specific purpose software**.

Example Inventory management system, railway reservation software, payroll management system, metrological department software, hotel management system, library management system.

Note SOUL 3.0 has been specifically designed to perform tasks related to library management, which makes it an application software.

Examples of Common Application Softwares

1. Word Processor Software

- Software like Microsoft Word and Google Docs are used for creating, editing and formatting text documents.
- They offer features like spell check, text formatting and their ability to insert images and tables, makes them ideal for writing reports, letters and essays.

2. Spreadsheet Software

- Applications such as Microsoft Excel and Google Sheets allow users to organize, analyze and manipulate data in tabular form.
- Their functions for calculations, graphing tools and pivot tables, makes them essential for financial analysis.

3. Presentation Software

- Tools like Microsoft PowerPoint and Google Slides enable users to create visual presentations using slides.
- They support multimedia elements such as images, videos and animations. It makes them useful for making educational and business presentations.

4. Database Management System (DBMS)

- A database management system is a set of programs that enables users to define, create and maintain the database, it also provides controlled access to the database.
- Software like Microsoft Access and MySQL help users create, manage and manipulate databases.

5. Email Clients

- Applications such as Microsoft Outlook and Gmail help users to manage their email accounts.
- They provide tools for organizing emails, scheduling appointments and maintaining contact lists.

6. Accounting Software

- Applications like Quick Books, ERP tools and Tally are used in business transactions.

7. Malicious Software

- These software's purpose is to harm computer.

Example Virus, Worms, Trojans, etc.

8. Desktop Publishing Software

- Softwares like Adobe Page Maker and Canva are used to manage text and graphics.

Other Categories of Software

1. Freeware Software

- Freeware software refers to applications that are available for free use but typically do not include access to the source code.
- Users can download and use these programs at no cost, although there may be restrictions on modifications and redistribution.
- These softwares do not have copyright issues.

2. Shareware Software

- It refers to the software, which is made available with a right to redistribute copies.
- After a certain period, a license fee is paid, otherwise it may stop running.

3. Firmware Software

- Firmware is specialized software embedded in hardware devices that controls their functions.
- It is stored in non-volatile memory and provides low-level control necessary for hardware operations.

4. Groupware Software

- Groupware software is a type of collaborative software designed to help teams work together more effectively, regardless of their physical locations.
- It facilitates communication, coordination and collaboration among group members.

5. Open Source Software

- These softwares are distributed with their source code available for modification.
- They are also called **free source software**.

6. Proprietary Software

- It is a software that is owned by an individual or a company. It is also known as **closed source software**.

7. Cloud Software

- Software that is accessed online instead of being installed on a computer is called cloud software.

Terms Related to Software

Testing

- Testing involves evaluating a software application to identify any defects or issues.
- It ensures that the software meets its requirements and functions as intended.

Bug

- A bug is a **coding error** in a computer program.

Debugging

- Debugging is the process of **finding** and **fixing** errors or bugs in the code.

Update

- An update refers to a modification or enhancement made to a software program to improve its performance, add new features, fix bugs or enhance security.

Patch

- A patch is a small piece of software designed to fix or improve an existing program.
- It can correct bugs, enhance functionality or close security vulnerabilities.

POST

- POST (Power-On Self-Test) is a check that happens when you turn ON your computer.
- It makes sure all the hardware is working properly before starting the operating system.
- If there's a problem, it may give an error message to let you know.

Install

- Install is the process of **adding software** to a computer, setting it up to run and creating necessary files.

Uninstall

- Uninstall is the process of **removing software** from a computer, deleting the application to free up space

Facts Drive

- BIOS is **firmware** that starts your computer when you turn it ON.
- A **software license** is a legal agreement that grants users the rights to use a software application under specific conditions.
- A **software package** is a collection of related software components bundled together for installation and use.
- A **linker** is a system program that combines multiple object files and libraries into one executable program.
- A **loader** is system software that loads the executable program into main memory.
- A **retail software** refers to applications specifically designed to assist businesses in managing their retail operations.

Important Abbreviations

OS Operating System
OSS Open Source Software
BIOS Basic Input/Output System

PYQs Oneliner

1. A **word processor** is an example of application software. *SSC CHSL 2024*
2. **Mozilla firefox** web browser is not a proprietary software. *RRB NTPC 2024*
3. **Microsoft office** is not open source software. *RRB NTPC 2024*
4. Application software includes a variety of programs that are designed to meet the information processing needs of **end users**. *SSC CHSL 2024*
5. **Database management system** software is utilised for managing extensive data collections and executing queries. *SSC CHSL 2024*
6. **Windows operating system** is an example of system software. *SSC CHSL 2024*
7. **System software** provides instructions for computer operations. *DSSSB TGT 2023*
8. **Disk defragmenter** rearranges files so that all parts of the files are next to each other. *CPCT 2023*
9. Quattro Pro is a **spreadsheet** program. *RRB NTPC 2021*
10. **WinZip** compresses large files into smaller files. *RRB NTPC 2021*
11. Firmware is the software that controls hardware and is stored in **ROM**. *IBPS Clerk 2020*
12. **File compression** reduces a file size by removing **unnecessary information**. *SSC CHSL 2019*
13. Linux, Unix and MySQL are examples of **open source software**. *SSC CHSL 2019*
14. The type of software used to perform tasks such as writing letters is called **application software**. *SSC CGL 2018*

Practice Exercise

Introduction to Software

1. Modern computers follow a set of instructions to perform any task. What are these instructions commonly called? *RRB NTPC 2021*
(a) Command (b) Program
(c) Language (d) Guidelines

2. Which of the following is a set of instructions, data or programs which are used to operate and execute specific tasks in a computer? *SSC CGL 2018*
(a) Processor (b) Hardware
(c) Malware (d) Software

3. Which of the following is not a characteristic of software? *SSC CGL 2018*
(a) It can be physically touched.
(b) It is prone to access (bugs).
(c) It needs regular updates and maintenance.
(d) It is designed to solve specific problems.

4. The term used to describe the intangible instructions that tell the computer what to do is
(a) hardware (b) software
(c) storage (d) input/output

5. Software refers to
(a) the physical components that a computer is made of
(b) firmware
(c) programs
(d) people ware

6. Which of the following is software?
(a) Keyboard (b) Internet Explorer
(c) Scanner (d) Mouse

7. The primary purpose of software is to turn data into
(a) information (b) programs
(c) objects (d) charts

8. The two broad categories of software are
(a) word processing and spreadsheet
(b) transaction and application
(c) windows and mac OS
(d) system and application

9. Which of the following is a completely new installation of an operating system or application on a computer? *CPCT 2024*
(a) A clean installation
(b) A headless installation
(c) An unattended installation
(d) A silent installation

Types of Software

10. Which of the following computer programs provides instructions for computer operations? *DSSSB TGT 2023*
(a) System software (b) System utility
(c) Magnetic card (d) System application

11. Which of the following is not a purpose of the system software? *DSSSB Patwari 2022*
(a) To control computer hardware
(b)To assist in architecture design of user's projects
(c) To provide basic functionality to computer
(d) To act as an interface between user applications and computer hardware

12. Which of the following is pre-installed on the computer and acts as a translator between the hardware and the software that uses the devices? *DSSSB Patwari 2022*
(a) Device controller (b) Device key
(c) Device driver (d) Device manager

13. Which type of software is used for operating computer hardware? *DSSSB Patwari 2022*
(a) Application software (b) System software
(c) Media player (d) MS office

14. Which of the following software rearranges files so that all parts of the files are next to each other? *CPCT 2023*
(a) Disk defragmenter (b) Backup
(c) File synchronization (d) Scheduling

15. Which of the following is/are an example of utility program? *RRB JE CBT-II 2022*
(a) All of the options (b) Antivirus software
(c) Network managers (d) File compression

16. Which of the following is a type of software which controls the internal activities in the computer and controls the functions of all parts of the computer? *SSC CGL 2020*
(a) Share ware
(b) Public domain software
(c) Application software
(d) Operating system

17. What is the name of a computer program that converts the whole program into machine language? *RRB NTPC 2021*
(a) Converter (b) Interpreter
(c) Simulator (d) Compiler

18. Which of the following is a computer utility program? *RRB NTPC 2021*
(a) Inventory control system
(b) Shareware
(c) Packet software
(d) Disk defragmentor

19. ....is a windows utility program, which eliminates unnecessary fragments and rearranges files and unused disk space to perform optimised operations. *SSC FCI 2018*
(a) Back up (b) Disk carpet
(c) Disk defragmentor (d) Restore

20. File compression reduces a file by removing
(a) old data *SSC CHSL 2019*
(b) unsaved data
(c) unnecessary information
(d) unused data

21. What is a backup? *SSC CGL 2020*
(a) Connecting your network to more components
(b) Copying and securing data from the original source to a different destination
(c) Filtering of old data from new data
(d) Accessing data on tape

22. Which of the following is an example of system software? *SSC CHSL 2024*
(a) Windows operating system
(b) Adobe photoshop
(c) Microsoft word
(d) Google chrome

23. What is the category of software that enables word processing, database management, graphic manipulation and spreadsheet creation? *Delhi Police 2023*
(a) Structure (b) Application
(c) Framework (d) System

24. It is a set of programs that enables your computer's hardware device and application software to work together.
(a) Management (b) Processing
(c) Utility (d) System software

25. A(n) ...... is a software that helps a computer to operate efficiently and keep track of data.
(a) application system (b) hardware system
(c) software system (d) operating system

26. A computer cannot boot if it does not have the
(a) compiler (b) loader
(c) operating system (d) assembler

27. The .... tells the computer how to use its components.
(a) utility (b) application
(c) operating system (d) network

28. Operating system is a
(a) application software (b) system software
(c) hardware (d) language

29. In computer terminology, which of the following best describes a device driver? *UGC NET 2019*
(a) Software that allows the user to control the operating system
(b) Hardware that allows the user to control the operating system
(c) Hardware that allows interaction between peripheral devices and the operating system
(d) Software that allows interaction between peripheral devices and the operating system

30. .... helps in converting programming language to machine language.
(a) Operating system (b) Device driver
(c) Language translator (d) Linker

31. Which of the following scenarios correctly illustrates the interdependence of system software and application software? *SSC CGL (T-II) 20.01.2025*
(a) An antivirus program relying on system utilities to perform disk scans and remove malware.
(b) A word processor functioning independently without the need for an operating system.
(c) An operating system requiring a media player to manage hardware resources.
(d) A device driver operating as application software to provide printing functionality.

32. The main purpose of .... is to resolve references among files.
(a) text editor (b) loader
(c) antivirus (d) linker

33. Which of the following system software resides in main memory always?
(a) Text editor (b) Assembler
(c) Linker (d) Loader

34. A kind of system software, which is responsible for loading and relocating of the executable program in the main memory
(a) loader (b) linker
(c) translator (d) presentation software

35. Which among the following is not an example of system software?
(a) Operating system (b) Debugger
(c) Software driver (d) Adobe photoshop

36. A software program that adds functionality to your computer or help your computer perform better is called as
(a) utility program (b) function program
(c) specialised program (d) manufacturer program

37. It can make copies of all information stored on a disk or either restore the entire disk.
(a) Restore utility
(b) Disk cleaner
(c) Backup software
(d) Defragmenter

38. What is backup?
(a) Connect the user's network to more component
(b) Copy to save a data from original source to other destination
(c) Filter on old data from new data
(d) Access data from tape

39. Disk cleaner helps to free
(a) data (b) recycle bin
(c) space (d) information

40. They can find files that are unnecessary to computer operation or take up considerable amounts of space.
(a) Antivirus
(b) Sweep
(c) Disk cleaner
(d) Disk formatting

41. Which of the following windows utilities erase unneeded files?
(a) Backup or restore wizard
(b) Disk cleanup
(c) Disk defragmenter
(d) Antivirus

42. Which of the following is not related to a utility software?
(a) Firewall software
(b) Antivirus program
(c) Disk compression software
(d) Railway reservation system

43. Utility programs include
(a) virus scanning software
(b) backup software
(c) disk defragmenter
(d) All of the above

44. Which type of computer application software is Quattro Pro? ***RRB NTPC 2021***
(a) Word processing software
(b) Spreadsheet software
(c) Database software
(d) Desktop publishing software

45. What is the function of WinZip? ***RRB NTPC 2021***
(a) This is a antivirus software
(b) It compresses large files into a smaller file
(c) It extracts smaller file from larger files
(d) It expands smaller files into a large file

46. CorelDraw is an example of....... ***SSC CHSL 2021***
(a) Database software
(b) Accounting software
(c) Spreadsheet software
(d) Desktop publishing software

47. Which of the following is a system software? ***RRB NTPC 2021***
(a) Graphics (b) macOS
(c) Unix (d) Linux

48. GIMP is a/an........ ***SSC CHSL 2021***
(a) Application software
(b) Diagnostic utility program
(c) Text editor
(d) Operating system

49. Which of the following software applications is not a part of microsoft office? ***RRB NTPC 2021***
(a) Excel (b) Acrobat reader
(c) Power point (d) Word

50. The type of software used to perform tasks such as writing letters is called........ ***SSC CGL 2018***
(a) GUI software (b) utility software
(c) application software (d) user needs software

51. What type of software is most useful for creating brochures, posters and newsletters? ***Delhi Police 2020***
(a) Spreadsheet software
(b) Web authoring software
(c) Multimedia authoring software
(d) Desktop publishing software

52. For which facility has the 'e-Drishti' software been launched? ***HPPSC (Pre) 2018***
(a) To monitor the implementation of schemes by the Prime Minister
(b) To see punctuality of trains by the Railway Minister
(c) To monitor law and order by Home Minister
(d) Night surveillance by soldiers on the border

53. Which type of application software would you use to track expenses and create a budget? ***UPSC EPFO 2024***
(a) Database software (b) Spreadsheet software
(c) Presentation software (d) Web browser

54. Software designed for a specific purpose/ application such as pay calculations, processing of examination result, etc. are known as
(a) utility software (b) system software
(c) application software (d) customised software

55. Application software
(a) is used to control the operating system
(b) is designed to help programmers
(c) performs specific task for computer users
(d) is used for making design only

56. Which of the following general purpose softwares allow you to do mathematical or financial calculation?
(a) Word processing program
(b) Spreadsheet program
(c) Presentation program
(d) Database program

57. Which of the following is an example of application software? *SSC CHSL 2024*
(a) A web browser
(b) A programming language
(c) An operating system
(d) A word processor

58. Which software is used to create presentations to show to customers or staff members?
(a) Report generation
(b) Graph generator
(c) Presentation software
(d) Picture generator

59. Application software includes a variety of programs that are designed to meet the information processing needs of.......... *SSC CHSL 2024*
(a) programmers (b) team leaders
(c) customers (d) end users

60. DTP is a tool for graphic designers and non- designers to create visual communications for professional. DTP stands for
(a) Device Transfer Protocol
(b) Desktop Publishing
(c) Device Transfer Programs
(d) All of the above

61. Which application software is used for a special purpose? *IBPS RRB PO Mains 2018*
(a) General purpose software
(b) Special purpose software
(c) Important software
(d) System software

62. Which of the following is not a hardware requirement of SOUL 3.0? *RSMSSB LDC 2025*
(a) RAM : Minimum 2 GB for 32-bit
(b) Screen resolution : Minimum 1366 × 768
(c) Processor speed : 1.8 GHz or higher
(d) Free hard disk space : Minimum 160 GB free

63. What application software is utilised for managing extensive data collections and executing queries? *SSC CHSL 2024*
(a) Paint
(b) Word processing software
(c) Database management system software
(d) Antivirus software

64. Which of the following is not an application software? *SSC CHSL 2023*
(a) Operating system (b) Graphic software
(c) Spreadsheet software (d) Word-processing software

Other Categories of Software

65. Which of the following web browsers is not a proprietary software? *RRB NTPC 2024*
(a) Internet explorer (b) Mozilla firefox
(c) Opera (d) Safari

66. Which among the following is not open source software? *RRB NTPC 2024*
(a) Microsoft office (b) Linux
(c) Android (d) Mozilla firefox

67. The software substituted for hardware and stored in ROM. *IBPS Clerk 2020*
(a) Synchronous software (b) Package software
(c) Firmware (d) Middleware

68. The users must agree to the .... terms and agreements when they use an open source software. *SBI PO Mains 2021*
(a) system (b) license
(c) community (d) programmer

69. Which of the following software's source codes is available for modification? *SSC CGL 2018*
(a) Application software (b) System software
(c) Proprietary software (d) Open source software

70. Example of open source software is *SSC CHSL 2019*
(a) linux (b) unix
(c) mySQL (d) All of these

71. Which of the following software is any computer software that is distributed with its source code available for modification? *SSC CGL 2018*
(a) Application software (b) System software
(c) Open source software (d) Proprietary software

72. Which of the following is not an open source software? *UPSSSC 2018*
(a) Linux (b) Microsoft office
(c) Mozilla firefox (d) Android

73. This software is copyrighted and bears the limits against use. *SSC CGL 2017*
(a) Proprietary software (b) Open source software
(c) Application software (d) System software

74. Which of the following is a software whose source code is available and can be customized and altered within the specified guideline laid down by the creator? *DSSSB Patwari 2022*
(a) Shareware (b) Demo software
(c) Freeware (d) Open source software

75. Where is firmware stored in a computer? ***RRB ALP 2024***
(a) RAM
(b) Hard disk
(c) ROM or flash memory
(d) Cache memory

Terms Related to Software

76. What is the primary purpose of software testing?
(a) To make the software more visually appealing
(b) To identify and fix defects in the software
(c) To increase the complexity of the code
(d) To add more features to the software

77. What term describes the process of identifying and removing errors in software code?
(a) Testing
(b) Debugging
(c) Development
(d) Deployment

78. What does the term bug refer to in software development?
(a) A feature of the program
(b) An error or flaw in the code
(c) A piece of hardware
(d) A completed module

79. What is the primary goal of debugging? ***SSC CHSL 2024***
(a) To write new code
(b) To identify and fix errors in the program
(c) To optimize the software for performance
(d) To create documentation

80. What does a bug report include in software debugging?
(a) A list of all the software's features
(b) Information about the error and steps to reproduce it
(c) User manual for the software
(d) All of the above

81. What is the purpose of a patch in software maintenance?
(a) To install the software
(b) To fix bugs or vulnerabilities
(c) To uninstall software
(d) To update the system's hardware

82. Which term refers to removing software from a computer system?
(a) Update (b) Uninstall
(c) Install (d) Patch

83. What does POST(Power-On-self-Test) ensure in a computer system?
(a) The system shuts down properly
(b) The computer performs basic hardware checks on startup
(c) The operating system is installed correctly
(d) The software is updated

84. What does it mean when software is updated? ***UGC-NET 2024***
(a) It is removed from the system
(b) It is made compatible with the latest hardware
(c) It is improved with new features or fixes
(d) It is uninstalled

Answers

1.	(b)	2.	(d)	3.	(a)	4.	(b)	5.	(c)	6.	(b)	7.	(a)	8.	(d)	9.	(a)	10.	(a)
11.	(b)	12.	(c)	13.	(b)	14.	(a)	15.	(a)	16.	(d)	17.	(d)	18.	(d)	19.	(c)	20.	(c)
21.	(b)	22.	(a)	23.	(b)	24.	(d)	25.	(d)	26.	(c)	27.	(c)	28.	(b)	29.	(d)	30.	(c)
31.	(a)	32.	(d)	33.	(d)	34.	(a)	35.	(d)	36.	(a)	37.	(c)	38.	(b)	39.	(c)	40.	(c)
41.	(b)	42.	(d)	43.	(d)	44.	(b)	45.	(b)	46.	(d)	47.	(a)	48.	(a)	49.	(b)	50.	(c)
51.	(d)	52.	(b)	53.	(b)	54.	(d)	55.	(c)	56.	(b)	57.	(d)	58.	(c)	59.	(d)	60.	(b)
61.	(b)	62.	(d)	63.	(c)	64.	(a)	65.	(b)	66.	(a)	67.	(c)	68.	(b)	69.	(d)	70.	(d)
71.	(c)	72.	(b)	73.	(a)	74.	(d)	75.	(c)	76.	(b)	77.	(b)	78.	(b)	79.	(b)	80.	(b)
81.	(b)	82.	(b)	83.	(b)	84.	(c)												

Operating System

- An operating system is a software that acts as a bridge between the user and the computer hardware.
- It manages all the hardware and software resources of a computer.
- Application programs usually require an operating system to function.
- It provides a user interface, which allows users to interact with the computer easily.
- The OS manages system resources such as CPU, memory and storage.
- Common operating systems include microsoft windows, macOS, linux and android.

In this Chapter

User Interface

- The user interface in an operating system (OS) is the component that allows users to interact with the computer.
- There are two main types of user interfaces – Command Line Interface and Graphical User Interface.

Command Line Interface

- A Command Line Interface (CLI) is a **text-based** user interface.
- It allows users to interact with the computer by **typing commands**.

  Example MS DOS, UNIX

Graphical User Interface

- A Graphical User Interface (GUI) is a **visual interface** that allows users to interact with the computer through graphical elements like icons, buttons and menus.
- It is user-friendly and intuitive, making it accessible for beginners.

  Example Windows, Ubuntu, MAC

> “Computer science is the operating system of all innovation.
>
> **~ Steve Ballmer**”

Characteristics of Operating System

- It provides communication between the computer's hardware and software.
- It manages processes, including multitasking and scheduling.
- It controls memory allocation and usage for running applications.
- It organizes and manages data storage through a file system.
- It ensures security and access control to protect system resources.
- It performs error detection and recovery mechanisms.
- It is able to handle hardware and software failures.
- It is necessary to start the computers.

Functions of Operating System

1. **Process Management** The OS manages the execution of processes, including scheduling, creation and termination. It allocates CPU time to different processes.
2. **Resource Management** The OS efficiently manages computer resources, such as CPU, memory, storage and I/O devices.
3. **Memory Management** The OS handles the allocation and deallocation of memory space for processes. It keeps track of memory usage.
4. **File Management** The OS organizes and manages files on storage devices. It provides a file system that allows users to create, read, write and delete files.
5. **Device Management** The OS manages hardware devices such as printers, hard drives and keyboards.
6. **Security and Access Control** The OS implements security measures to protect the system from unauthorized access.
7. **Networking** The OS manages network connections and communications, allowing devices to connect and communicate over networks.
8. **Job Management** It keeps track of time and resources used by various jobs and users.
9. **Backup and Recovery** It provides mechanisms for backing up data and recovering it in case of system failures, errors or disasters.

Types of Operating System

1. Batch Processing operating system

- In this technique, similar types of jobs are batched together and executed in time.

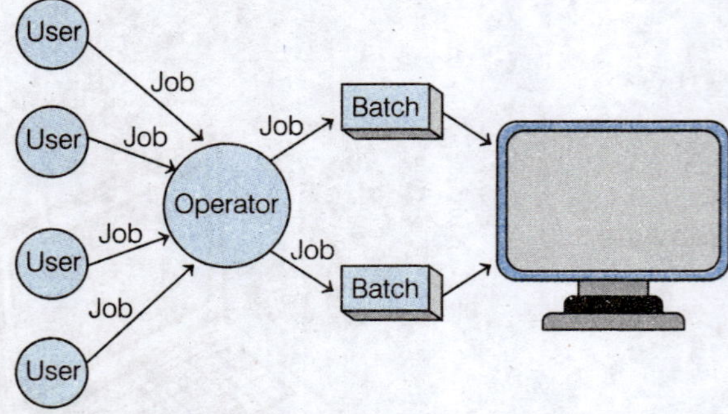

- Batch processing minimizes CPU idle time by grouping similar jobs together.

Example Bank statement, payroll systems

2. Single-User Operating System

- A single-user operating system is designed to support only one user at a time.

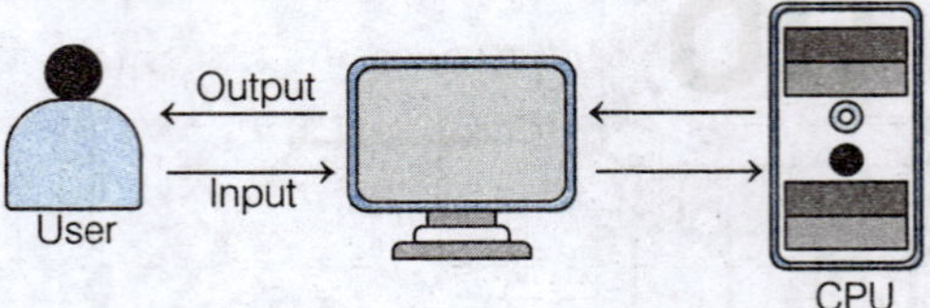

- They are designed to manage one task at a time.

Example MS-DOS and palm OS, palm handheld computers

3. Multi-User Operating System

- A multi-user operating system is designed to allow multiple users to access a computer's resources simultaneously.

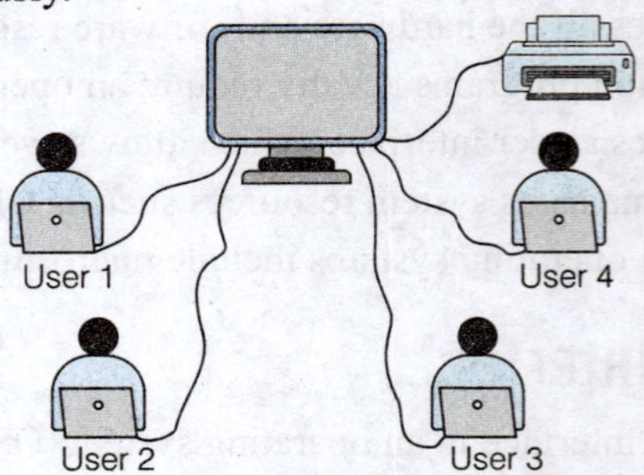

- Each user has a unique account and can run applications, store files and perform tasks independently.
- This operating system manages and allocates resources like CPU time, memory and storage to ensure fair access for all users.

Example UNIX, linux, windows server, ubuntu and main frame operating system

4. Multi Programming Operating System

- A multiprogramming operating system is designed to execute multiple programs simultaneously.

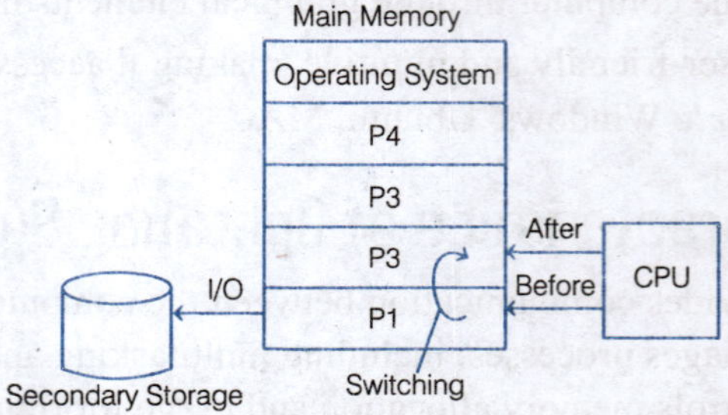

- It maximizes CPU utilization by keeping several processes in memory at once, allows the CPU to switch between them when one waits for I/O.
- It uses scheduling algorithms to manage program execution efficiently.

5. Multi-Processing Operating System

- In multi-processing operating system more than one CPU (processor) is used for the execution of the resources.
- It is also called **parallel processing** system.

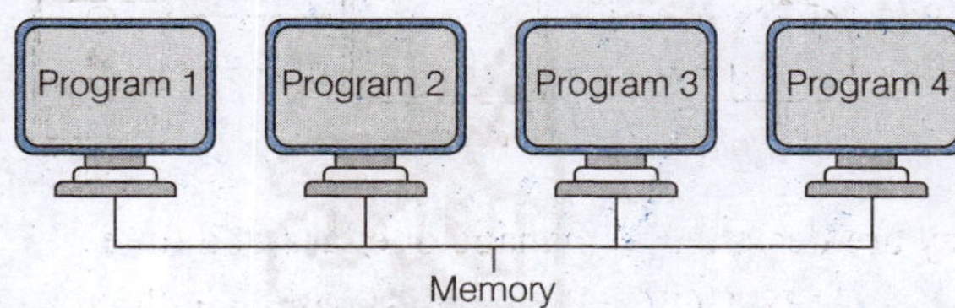

- This setup is commonly used in servers, scientific computing and applications that require heavy processing power.
- It allows faster data processing and better performance for complex tasks.

Example Windows XP, unix, windows NT

6. Time Sharing Operating System

- In time sharing operating system, each user gets the time of the CPU as they use a single system.

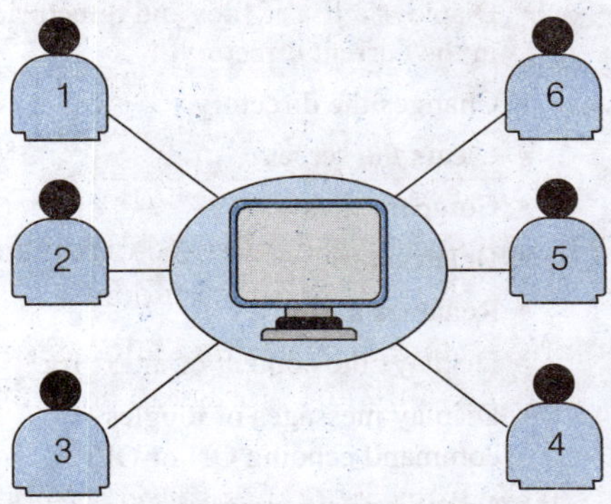

- The time that each task gets to execute is called **time slice** or **time quantum**.
- It makes the system more efficient, as users can work on their tasks without waiting long for their turn.

Example Unix, openVMS, multics

7. Multi-Tasking Operating System

- These are designed to enable multiple applications to run simultaneously.

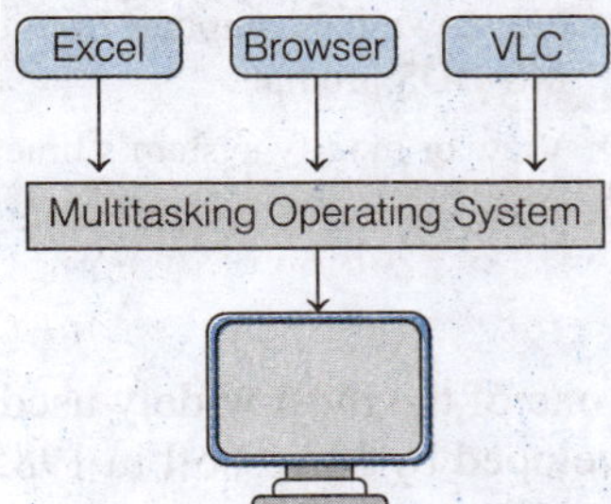

- It manages this by quickly switching between tasks, giving each one a small time slice to execute.

Example MacOS, microsoft windows

8. Real Time Operating System (RTOS)

- A real-time operating system is designed to process the input given by the user and provide output in real time.

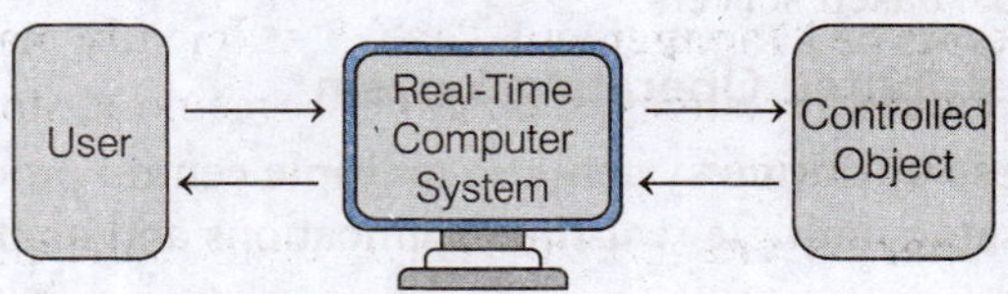

- In RTOS, the time for executing tasks is fixed in advance.
- The time taken in execution of the program is called **response time**.
- It is commonly used in systems where delays could lead to failure or risks, such as medical devices, industrial control systems and automotive systems.

Example Linux

- This is classified into two types
  (i) **Hard Real-Time Operating System** guarantee that critical tasks complete on time.
  (ii) **Soft Real-Time Operating System** allows a system to continue execution even if it is unable to complete a task's deadline.

9. Embedded Operating System

- An operating system that is designed to use a processor located inside a device is called an **embedded operating system**.
- These are designed to perform specific tasks.
- Embedded operating systems are commonly found in devices like washing machines, microwaves, traffic lights and smart home gadgets.

10. Network Operating System

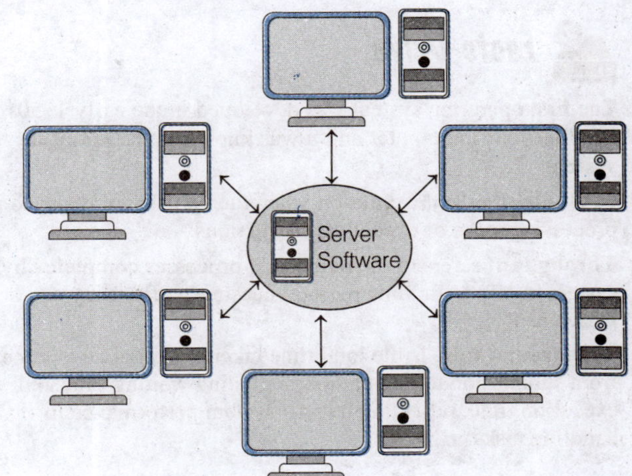

- These systems run on a server and provide the capability to manage data, users, groups, security, applications and other network functions.
- This allows shared file and printer access among multiple computers in a network.

Example Windows server, novell netware and linux-based servers.

11. Distributed Operating System

- These operating system use multiple central processors to serve multiple real-time applications and multiple users.

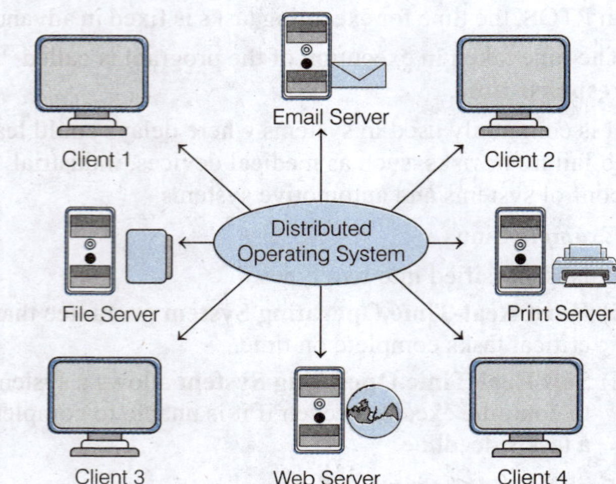

- Data processing jobs are distributed among the processors accordingly.
- These systems are also referred to as **loosely coupled systems**.
- These systems are commonly used in cloud computing, scientific research and large-scale enterprise systems to achieve high efficiency and reliability.

Example MICROS, LOCUS

Facts Drive

- The first operating system was developed in the early 1950s for the UNIVAC I computer and it was known as the **monitor system**.
- CPU **idle time** is the duration when the CPU is not engaged in processing tasks or executing instructions.
- **Throughput** refers to the number of processes completed by a system in a specific time period, measuring efficiency and a performance.
- **Turnaround time** is the total time taken to complete a process from submission to completion, including waiting time and execution time, reflecting overall system performance in handling tasks.

Some Popular Operating System

1. MS DOS

- MS-DOS (Microsoft Disk Operating System) is a command-line operating system released in 1981.

- It is a **text-based** user interface operating system.
- In this operating system only keyboard is used to give instructions and commands.
- DOS commands are classified into two parts- Internal Commands and External Commands.
- Some useful DOS commands are

Command	Description	Type
Mkdir/MD	▪ Creates a new directory	Internal
dir	▪ Displays a list of files and directories in the current directory.	Internal
cd	▪ Changes the directory	Internal
cls	▪ Clears the screen	Internal
comp	▪ Compare files	External
del	▪ Deletes a file	Internal
ren	▪ Renames a file	Internal
type	▪ Displays the content of a text file	Internal
echo	▪ Display messages or toggles command echoing ON or OFF.	Internal
cmd	▪ Opens a new command prompt window or session	Internal
power	▪ Conserve power with computer portables	External
exit	▪ Close the command prompt	Internal
xcopy	▪ Copy multiple files, directories, drives from one location to another	External
erase	▪ Erase files from computer	Internal
start	▪ Start a separate window in windows from the MS-DOS prompt	Internal
shutdown	▪ Shutdown the computer from the MS-DOS prompt	External
time	▪ View or modify system's time	Internal
date	▪ View or modify system's date	Internal

2. Windows

- Windows is one of the most widely used operating systems, developed by Microsoft in 1985.

- Windows have many versions like Windows 95, Windows 98, Windows 7, Windows 8, Windows 10 etc.

3. macOS

- macOS is developed by Apple for its line of **Macintosh** computers, initially released in 1984.

- It is also known as macintosh computer, apple macintosh, thin mac, fat mac.
- **GUI** was used for very first time in mac computers.

4. Linux

- Linux is an open-source, multi-user operating system kernel that was first created by **Linus Torvalds** in 1991.

- It comes in various distributions, such as Ubuntu, Fedora and CentOS.
- Some useful Linux commands are

Command	Use
RENAME	▪ Renames a file or directory
PWD	▪ Prints the current working directory
MKDIR	▪ Creates a new directory
RMDIR	▪ Removes an empty directory
WC-1	▪ Counts the number of lines in a file
RAWRITE	▪ A utility used to write raw disk images to a disk
WHO	▪ Displays who is logged into the system
CD	▪ Changes the current directory.
TOUCH	▪ Updates the timestamp of a file or creates an empty file if it doesn't exist.
LS	▪ Lists files and directories in the current directory
CAT	▪ Concatenates and displays the contents of files
HEAD	▪ Displays the first few lines of a file
GREP	▪ Searches for a specified pattern in files and displays matching lines
OD	▪ Displays file contents in octal, hexadecimal or ASCII format
SORT	▪ Sorts lines of text files

5. iOS

- iOS is a mobile operating system developed by Apple, specifically for iPhones and iPads.

6. Unix

- Unix is a stable, multi-user, multi-tasking system for servers, desktops and laptops.

- It is based on character user interface operating system.
- Unix operating system is made up of three parts- Kernel, Shell and Programs.

7. Ubuntu

- Ubuntu is a popular open-source operating system based on the linux kernel, developed by Canonical Ltd.

- It was first released in 2004.
- It features a clean interface, primarily using the GNOME desktop environment.
- It has features of GUI as well as Linux operating system.
- It is mainly used in universities and research institutes.

8. Chrome

- It is Linux based operating system developed by Google in 2009.

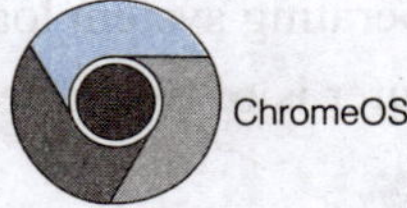

- It is specifically designed to work with online web applications.

9. Android

- Android is a mobile operating system developed by Google, primarily for smartphones and tablets.

- It is based on the linux kernel and is known for its wide range of applications.

- Some popular Mobile Operating system are IOS android OS, Ali OS, Blackberry, Color OS, Symbian OS, Meego OS

Android version and their release year

Version	Code Name	Release Year
1.0-1.1	–	2008
1.5	Cupcake	2009
1.6	Donut	2009
2.0-2.1	Eclair	2009
2.2	Froyo	2010
2.3	Gingerbread	2010
3.0-3.2	Honeycomb	2011
4.0	Ice Cream Sandwich	2011
4.1-4.3	Jelly Bean	2012
4.4	KitKat	2013
5.0-5.1	Lollipop	2014
6.0	Marshmallow	2015
7.0-7.1	Nougat	2016
8.0-8.1	Oreo	2017
9	Pie	2018
10	Android 10	2019
11	Android 11	2020
12	Android 12	2021
13	Android 13	2022
14	Android 14	2023
15	Android 15	2024

Operating System Basics

Booting

- The process of starting up a computer or computer appliance until it can be used.
- It begins the moment you turn ON the computer and ends when the operating system loads.
- Booting in computer is of two types

1. Cold Booting

- The process when a computer is turned ON after it has been completely shut down is known as cold booting.

2. Warm Booting

- Warm booting occurs when the computer is restarted by pressing the combination of Ctrl + Alt + Del or by restart button.

Process State in Operating System

- In an operating system, a process state is the status of a process at a given time.
- These states helps in managing process scheduling and resource allocation.
- Process goes through different states throughout the life cycle.

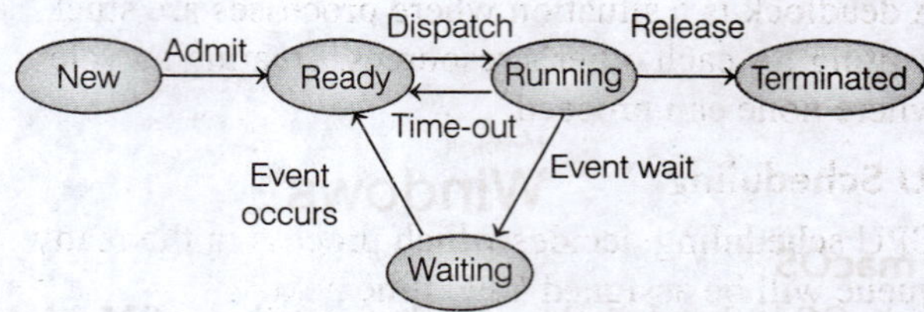

1. **New** The process is created but not yet ready to execute.
2. **Ready** The process is loaded and waiting for CPU time to execute.
3. **Running** The process is actively being executed by the CPU.
4. **Waiting (Blocked)** The process is paused, waiting for a resource or event.
5. **Terminated** The process has completed its execution or was stopped.

Process Control Block

- PCB is a data structure used by OS to maintain every process in the system.

Process-id
Process state
Process priority
Accounting information
Program counter
CPU register
PCB pointers
....

Process Control Block

- It is also called **task control block.**
- It contains all the information needed to manage and track the process throughout its lifecycle.

Some Important Terms

Scheduler

- A scheduler manages the execution of processes by determining which process runs at any given time.

Dispatcher

- A dispatcher is responsible for switching the CPU's control from one process to another.
- It works closely with the scheduler and handles the actual task of context switching

Dead Lock

- A deadlock is a situation where processes are stuck waiting for each other's resources, creating a cycle where none can proceed.

CPU Scheduling

- CPU scheduling decides which process in the ready queue will be assigned CPU time next.
- The goal is to optimize CPU use, maximize throughput and ensure fair and efficient task management.

Swapping

- Swapping is the process of temporarily moving a process from main memory (RAM) to a storage disk and then back to memory when needed.

Facts Drive

- The first mobile operating system is generally considered to be IBM's **Simon Personal Communicator**, which was released in 1994.
- **Kernel** is the core component of an operating system responsible for managing system resources and facilitating communication between hardware and software
- In 2011 **android** became the most popular operating system in the world, surpassing Windows in terms of internet usage on devices, showcasing the rise of mobile technology.
- **Demand paging** refers to the memory management scheme that loads pages into memory only when they are needed, rather than loading all pages at the start of a program.

Important Abbreviations

OS Operating System
CLI Command Line Interface
GUI Graphical User Interface
RTOS Real Time Operating System
NOS Network Operating System
DOS Disk Operating System
PCB Process Control Block

PYQs Oneliner

1. **COPY** command in MS-DOS is used to copy files from one directory to another. *SSC CGL 2024*
2. In Linux, you can change your working directory using **cd command** followed by the path name to which you want to move. *CPCT 2024*
3. The operating system of the computer is an example of **system software.** *RRB NTPC 2021*
4. **Kernel** is the core of an operating system. *SSC CHSL 2021*
5. **Operating system** is required for booting the computer. *RRB NTPC 2021*
6. MS- DOS is an operating system which contains **command line interface**. *RRB NTPC 2021*
7. **Android** is an open source operating system. *SSC CHSL 2021*
8. **Candy bean** is not the version of Android operating system. *RRB NTPC 2021*
9. **Unix** is a multi-user operating system. *RRB NTPC 2021*
10. **MS-DOS** is a single user operating system. *SBI PO MAINS 2021*
11. The first MS Windows operating system was introduced in early **1985**. *IBPS CLERK 2020*
12. **Kernel** is the core part of Linux and is responsible for all major activities. *UPPCL 2019*
13. If the computer has no **operating system**, then the computer cannot boot. *SSC MTS 2019*
14. **CLS** is used to clear the screen in MS-DOS. *HSSC 2018*
15. **Linus Torvalds** developed the operating system Linux, which was initially started as a project by a student of Finland. *SSC CGL 2018*
16. **Intel** is not an operating system. *SSC CGL 2018*

Practice Exercise

Introduction to Operating System

1. Which type of computer program acts as a bridge between a computer user and the computer hardware?
(a) Random access memory
(b) User thread
(c) Operating system
(d) Kernel

2. The operating system of the computer is an example of.......... *RRB NTPC 2021*
(a) hardware (b) system software
(c) application software (d) application platform

3. The interface between the user and the computer hardware is known as .... *RRB NTPC 2021*
(a) operating system (b) operating unit
(c) software (d) modem

4. A user interface that is part of .... allow the user to enter and receive information. *SSC CHSL 2021*
(a) computer network (b) operating system
(c) computer hardware (d) data science

5. Which of the following defines an operating system? *RRB NTPC 2021*
(a) It is a software which is used to convert source program instructions into set programs.
(b) It is a set of programs which are used to convert high level language into low level language.
(c) It is a set of programs that control the way a computer works and run other programs.
(d) It is the actual way of working on the computer.

6. .... is a complex software which is responsible for arranging the hardware resources and functionality of a computer system. *UPPCL 2019*
(a) Operating system (b) Word processor
(c) Compression software (d) Utility software

7. Which of the following is required for booting the computer? *RRB NTPC 2021*
(a) Translator (b) Assembler
(c) Compiler (d) Operating system

8. Which of the following statements is/are correct? *UPPCL 2018*
1. An operating system is the interface between a human and a machine.
2. Operating system is an application program.
(a) 1 is true, 2 is false (b) 1 is false, 2 is true
(c) Both 1 and 2 are true (d) Both 1 and 2 are false

9. If the computer has not ...., then the computer cannot boot. *SSC MTS 2019*
(a) operating system (b) loader
(c) compiler (d) linker

10. .... is an automatic process that runs from the time the computer's power button is turned ON until the system is ready to use. *SSC CHSL 2021*
(a) Saving (b) Implementation
(c) Booting (d) Loading

11. Which of the following best describes the computer booting process? *UPPCL 2019*
(a) Moving the operating system from the hard disk to the main memory and preparing the computer to execute the programs of the users
(b) Merging fragmented files to speed up the computer system
(c) Creating a backup of the operating system
(d) Refreshing files and application programs on high-disc

12. Which of the following is the type of software that controls the internal operations in the computer?
(a) Shareware
(b) Public domain software
(c) Application software
(d) Operating system software

13. .... controls the way in which the computer system does function and provides a means by which users can interact with the computer.
(a) Operating system (b) Motherboard
(c) Platform (d) Application software

14. A collection of programs that controls how your computer system runs and processes information is called
(a) operating system (b) computer
(c) office (d) compiler

15. It is the program that manages the hardware of the computer system including the CPU, memory storage devices and input/output devices.
(a) Software (b) Operating system
(c) Hardware (d) System software

16. Which of the following is the correct reason to use an operating system?
(a) To manage resources
(b) To control the hardware
(c) To provide an interface between the hardware and user
(d) All of the above

17. A program in execution is called
(a) process (b) instruction
(c) procedure (d) function

18. What is the role of an operating system in a computer system?
(a) It provides a user interface for interaction.
(b) It handles communication between hardware & software.
(c) It manages system resources.
(d) All of the above

19. ……… is a set of programs that are used to manage the database. *CPCT 2024*
(a) Hardware (b) Software
(c) Administrator (d) Data

User Interface

20. The first graphical user interface was designed by
(a) Apple Inc. (b) Microsoft
(c) Xerox Corporation (d) None of these

21. The full form of CUI is ………… *CPCT 2024*
(a) Character User Interface
(b) Character Under Interface
(c) Command User Interchange
(d) Command Under Interchange

22. Which of the following operating system is a command line user interface operating system? *Selection Post 2023*
(a) Android (b) MS-DOS
(c) MS-Windows (d) Linux

23. MS-DOS is an operating system that has a/an *RRB NTPC 2021*
(a) command line interface
(b) voice line interface
(c) open source origin
(d) graphical user interface

Functions of Operating System

24. Which of the following is the primary function of an operating system? *SSC CGL 2020*
(a) Ordering resources (b) Managing resources
(c) Mapping utilities (d) Both (a) and (b)

25. Which of the following is a function of the operating system?
(a) Memory management
(b) Process management
(c) File management
(d) All of the above

26. Which one of the following is not the function of operating system?
(a) Resource management (b) File management
(c) Taking input (d) Processor management

Types of Operating System

27. Match the column Functions with the column descriptions.

	Functions		Descriptions
(a)	Multiprocessing	(i)	Two or more users can work with programs and share peripheral devices, such as printers, at the same time.
(b)	Multithreading	(ii)	The computer can have two or more central processing units (CPUs) that programs share.
(c)	Multiuser	(iii)	A program can be broken into smaller parts that can be loaded as needed by the operating system.

(a) a-ii, b-i, c-iii
(b) a-i, b-iii, c-ii
(c) a-ii, b-iii, c-i
(d) a-iii, b-ii, c-i

28. Which of the following operating systems guarantees a response within specified time constraints?
(a) Time sharing operating system *SSC CHSL 2021*
(b) Distributed operating system
(c) Real-time operating system
(d) Interactive operating system

29. Which of the following is a multi user operating system?
(a) MS-DOS (b) Unix
(c) Windows 7 (d) iOS

30. Which of the following is a single-user operating system? *SBI PO Mains 2021*
(a) Windows (b) MAC
(c) MS-DOS (d) None of these

31. Why do desktop and laptop operating systems require more advanced memory management techniques than embedded systems? *SSC CGL (T-II) 20.01.2025*
(a) They utilise more hardware resources and need dynamic memory allocation.
(b) Memory management is not necessary for desktop and laptop operating systems.
(c) They run only one application at a time, simplifying memory management.
(d) They rely on static memory allocation due to limited hardware resources.

32. Grouping and processing all of a firm's transactions at one time, is called
(a) a database management system
(b) batch processing
(c) a real time system
(d) on-time system

33. .... is used for very large files or where a fast response time is not critical. The files to be transmitted are gathered over a period and then send together as a batch.
(a) Batch processing (b) Online processing
(c) File processing (d) Data processing

34. Which of the following system is a function of dedicated PCs?
(a) Meant for a single user
(b) Meant for the single task
(c) Deal with single software
(d) Deal with only editing

35. Windows operating system is ...... and ....
(a) multitasking, multi user
(b) multi user, single tasking
(c) single user, multitasking
(d) single tasking, single user

36. Operating system that allows only one user to work on a computer at a time is known as
(a) single user operating system
(b) multi user operating system
(c) single tasking operating system
(d) multitasking operating system

37. An operating system is said to be multi user, if
(a) more than one programs can run simultaneously
(b) more than one users can work simultaneously
(c) Either (a) or (b)
(d) None of the above

38. ...... provides process and memory management services that allow two or more tasks, jobs or programs to run simultaneously.
(a) Multitasking (b) Multithreading
(c) Multiprocessing (d) Multicomputing

39. Which of the following terms explains the execution of more than one file at the same time on a single processor?
(a) Single tasking (b) Multitasking
(c) Scheduling (d) Multiprocessing

40. ...... is a feature for scheduling and multi-programming to provide an economical interactive system of two or more users.
(a) Time sharing (b) Multisharing
(c) Time tracing (d) Multiprocessing

41. The simultaneously processing of two or more programs by multiple processors, is
(a) multiprogramming (b) multitasking
(c) time sharing (d) multiprocessing

42. Real time systems must have
(a) pre-emptive kernels (b) non-pre-emptive kernels
(c) Both (a) and (b) (d) Either (a) or (b)

43. RTOS stands for
(a) Real Time Operating System
(b) Reliable Time Operating System
(c) Reboot Time Operating System
(d) None of the above

44. A multi-programming system can be defined as a *CPCT 2024*
(a) computer system that permits multiple users to run programs at the same time
(b) computer system that permits to run similar programs at multiple time
(c) computer system that permits multiple programs simultaneously on a single processor
(d) computer program that runs on multiple processors

45. In a multi-user operating system, what does a user need in order to log in?
(a) A Password (b) A Username
(c) Both (a) and (b) (d) None of these

Some Popular Operating Systems

46. In Linux, you can change your working directory using ………… command followed by the path name to which you want to move. *CPCT 2024*
(a) usr (b) ls (c) cd (d) pwd

47. Ubuntu, Mint and Feadora are versions of
(a) Apple MAC OS X (b) MS DOS
(c) Linux (d) Windows 10

48. When were MS windows operating systems proposed? *IBPS Clerk 2020*
(a) 1994 (b) 1990 (c) 1992 (d) 1985

49. What is Ubuntu in the context of computer? *SSC CHSL 2021*
(a) An open-source operating system sponsored by Canonical Limited
(b) An anti-virus software from Microsoft
(c) Microsoft to launch an android-based search engine
(d) A search engine of the mozilla foundation

50. Which of the following is an open source operating system used to manage computer hardware and software? *RRB NTPC 2021*
(a) Microsoft windows (b) Macintosh
(c) Linux (d) Apple

51. MS DOS is an operating system which contains.............. *RRB NTPC 2021*
(a) open source origin (b) voice line interface
(c) graphical user interface (d) command line interface

52. Which of the following is a multi-user operating system? *RRB NTPC 2021*
(a) MS-DOS (b) Unix
(c) Windows 7 (d) iOS

53. Which command is used to clear the screen in MS-DOS? *HSSC 2018*
(a) Wipe (b) CLS
(c) Clear (d) Clear screen

54. What is not correct regarding the GNU operating system? *CGPSC (Pre) 2021*
(a) Its full form is GNU's Not Unix.
(b) It was started by Richard Stallman.
(c) It is an open source software.
(d) It is not compatible with Unix.

55. Which of the following is an open source operating system? *SSC CHSL 2021*
(a) Windows 10 (b) iOS
(c) Windows Vista (d) Android

56. Which of the following is not a version of android mobile operating system? *RRB NTPC 2021*
(a) Pie (b) Lollipop
(c) Candy Bean (d) Marshmallow

57. The primary purpose of the Windows operating system is
(a) to make the most efficient use of the computer hardware
(b) to allow people to use the computer
(c) to keep systems programmer's employed
(d) to make computers easier to use

58. The first version of Unix was developed by
(a) Ken Thompson (b) Presper Eckert
(c) JW Mauchly (d) Herman Hollerith

59. Which of the following is an operating system?
(a) Linux (b) Debugger
(c) Mozilla (d) Google Chrome

60. Linux is a type of …….. software.
(a) shareware (b) commercial
(c) proprietary (d) open source

61. Which one of the following is not an operating system? *SSC CGL 2018*
(a) Linux (b) Unix
(c) Intel (d) Windows

62. Who developed the operating system Linux started as a project by a student of Finland? *SSC CGL 2018*
(a) Barbara Liskov
(b) Linus Torvalds
(c) Leonard M. Adleman
(d) Leslie Lamport

63. Which of the following operating systems was first developed by Microsoft?
(a) Windows ME (b) Windows NT
(c) Windows 97 (d) MS-DOS

64. Which of the following operating systems is also known as single user operating system?
(a) Windows (b) Linux
(c) Unix (d) DOS

65. The main difference between Windows and DOS is the ability to
(a) multitasking (b) speed up
(c) run a program (d) run without power

66. '>' symbol in DOS commands is used to
(a) compare two values (b) redirect input
(c) redirect output (d) filter data

67. Which of the following is not an external command of DOS?
(a) Label (b) Format
(c) Chkdsk (d) Cls

68. Which command in MS-DOS is used to copy files from one directory to another? *SSC CGL 2024*
(a) Copy (b) Del (c) Move (d) Rename

69. DEL command is used to
(a) delete files (b) delete directory
(c) delete lables (d) Both (a) and (b)

70. This command is used to display a list of files and sub-directories that are in the directory you specify.
(a) Der (b) Dis (c) Dir (d) Dar

71. Which command is used to delete file from a directory in DOS?
(a) Ren (b) Del (c) Cd (d) Md

72. In MS-DOS, which of the following commands is used to delete directory with all sub-directories and files?
(a) Delete (b) Del (c) Deltree (d) Move

73. Which one of the following DOS command sends contents of the screen to an output device?
(a) Break (b) Disk Copy
(c) More (d) Assign

74. In DOS, the DIR command is used to
(a) display content of a file
(b) delete file
(c) display list of files and sub-directories
(d) copy files

75. A command, in DOS, used to set a name to a disk, is
(a) Vol (b) Ren (c) Label (d) Cls

76. In DOS, the label command is used to
(a) create the label of disk
(b) change the label of disk
(c) remove the label of disk
(d) Both (a) and (b)

77. Which among the following is not a mobile operating system?
(a) Android (b) Safari (c) Symbian (d) iOS

78. Which of the following is an operating system? *CPCT 2024*
(a) DragonFlyBSD (b) MS-word
(c) MS-paint (d) MS-powerpoint

79. Which mobile operating system is associated with devices like the iPhone and iPod?
(a) Windows phone (b) Symbian
(c) Android (d) iOS

80. Which company developed the android mobile operating system? *SSC CHSL 2024*
(a) Microsoft (b) Google
(c) Apple inc. (d) Symbian Ltd.

81. The operating system which does not support multitasking is
(a) Windows (b) Linux
(c) Ms-Dos (d) MacOS

Operating System Basics

82. Which of the following is the core of an operating system? *SSC CHSL 2021*
(a) Kernel (b) Genics
(c) Device Driver (d) Ventura

83. Which of the following is the core part of Linux and is responsible for all major activities? *UPPCL 2019*
(a) Editor (b) GUI
(c) Shale (d) Kernel

84. The process of loading an operating system into the computer's main memory (RAM)is known as.......
(a) waiting time (b) response time
(c) turnaround time (d) boot

85. Which process checks to ensure the components of the computer are operating and connected properly?
(a) Booting (b) Processing
(c) Saving (d) Editing

86. What happens when you boot up a PC?
(a) Portions of the operating system are copied from disk into memory
(b) Portions of the operating system are copied from memory onto disk
(c) Portions of the operating system are compiled
(d) Portions of the operating system are emulated

87. Restart of computer is called ...... when computer is already ON.
(a) cold booting (b) warm booting
(c) shut down (d) logging OFF

88. What is the state of a process when it is being created in an operating system?
(a) Ready (b) Running
(c) New (d) Waiting

89. Which of the following is not the state of a process?
(a) New (b) Old
(c) Waiting (d) Running

90. Which of the following is stored in the process control block (PCB) of a process? *SSC CHSL 2024*
(a) Process state (b) CPU registers
(c) Program counter (d) All of these

91. The main function of the dispatcher in an operating system is to
(a) assign a ready process to the CPU.
(b) swapping a process to disk.
(c) suspend some processes when CPU load is high.
(d) bring processes from disk to main memory.

92. How many states can a process be in within an operating system?
(a) 4 (b) 5 (c) 3 (d) 6

93. Which of the following is true about the process control block (PCB)?
(a) It holds all information about a process.
(b) It is created and deleted during the process execution.
(c) It is used to manage process states.
(d) All of the above

Answers

1. (c)	2. (b)	3. (a)	4. (b)	5. (c)	6. (a)	7. (d)	8. (a)	9. (a)	10. (c)
11. (a)	12. (d)	13. (a)	14. (a)	15. (b)	16. (d)	17. (a)	18. (d)	19. (b)	20. (c)
21. (a)	22. (b)	23. (a)	24. (b)	25. (d)	26. (c)	27. (c)	28. (c)	29. (b)	30. (c)
31. (a)	32. (b)	33. (a)	34. (b)	35. (a)	36. (a)	37. (b)	38. (a)	39. (b)	40. (a)
41. (d)	42. (a)	43. (a)	44. (c)	45. (c)	46. (c)	47. (c)	48. (d)	49. (a)	50. (c)
51. (d)	52. (b)	53. (b)	54. (d)	55. (d)	56. (c)	57. (a)	58. (a)	59. (a)	60. (d)
61. (c)	62. (b)	63. (d)	64. (d)	65. (a)	66. (c)	67. (d)	68. (a)	69. (d)	70. (c)
71. (b)	72. (c)	73. (b)	74. (c)	75. (c)	76. (d)	77. (b)	78. (a)	79. (d)	80. (b)
81. (c)	82. (a)	83. (d)	84. (d)	85. (a)	86. (a)	87. (b)	88. (c)	89. (b)	90. (d)
91. (a)	92. (b)	93. (d)							

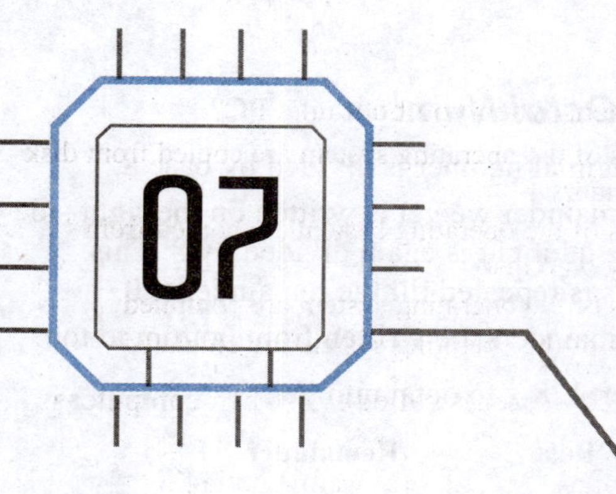

Number System and Logic Gates

Number System

- The language we use to communicate with each other is comprised of words and characters.
- We understand numbers, characters and words whereas computers only understand the numbers.
- Number system is a way to represent or express numbers in the computer system architecture.
- In daily life, we use numbers like 0,1,2,3,4,5,6,7,8,9 which are a part of decimal number system. For computers, we combine these digits to create higher numbers.

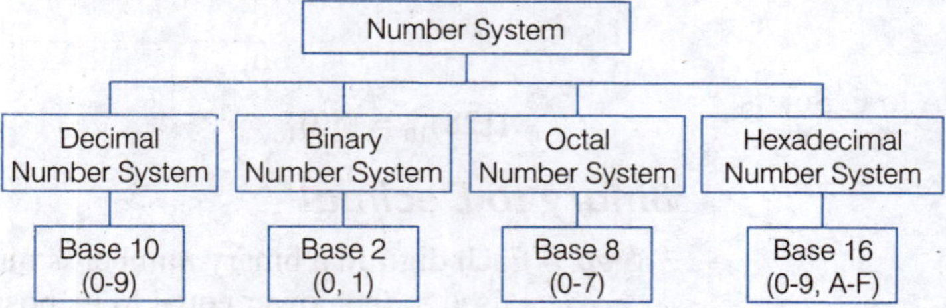

- Each number system has a base value, a face value and a positional value.

Base Value	▪ The total number of digits used to represent a number in a number system is called its base value. ▪ **Example** In Binary number system, there are total two digits (0,1) so its base value is 2.
Positional Value	▪ The position of digits in a number is counted from **right to left**. The right most digit will have a positional value of 0, the second right digit will have a positional value of 1, the third right digit will have a positional value of 2 and so on. ▪ **Example** In the number, 5467. ▪ Positional value of 7 is 0, face value of 6 is 1, positional value of 4 is 2 and the positional value of 5 is 3.
Face Value	▪ Face value is the actual value of a digit. ▪ Example, face value of digit 6 in number 5467 (decimal number system) will be 6 itself.

Note If we divide any number by 0, the computer shows an error.

In this Chapter

- Number System
- Number System Conversion
- Computer Codes
- Logic Gates

"Computers are composed of nothing more than logic gates stretched out to the horizon in a vast numerical irrigation system.

~ Stan Augarten"

Types of Number System

Number system is classified into four types

1. Decimal number system

- The number system that we use in our day-to-day life is the decimal number system.
- Decimal number system has **base 10** as it uses 10 digits from 0 to 9.
- It is also known as **base 10 system**.

Example $723_{10}, 32_{10}, 4257_{10}$ etc.

2. Binary number system

- It has only two digits 0 and 1, so its base is 2.
- Digits 0 and 1 are called **bits** and 8 bits together make a **byte**.
- It is also called **base 2 system**.

Example $10001_2, 111101_2, 1010101_2$ etc.

3. Octal number system

- It has eight digits (0, 1, 2, 3, 4, 5, 6, 7), so its base is 8.
- The three binary digits can be represented with a single octal digit.
- It is also called **base 8 system**.

Example $35_8, 23_8$ and 141_8 etc.

4. Hexadecimal number system

- It is an **alpha numeric** system.
- It has 16 digits that ranges from 0 to 9 and A to F. So, its base is 16.
- It is also called **base 16 system**.

Example $7B3_{16}$, $6F_{16}$ and $4B2A_{16}$

Number System Conversion

Decimal to Binary Number

Step 1 The decimal number is divided by base 2.

Step 2 The remainder we get, is written on the right side and the quotient is again divided by 2. This process is repeated till the remainder is 0.

Step 3 The remainders are written from bottom to top.

Example Convert $(25)_{10}$ to binary number.

Base		Remainder
2	25	1
2	12	0
2	6	0
2	3	1
2	1	1
	0	

$\therefore \quad (25)_{10} = (11001)_2$

Decimal to Octal Number

Step 1 The decimal number is divided by base 8.

Step 2 The remainder we get is written on the right side and the quotient is again divided by 8. This process is repeated till the remainder is 0.

Step 3 The remainders are written from bottom to top.

Example Convert 128_{10} to octal number.

Base		Remainder
8	128	0
8	16	0
8	2	2
	0	

$\therefore \quad (128)_{10} = (200)_8$

Decimal to Hexadecimal

Step 1 The decimal number is divided by base 16.

Step 2 The remainder we get is written on the right side and the quotient is again divided by 16. This process is repeated till the remainder is 0.

Step 3 The remainders are written from bottom to top.

Example Convert 128_{10} to hexadecimal number.

Base		Remainder
16	128	0
16	8	8
	0	

$\therefore \quad (128)_{10} = (80)_{16}$

Binary to Decimal

Step 1 Each digit in a binary number is multiplied by 2 raised to the power equal to its positional value.

Step 2 The multiplication process begins from the R.H.S.(Right Hand Side).

Step 3 All the multiplied values are added.

Example Convert $(1101)_2$ to a decimal number.

$$1\times 2^3 + 1\times 2^2 + 0\times 2^1 + 1\times 2^0$$

$$= 8 + 4 + 0 + 1$$

$$= 13$$

$\therefore \quad (1101)_2 = (13)_{10}$

Binary to Octal

Step 1 Form the pairs of three from the right hand side of the given binary number.

Step 2 If there is a difficulty in forming groups of three, 0 can be added to the left hand side.

Step 3 After this, the octal numbers for the formed groups are placed.

Example Convert $(1101)_2$ into an octal number.

Step 1 1 <u>1 0 1</u>

Step 2 Now we have difficulty in forming another group of 3 so, we add two zeroes on the left of 1.

	<u>0 0 1</u>	<u>1 0 1</u>
Step 3 Octal number	1	5

So, our answer is $(15)_8$.

Binary to Hexadecimal

Step 1 Form the pairs of four from the right hand side of the given binary number.

Step 2 If there is a difficulty in forming groups of four, 0 can be added to the left hand side.

Step 3 After this, the hexadecimal numbers for the formed groups are placed.

Example Convert $(111101)_2$ into an hexadecimal number.

Step 1 1 1 <u>1 1 0 1</u>

Step 2 Now we have difficulty in forming another group of four so, we add two zeroes on the left of 1.

	<u>0 0 1 1</u>	<u>1 1 0 1</u>
Step 3 Hexadecimal number	3	13=D

So, our answer is $(3D)_{16}$.

Octal to Binary

To convert octal to binary, the binary code for each octal number is given.

3 Binary Bits	Octal
000	0
001	1
010	2
011	3
100	4
101	5
110	6
111	7

Example Convert $(35)_8$ to binary.

We know, 3= 011

5=101

$\therefore \quad (35)_8 = (011101)_2$.

Octal to Decimal

Step 1 Each digit in an octal number is multiplied by 8 raised to the power equal to its positional value.

Step 2 The multiplication process begins from the R.H.S.(Right Hand Side).

Step 3 All the multiplied values are added.

Example Convert 22_8 to decimal number.

$$2\times 8^1 + 2\times 8^0 = 16+2=18$$

$$\therefore \quad (22)_8 = (18)_{10}$$

Octal to Hexadecimal

Step 1 Convert octal number to binary number.

Step 2 Convert binary number to hexadecimal number

Example Convert 22_8 to a hexadecimal number.

Step 1 Convert 22 to binary number.

2 = 010 So, 22 = 010010

Step 2 Now convert 010010 to hexadecimal number by forming groups of four.

So, 01 <u>0010</u>

Putting two 0s on the left, we get, 0001

So, the groups are	<u>0001</u>	<u>0010</u>
Hexadecimal number	1	2

$\therefore \quad 22_8 = 12_{16}$ or C_{16}.

Hexadecimal to Binary

To convert a hexadecimal number to a binary number, we write the code for the hexadecimal number.

Hexadecimal Number	Binary
0	0000
1	0001
2	0010
3	0011
4	0100
5	0101
6	0110
7	0111
8	1000
9	1001
A	1010
B	1011
C	1100
D	1101
E	1110
F	1111

Example Convert $(6B)_{16}$ to a binary number.

We know, 6 B

0110 1011

$\therefore \quad (6B)_{16} = (01101011)_2$.

Hexadecimal to Octal

Change hexadecimal number to binary number and then change it to octal number by forming groups of three.

Example Convert $(65C)_{16}$ to octal number.

Step 1 6 5 C
0110 0101 1100

Step 2 Form groups of 3.
So, 011001011100.

011	001	011	100
3	1	3	4

So, the octal number is $(3134)_8$.

Hexadecimal to Decimal

Step 1 Each digit in a hexadecimal number is multiplied by 16 raised to the power equal to its positional value.

Step 2 The multiplication process begins from the R.H.S.(Right Hand Side).

Step 3 All the multiplied values are added.

Example Convert 121_{16} to decimal number.

$$1\times16^2+2\times16^1+1\times16^0=16\times16+2\times16+1\times1=289$$

$$\therefore\ (121)_{16}=(289)_{10}$$

Computer Codes

- Computers and digital circuits process information in the binary format.
- Each character is assigned 7 or 8 bit binary code to indicate its character which may be numeric, alphabet or special symbol.
- The processing on information can be done only, if its code is known.

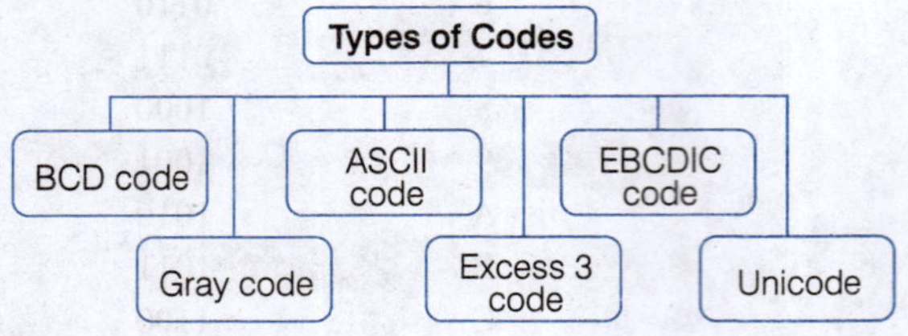

BCD (Binary-Coded Decimal) code

- Four-bit code that represents one of the ten decimal digits from 0 to 9.
  Example $(37)_{10}$ is represented as 0011 0111 using BCD code, rather than $(100101)_2$ in straight binary code.
- Thus, BCD code requires more bits than straight binary code.

ASCII (American Standard Code for Information Interchange) code

- It is a 7-bit or 8-bit alphanumeric code.
- 7-bit code is standard ASCII code. It supports 128 characters.
- Standard ASCII series lies from 00h to 7Fh, where 00h-1Fh are used as control characters and 20h-7Fh as graphics symbols.
- 8-bit code is extended ASCII code. It supports 256 symbols, where special graphics and maths symbols are added.

EBCDIC (Extended Binary Coded Decimal Interchange Code) code

- 8-bit alphanumeric code developed by IBM, supports 256 symbols.
- It was mainly used in IBM mainframe computers.

Gray code

- It differs from leading and following number by a single bit.
- Gray code for 2 is 0011 and for 3 is 0010.
- No weights are assigned to the bit positions.
- Extensively used in shaft encoders.

Excess-3 code

- 4-bit code obtained by adding binary 0011 to the natural BCD code of the digit.
  Example Decimal 2 is coded as 0010 + 0011 = 0101 as Excess-3 code.
- It is not weighted code.
- It is a self-complimenting code, means 1's complement of the coded number yields 9's complement of the number itself.
- It is used in digital system for performing subtraction operations.

Unicode

- A standard for representing characters as integers.
- Unlike ASCII, which uses 7 or 8 bits for each character, Unicode uses 16 bits, which means that it can represent more than 65,000 unique characters.
- It is necessary for some other languages, such as Greek, Chinese and Japanese.

Logic Gates

- It is a basic building block of a digital circuit.
- The relationship between the input and the output is based on a certain logic.

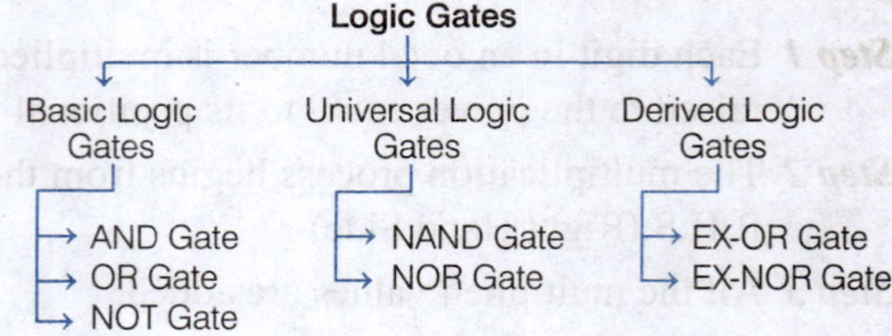

- These gates are implemented using electronic switches like transistors, diodes and perform boolean or logical operations.
- A **truth table** in logic gates is a table that lists all the possible combinations of inputs and their corresponding outputs.

1. Basic Logic Gates

There are three basic logic gates

AND Gate

- In digital electronics, the AND gate is one of the basic logic gates that performs the logical **multiplication** of inputs applied to it.
- It generates the output 1 when all inputs are 1.
- 1 is called a **high** or **logic 1**, 0 is called **low** or **logic 0**.

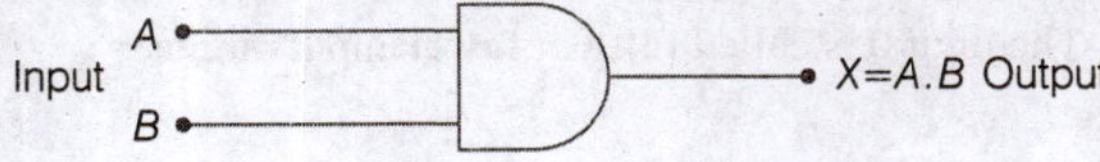

The truth table of AND gate for two variables

A	B	$X = A.B$
0	0	0
0	1	0
1	0	0
1	1	1

OR Gate

- In digital electronics, this is a type of basic logic gate which produces a 0 output only when its all inputs are 0.
- For all other input combinations, the output of the OR gate is high or logic 1.
- The primary function of the OR gate is to perform the logical sum(addition) operation.

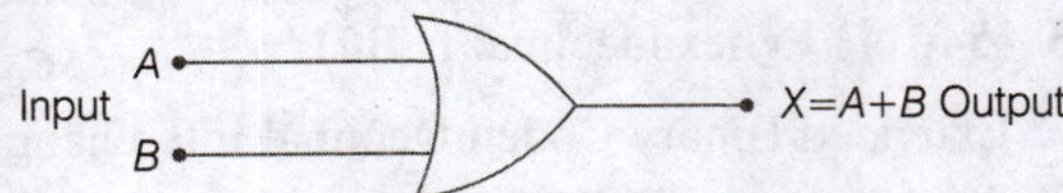

The truth table of OR gate for two variables

A	B	$X = A + B$
0	0	0
0	1	1
1	0	1
1	1	1

NOT Gate

- In digital electronics, the NOT gate is another basic logic gate used to perform compliment of an input signal applied to it. It takes only one input and one output.
- The output of the NOT gate is **complement** (opposite) of the input applied to it.
- If we apply a 0 input to the NOT gate, it gives 1 output and *vice-versa*.
- The NOT gate is also known as **inverter**, as it performs the inversion operation.

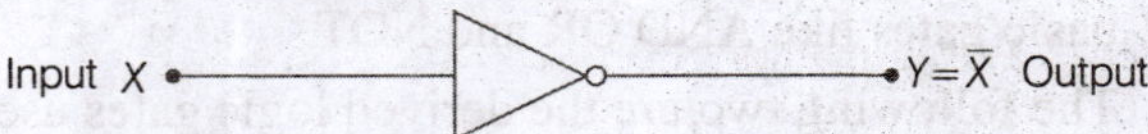

The truth table of NOT gate

X	$Y = \overline{X}$
0	1
1	0

2. Universal Logic Gates

Universal logic gates are NAND and NOR gates, which can be used to implement any Boolean function without using any other logic gates.

NAND Gate

- This is known as NOT AND gate. It has the same parameters as the AND gate but the **output** is **inverted**.
- Usually, a NAND gate has **two or more inputs** attached to it and has only **one output**.
- If all the inputs are TRUE (high) the output is FALSE (low) otherwise the output is TRUE (high) all the time.
- TRUE=1, FALSE=0.

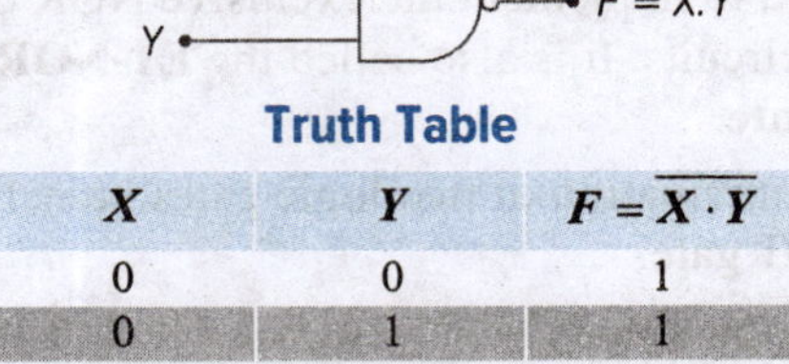

Truth Table

X	Y	$F = \overline{X \cdot Y}$
0	0	1
0	1	1
1	0	1
1	1	0

NOR Gate

- It has the same parameters as the OR gate, but the output is **inverted**.
- This is also known as NOT OR gate.
- Usually, NOR gate has **two** or **more inputs** attached to it and has only **one output**.
- If any input is TRUE (high) the output is FALSE (low) otherwise the output is TRUE (high) all the time.

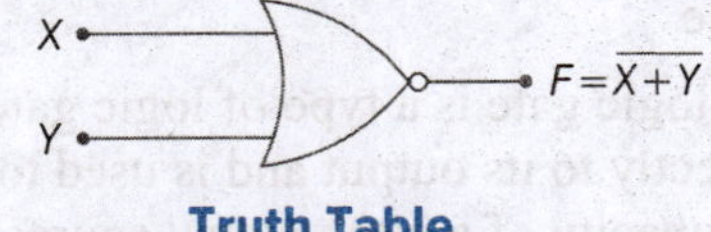

Truth Table

X	Y	$F = \overline{X + Y}$
0	0	1
0	1	0
1	0	0
1	1	0

3. Derived Logic Gates

- Derived logic gates are logic gates that are derived from basic gates like AND OR and NOT.
- The following two are the derived logic gates used in digital systems

XOR Gate

- It is also referred to as **exclusive OR gate** or **Ex-OR gate**.
- The XOR gate can take only **two inputs** at a time and give an output.
- The output of the XOR gate is 1 only when its two inputs are different.

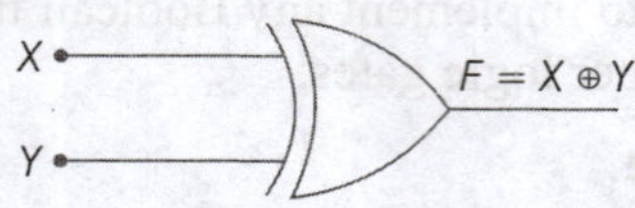

Truth Table

X	Y	$F = X \oplus Y$
0	0	0
0	1	1
1	0	1
1	1	0

XNOR Gate

- It is used to implement the exclusive NOR operation in digital circuits. It is also called the **Ex-NOR** or **exclusive NOR gate**.
- It is a combination of two logic gates namely, XOR gate and NOT gate.
- The output of an XNOR gate is 1 when its both inputs are similar. Otherwise the output is 0.

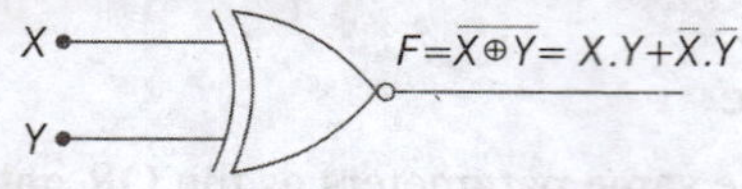

Truth Table

X	Y	$F = X \odot Y$
0	0	1
0	1	0
1	0	0
1	1	1

Buffer Gate

- A buffer logic gate is a type of logic gate that passes its input directly to its output and is used to increase the current capacity of a weak signal source.
- If the input is **1**, the buffer outputs **1**.
- If the input is **0**, the buffer outputs **0**.

The truth table of buffer gate

Input	Output
0	0
1	1

Facts Drive

- Boolean algebra was invented by a British Mathematician, **George Boole**.
- Division Remainder Method is used to convert decimal number system to any other number system.
- The digit 1 is called **true** or **high** input output.
- The digit 0 is called **false** or **lower** input output.

PYQs Oneliner

1. The size of each ASCII character is **8 bits**. *SSC CGL (T-II) 20.01.2025*
2. Computers use the **binary** number system to store data and perform calculations. *CPCT 2024*
3. The radix (r) value of the octal number system is **8**. *CPCT 2024*
4. The decimal equivalent of binary 101 is **5**. *CPCT 2024*
5. $(22)_8$ into its corresponding decimal number is 18. *SSC CGL 2023*
6. $(5401)_8$ to hexadecimal is **B01**. *SSC CGL 2022*
7. Extended Binary Coded Decimal Interchange Code is the full form of **EBCDIC**. *SSC CHSL 2021*
8. American Standard Code for Information Interchange is the full form of **ASCII**. *SSC CHSL 2021*
9. The hexadecimal representation of 1110 is **E**. *IBPS Clerk 2020*
10. **100000** is the binary representation of 32. *RRB JE 2019*
11. 0 and 1 digits are used in the **binary** number system. *RRB JE 2019*

Practice Exercise

Number System

1. Computers use the .... number system to store data and perform calculations. *CPCT 2024*
(a) binary (b) decimal
(c) hexadecimal (d) octal

2. The radix (r) value of the octal number system is .... *CPCT 2024*
(a) 16 (b) 8
(c) 2 (d) 10

3. The hexadecimal digits are 1 to 0 and A to ....
(a) E (b) F
(c) G (d) D

4. The main advantage of hexadecimal numbers is the ease of conversion from hexadecimal to.......
(a) decimal (b) binary
(c) ASCII (d) BCD

5. How many bytes are there in 1011 1001 0110 1110 numbers?
(a) 1 (b) 2
(c) 4 (d) 8

6. When numbers, letters or words are represented by a special group of symbols, this process is called
(a) decoding (b) encoding
(c) coding (d) None of these

7. The total number of digits used to represent a number in a number system is called its
(a) face value (b) base value
(c) positional value (d) None of these

8. Base value of binary number system is ....
(a) 8 (b) 16
(c) 10 (d) 2

9. Decimal number system has base 10 as it uses 10 digits from
(a) 1 to 10 (b) 1 to 9
(c) 0 to 9 (d) 0 to 10

10. How many bits together make a byte ?
(a) 10 (b) 8 (c) 4 (d) 2

11. The A to F alphabets represent
(a) 10 to 15 decimal numbers
(b) 1 to 15 decimal numbers
(c) 0 to 12 decimal numbers
(d) 10 to 20 decimal numbers

12. How many digits are there in binary number system ?
(a) 8 (b) 16
(c) 2 (d) 10

13. Which of the following is an example of a binary number ?
(a) 6AH1 (b) 1234
(c) 006 (d) 0111

14. Which of the following number systems is alphanumerical ?
(a) Binary (b) Octal
(c) Hexadecimal (d) Decimal

15. Bit is the short form for
(a) binary integer (b) binary task
(c) binary digit (d) binary interceptor

16. A .... bit is an extra bit included with a binary message to make the total number of 1s either odd or even. *SSC CHSL 2023*
(a) exclusive (b) parity
(c) complementary (d) checker

17. The positional value in number system is calculated from ....
(a) left to right (b) right to left
(c) top to bottom (d) None of these

18. How many characters can be made from 1 byte to 28 bytes ?
(a) 255 (b) 256
(c) 343 (d) 295

19. Which number system is used to store data and perform calculations on it ?
(a) Binary number system (b) Boolean number system
(c) ASCII code (d) All of these

Number System Conversion

20. What is the binary equivalent of the decimal number 10.25? *DSSSB TGT 2023*
(a) 1010.01 (b)1011.01
(c)1101.01 (d) 1111.01

21. The decimal equivalent of binary 101 is .... *CPCT 2024*
(a) 2 (b) 3 (c) 6 (d) 5

22. The input hexadecimal representation of 1110 is .... *IBPS Clerk 2020*
(a) 0111 (b) E (c) 15 (d) 14

23. Convert $(22)_8$ into its corresponding decimal number. *SSC CGL 2023*
(a) 28 (b) 18 (c) 81 (d) 82

24. Convert $(5401)_8$ to hexadecimal. *SSC CGL 2022*
(a) A01 (b) A02 (c) B01 (d) C01

25. In computer number system, what is the binary value for decimal number $(5)_{10}$ *SSC Selection Post 2023*
(a) $(1010)_2$ (b) $(101)_2$
(c) $(11)_2$ (d) $(1100)_2$

26. The octal equivalent of 111 010 is.....
(a) 81 (b) 72
(c) 71 (d) All of these

27. How would you represent 10111 in the decimal number system?
(a) 23 (b) 24
(c) 25 (d) 22

28. The decimal equivalent of $(1011.011)_2$ is equal to
(a) 11.375 (b) 10.123
(c) 11.175 (d) 9.234

29. The binary equivalent of the hexadecimal number 7 BD is.....
(a) 01111 0111101 (b) 111010111101
(c) 101110111101 (d) All of these

30. Convert hexadecimal to decimal: (1E2) = ?
(a) 480 (b) 483
(c) 482 (d) 484

31. To convert a binary number to an octal number, we divide the binary number into groups of ....
(a) three (b) four
(c) two (d) None of these

32. The binary code 1101 is equal to .... in hexadecimal number system.
(a) 10=A (b) 13=D
(c) 15=F (d) 12=C

Computer Codes

33. Binary Coded Decimal (BCD) numbers express each digit as a group of 4 ....
(a) byte (b) nibble
(c) bit (d) All of these

34. It is an 8-bit alphanumeric code developed by IBM, supports 256 symbols.
(a) EBCDIC (b) Unicode
(c) Gray code (d) BCD code

35. This code is extensively used in shaft encoders.
(a) EBCDIC (b) Unicode
(c) Gray code (d) BCD code

36. What is the size of each ASCII character in bits? *SSC CGL (T-II) 20.01.2025*
(a) 4 bits (b) 16 bits
(c) 8 bits (d) 5 bits

Logic Gates

37. Which of the following algebraic functions represents NAND gate? *DSSSB TGT 2023*
(a) (xy)' (b) (x+y)'
(c) x+y (d) x*y

38. An OR gate has 6 inputs, how many input words are in its truth table?
(a) 64 (b) 32 (c) 16 (d) 128

39. Which of the following logical operations is represented by the + sign in Boolean algebra?
(a) Inversion (b) AND
(c) OR (d) Complementation

40. The output of a NOR gate is HIGH, if ....
(a) all inputs are HIGH (b) any input is HIGH
(c) any input is LOW (d) all inputs are LOW

41. If the input to a NOT gate is A and the output is X, then ....
(a) $X = A$ (b) $X = \overline{A}$
(c) $X = 0$ (d) None of these

42. What is the Boolean expression for a three-input AND gate?
(a) $X = A \cdot B \cdot C$ (b) $X = A + B + C$
(c) $X = (A + B + C)$ (d) $X = (A \cdot B \cdot C)$

43. Write the Boolean expression for an inverter logic gate with input X.
(a) $A = \overline{X}$ (b) $A = X$
(c) $A = 0$ (d) $A = 1$

44. A 2-input NOR gate is equivalent to a ....
(a) negative-OR gate (b) negative-AND gate
(c) negative-NAND gate (d) None of these

45. The NOR logic gate is the same as the operation of the .... gate with an inverter connected to the output.
(a) OR (b) AND
(c) NAND (d) None of these

46. The NOR logic gate is a .... gate.
(a) basic logic gate
(b) derived logic gate
(c) universal logic gate
(d) None of the above

47. The basic logic gate whose output is the complement of the input is the
(a) OR gate (b) AND gate
(c) inverter (d) buffer

48. Identify the gate

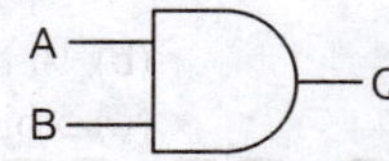

(a) AND (b) NAND
(c) OR (d) XOR

49. The output in an OR gate will be 0 when
(a) A=0,B=1
(b) A=0,B=0
(c) A=1,B=0
(d) None of the above

50. A .... is a table that lists all the possible combinations of inputs and their corresponding outputs.
(a) file (b) record
(c) maths table (d) truth table

51. It has the same parameters as the AND gate but the output is inverted.
(a) NAND gate (b) NOR gate
(c) XNOR gate (d) NOT gate

52. The output of the XOR gate is high or logic 1 only when its two inputs are
(a) same (b) different
(c) not defined (d) zero

53. It is a combination of two logic gates namely, XOR gate and NOT gate.
(a) NAND gate (b) NOR gate
(c) XNOR gate (d) NOT gate

54. Which of the following is a universal gate ?
(a) XOR (b) NAND
(c) XNOR (d) Both (a) & (c)

55. Which of the following is a basic gate ?
(a) AND gate (b) OR gate
(c) NOT gate (d) All of these

56. A .... gate produces the same output as the input.
(a) AND (b) buffer
(c) OR (d) inverter

57. Logic gates perform ....
(a) mathematical operations
(b) boolean operations
(c) alphanumerical opertions
(d) None of the above

58. In logic gates, 1 is known as ....
(a) true (b) false
(c) zero (d) complement

59. If the inputs for an OR gate are 0 and 1 respectively, its output will be
(a) 1 (b) 0
(c) Error (d) None of these

60. Which gate is used to perform logical multiplication?
(a) AND (b) OR
(c) NOT (d) EXOR

61. A NAND gate has the following expression
(a) Y = (A + B)' (b) Y = A - B
(c) Y = (A *B)' (d) None of these

Answers

1.	(a)	2.	(b)	3.	(b)	4.	(b)	5.	(b)	6.	(b)	7.	(b)	8.	(d)	9.	(c)	10.	(b)
11.	(a)	12.	(c)	13.	(d)	14.	(c)	15.	(c)	16.	(b)	17.	(b)	18.	(a)	19.	(a)	20.	(a)
21.	(d)	22.	(b)	23.	(b)	24.	(c)	25.	(b)	26.	(b)	27.	(a)	28.	(a)	29.	(a)	30.	(c)
31.	(a)	32.	(b)	33.	(c)	34.	(a)	35.	(c)	36.	(c)	37.	(a)	38.	(a)	39.	(c)	40.	(d)
41.	(b)	42.	(a)	43.	(a)	44.	(a)	45.	(a)	46.	(c)	47.	(c)	48.	(a)	49.	(b)	50.	(d)
51.	(a)	52.	(b)	53.	(c)	54.	(b)	55.	(d)	56.	(b)	57.	(b)	58.	(a)	59.	(a)	60.	(a)
61.	(c)																		

Programming Concepts

In this Chapter
- Computer Programming Languages
- Language Translator Software
- Algorithm
- Flowchart
- Pseudo Code

- Programming is the process of creating instructions, that tell a computer how to perform a task.
- These instructions are written in a **programming language**, which acts like a **translator** between humans and computers.
- By using programming, we can create software, websites, games and even control hardware like robots.

Computer Programming Languages

- Programming languages are the code used by a programmer to communicate with a computer.
- It is a formal system used to write instructions that a computer can understand and execute to perform specific tasks.
- Each programming language has its own syntax, which is the set of rules for writing code.
- These languages are classified into following categories

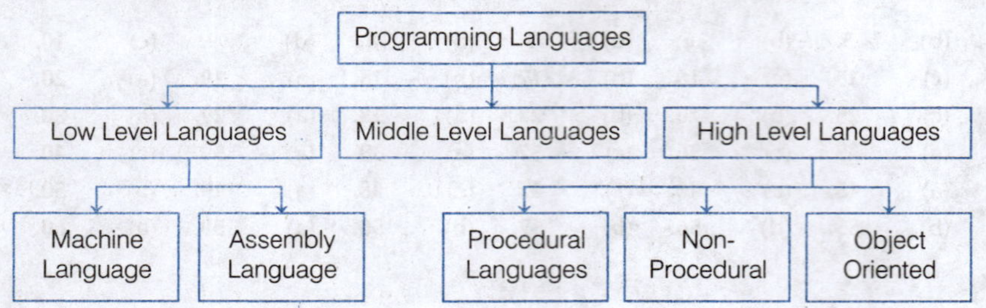

"Programming is not about what you know, it is about what you can figure out.

~ Chris Pine"

Low-Level Languages (LLL)

- It is a **machine dependent** programming language.
- The program written in LLL runs very fast as they don't need any compiler or interpreter.
- It is further divide into two parts.

1. Machine Language

- It is also called **object code** or **machine code**.
- This language was used in first generation of computer.
- It helps the programmer to execute the programs faster than the high-level programming language.

2. Assembly Language

- It represents the set of instructions in a symbolic and human-understandable code.
- It uses **mnemonics** (symbolic codes) like MOV, ADD and SUB to represent machine-level instructions.
- **Assembler** is used to convert assembly language into machine language.

Medium-Level (Mid-level) Languages

- Mid-level languages combine features of both low-level and high-level programming languages.
- These are also known as **intermediate programming language** and **pseudo language**.

High-Level Languages (HLL)

- HLL are designed for developing user-friendly software programs and websites.
- These are easy to read, write and maintain.
- These are not directly understood by computer.
- These languages use **language translator** (compiler or interpreter) to translate code into machine language.

  Example Python, JAVA, JavaScript, PHP, C, C++, FORTRAN, Pascal etc.
- High level languages are classified into three categories

1. Procedural Language

- Procedural language follows a sequential step-by-step approach to solve problems.
- It divides a program into small procedures called **routines** or **functions**.

  Example C, Pascal and FORTRAN

2. Non-Procedural Language

- In this, user has to specify only what to do and not how to do.
- These are also known as **applicative** or **functional languages**.
- This is based on queries.

  Example SQL, Prolog and XSLT

3. Object Oriented Language

- It is based upon **objects**.
- In object oriented language, functions and data are used together, which is called **class**.
- They promote code reuse and modularity.

  Example Java, C++ and Python

Some High Level Languages and their Application Areas

Language	Year	Developer	Application Area	Nature
FORTRAN	1957	IBM	Scientific and engineering computations	Compiled
ALGOL	1958	A committee of European and American computer scientists	Scientific purpose	Compiled
LISP	1958	John McCarthy	AI research, symbolic computing	Compiled and Interpreted
COBOL	1959	CODASYL& Grace Hopper	Business, finance, administrative systems	Compiled
BASIC	1964	John G. Kemeny& Thomas E. Kurtz	Education, early programming learning	Interpreted
Pascal	1970	Niklaus Wirth	Education	Compiled
C	1972	Dennis Ritchie	System programming, OS development	Compiled
C++	1985	Bjarne Stroustrup	Game development, system software	Compiled
Python	1991	Guido van Rossum	Data science, AI, web development	Interpreted
Java	1995	Sun Microsystems	Web apps android apps	Compiled
SQL	1970s	IBM	Database management	Declarative, query language
Ruby	1995	Yukihiro Matsumoto	Web development	Interpreted

Generations of Languages

1st Generation (1GL)	Machine language
2nd Generation (2GL)	Assembly language
3rd Generation (3GL)	C, FORTRAN, COBOL
4th Generation (4GL)	Oracle, SQL
5th Generation (5GL)	Visual basic, LISP, Mercury

Language Translator Software

- A language translator is a program that translates a program written in a given programming language into machine language.
- There are three main types of language translator softwares.

Assembler

- An assembler is a program that converts assembly language into machine code or object code.
- It scans the program in **phases**.
- Assembly language uses **mnemonics** that are easier for humans to understand compared to machine code.
- It requires less memory and less execution time to execute program.

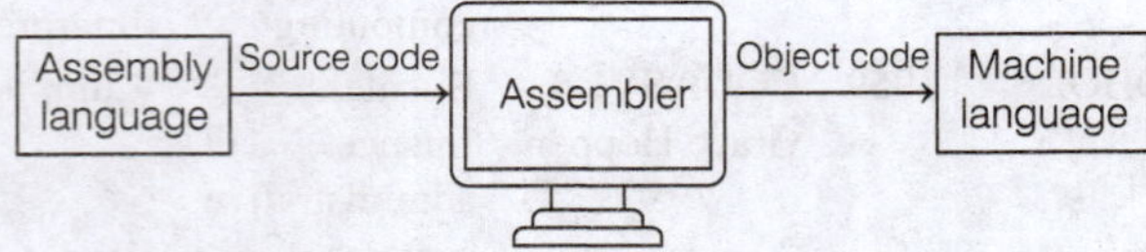

Compiler

- A compiler is a program that translates high-level programming language into machine language.
- It processes the entire source code before execution, by creating an executable file or object code.
- It translates all the **code at once**.
- It reports all the error of the program along with the line number.
- It requires more memory for storing the compiled execution.

Interpreter

- An interpreter is a program that translates and executes high-level programming code **line-by-line**.
- Errors are displayed line by line.
- Program execution cannot resume until the error is rectified by user.
- It executes directly without producing any intermediate code.
- It requires less memory as it stores and executes code directly.

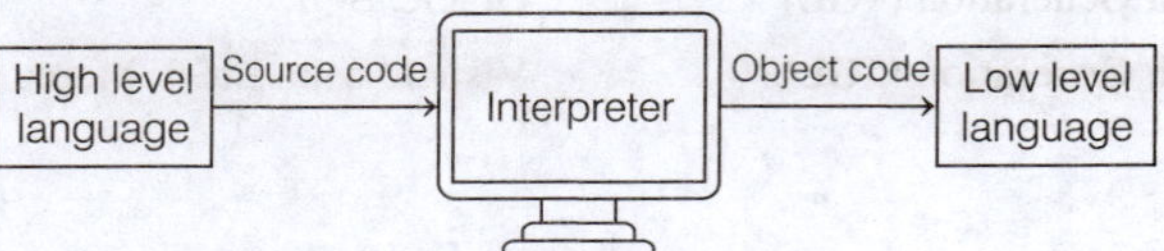

Facts Drive

- The first ever computer program was written by **Lady Ada Augusta /Ada Lovelace** for Charles Babbage's analytical engine in the 1840s.
- A **program** is a set of instructions written in a programming language that tells a computer how to perform specific tasks or solve problems.
- A **programmer**, also known as a software developer or coder, is a person who writes and maintains computer programs.
- The first compiler was developed by **Grace Hopper** in 1952.
- **Source code** is the human-readable instruction written in a programming language before they are compiled or interpreted.
- **Object code** is the machine-readable code generated by a compiler after translating high-level programming code.
- **Smalltalk**, developed in the 1970s, was one of the first true object-oriented programming language.

Algorithm

- An algorithm is a **finite sequence** of instructions for solving a specific problem.
- It provides a clear plan for writing code.
- The characteristics of a good algorithm are- correctness, efficiency, clarity, output, finiteness, precision, language independence.

Flowchart

- A flowchart is a **diagrammatic representation** of an algorithm.
- It uses different shapes to show the sequence of tasks and decisions.
- Useful for planning, problem-solving, debugging and optimizing programs.

Symbols Used in Flowchart

Symbol	Shape	Description
Start/Stop	(oval)	Used to represent start and end of the flowchart. This is also called **terminal**.
Processing	(rectangle)	Used for arithmetic operations and data manipulation.
Decision	(diamond)	Indicates a decision point with two alternatives, True or False.
Input/Output	(parallelogram)	Used for input or output operations.

Symbol	Shape	Description
Flow line/arrow		▪ Shows the direction or flow from one step to the next.
Connector		▪ Connects parts of a flowchart when they are too far apart.
Hexagon symbol		▪ Used to represent loops in a program. ▪ It is also called **preparation symbol**.
Document symbol		▪ Used to indicate a document or a report that is part of the process.

Rules for making a Flowchart

- Every flowchart should have a clear start and end point.
- Avoid overcrowding the flowchart with too many steps.
- Arrows should be used to indicate the direction of the flow of the process.
- If the flow chart is large and complex, then connector symbols should be used.

Example Flowchart of sum of two numbers

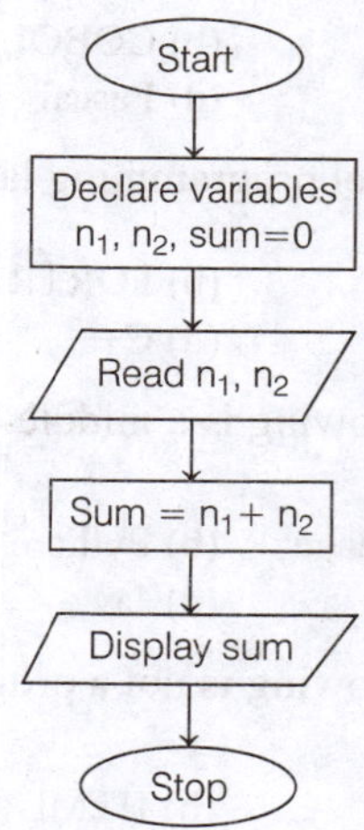

Advantages of Flowchart

- Easy technique to understand logic.
- Efficient coding.
- Proper documentation.

Disadvantages of Flowchart

- Time consuming.
- Hard to modify.
- Difficult to draw for big programs.

Pseudo Code

- Pseudo code is an informal way of describing a program.
- It does not follow any syntax easily.
- It helps you plan how a program will work without getting into the technical details.

Example

1. Start
2. Input n1 and n2
3. Sum= n1+n2
4. Print Sum
5. Stop

Important Abbreviations

HLL High Level Language
LLL Low Level Language
FORTRAN Formula Translation
LISP List Processing
COBOL Common Business Oriented Language
BASIC Beginner's All- purpose Symbolic Instruction Code
SQL Structured Query Language

PYQs Oneliner

1. A computer can only understand **machine language** directly. *CPCT 2024*
2. **LISP** is a fifth generation language. *CPCT 2024*
3. **Compiler** is the translator that translates source code into object code. *DSSSB TGT 2023*
4. **Flowchart** is the graphical representation of an algorithm. *DSSSB TGT 2023*
5. **C++** is an example of object oriented language. *SSC CHSL 2023*
6. **FORTRAN** is a high level language, suitable for scientific and engineering applications. *DSSSB Patwari 2022*
7. **John Backus** created the first high level computer programming language. *SSC CHSL 2021*
8. **Dennis Ritchie** created the language C. *SSC CHSL 2021*
9. The programming language Java was invented by **James Gosling**. *RRB NTPC 2021*
10. The full form of DFD is **Data Flow Diagram**. *UPPSC 2019*

Practice Exercise

Computer Programming Languages

1. Which of the following high-level language is suitable for scientific and engineering applications? ***DSSSB Patwari 2022***
(a) PROLOG (b)FORTRAN
(c) COBOL (d) LISP

2. In computer system, which of the following is not a programming language?
(a) COBOL (b) FORTRAN
(c) Pascal/PASCAL (d) Lotus/LOTUS

3. Which of the following language program written on one computer may not work on another computer with a different processor? ***DSSSB Patwari 2022***
(a) Machine language (b) High-level language
(c) Procedural language (d) Object based language

4. Which of the following programming language is used in general for artificial intelligence based problems? ***CPCT 2024***
(a) C (b) Python
(c) Assembly (d) BASIC

5. In 1970, Alan Kay invented the first object-oriented programming language called ………… ***CPCT 2024***
(a) Tablet comp (b) Kiddi comp
(c) Kudo comp (d) Smalltalk

6. A computer can only understand ………… directly. ***CPCT 2024***
(a) machine language
(b) algorithms
(c) high-level language
(d) middle-level language

7. Which of the following is a fifth generation language? ***CPCT 2024***
(a) COBOL (b) LISP
(c) Java (d) BASIC

8. Which generation of computer languages includes structured query language (SQL)? ***CPCT 2024***
(a) Fourth generation languages(4GL)
(b) Second generation languages(2GL)
(c) Third generation languages(3GL)
(d) Fifth generation languages(5GL)

9. Which language is optimised for web and internet applications? ***CPCT 2024***
(a) Java (b) Cobol (c) C++ (d) C

10. Which of the following is an example of a high-level programming language? ***SSC CGL 2022***
(a) Assembly language
(b) Machine language
(c) Python
(d) Binary language

11. What does COBOL stand for? ***IBPS SO 2021***
(a) Common Binary Language
(b) Common Business-Oriented Language
(c) Coded Binary Object Language
(d) Code Binary Online Language

12. Which language is often referred to as the mother of all programming languages? ***RRB NTPC 2020***
(a) Python (b) Java
(c) C (d) Assembly Language

13. The first programming language developed was ***IBPS Clerk 2018***
(a) FORTRAN (b) COBOL
(c) BASIC (d) Pascal

14. The first high-level programming language was ***IBPS SO 2020***
(a) BASIC (b) FORTRAN
(c) Pascal (d) C++

15. Which of the following is a middle-level programming language? ***RRB NTPC 2019***
(a) Assembly language (b) Python
(c) C (d) Java

16. Which of the following is not a programming language? ***SSC CGL 2019***
(a) Java (b) HTML
(c) Python (d) C++

17. Which of the following is not an example of a high-level programming language? ***IBPS SO 2018***
(a) Python (b) Java
(c) Assembly (d) Ruby

18. The Python programming language was created by ***IBPS SO 2021***
(a) Dennis Ritchie (b) Bjarne Stroustrup
(c) Guido van Rossum (d) James Gosling

19. Python is an example of which type of programming language? ***IBPS Clerk 2019***
(a) Low-level language (b) High-level language
(c) Assembly language (d) Machine language

20. The C programming language was developed by *SSC CPO 2019*
(a) James Gosling (b) Guido van Rossum
(c) Dennis Ritchie (d) Charles Babbage

21. Which of the following is a database query language? *IBPS PO 2020*
(a) Python (b) SQL
(c) Java (d) C++

22. What does IDE stand for in software development? *RRB NTPC 2020*
(a) Internal Data Encoding
(b) Integrated Development Environment
(c) Intelligent Debugging Engine
(d) Internet Data Explorer

23. Find the odd one out among the following. *RSMSSB LDC 2025*
(a) COBOL (b) JAVA
(c) FORTRAN (d) EXCEL

Language Translator Software

24. Which of the following is a translator that translates source code into object target code? *DSSSB TGT 2023*
(a) Language processor (b) Interpreter
(c) Compiler (d) Assembler

25. Which of the following options best describes the truthfulness of the following statements? *DSSSB Patwari 2022*
(I) Assembler is a software that converts a program written in assembly language into machine code.
(II) Compiler converts a high level source code line-by-line into equivalent machine executable form.
(a) (I) False (II) False (b) (I) True (II) True
(c) (I) True (II) False (d) (I) False (II) True

26. A/an ………… converts and executes one statement at a time. *CPCT 2024*
(a) complier (b) interpreter
(c) converter (d) loader

27. Which of the following is an example of a language translator software? *SSC CHSL 2019*
(a) Compiler (b) Operating system
(c) Database (d) Web browser

28. The process of converting source code into machine code using a compiler is called *SSC CHSL 2018*
(a) compilation (b) interpretation
(c) execution (d) debugging

29. What is the main function of a compiler? *SSC CHSL 2019*
(a) Converts machine code to high-level code
(b) Converts assembly language to binary code
(c) Converts high-level language to machine code
(d) Converts machine language to assembly code

30. What is the role of an interpreter in programming? *RRB JE 2018*
(a) Converts entire source code into machine code at once
(b) Converts machine code back to source code
(c) Converts source code into machine code line by line
(d) Converts assembly code to binary

31. Which of the following software is used to translate assembly language into machine code? *IBPS Clerk 2019*
(a) Compiler (b) Interpreter
(c) Assembler (d) Debugger

32. Which type of translator converts the entire program into machine code at once? *IBPS SO 2020*
(a) Interpreter (b) Compiler
(c) Assembler (d) Debugger

Algorithm

33. An/A … is a finite set of instructions which, when followed, accomplish a particular task. *SSC CHSL 2021*
(a) array (b) algorithm
(c) data (d) node

34. The primary goal of an algorithm is to *IBPS SO 2021*
(a) create hardware components
(b) generate random outputs
(c) solve a specific problem efficiently
(d) translate high-level code into machine code

35. An algorithm should always have which of the following characteristics? *RRB JE 2020*
(a) Infinite steps
(b) Clear and unambiguous instructions
(c) Only graphical representation
(d) Requires special software to run

36. Which of the following is not a characteristic of a good algorithm? *SSC CHSL 2019*
(a) Finiteness (b) Ambiguity
(c) Definiteness (d) Input and output

37. Which of the following is an example of an algorithm? *RRB ALP 2021*
(a) A recipe for baking a cake
(b) A web browser
(c) A computer hardware device
(d) A programming language

38. Which of the following statements is true about algorithms?
(a) An algorithm must always have a graphical representation
(b) An algorithm can have infinite steps
(c) An algorithm must have a finite number of steps
(d) Algorithms do not require inputs

Flowchart and Pseudo Code

39. Which symbol in a flowchart is used to represent a decision or conditional branch?
(a) Rectangle (b) Diamond
(c) Oval (d) Circle

40. In a flowchart, what does a rectangle symbol typically represent?
(a) Decision point (b) Input or output
(c) Process or operation (d) Start/End

41. Which of the following best describes the flow of a flowchart?
(a) Top to bottom, left to right
(b) Right to left only
(c) Diagonally
(d) Random directions

42. What is the purpose of a flowchart in the programming development process?
(a) To execute code
(b) To represent algorithms visually
(c) To perform data analysis
(d) To compile the program

43. Which symbol would you use in a flowchart to denote a connection point or flow direction?
(a) Arrow (b) Diamond
(c) Parallelogram (d) Circle

44. Which of the following is a graphical representation of an algorithm? ***DSSSB TGT 2023***
(a) Flowchart (b) Source code
(c) Program (d) Pseudo code

45. Which of the following is the primary purpose of a flowchart?
(a) To display data in graphical format
(b) To illustrate the flow of processes of operations
(c) To generates random numbers
(d) To store data

46. Which flowchart symbol is used to represent an input/output operation?
(a) Rectangle
(b) Parallelogram
(c) Oval
(d) Diamond

47. Which symbol in a flowchart represents the start or end of a process? ***UPSC CDS 2024***
(a) Rectangle (b) Diamond
(c) Parallelogram (d) Oval

48. A flowchart helps in ***IBPS PO 2024***
(a) undesrtanding the logic of program.
(b) writing complex code directly.
(c) designing hardware systems.
(d) None of the above

49. Which of the following is not a type of a flowchart symbol?
(a) Start/End (b) Process
(c) Decision (d) Calculation

50. Which of the following is a method of describing computer algorithms using a combination of natural language and programming language? ***SSC CHSL 2021***
(a) Node (b) Pseudo code
(c) Flowchart (d) Array

Answers

1. (b)	2. (d)	3. (a)	4. (b)	5. (d)	6. (a)	7. (b)	8. (a)	9. (a)	10. (c)
11. (b)	12. (c)	13. (a)	14. (b)	15. (c)	16. (b)	17. (c)	18. (c)	19. (b)	20. (c)
21. (b)	22. (b)	23. (d)	24. (c)	25. (c)	26. (b)	27. (a)	28. (a)	29. (c)	30. (c)
31. (c)	32. (b)	33. (b)	34. (c)	35. (b)	36. (b)	37. (a)	38. (c)	39. (b)	40. (c)
41. (a)	42. (b)	43. (a)	44. (a)	45. (b)	46. (b)	47. (d)	48. (a)	49. (d)	50. (b)

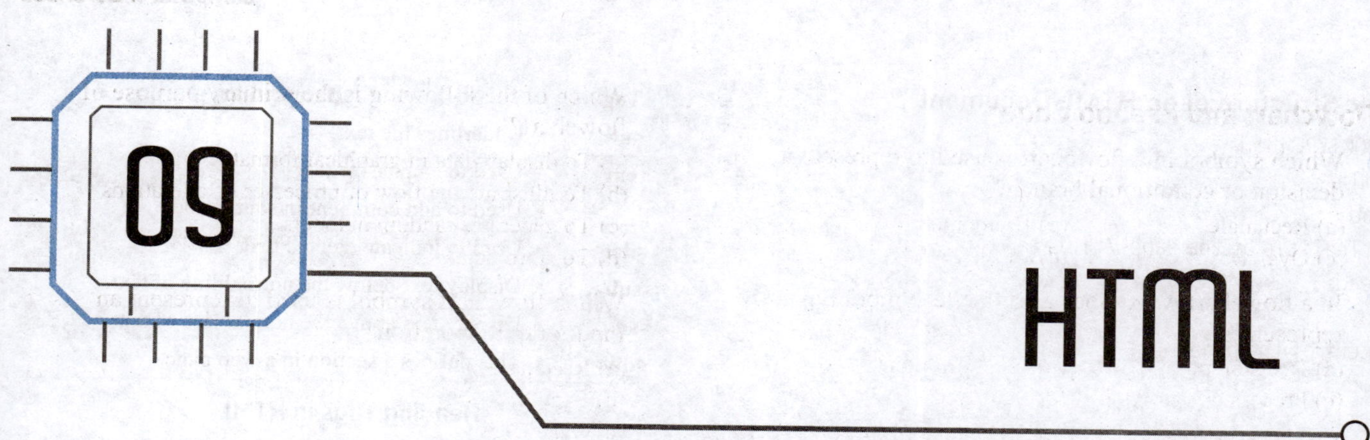

09 HTML

- HTML stands for **Hypertext Markup Language**.
- It is the markup language, used to create and design a **webpage** or **website**.
- It requires a program (known as **browser**) to display the web page.
- HTML uses tags to structure the content of the webpage.
- It was invented by a British computer scientist, **Tim Berners-Lee** in 1993.

Evolution of HTML

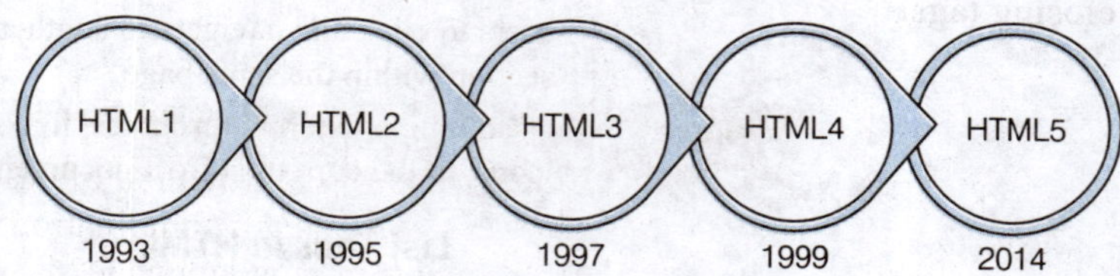

Structure of HTML

- HTML is structured in a hierarchical way using various elements and tags.
- The basic structure of an HTML contains three parts
  1. **Main Container** <html></html>
  2. **Head Section** <head></head>
  3. **Body Section** <body></body>

Main Container

- This defines the structure and content of an HTML document.
- It is the root of an HTML document.
- It contains all the elements inside it.

Head Section

- It contains the **metadata** (data about data).

Body Section

- It contains the actual content that appears on the webpages.

In this Chapter

- Evolution of HTML
- Structure of HTML
- HTML Tags
  - Container Tags
  - Empty Tags

"Before software can be reusable, it first has to be usable."

~ Ralph Johnson

Basic Structure of an HTML Document

```
<! DOCTYPE html>
<html>
<head>
<title>Title of the Page</title>
</head>
<body>
Content of the page
</body>
</html>
```

Note DOCTYPE declares the document type.

HTML Tags

- In HTML, tags are the building blocks used to create and structure content on a webpage.
- Tags are special keywords enclosed in **angle brackets**, like <p> or <h1>.
- HTML tags can be classified into two categories

1. Container Tags

- These tags have both an opening and closing tag.
- The content goes between the opening and closing tags.

Example **Heading tag** <h1></h1>,
HTML tag <html></html>

2. Empty Tags

- They do not need a closing tag.
- These tags are also called **self-closing tags**.
- They are used for elements that do not have any content inside them.

Example **Line break tag**
, **Image tag** <img>

Basic HTML tags

Tags	Description
<html>	▪ Defines the start and end of an HTML document. ▪ It is the fundamental tag of HTML.
<head>	▪ This tag is used to make header in webpages. ▪ It contains metadata about the HTML document.
<title>	▪ Used to give the title of the web page.
<body>	▪ Used to create main content.
<p>	▪ It defines a paragraph of text.
<img>	▪ It is used to insert an image into an HTML document.

Text formatting tags

Tag	Description
<b>	▪ Used to bold the text
<i>	▪ Used to make the text italic
<u>	▪ Underlines the text.
<em>	▪ Used to emphasize text.
<!_ _>	▪ Used to add comment in source code.
<del>	▪ Used to indicate deleted text.
<sub>	▪ Display text below the normal line of text.
<sup>	▪ Display text above the normal line of text.
<div>	▪ This defines a section in a web page.

Heading Tags in HTML

Tag	Description
<h1>	▪ Defines the main heading of the page (largest size).
<h2>	▪ Defines a subheading slightly smaller than <h1>.
<h3>	▪ Defines a sub-subheading below <h2>.
<h4>	▪ Defines a section heading below <h3>.
<h5>	▪ Defines a section heading below <h4>.
<h6>	▪ Defines the smallest heading, often used last.

Linking Tags in HTML

Tag	Description
<a>	▪ Used to define a hyperlink in the webpage, allows users to click and navigate to another webpage or section within the same page.
<link>	▪ Used to link external resources, like stylesheets or icons, to the current HTML document.

List Tags in HTML

Tag	Description
<ul>	▪ Used to create an unordered list (bulleted list).
<ol>	▪ Used to create an ordered list (numbered list).
<li>	▪ Used to define a list item within <ul> or <ol>.
<dl>	▪ Used to create a definition list for terms and descriptions.
<dt>	▪ Used to define term in a definition list.
<dd>	▪ Used to define the description or details of a term in a definition list.

Table Tags in HTML

Tag	Description
<table>	▪ Used to define the table structure.
<tr>	▪ Used to define a table row.
<th>	▪ Used to define a header cell.
<td>	▪ Used to define a data cell in a table.
<caption>	▪ Adds a title or caption to the table.
<thead>	▪ Groups the header content of a table.
<tbody>	▪ Groups the body content of a table.
<tfoot>	▪ Groups the footer content of a table.

Form Tags in HTML

Tag	Description
<form>	▪ Used to define an HTML form for user input.
<input>	▪ Used to define an input field where user can enter data.
<textarea>	▪ Used to define a multi-line text input field for larger text entries.
<button>	▪ Used to define a clickable button to submit or reset a form.
<select>	▪ Used to define a dropdown list for selecting options.
<option>	▪ Used to define an option inside a <select> dropdown list.
<label>	▪ Used to define a label for an input element, enhancing accessibility.
<fieldset>	▪ Used to group related elements in a form.

Facts Drive

- **<hr>** tag is used to create a horizontal rule (line) on a webpage.
- HTML is a **case insensitive** language, it means both uppercase and lowercase can be used.
- The words that are placed inside the opening HTML tag are called **attributes**.
- The <marquee> tag is used to display text with a scrolling effect.

PYQs Oneliner

1. <html> tag indicates start of the HTML document. *CPCT 2024*
2. **<Link>** tag in HTML is used to link external files like CSS. *UPSC IES 2021*
3. HTML stands for **Hyper Text Markup Language.** *SSC CHSL 2020*
4. **<a>** HTML tag is used to define a **hyperlink**. *RRB NTPC 2020*
5. **href** attribute in the <a> tag is used to specify the destination URL. *SSC CGL 2019*
6. **<h1>** tag is used to define the largest heading in HTML. *SSC CGL 2019*
7. **<input>** tag is used to define an input field where the user can type text. *IBPS Clerk 2019*
8. **<ol>** tag is used to create a numbered list in HTML. *IBPS SO IT Officer 2019*
9. **<strong>** HTML element is used to define important text. *RRB NTPC 2019*
10. **<select>** tag is used to create a dropdown list in HTML. *IBPS Clerk 2018*

Practice Exercise

Introduction to HTML

1. What does HTML stand for? *SSC CHSL 2020*
(a) Hyperlinks and Text Markup Language
(b) Hyper Text Markup Language
(c) Home Tool Markup Language
(d) Hyper Text Managing Links

2. An HTML program is saved by using the .... extension.
(a) .ht (b) .html
(c) .hml (d) None of these

3. What is the default alignment of text in an HTML document? *SSC CGL 2020*
(a) Left (b) Center
(c) Right (d) Justify

4. Who is considered as the 'Father of HTML'?
(a) Brendan Eich
(b) Rasmus Lerdorf
(c) Tim Berners Lee
(d) Sergey Brin

Structure of HTML

5. What is the correct syntax of doctype in HTML5?
(a) <!doctype html> (b) <doctype html!>
(c) <doctype html> (d) </doctype html>

6. The correct sequence of HTML tags for starting a webpage is
(a) Head, title, HTML, body
(b) HTML, body, title, head
(c) HTML, head, title, body
(d) HTML, head, body, title

7. What if one does not use the doctype in the starting of HTML document?
(a) Browser finds the document in quirky mode
(b) Browser finds a document in standard mode
(c) Browser stops working
(d) Browser crashes after showing the page

HTML Tags

8. Which of the following defines the title of a work?
(a) <cite> (b) <hr>
(c) <a> (d) <address>

9. Which of the following are the boldface tags instructions for the web browser? *SSC Selection Post 2023*
(a)
 and </Br> (b) <Bl> and </BI>
(c) <Bo> and </Bo> (d) <B> and </B>

10. Which of the following element is responsible for making the text bold in HTML?
(a) <pre> (b) <a>
(c) <b> (d)

11. What is the correct way to make a comment in HTML? *SSC GD 2019*
(a) <!-- This is a comment -->
(b) // This is a comment
(c) /* This is a comment */
(d) # This is a comment

12. Which tag is used to create a drop-down list in HTML? *UPSC CDS 2018*
(a) <dropdown> (b) <select>
(c) <option> (d) <list>

13. What is the correct HTML tag for inserting a line break?
(a)
 (b) <lb>
(c) <break> (d) <line>

14. How to create an unordered list (a list with the list items in bullets) in HTML? *IBPS SO IT Officer 2019*
(a) <ul> (b) <ol>
(c) <li> (d) <i>

15. Which character is used to represent the closing of a tag in HTML?
(a) \ (b) !
(c) / (d) .

16. How to create a hyperlink in HTML?
(a) <a href = "…"> </a> (b) <a url = "…." /a>
(c) <a link = "….> </a> (d) <a> …. < /a>

17. How to create an ordered list (a list with the list items in numbers) in HTML?
(a) <ul> (b) <ol>
(c) <li> (d) <i>

18. Which of the following defines a section in a web page?
(a) <div> (b) <del>
(c) <sup> (d) <sub>

19. How to insert an image in HTML?
(a) <img href = "…" /> (b) <img url = "…" />
(c) <img link = "…" /> (d) <img src = "…." />

20. Which of the following tag is used to make the underlined text?
(a) <i> (b) <ul> (c) <u> (d) <pre>

21. Which of the following tag is used to define options in a drop-down selection list?
(a) <select> (b) <list>
(c) <dropdown> (d) <option>

22. Which of the following tag is used to add rows in the table?
(a) <td> and </td> (b) <th> and </th>
(c) <tr> and </tr> (d) None of these

23. Which tag is used to insert a horizontal line in HTML? *RRB NTPC 2019*
(a) <hr> (b) <line>
(c) <hline> (d) <separator>

24. Which of the following is the container for <tr>, <th> and <td> ?
(a) <data> (b) <table>
(c) <group> (d) All of these

25. How to insert a background image in HTML?
(a) <body background = "img.png">
(b) <img background = "img.png">
(c) <bg-image = "img.png">
(d) None of the above

26. Which of the following is the correct way to create a list using the lowercase letters?
(a) <ol alpha = "a" >
(b) <ol type = "a">
(c) <ol letter = "a">
(d) None of the above

27. Which of the following HTML attribute is used to define inline styles?
(a) style (b) type
(c) class (d) None of these

28. Which of the following is the paragraph tag in HTML?
(a) <p> (b) <b>
(c) <pre> (d) None of these

29. Which HTML tag is used to define a description list? *RRB JE 2020*
(a) <dl> (b) <dt>
(c) <dd> (d) All of these

30. The tags in HTML are
(a) case-sensitive
(b) in upper case
(c) not case sensitive
(d) in lowercase

31. Which of the following is the root tag of the HTML document?
(a) <body> (b) <head>
(c) <title> (d) <html>

32. Which of the following tag is used to create a combo box (or drop-down box)?
(a) <list>
(b) <select>
(c) <input type = "dropdown">
(d) <ul>

33. How do you create a table row in HTML?
SSC CHSL 2020
(a) <td> (b) <th>
(c) <tr> (d) <row>

34. Which tag is used to display bold text in HTML?
RRB JE 2019
(a) <strong> (b) <b>
(c) Both (a) and (b) (d) <bold>

35. Which tag is used to define a description list in HTML?
IBPS SO IT Officer 2020
(a) <dl> (b) <dt> (c) <dd> (d) <list>

36. Which tag is used to create a button in HTML?
SSC GD 2020
(a) <btn> (b) <button>
(c) <input type="button"> (d) Both (b) and (c)

37. Which tag is used to display text in italics in HTML?
RRB ALP 2018
(a) <i> (b) <em>
(c) Both (a) and (b) (d) <italic>

38. .... tag indicates start of the HTML document.
CPCT 2024
(a) <html> (b) <body>
(c) <title> (d) <head>

39. Which tag is used to insert the largest heading in HTML?
(a) <h1> (b) <h3>
(c) <h6> (d) None of these

40. Which HTML tag is used to display text along with a scrolling effect?
(a) <scroll> (b) <marquee>
(c) <div> (d) <em>

41. What is the correct HTML tag for creating a text input field?
(a) <text area> (b) <input text>
(c) <input type = "text"> (d) <text field>

42. Which tag is used to create a table header in HTML?
(a) <thead> (b) <header>
(c) <th> (d) <head>

43. Which tag in HTML is used to add a title to a table?
(a) <thead> (b) <caption>
(c) <header> (d) <title>

44. What is the purpose of the <link> tag in HTML?
(a) To link external resources like stylesheets
(b) To create hyperlinks
(c) To link internal elements on the page
(d) To add a video to the page

45. What is the primary purpose of the <label> tag in HTML?
(a) To add styles to input elements
(b) To define a label for an input element.
(c) To group multiple input elements
(d) To define a placeholder text for input

Answers

1.	(b)	2.	(b)	3.	(a)	4.	(c)	5.	(a)	6.	(c)	7.	(a)	8.	(a)	9.	(d)	10.	(c)
11.	(a)	12.	(b)	13.	(a)	14.	(a)	15.	(c)	16.	(a)	17.	(b)	18.	(a)	19.	(d)	20.	(c)
21.	(d)	22.	(c)	23.	(a)	24.	(b)	25.	(a)	26.	(b)	27.	(a)	28.	(a)	29.	(a)	30.	(c)
31.	(d)	32.	(b)	33.	(c)	34.	(c)	35.	(a)	36.	(d)	37.	(c)	38.	(a)	39.	(a)	40.	(b)
41.	(c)	42.	(c)	43.	(b)	44.	(a)	45.	(b)										

Microsoft Windows

- Microsoft Windows is a **graphical operating system** developed by **Microsoft**.
- It was first introduced in 1985.
- It provides a graphical user interface (GUI) that allows users to interact with the computer through icons.
- It allows users to view and store files, run the software, play games, watch videos and provides a way to connect to the internet.
- Expanded form for Microsoft windows is Microsoft Wide Interactive Network Development for Office Work Solution.

In this Chapter

- Evolution of Windows Operating System
- Main Components of Window
- Files & File Extensions in Windows

"Computing is not about computers anymore. It is about living.

~ **Nicholas Negroponte**"

Evolution of Windows Operating System

- The given table contains history of windows from edition MS-DOS to Windows 11.

Version/Year	Logo	Key Features & Developments
MS-DOS (1981)		▪ Originally developed by Microsoft for IBM. ▪ It was a **text-based interface** that allows users to interact with computer using command lines.
Windows 1.0 (1985)		▪ First graphical user interface for MS-DOS. ▪ It introduced multitasking, use of the mouse and various built in programs.
Windows 2.0 (1987)		▪ It allows users to overlap and resize application windows. ▪ Launched with windows **keyboard shortcuts.** ▪ **MS Excel** and **Word** was introduced for the first time.
Windows 3.0 (1990)		▪ Major improvements in performance and interface. ▪ Introduced **Program Manager** for app launching. ▪ **Computer gaming** was also introduced.
Windows 95 (1995)		▪ Introduced the **Start Menu**, Taskbar and plug and play hardware support. ▪ First version to include Internet Explorer.
Windows 98 (1998)		▪ Enhanced support for the Internet, USB devices and improved performance over Windows 95. ▪ Windows Media Player and CD/DVD player were introduced. ▪ It was a mutli-programming operating system.

Version/Year	Logo	Key Features & Developments
Windows ME (2000)		▪ Enhanced multimedia and home networking. ▪ Windows Movie Maker was introduced. ▪ Meant for home users. ▪ Launched internet explorer 5.5.
Windows XP (2001)		▪ Combined the best features of Windows 2000 and Windows 98. ▪ Better multimedia and gaming support. ▪ Major drawback of windows XP was its security.
Windows Vista (2006)		▪ Introduced new Aero Glass interface. ▪ Improved media management (Windows Media Center). ▪ New search functionality in the Start Menu.
Windows7 (2009)		▪ Focused on speed, stability and security. ▪ New taskbar with better app management and previews. ▪ Improved device management and network features.
Windows8 (2012)		▪ Introduction of Modern UI (Metro). ▪ Removal of the Start Menu in favor of the Start Screen. ▪ New Windows Store for apps. ▪ Enhanced support for tablets and touchscreens.
Windows10 (2015)		▪ Combined Windows 7 and 8 features. ▪ Introduced **Cortana**, a digital assistant. ▪ Spinning tool was available for taking screen shot. ▪ Edge browser replaced Internet Explorer.
Windows11 (2021)		▪ Redesigned Start Menu and Taskbar. ▪ Enhanced support for virtual desktops. ▪ Improved gaming performance.

Main Components of Window

- MS Windows is a graphical user interface element used to display the contents of an application for the user to view and interact with computer.
- Windows operating system consists of several components that work together to provide a user-friendly experience.

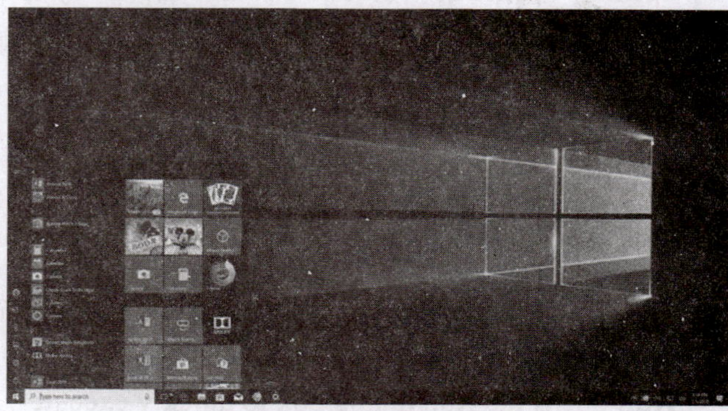

- These components manage both the hardware and software, allowing the system to run smoothly.

Key Components

My Computer/This PC

- This is the file manager of the computer, that saves all the data.
- It is an icon that looks like a computer, in older versions of Windows.

My Document

- It is a default location for storing personal documents.

Desktop

- Main workspace area where you can place files, folders and shortcuts.
- It provides easy access to frequently used items.

Icons

- Icons are the small graphical representation of files, applications or shortcuts on the desktop.
- It allows quick access to programs or documents.

Desktop Background

- The background image or colour of the desktop.
- It can be customised with images or solid colours.

Start Menu

- It is accessible from the Taskbar.
- It provides quick access to applications, settings and files.
- It includes Live Tiles for dynamic content.
- The main options you typically find in the Start Menu include
  - **All Apps** displays a list of all the installed applications.
  - **Pinned Apps** frequently used or favorite apps pinned for quick access.

- **Power Options** provides options like Sleep, Restart and Shut Down.
- **Settings** opens the Windows Settings app for system configuration.
- **File Explorer** opens the file management system to access folders and files.
- **Search Bar** allows you to search for apps, files or web content.
- **User Account** provides access to account settings or allows you to sign out, lock or switch users.
- **Help and Support** provides access to Windows Help resources (available in older versions).
- **Run** opens the Run dialog box to quickly execute commands or programs (shortcut: Windows + R).

Cortana

- It is a built-in virtual assistant.
- Located on the Taskbar for voice commands and searches.

Search Box

- Located next to Cortana, it is used to search for apps, files or settings on the PC.

Windows Explorer (File Explorer)

- It is a file management system for browsing and organizing files and folders.
- Accessible through the Taskbar or Start Menu.

Minimise, Maximise, Close Buttons

- Found at the top-right corner of every window.
- Minimize reduces the window to the Taskbar.
- Maximize expands the window to full screen.
- Close button closes the window.

Recycle Bin

- A container for deleted files that can be restored or permanently deleted.
- Located on the desktop for easy access to deleted items.
- We can delete files permanently with the use of **shift +delete** shortcut key.

Control Panel

- A tool that provides advanced settings and management options for the system.
- Allows users to manage hardware, software, user accounts, network settings, etc.
- Accessible from the Start Menu or by searching.

Virtual Desktop

- It allows users to create multiple desktops for improved multitasking.
- Accessible from the Task View button on the Taskbar.

Task Bar

- Located at the bottom of the screen.
- Displays running applications and system icons.
- Contains the Start Menu, Task View and system tray (clock, notifications).

Notification Area (System Tray)

- Found on the right side of the Taskbar.
- It displays system notifications, battery status, network connection and other background processes.

Action Center

- It is located in the system tray (right side of the screen).
- It displays notifications for messages, updates and app alerts.

Title Bar

- Displays the name of the current window or application.
- Located at the top of each window, it allows you to move the window around.

Scroll Bar

- It provides a way to scroll through content when it exceeds the window size.
- Found on the right (vertical) or bottom (horizontal) edges of a window.

Menu Bar

- It displays menus with options for various tasks, like File, Edit and View.
- Often located at the top of the window in most applications.

Status Bar

- It displays information about the current window or application.
- Located at the bottom of the window, showing details like file size, progress or cursor position.

Files & File Extensions in Windows

File

- A file is a collection of data or information stored on a computer that can be accessed, modified or saved.
- In a graphical user interface (GUI) like Microsoft Windows, files are shown as unique icons that relate to the program that opens the file.

File Extension

- File extensions are the part of the filename that is after the dot.

  Example a text file like myfile.txt has **txt** as its extension.

- The extension tells Windows which program or application should be used to open the file.
- It helps to identify the file type.

Some Common File Extensions

- **.txt** text file
- **.doc** Microsoft Word document
- **.docx** Microsoft Word open XML document - Word 2007 or later
- **.xls** Microsoft Excel spreadsheet
- **.xlsx** Microsoft Excel open XML spreadsheet - Excel 2007 or later
- **.pptx** Microsoft PowerPoint open presentation document - PowerPoint 2007 or later
- **.html** Web page (Hypertext Markup Language) file
- **.mp3** audio (music) file
- **.pdf** Adobe Portable Document Format file (Adobe Reader)
- **.jpg** JPEG image file (usually a photo)
- **.bak** Backup File
- **.tmp** Temporary File
- **.zip** Zipped File
- **.mp4** MPEG-4 video file
- **.wav** Windows Sound File

Windows Accessories

Accessory	Description
Calculator	▪ A basic calculator app with standard, scientific and programming modes.
Paint	▪ A simple graphics editor for creating and editing images.
WordPad	▪ A basic word processing application with text formatting tools, suitable for simple documents.
Notepad	▪ A simple text editor for creating and editing plain text files.
Snipping Tool	▪ A screenshot tool that allows users to capture portions of the screen.
Sticky Notes	▪ A digital version of sticky notes for writing down quick reminders or notes.
Windows Media Player	▪ A media player that supports audio and video playback.
Narrator	▪ A screen reader tool that reads text on the screen aloud.
Magnifier	▪ A screen magnification tool that allows users to zoom in on parts of the screen for easier viewing.
Mail	▪ A built-in email application for managing multiple email accounts.
Calendar	▪ A personal calendar app for scheduling appointments, meetings and events.
File Explorer	▪ A file management tool to browse, organize and access files and folders. ▪ Includes a built-in search function for quickly locating files.
Microsoft Edge	▪ The default web browser in Windows 10 and 11, replacing internet explorer.

Important Run Commands for Windows

Command	Application
cmd	▪ Opens command prompt
control panel	▪ Opens control panel
explorer	▪ Opens file explorer
msconfig	▪ Opens system configuration utility
services.msc	▪ Opens services manager
regedit	▪ Opens registry editor (be cautious!)
taskmgr	▪ Opens task manager
devmgmt.msc	▪ Opens device manager
compmgmt.msc	▪ Opens computer management
diskmgmt.msc	▪ Opens disk management
ncpa.cpl	▪ Opens network connections
firewall.cpl	▪ Opens windows firewall settings
inetcpl.cpl	▪ Opens internet properties (internet options)
notepad	▪ Opens notepad
calc	▪ Opens calculator
control printers	▪ Opens devices and printers
osk	▪ Opens on-screen keyboard
cleanmgr	▪ Opens disk cleanup utility
perfmon	▪ Opens performance monitor
charmap	▪ Opens character map
rstrui.exe	▪ Opens system restore
%temp%	▪ Opens temp folder to delete temporary files
winword	▪ Opens MS Word
powerpnt	▪ Opens PowerPoint
excel	▪ Opens MS Excel
msaccess	▪ Opens MS Access
write	▪ Opens word pad
snipping tool	▪ Opens snipping tool
desk.cpl	▪ Opens display settings
ms paint	▪ Opens paint
iexplore	▪ Open internet explorer
chrome	▪ opens google chrome
hdwwiz.cpl	▪ Opens add hardware wizard
downloads	▪ Opens download folder
powercfg.cpl	▪ Opens power option

Windows Shortcut Keys

Shortcut Key	Description
Ctrl+A	▪ Select all content
Ctrl+ C	▪ Copy selected item to clipboard
Ctrl+X	▪ Cut selected items to clipboard
Ctrl+V	▪ Paste content from clipboard
Ctrl+Z	▪ Undo an action
Ctrl+Y	▪ Redo an action
Ctrl+Shift+N	▪ Create new folder on desktop or File Explorer
Alt+F4	▪ Close Active Window.
Ctrl+D	▪ Delete selected item to the Recycle Bin
Shift+Delete	▪ Delete the selected item permanently, skipping Recycle Bin
Esc	▪ Close a dialog box of menu or exit full screen modes
Alt+Tab	▪ Switch between open apps
Windows logo key	▪ Open start menu
F1	▪ Open help window
F2	▪ Rename selected item
Ctrl+Shift+Esc	▪ Open Task Manager

Facts Drive

- Microsoft is a leading tech company founded in 1975 by **Bill Gates** and **Paul Allen**.
- The Microsoft campus is the corporate headquarters of Microsoft Corporation, located in **Redmond, Washington, United States**
- The Windows 10 Start Menu has **live tiles** that update in real-time, showing you news, weather and social media posts directly from the Start screen.
- The **Blue Screen of Death (BSOD)** in Windows is an error screen that appears when the operating system encounters a serious issue that it cannot recover from.
- **Windows defender** is an antivirus and malware protection feature included in your operating system.
- **Windows firewall** prevents unauthorized access from outside to get into your computer.

Important Abbreviations

MS-DOS Microsoft Disk Operating System
BSOD Blue Screen of Death
XP Experience (refers to Windows XP)
UI User Interface
CMD Command Prompt
OSD On Screen Display

PYQs Oneliner

1. **F2** is commonly used to rename a file or folder in windows OS. ***SSC CHSL 2024***
2. **Win + E** keyboard shortcut opens file explorer (previously known as windows explorer) in windows 10. ***SSC CHSL 2024***
3. **Ctrl + Shift + N** ip used to 'create a new folder' in windows. ***Selection Post 2023***
4. **.txt** file extension is commonly associated with the files that can be opened in Notepad on Windows. ***SSC MTS 2021***
5. **Windows 11** is the latest version of the Windows operating system as of 2024. ***RRB NTPC 2021***
6. **taskmgr** is the command used to open the Task Manager in Windows. ***RRB ALP 2020***
7. **Windows Vista** version of Windows first introduced the 'Aero' user interface. ***IB ACIO 2020***
8. **Microsoft Edge** is the default internet browser in Windows 10. ***SSC CGL 2018/2020***
9. **Windows key** is used to open the "Start" menu in Windows 10. ***SSC CHSL 2019***
10. **Alt+F4** key is used to shut down the windows operating system. ***SSC CGL 2019***
11. **Ctrl+Shift+Esc** is the shortcut key to open Task Manager in Windows 10. ***RRB NTPC 2019***

Practice Exercise

Introduction to Microsoft Windows

1. Which of the following is an example of a system software?
(a) Windows 7 (b) MS Word 2010
(c) MS PowerPoint 2010 (d) Openoffice Writer

2. Factor making Windows popular is
(a) multitasking capacity
(b) desktop features
(c) user friendly
(d) being inexpensive

3. Microsoft Windows is a .... software.
(a) freeware (b) proprietary
(c) disk defragmenter (d) open source

Evolution of Windows Operating System

4. Which of the following is not a feature of Windows 98?
(a) It supports Internet Explorer 4.0.1.
(b) It also supports many peripheral devices USB, DVD.
(c) It was the first operating system to use the WDM.
(d) It provides multiple firewall.

5. Windows XP released in
(a) 2000 (b) 1998
(c) 1999 (d) 2001

6. Which of the following is not a version of the Windows operating system software for the PC?
(a) ME (b) 98
(c) XP (d) Linux

7. Which of the following is a feature of Windows 10? *IBPS Clerk 2020*
(a) Start Menu (b) Task View
(c) Cortana (d) All of these

8. What is the maximum number of virtual desktops that can be created in Windows 10? *RRB NTPC 2020*
(a) 4 (b) Unlimited
(c) 8 (d) 10

9. Which Windows 10 feature allows you to search for files, applications and settings quickly? *SSC CHSL 2018*
(a) Cortana (b) File Explorer
(c) Start Menu (d) Taskbar

10. What is the default web browser in Windows 10? *SBI Clerk 2020*
(a) Internet Explorer (b) Google Chrome
(c) Microsoft Edge (d) Firefox

11. In file explorer of Windows 11, which of the following includes the 'hidden items' options? *SSC CGL 2023*
(a) Home (b) File
(c) View (d) Share

12. Which of the following keys will you press in Windows 10 to turn the volume up? *SSC CHSL 2021*
(a) F4 (b) F5 (c) F6 (d) F8

13. Which version of Windows introduced the Start button?
(a) Windows 95 (b) Windows XP
(c) Windows 98 (d) Windows 7

Main Components of Window

14. Which of the following is not an in-built software application found in MS Windows?
(a) Paint (b) CD Player
(c) Disk Defragmentor (d) MS Word

15. What is Windows Explorer?
(a) Personal Computer (b) Network
(c) File Manager (d) Drive

16. Background of screen is known as
(a) application (b) window
(c) desktop (d) frame

17. The background image of desktop is called as
(a) graphics (b) deskcover
(c) wallback (d) wallpaper

18. Graphical pictures that represent an object like file, folder, etc. are
(a) task bar (b) windows
(c) desktop (d) icons

19. A/An .... contains programs that can be selected.
(a) pointer (b) menu (c) icon (d) button

20. All the deleted files go to
(a) recycle bin (b) task bar
(c) tool bar (d) computer

21. What is the role of User Account Control (UAC) in Windows when modifying system settings? *SSC CGL (T-II) 20.01.2025*
(a) To monitor memory usage and performance
(b) To adjust display settings
(c) To automate software updates
(d) To prompt for permission before making system-wide changes

22. The taskbar is located
(a) on the start menu
(b) at the bottom of the screen
(c) on the quick launch toolbar
(d) at the top of the screen

23. Which of the following refers to the rectangular area for displaying information and running programs?
(a) Desktop (b) Dialog box
(c) Menu (d) Window

24. Title bar, ribbon, status bar, views and document workspace are components of .... program.
(a) windows (b) browser (c) explorer (d) website

25. Match the file locating features in column A with their corresponding functionalities in column B.
SSC CGL (T-II) 18.01.2025

Column-A	Column-B
A. Search Bar	1. Displays files and folders recently accessed
B. Quick Access	2. Allows grouping and sorting of files by attributes
C. Wildcards	3. Refines searches for files with partial names
D. File Sorting	4. Locates files and folders by typing keywords

(a) 1-b, 2-d, 3-a, 4-c (b) 1-a, 2-c, 3-b, 4-d
(c) 1-c, 2-b, 3-a, 4-d (d) 1-d, 2-a, 3-c, 4-b

26. In windows, the maximise, minimise and close buttons appear on .... bar.
(a) task (b) title (c) menu (d) status

27. Date and time are available on the desktop at
(a) recycle bin (b) menu bar
(c) task bar (d) title bar

28. Commands at the top of the screen such as file, edit, font, tools to operate and change things within program comes under
(a) tool bar (b) menu bar
(c) word processor (d) desktop

29. Help menu is available at which button?
(a) End (b) Start
(c) Turn OFF (d) Restart

30. .... is a easy-to-use interface to play digital media files.
(a) WordPad (b) Media Player
(c) Notepad (d) Games

31. Which of the following displays programs that are currently running in Windows 10 OS? *CPCT 2024*
(a) Menu bar (b) Task bar
(c) Title bar (d) Status bar

32. Which program do you use to manage folders and files in Windows10? *CPCT 2024*
(a) Accessories (b) Control panel
(c) File explorer (d) Office

33. What does the 'this PC' or 'my computer' icon represent in windows?
(a) The operating system settings
(b) Your email box
(c) The hardware and storage devices on your computer
(d) The recycle bin

34. What is the purpose of the 'Quick Access' section in windows explorer (file explorer)? *SSC Selection Post 2023*
(a) To provide quick access to the internet.
(b) To display shortcuts to frequently used folders and files.
(c) To play multimedia files, such as videos and music.
(d) To view recently visited websites.

Files & File Extensions in Windows

35. A saved document is referred to as a
(a) file (b) word (c) folder (d) project

36. The name given to a document by the user is called
(a) filename (b) program (c) data (d) record

37. Information kept about a file includes
(a) print setting (b) deletion data
(c) Both (a) and (b) (d) size

38. A file is often referred to as a
(a) wizard (b) document (c) pane (d) device

39. Which of the following statements is a false regarding file names?
(a) Every file in the same folder must have a unique name.
(b) The file name comes before the dot (.).
(c) File extension is another name for the type.
(d) The file extension comes before the dot (.) followed by the file name.

40. File extensions are used in order to
(a) name the file
(b) ensure the file name is not lost
(c) identify the file
(d) identify the file type

41. Which of the following contained at the end of the file name and help to determine the type of file?
(a) File property (b) File type
(c) File name (d) File extension

42. Which file extension is most commonly used for executable installation files on a Windows system?
SSC CGL (T-II) 20.01.2025
(a) exe (b) mp3
(c) txt (d) jpg

43. The Windows sound file has the extension ....
(a) .wpd (b) .wav (c) .gif (d) .txt

44. What is the default file extension for Notepad files?
(a) .der (b) .txt (c) .pdf (d) .rtf

Windows Accessories

45. Which operation can one directly perform using File Explorer in Windows? *SSC CGL (T-II) 18.01.2025*
(a) Run diagnostic tests
(b) Modify system settings
(c) Move, copy or delete files
(d) Manage user accounts

46. What type of files can be created using the windows Paint accessory?
(a) .txt (b) .png
(c) .jpg (d) Both (b) and (c)

47. Which of the following is not an accessory in Windows? *RRB JE 2023*
(a) Calculator (b) Notepad
(c) Paint (d) Device Manager

48. Which accessory in Windows allows you to view and manage files and folders on your computer? *RRB NTPC 2023*
(a) Paint (b) File Explorer
(c) Command Prompt (d) Calculator

49. Which of the following is the default file manager in Windows 10? *IBPS PO 2019*
(a) Windows Explorer (b) File Explorer
(c) My Computer (d) System Explorer

50. Which of the following is not a windows application?
(a) Notepad (b) Wordpad
(c) Calculator (d) Tweetbot

51. Which one is the default word processor for Microsoft Windows?
(a) MS word (b) MS paint
(c) Notepad (d) Wordpad

52. The keyboard shortcut .... will launch the Start Menu. *CPCT 2024*
(a) Esc (b) Shift (c) Windows (d) Ctrl

53. Which of the following app is the best way to write quick notes on your Windows 10 desktop by signing upwith Microsoft account? *CPCT 2024*
(a) Sticky pad (b) Adobe Reader
(c) Sticky notes (d) Sketchbook

54. Which windows accessory allows you to zoom in on the screen?
(a) Notepad (b) Snipping tool
(c) Magnifier (d) File explorer

55. What is the primary purpose of the snipping tool in windows?
(a) To edit images (b) To record videos
(c) To create animations (d) To take screenshots

56. Which accessory in windows is helpful for creating and managing appointments?
(a) Calendar (b) Clock
(c) Notepad (d) WordPad

Windows Shortcut Keys

57. Which of the following keyboard shortcuts is commonly used to rename a file or folder in Windows OS? *SSC CHSL 2024*
(a) Ctrl+ R (b) F2
(c) Ctrl+ F5 (d) ALT+ Enter

58. Which keyboard shortcut opens file explore (previously known as windows explorer) in Windows 10? *SSC CHSL 2024*
(a) Ctrl+ P (b) Alt+ Tab
(c) Ctrl+ C (d) Win + E

59. In Windows 11, to open File explorer you press the …on the keyboard. *SSC CHSL 2023*
(a) Windows logo key + W (b) Windows logo key + O
(c) Windows logo key + E (d) Windows logo key + F

60. Which of the following shortcut keys represents the correct sequence for copy, paste and cut commands?
(a) Ctrl + V; Ctrl+C; Ctrl+V
(b) Ctrl + C; Ctrl+V; Ctrl+X
(c) Ctrl + X; Ctrl+C; Ctrl+V
(d) Ctrl + C; Ctrl+X; Ctrl+V

Answers

1.	(a)	2.	(c)	3.	(b)	4.	(d)	5.	(d)	6.	(d)	7.	(d)	8.	(b)	9.	(a)	10.	(c)
11.	(c)	12.	(d)	13.	(a)	14.	(d)	15.	(c)	16.	(c)	17.	(d)	18.	(d)	19.	(b)	20.	(a)
21.	(d)	22.	(b)	23.	(d)	24.	(a)	25.	(d)	26.	(b)	27.	(c)	28.	(b)	29.	(b)	30.	(b)
31.	(b)	32.	(c)	33.	(c)	34.	(b)	35.	(a)	36.	(a)	37.	(d)	38.	(b)	39.	(d)	40.	(d)
41.	(d)	42.	(a)	43.	(b)	44.	(b)	45.	(c)	46.	(d)	47.	(d)	48.	(b)	49.	(b)	50.	(d)
51.	(a)	52.	(c)	53.	(c)	54.	(c)	55.	(d)	56.	(a)	57.	(b)	58.	(d)	59.	(c)	60.	(b)

Microsoft Word

- Microsoft Word is a word processing software developed by Microsoft.
- It was first introduced in 1983.
- It is one of the most widely used application for creating, editing and formatting text documents.
- It is a part of the **Microsoft Office suite** and is available for both Windows and Mac operating systems.
- Word allows users to create a variety of documents, such as letters, reports, resumes, brochures and more, with powerful formatting and design tools.

In this Chapter

- Components of MS Word Window
- MS Word Menu Bar Tabs
- Other Features of MS Word

How to start the MS word?

- Click Start → All Program → Microsoft Office → Microsoft Word

Components of MS Word Window

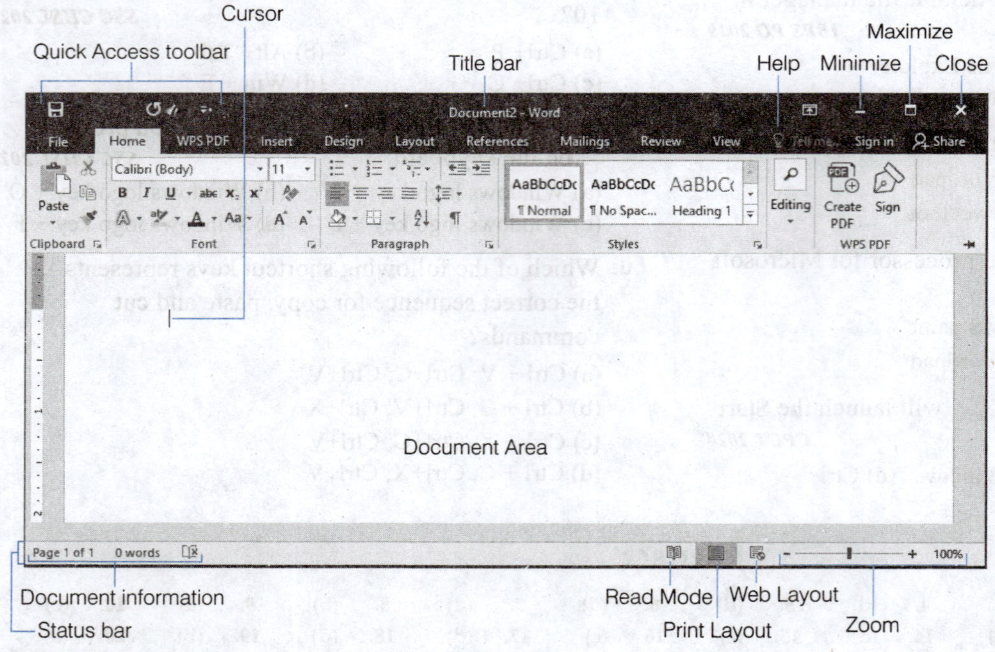

> Everybody should learn to program a computer because it teaches you how to think.
>
> **~ Steve Jobs**

Title Bar

- Located at the top of the window.
- It displays the name of the current document and the application (Microsoft Word).

- If the document has not been saved yet, it will show the default name, such as **Document1**.
- It also contains minimize, maximize and close buttons at the upper right corner.

Menu Bar

- Situated below the title bar, it includes various tabs such as Home, Insert, Design, Layout, etc.
- Each tab contains different commands and features for document creation, formatting and editing.

Ribbon

- It contains multiple tabs such as File, Home, Insert, Design, Page Layout, References, Mailings, Review and View, etc.
- A ribbon can replace both the traditional menu bar and tool bar.

Ruler

- Located at the top and left side of the document area (visible in Print Layout view).
- The horizontal ruler helps in adjust margins, tab stops and text alignment.
- The vertical ruler on the left displays the page margins.

Quick Access Toolbar

- Located at the upper-left corner, of the window.
- It provides quick access to frequently used commands, such as Save, Undo, Redo and Print.

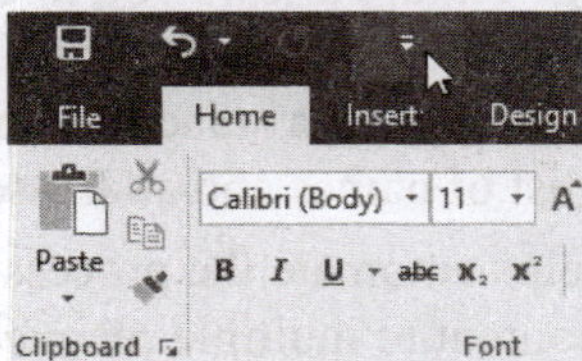

Document Area

- The main area, where you input and view the content of your document.
- It is the large white space in the center of the window where text, images, tables and other elements are displayed.

Scroll Bars

- Vertical and horizontal scroll bars are located on the right and bottom edges of the document area.
- They allow users to navigate through long or wide documents, making it easier to view different sections.

Status Bar

- Located at the bottom of the window, it displays helpful information about the current document.
- It shows the page number, word count and whether the document is in Print Layout or other viewing modes.

Zoom Control

- Located at the bottom-right corner of the window.
- It allows you to zoom in or out on the document for better visibility.

View Buttons

- Found at the right side of the status bar.
- Let you toggle between different document views such as Print Layout, Web Layout, Outline View and Draft View.

Help Button

In MS Word 2016, there is no traditional Help button as in older version, but there are several ways to access help and support.

(i) **Tell me** Use the search bar at the top ("Tell me what you want to do") to find commands or help.

(ii) **File Tab** Click File → Account → Help for links to support and what's new.

MS Word Menu Bar Tabs

- The Menu Bar Tabs in Microsoft Word 2016 are part of the Ribbon interface.
- Each tab focuses on specific tasks, making it easier for users to find and use features.
- Microsoft Word 2016 includes 9 main tabs on the Ribbon interface.

1. File Tab

- It provides access to the Backstage View for file-related operations.
- It includes options like Save, Save As, Open, Close and Print.
- It allows sharing, exporting and setting document properties.

2. Home Tab

- It contains basic text formatting tools like Font (bold, italic, underline) and Styles.
- It offers Clipboard options such as Cut, Copy, Paste and Format Painter.
- It manage paragraph settings such as alignment spacing etc.
- It has the Editing group for Find, Replace and Select commands.

3. Insert Tab

- It lets users insert elements like tables, pictures, shapes and charts.
- It includes options for adding Headers, Footers and Page Numbers.
- It provides tools to insert Links (e.g., hyperlinks, bookmarks) and Text Boxes.

4. Design Tab

- Apply pre-designed themes and templates to the document.
- Customize Page Borders, Colors and Effects for styling.
- It modifies the document's overall appearance easily.

5. Layout (Page Layout) Tab

- It configures page settings like Margins, Orientation and Paper Size.
- It customize indentation, spacing and columns.
- It manages document alignment and breaks.

6. References Tab

- It provides tools for managing Table of Contents, Footnotes and Endnotes.
- It helps insert and manage Citations, Bibliographies and References.
- It includes options for creating an Index and Table of Authorities.
- It is useful for academic and professional document formatting.

7. Mailings Tab

- It is designed for creating and managing Mail Merge documents.
- It allows users to create personalised letters, labels and envelopes.
- It includes options for Insert Merge Fields and Previewing Merged Data.
- It offers features to send merged documents directly to the printer or email.

8. Review Tab

- It focuses on proofreading and collaboration tools like Spelling & Grammar and Thesaurus.
- It includes options for Comments, allows users to add or review feedback.
- Provides tools for comparing or protecting documents from unauthorised changes.

9. View Tab

- It offers different document views like Print Layout, Web Layout and Outline View.
- It provides tools to show or hide elements like Rulers, Gridlines and Navigation Pane.
- It contains a Zoom Slider to adjust the document's zoom level.

Other Features of MS Word

Header and Footer

- In Microsoft Word, headers and footers are sections of a document that appear at the top (header) or bottom (footer) of each page.
- They are often used to display information that repeats throughout the document, such as titles, page numbers and dates.
- Header and Footer options are found in insert tab of ribbon.

Mail Merge

- The Mail Merge feature allows you to create personalised documents (such as letters, labels or envelopes) by combining a standard template with a data source (like a list of names and addresses).
- This feature helps automate the process of sending personalised content to multiple recipients.

Thesaurus

- The Thesaurus feature helps you find synonyms (words with similar meanings) and antonyms (words with opposite meanings) for any selected word.
- Shortcut key to open thesaurus is **Shift + F7**.

Change Case

- The Change Case allows you to quickly change the capitalisation of selected text without having to retype it.

- It is especially useful when you want to adjust the case formatting to match a style or preference.

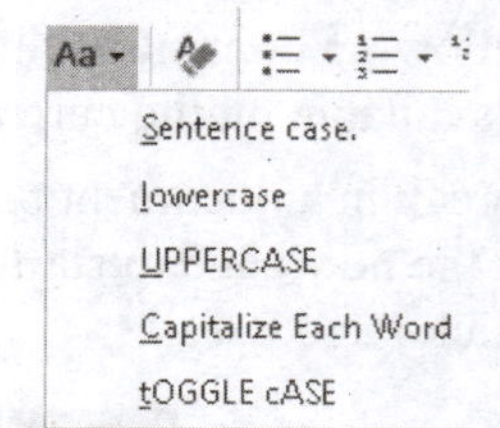

Different type of change case

Case	Description	Example
Sentence Case	▪ Capitalises the first letter of the first word in the sentence and leaves the rest in lowercase.	This is an example.
Lower Case	▪ Converts all letters in the selected text to lowercase.	this is an example.
Upper Case	▪ Converts all letters in the selected text to uppercase.	THIS IS AN EXAMPLE.
Capitalize Each Word	▪ Capitalises the first letter of each word in the selected text.	This Is An Example.
Toggle Case	▪ Switches the case of each letter (lowercase becomes uppercase and *vice-versa*).	"tHIS IS AN EXAMPLE." becomes "This is an example."

Find and Replace

- The Find and Replace feature allows you to quickly locate specific words, phrases or characters in your document and replace them with something else.
- It's a great tool for editing and proofreading, especially in long documents.
- For this, we use the shortcut key **Ctrl+H.**

Auto Correct

- The Auto Correct feature automatically fixes common typing errors and misspellings as you type.
- It makes your writing process faster and more accurate.
- It helps to improve efficiency by correcting mistakes without having to manually edit them.

Spell Check and Grammar

- The Spell Check and Grammar feature helps you identify and correct spelling and grammatical errors in your document automatically.
- It ensures that your writing is clear, professional and error-free.

Footnotes and Endnotes

- In MS Word, footnotes and endnotes are used to provide additional information, references or citations within a document.
- **Footnotes** appear at the bottom of the page, where the reference is made.
- **Endnotes** appear at the end of the document.

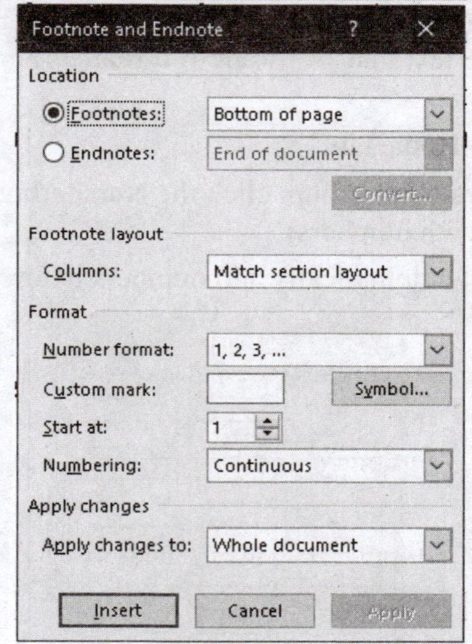

Bullets and Numbering

- The Bullets and Numbering feature helps you in organising lists in a visually clear way, making it easier to read and follow.
- This feature allows you to create ordered (numbered) or unordered (bulleted) lists.

How to Use Bullets and Numbering?

1. Bullets

- Bullets are used for **unordered lists,** where the order of the items does not matter.

How to Use

- Select the text that you want to format as a bulleted list.
- Go to the Home tab.
- In the Paragraph group, click the Bullets button (a list icon with dots).

- Word will automatically add bullet points before each selected line or paragraph.

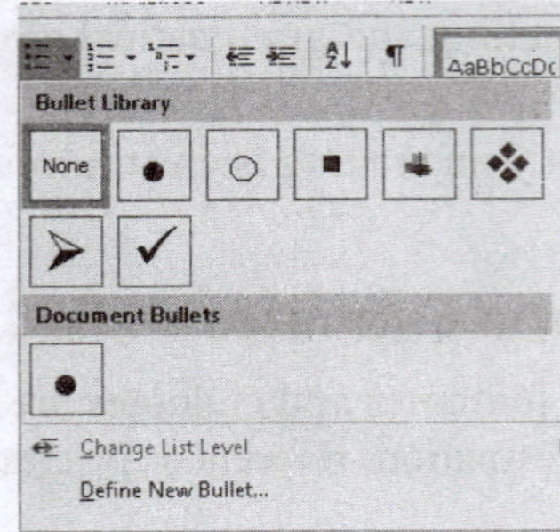

2. Numbering

- Numbering is used for ordered lists, where the sequence of items matters.

How to Use

- Select the text that you want to format as a numbered list.
- Go to the Home tab.
- In the Paragraph group, click the Numbering Library (a list icon with numbers).
- Word will automatically add numbers before each item.

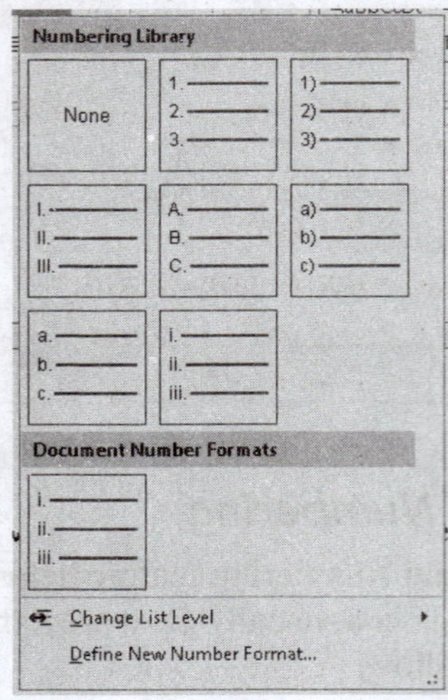

Clip Art

- The Clipart feature allows you to insert images, illustrations and other graphical content into your document to make it more visually appealing.

Word Art

- The WordArt feature allows you to create stylised text with special effects, makes your text stand out with colorful designs, special fonts and 3D-like appearances.

Page Break

- A page break starts a new page in the document.
- It ensures the following content begins on a new page, even if space is available on the current page.
- To insert page break in a document place the cursor where you want the new page to start, then go to the Insert tab and click Page Break.

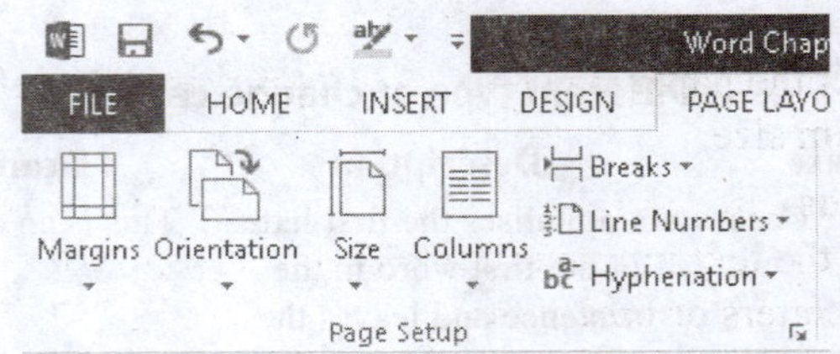

Section Break

- A Section Break divides a document into sections, allows you to apply different formatting to each section.
- To insert section break place the cursor where you want the break, go to the Layout tab, click Breaks and choose the type of section break (Next Page, Continuous, Even Page or Odd Page).

Page Orientation

- The Page Orientation allows you to set the layout of your page, either Portrait or Landscape.
- Portrait orientation is vertical, with the height being greater than the width.
- Landscape orientation is horizontal, with the width greater than the height.

Page Setup

- The Page Setup allows you to customize the layout and formatting of your document's pages, including margins, orientation, size and more.
- It provides a way to control how your document appears when printed.

How to Access Page Setup

- Go to the Layout tab on the ribbon.
- In the Page Setup group, you'll find options for Margins, Orientation, Size, Columns and Breaks.

Page Setup Options

Here are the following Page Setup options.

Margins

- Adjust the space around the edges of the page. Options include Normal, Narrow, Wide or Custom margins.

- In MS Word, you can set the following margin types:
  (i) Left Margin
  (ii) Right Margin
  (iii) Top Margin
  (iv) Bottom Margin

Orientation

- Choose between Portrait (vertical) or Landscape (horizontal) layout for your pages.

Size

- Select the paper size (e.g., A4, Letter, etc.) or define a custom size.

Columns

- Split the text into multiple columns (useful for newsletters or brochures).

Line Numbers

- Add line numbers to the document for reference or legal documents.

Hyphenation

- Enable or adjust automatic hyphenation for better text flow.

Page Background

- The Page Background feature allows you to add color, patterns and images to the background of your document pages, making them more visually appealing or distinctive.

Page Background Options

Page background options are given below

Page Color

- It adds a solid color or gradient to the background of your page.
- You can choose from a variety of colors or create a custom color.

Page Borders

- It allows you to add borders around the entire page.
- You can customize the style, color, width and type of border (e.g., solid, dashed, double lines, etc.).

Watermark

- It adds a faint image or text to the background of your document (commonly used for branding or marking the document as Confidential).
- You can choose a preset watermark (like Confidential or Draft) or create a custom watermark with your own image or text.

Closing a Word Program

- To close MS Word, follow these steps

Using the Close Button

- Click on the ☒ in the top-right corner of the Word window.

Using the File Menu

- Click on the File tab.
- Select Exit or Close.

Keyboard Shortcut

- Press keyboard shortcut Alt + F4 to close the program quickly.

MS Word Shortcut Keys

Keys	Functionality
Ctrl+ N	▪ Create a new Word document
Ctrl + O	▪ Open an existing Word document
Ctrl + W	▪ Close Word document
Ctrl + S	▪ Save Word document
F12	▪ Open save as dialog box
Ctrl+C	▪ Copy the selected text
Ctrl+ X	▪ Cut the selected text
Ctrl+ V	▪ Paste the text
Ctrl+ B	▪ Apply bold effect to the selected text
Ctrl+ I	▪ Apply italic effect to the selected text
Ctrl+ U	▪ Underline the selected text
Ctrl+Shift+D	▪ Double underline the text
Ctrl+Shift+K	▪ Change text to small caps
Ctrl+ A	▪ Select all
Ctrl+Q	▪ Remove paragraph formatting
Ctrl+F	▪ Open a find dialog box
Ctrl + P	▪ Print Word document/print preview
Ctrl+F6	▪ Switch between multiple Word documents
Ctrl + D	▪ To Open Font dialog box
Ctrl + Shift + N	▪ Apply normal style
Ctrl+Shift +W	▪ Apply/remove words underline
Ctrl+L	▪ Left-align selected text
Ctrl+R	▪ Right-align selected text
Ctrl + E	▪ Center-align selected text
Ctrl + J	▪ Justify-align selected text
Ctrl + Y	▪ Redo undone action
Ctrl+ Z	▪ Undo an action
Shift+ F3	▪ Change case
Ctrl + K	▪ Insert a hyperlink
Alt + H	▪ Opens the Home tab
Ctrl + Shift + C	▪ Copy the format of the selection into Clipboard

Keys	Functionality
Delete / Backspace	▪ Delete one character to the right / to the left of cursor (or delete selection)
Ctrl+ Delete / Ctrl +Backspace	▪ Delete one word to the right / to the left
Ctrl+ Shift+< / Ctrl+ Shift+>	▪ Decrease / Increase font size by one value
Ctrl + Right Arrow	▪ Move the cursor to the right one word
Ctrl+ Left Arrow	▪ Move the cursor to the left one word
Ctrl+ Down Arrow	▪ Move the cursor down one paragraph
Ctrl+ Up Arrow	▪ Move the cursor up one paragraph
Ctrl+Shift+V	▪ Paste unformatted or plain text

Facts Drive

- The default font in MS Word is **Calibri**, but it was changed to Calibri from Times New Roman in 2007.
- In Word 2016, you can use **Ink to Text** to convert your handwritten notes into typed text using a stylus or touch screen.
- In MS Word, the minimum and maximum zoom percentages are **10%** and **500%** respectively.
- MS Word primarily uses the **.docx** file format, introduced in Word 2007. It replaced the older .doc format, offering better compatibility and smaller file sizes.

PYQs Oneliner

1. **Ctrl+Shift+L** keyboard shortcut is used for adding bullets in MS Word 2010. ***SSC CGL (T-II) 18.01.2025***
2. **Ctrl+M** keyboard shortcut is used to increase the indent in a paragraph in MS Word 2010. ***SSC CGL (T-II) 20.01.2025***
3. **Page Layout** tab in MS Word is used to set page margins and orientation. ***CPCT 2024***
4. **Ctrl+ S** keyboard shortcut is used to save a document in MS Word. ***SSC CHSL 2024***
5. **.docx** is the default file extension for MS Word documents. ***SSC CHSL 2020***
6. **Backspace** key is used to delete the character to the left of the cursor. ***SSC CGL 2020***
7. Themes option in MS Word allows you to apply **pre-designed** documents themes. ***SSC CGL 2020***
8. **Quick Access Toolbar** feature in MS Word helps to quickly access the frequently used commands. ***SSC CGL 2019***
9. **Print Layout** view in MS Word allows you to see how your document will look when printed. ***SSC CHSL 2019***

Practice Exercise

Introduction to Microsoft Word

1. Microsoft Office Word is a/an
   (a) area in the computer's main memory in which Microsoft Office text files are stored temporarily.
   (b) program included with Windows 2000 that can be used only to create or edit text files, smaller than 64k, that do not require formatting.
   (c) classified password that prevents unauthorized users from accessing a protected Microsoft Office item or document.
   (d) full featured Word processing program that can be used to create and revise professional looking documents easily.

2. You can start MS Word by using which button?
   (a) New (b) Start
   (c) Program (d) All of these

3. MS Word is a
   (a) tabular data formatting software
   (b) word processing software
   (c) presentation software
   (d) e-mail client

4. MS Word 2010, opens a new document with the temporary name as... . ***Delhi Police 2022***
   (a) book (b) book1
   (c) document 1 (d) document

5. MS Word is a text or document editing application program that comes in the package of MS Office Suite. Which among the given options is not related with MS Word?
   (a) Page Layout (b) Antivirus
   (c) Mailings (d) Format Painter

6. The valid format of MS Word is
(a) .jpeg (b) .png
(c) .docx (d) .exe

7. Which of the following is the use of a word processor?
(a) Make a presentation
(b) Maintain inventory
(c) Type a biography
(d) Maintain inventory

Components of MS Word Window

8. Which of the following is not a component of the MS Word window? *SSC CGL 2020*
(a) Title Bar (b) Status Bar
(c) Taskbar (d) Ribbon

9. What is the function of the Quick Access Toolbar in MS Word? *SSC CHSL 2018*
(a) It provides access to all the documents on your computer.
(b) It displays commonly used commands for easy access.
(c) It is used to save documents automatically.
(d) It shows the system tray icons.

10. Which component of the MS Word window shows the name of the open document? *SSC CGL 2019*
(a) Status Bar (b) Title Bar
(c) Ribbon (d) Scroll Bar

11. Which part of the MS Word window contains options like File, Home, Insert and Design? *SSC CHSL 2020*
(a) Title Bar (b) Ribbon
(c) Toolbar (d) Quick Access Toolbar

12. The area in the MS Word window where you can view and edit your document is called *SSC CGL 2020*
(a) Document Window (b) Viewport
(c) Work Area (d) Canvas

13. Which component of the MS Word window displays information such as page number, word count and language settings? *SSC CHSL 2019*
(a) Title Bar (b) Status Bar
(c) Scroll Bar (d) Task Pane

14. What is the primary function of the Ruler in MS Word? *SSC CGL 2020*
(a) To create a table of contents
(b) To adjust margins, indents and tabs
(c) To check spelling and grammar
(d) To align text in a paragraph

15. Which part of the MS Word window contains options like New, Open, Save and Print? *SSC CGL 2018*
(a) Quick Access Toolbar (b) Ribbon
(c) File Tab (d) Task Pane

16. What does the Status Bar in MS Word display?
SSC CGL 2021
(a) The active sheet's name
(b) The document's title
(c) Page number, word count and language settings
(d) Formatting options

17. Which feature in MS Word helps to quickly access the frequently used commands? *SSC CGL 2019*
(a) Quick Access Toolbar (b) Task Pane
(c) Ribbon (d) Action Pane

18. Which of the following is not a part of MS Word?
(a) Font (b) Bold
(c) Italic (d) Magic tool

19. Which of the following tools can be used in MS Word?
(a) Bullets (b) Hyperlinks
(c) Highlights (d) All of these

MS Word Menu Bar Tabs

20. In MS Word, Spelling Check is a feature available in which tab?
(a) File (b) Home (c) Insert (d) Review

21. Which tab in MS Word allows you to insert page numbers? *SSC CGL 2019*
(a) Insert (b) Layout (c) View (d) Design

22. Which tab in MS Word contains the Page Break option? *SSC CHSL 2019*
(a) Insert Tab (b) Layout Tab
(c) Design Tab (d) View Tab

23. Which MS Word tab provides tools for adding headers, footers and page numbers? *IBPS PO 2023*
(a) References (b) Design
(c) Insert (d) Review

24. Which tab in MS Word is used to change the document view, such as switching to Print Layout or Outline view? *SSC GD 2022*
(a) File (b) View
(c) References (d) Layout

25. In MS Word, which tab allows you to apply themes to the document? *RRB Group D 2023*
(a) Home (b) Design (c) Layout (d) View

26. Which of the following item is included in the 'References' menu of Microsoft Word (Office 2019)? *RSMSSB LDC 2025*
(a) Tables (b) Citations and Bibliography
(c) Comments (d) Proofing

27. In MS Word, the Save As option is found under which tab? *UPSC CDS 2021*
(a) Home (b) File (c) Insert (d) Review

28. Which tab in MS Word contains the Find and Replace feature? *UPSC CAPF 2022*
(a) Review (b) Home
(c) Layout (d) References

29. To change the orientation of the page in MS Word, which tab should you use? *SSC CHSL 2022*
(a) Layout (b) Insert (c) File (d) Design

30. Which option in MS Word allows a user to align text within a document to the left, center, right or justify it across the page? *SSC CGL (T-II) 20.01.2025*
(a) Font Style: Changes the appearance of text but does not affect its alignment
(b) Paragraph Alignment: Adjusts the alignment of text to the left, center, right or justifies it
(c) Line Spacing: Adjusts the space between lines of text but does not affect text alignment
(d) Text Direction: Changes the orientation of the text, such as vertical or horizontal, but not its alignment

31. What is the default font face in an MS Word 2010 document? *Delhi Police 2022*
(a) Times New Roman (b) Italic
(c) Calibri (d) Arial

32. We can add a table in MS word document from which of the following tabs? *SSC CHSL 2024*
(a) View Tab (b) Home Tab
(c) Design Tab (d) Insert Tab

33. The moderate margin of a page in MS Word can be applied to the page from which of the following? *SSC CHSL 2024*
(a) Page Layout Tab (b) Design Tab
(c) Review Tab (d) View Tab

34. Where is the save button in MS Word? *SSC CHSL 2024*
(a) Top left corner of a word window
(b) Bottom right corner of a word window
(c) Bottom left corner of a word window
(d) Top right corner of a word window

35. To create a new MS Word document, which of the following steps is correct? *SSC CHSL 2024*
(a) File Tab → Open (b) File Tab → Start
(c) File Tab → New (d) File Tab → Recent

Other Features of MS Word

36. In MS Word 2010, Page number option comes under which of the following menus? *Delhi Police 2023*
(a) Pages (b) Header and Footer
(c) Home Tab (d) Page Layout

37. In MS Word, which of the following is used to find synonyms for a selected word? *SSC CGL 2018*
(a) Thesaurus (b) Spell Checker
(c) Find and Replace (d) AutoCorrect

38. Which of the following is used to remove the formatting applied to text in MS Word? *SSC CGL 2020*
(a) Clear Formatting (b) Undo
(c) Reset (d) Delete Formatting

39. Instead of retyping the same text in MS Word 2010, we can use ……… to reduce time and efforts. *Delhi Police 2022*
(a) copy + undo (b) paste + undo
(c) copy + paste (d) cut + copy

40. Where header appears?
(a) Top (b) Bottom
(c) Centre (d) All of these

41. In MS Word, which feature allows you to create a list of items that can be clicked to navigate to specific sections of a document? *SSC CHSL 2019*
(a) Hyperlinks (b) Bookmarks
(c) Cross-references (d) Table of Contents

42. Which of the following is not a valid paragraph alignment option in MS Word? *SSC CGL 2021*
(a) Left (b) Right
(c) Center (d) Justify Full

43. What does the Spelling & Grammar feature in MS Word do? *SSC CHSL 2018*
(a) Checks only spelling errors
(b) Checks only grammar errors
(c) Checks both spelling and grammar errors
(d) Suggests synonyms for incorrect words

44. In MS Word 2010, creating a large capital letter used as a decorative element at the beginning of a paragraph or section refers to *Delhi Police 2022*
(a) Header (b) Smart Art
(c) Drop Cap (d) Watermark

45. Which keyboard shortcut is used for adding bullets in MS Word 2010? *SSC CGL (T-II) 18.01.2025*
(a) Ctrl + Alt + L (b) Ctrl + L
(c) Shift + L (d) Ctrl + Shift + L

46. Which feature of MS Word helps in creating list?
(a) Word art (b) Bullets and numbering
(c) Scaling (d) Word wrap

47. The process of merging data from a data source into a main document in a word-processing application is called…. *SSC CHSL 2024*
(a) data concatenation (b) mail merge
(c) data accumulation (d) data integration

48. A picture of graphic that can be added to MS Word is called?
(a) WordArt (b) ClipArt
(c) Themes (d) Drawings

49. In MS Word, which option allows you to align text in a way that it appears vertically at the bottom of a cell or text box? *SSC CHSL 2024*
(a) Distributed alignment (b) Justify alignment
(c) Center alignment (d) Bottom alignment

50. In MS Word, which feature allows you to create different headers and footers for odd and even pages in a document? *SSC CHSL 2024*
(a) Different First Page (b) Page Breaks
(c) Different Odd and Even Pages
(d) Section Breaks

51. In MS Word, a number printed above the base line is called .... *SSC CHSL 2024*
(a) superscript (b) strikethrough
(c) above BL (d) subscript

52. In MS Word, which option allows you to copy the selected text or object to the clipboard while simultaneously removing it from its original location? *SSC CHSL 2024*
(a) Drag and Drop (b) Paste
(c) Copy (d) Cut

53. Which of the following is the fastest way to open the Help window in MS Word? *SSC CHSL 2024*
(a) Type 'help' in the search bar and then press enter
(b) Click the Microsoft office button and then click Help
(c) Press F1
(d) Click the Help button on the ribbon

MS Word Shortcut Keys

54. Which keyboard shortcut is used to increase the indent in a paragraph in MS Word 2010? *SSC CGL (T-II) 20.01.2025*
(a) Ctrl + U (b) Ctrl + D
(c) Ctrl + M (d) Ctrl + K

55. What is the shortcut key to open the Find and Replace dialog box in MS Word? *SSC CHSL 2019*
(a) Ctrl + F (b) Ctrl + H
(c) Ctrl + R (d) Ctrl + N

56. To underline the text we used the .... command in MS Word.
(a) Ctrl+B (b) Ctrl+A (c) Ctrl+N (d) Ctrl+U

57. To save a document in MS Word, which shortcut key do you use? *IBPS Clerk 2019*
(a) Ctrl + S (b) Ctrl + P
(c) Ctrl + D (d) Ctrl + O

58. How can you align text to the center in MS Word? *RRB NTPC 2022*
(a) Ctrl + R (b) Ctrl + E
(c) Ctrl + J (d) Ctrl + L

59. Which shortcut key opens the Save As dialog box in MS Word? *SSC CHSL 2021*
(a) F9 (b) F8 (c) F10 (d) F12

60. Which of the following is the correct option to convert text into superscript? *Delhi Police 2023*
(a) Shift + S (b) Ctrl + shift + +
(c) Ctrl + Shift + U (d) Ctrl + Shift + S

61. Which key combination is used to go to the next spell check in MS Word?
(a) F7 (b) Ctrl + F7
(c) Alt + F7 (d) Shift + F7

62. What does the shortcut key Ctrl + P do in MS Word? *SSC CHSL 2019*
(a) Open a new document (b) Print a document
(c) Open the print preview (d) Paste text

63. What is the function of Shift + F3 in MS Word? *IBPS PO 2020*
(a) Open the Thesaurus
(b) Change the case of selected text
(c) Repeat the last action
(d) Save as

64. What does Ctrl + D do in MS Word? *RRB NTPC 2021*
(a) Opens the font options (b) Deletes the selected text
(c) Inserts a page break (d) Aligns text to the center

65. Which shortcut key is used to close the MS Word application?
(a) Ctrl + Q (b) Alt + F4
(c) Ctrl + W (d) Ctrl + F4

66. In MS Word, a document may be printed using.... . *SSC CHSL 2024*
(a) Ctrl + X (b) Ctrl + C
(c) Ctrl + P (d) Ctrl +V

Answers

1. (d)	2. (b)	3. (b)	4. (c)	5. (b)	6. (c)	7. (c)	8. (c)	9. (b)	10. (b)
11. (b)	12. (a)	13. (b)	14. (b)	15. (c)	16. (c)	17. (a)	18. (d)	19. (d)	20. (d)
21. (a)	22. (a)	23. (c)	24. (b)	25. (b)	26. (b)	27. (b)	28. (b)	29. (a)	30. (b)
31. (c)	32. (d)	33. (a)	34. (a)	35. (c)	36. (b)	37. (a)	38. (a)	39. (c)	40. (a)
41. (d)	42. (d)	43. (c)	44. (c)	45. (d)	46. (b)	47. (b)	48. (b)	49. (d)	50. (c)
51. (a)	52. (d)	53. (c)	54. (c)	55. (b)	56. (d)	57. (a)	58. (b)	59. (d)	60. (b)
61. (a)	62. (c)	63. (b)	64. (a)	65. (b)	66. (c)				

Microsoft Excel

- MS Excel is a **spreadsheet program** introduced by **Microsoft Corporation** in 1985.
- It is also known as Microsoft Excel.
- It is widely used for organizing, analyzing and storing data in **tabular** form.
- It allows you to perform calculations, create charts and manage large sets of information efficiently.
- Excel uses a **grid system** made up of rows and columns to store data in cells.

In this Chapter

- Terms Related to MS Excel
- Main Components of MS Excel Window
- Open, Insert, Rename, Move Excel Workbook
- Main Functions Used in MS Excel
- Charts in MS Excel

"You can not make decision without data and Excel provides that data.

~ **Peter Drucker**"

How to start MS Excel?

- Click Start → All Programs → Microsoft Office → Microsoft Excel

Uses of MS Excel

- Data Formatting
- Data Management
- Chart Creation
- Mathematical Calculations
- Time Management
- Accounting and Budgeting
- Financial Modelling

Advantages of MS Excel

- Saves time
- Increase productivity
- Table creating ability
- Proficient in spreadsheet
- Recover data easily

Terms Related to MS Excel

Spreadsheet

- Spreadsheet is also known as **worksheet**.
- In spreadsheet, data is stored in tabular format using rows and columns.

Example Microsoft Excel, Google Sheets, LibreOffice Calc, etc.

Workbook

- The entire Excel file that contains your work is called a **workbook**.

- Workbook is basically a collection of multiple worksheets/spreadsheets.
- Excel workbook is saved with the **.xlsx** file extension.

Cell

- Cell is a box which is intersection of a row and column in a worksheet.
- It is the smallest unit in an Excel worksheet.
- It is known as the **basic building block** of Excel.
- The cell in which user is working is called **active cell.**

Cell Address/Reference

- The location of a cell is called **cell address.**

  Example B3 refers to the cell in column B and row 3.

Formula

- An expression that performs calculations or logical operations.
- In excel, a formula always starts with an **equal sign (=).**

  Example =A1+B1 adds the contents of cells A1 and B1.

Function

- A predefined formula that performs a specific calculation or operation on data.

  Examples SUM () for addition, AVERAGE () for mean and COUNT () for counting entries.

Cell Range

- A cell range in excel refers to a group of two or more cells selected or referenced together.

  Example A1:A5

AutoSum

- It is a quick way to sum up a range of numbers.
- It is found on the Home tab and uses the SUM () function.
- It saves time when adding columns or rows of data.

Fill Handle

- It is a small square at the bottom-right corner of a selected cell.
- We can drag it to copy data or formulas to adjacent cells.
- We can also fill patterns like dates or sequences using fill handle.

Main Components of MS Excel Window

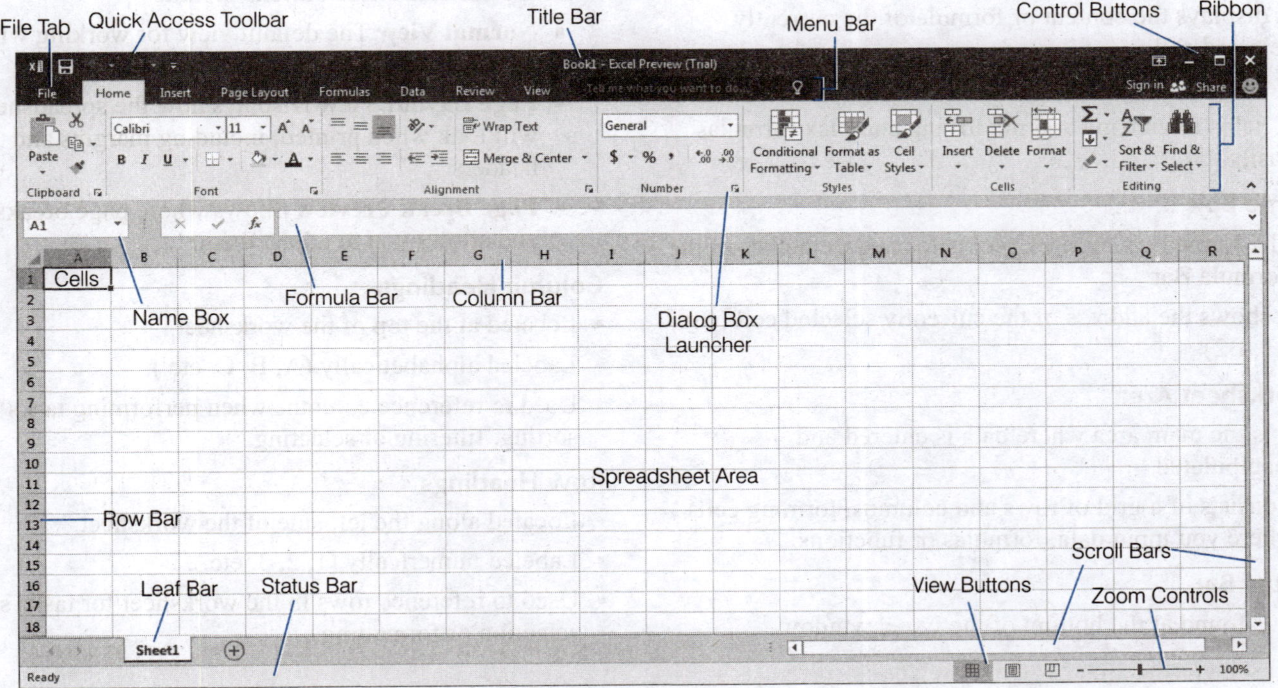

Title Bar

- It is located at the top of the window.
- It displays the name of the workbook.
- It often includes control buttons like Minimize, Maximize and Close on the right side.

Quick Access Toolbar

- This is located at the upper left corner of the screen.
- Its objective is to show the most frequently used excel commands.

Menu Bar

- Found just below the Title Bar.
- It contains drop-down menus such as File, Home, View, Insert, Formula, Page Layout, Window, etc.

Ribbon

- A toolbar located below the Menu Bar.
- Organized into multiple tabs like Home, Insert, Page Layout, Formulas, Data, Review, View, etc.
- Each tab contains groups of related commands, such as font settings, alignment, data tools, etc.

Formula Bar

- It is a toolbar located just below the Ribbon.
- It displays the content or formula of the currently selected cell.
- You can use it to enter or edit data and formulas.
- It helps in viewing and modifying complex formulas easily.

Name Box

- The Name Box in MS Excel is located to the left of the Formula Bar.
- It shows the address of the currently selected cell (e.g., A1, B2).

Worksheet Area

- It is the main area where data is entered and manipulated.
- Consists of a grid of rows and columns, forming cells where you input data, formulas or functions.

Status Bar

- It is found at the bottom of the Excel window.
- Displays information about the current state of the worksheet, such as the current cell mode, the sum of selected cells and calculation status.
- Can be customized to show additional information like average, count, etc.

Sheet Tab

- It is located at the bottom of the workbook window.
- It shows the names of all the worksheets (e.g., Sheet1, Sheet2, etc.) within the workbook.
- You can use it to switch between worksheets by clicking on a tab.

Scroll Bars

- Located on the right side (vertical) and at the bottom (horizontal) of the window.
- Used to navigate through large worksheets by scrolling up, down, left or right.
- Help you move across different sections of the worksheet when the content exceeds the viewable area.

View Button

- In MS Excel, the View Buttons are located at the bottom-right corner of the window.
- It provides quick access to different viewing modes of the worksheet. These buttons include
  - **Normal View** The default view for working with spreadsheets.
  - **Page Layout View** Displays how the spreadsheet will look when printed, including margins and headers.
  - **Page Break Preview** Shows where page breaks are and allows you to adjust them.

Column Headings

- Located at the top of the worksheet.
- Labeled alphabetically (A, B, C, etc.).
- Used to reference columns when performing tasks like sorting, filtering or selecting.

Row Headings

- Located along the left side of the worksheet.
- Labeled numerically (1, 2, 3, etc.).
- Used to reference rows in the worksheet for tasks such as selection or formatting.

Open, Insert, Rename and Move Excel Workbook

Task	Description
Open Excel Workbook	▪ **Start Menu** Click on Start > All Programs > Microsoft Office> MS Excel ▪ **Shortcut Key** Press Windows + R, type excel and hit Enter. ▪ **Desktop** Double-click the Excel shortcut. ▪ **Cortana** Search for Excel and press Enter.
Insert New Worksheet in Workbook	▪ **Ribbon** Go to Home > Insert > Insert Sheet. ▪ **Right-click** Right-click a sheet tab > Insert > Worksheet. ▪ **Shortcut** Press Shift + F11. ▪ **+ Button** Click the insert sheet icon (+) next to sheet tabs.
Rename a Worksheet	▪ **Right-click Method** Right-click the sheet tab > Rename > Type the new name. ▪ **Double-click Method** Double-click the sheet tab > Type the new name and press Enter. ▪ **Ribbon** Go to Home tab > Format > Rename Sheet. ▪ **Keyboard Shortcut** Press Alt + H + O + R in sequence to rename the sheet.
Moving a Worksheet	▪ **Drag and Drop** Click and hold the sheet tab, then drag it to a new position and release. ▪ **Ribbon** Go to the Home tab > Format > Move or Copy Sheet > Choose the new position and click OK. ▪ **Right-click Method** Right-click the sheet tab > Move or Copy > Select the new position and click OK.

Note The default name of worksheets in Excel are Sheet1, Sheet2, Sheet3.... These names are assigned sequentially as you add new worksheets.

Main Functions Used in MS Excel

- A predefined formula that performs a specific calculation or operation on data.
- They can simplify complex calculations and automate repetitive tasks.

Math & Trig Functions

Function	Description	Example	Result
SUM()	▪ Adds all numbers in a range	=SUM(A1:A10)	Sum of range
ROUND()	▪ Rounds a number to specified digits	=ROUND(5.678, 2)	5.68
INT()	▪ Rounds down to nearest integer	=INT(4.99)	4
MOD()	▪ Returns remainder after division	=MOD(10,3)	1
ABS()	▪ Returns absolute value	=ABS(-8)	8
POWER()	▪ Raises number to a power	=POWER(2,3)	8
SQRT()	▪ Returns square root	=SQRT(16)	4
EVEN()	▪ Rounds a number up to the nearest even integer	=EVEN(3)	4
ODD()	▪ Rounds a number up to the nearest odd integer	=ODD(4)	5
PI()	▪ Returns value of Pi	=PI()	3.1416
FACT()	▪ Returns the factorial of a number	=FACT(5)	120
ROMAN()	▪ Converts a number to roman numeral	=ROMAN(10)	X
CEILING()	▪ Rounds a number up to the nearest multiple of a given value	=CEILING(7.5,2)	8
FLOOR()	▪ Rounds a number down to the nearest multiple of a given value	=FLOOR(7.5,2)	6

Date & Time Functions

Function	Description	Example	Result
TODAY()	▪ Returns the current date	=TODAY()	Today's date
NOW()	▪ Returns the current date and time	=NOW()	Today's date and time
DATE()	▪ Returns the date value based on year ,month ,and day	=DATE(2024,12,31)	12/31/2024
TIME()	▪ Returns the time value based on hour, minute and second	=TIME(12,30,0)	12:30:00 PM

Function	Description	Example	Result
HOUR()	▪ Returns the hour from a given time	=HOUR("12:30:00 PM")	12
MINUTE()	▪ Returns the minute from a given time	=MINUTE("12:30:00 PM")	30
SECOND()	▪ Returns the second from a given time	=SECOND("12:30:30 PM")	30

Text Functions

Function	Description	Example	Result
UPPER()	▪ Converts text to uppercase	=UPPER("Hello")	HELLO
LOWER()	▪ Converts text to lowercase	=LOWER("Hello")	hello
CONCATENATE()	▪ Combines multiple text strings into one	=CONCATENATE("Hello", " ", "World")	Hello World
LEFT()	▪ Returns the first N characters from a text string	=LEFT("Hello", 3)	Hel
RIGHT()	▪ Returns the last N characters from a text string	=RIGHT("Hello", 3)	llo
MID()	▪ Returns a specific number of characters from a text string, starting at a specified position	=MID("Hello", 2, 3)	ell
LEN()	▪ Returns the length of a text string	=LEN("Hello")	5
TRIM()	▪ Removes extra spaces from text (except for single spaces)	=TRIM(" HelloWorld ")	"Hello World"
EXACT()	▪ Compares two text strings and returns TRUE if they are exactly the same	=EXACT("Hello", "hello")	FALSE

Statistical Functions

Function	Description	Example	Result
AVERAGE()	▪ Returns the average (arithmetic mean) of a set of numbers	A B C D E [5] [4] [3] [2] [1] =AVERAGE(A1:E1)	=3
MEDIAN()	▪ Returns the median (middle value) of a set of numbers	A B C D E [5] [4] [3] [2] [1] =MEDIAN(A1:E1)	=3
MODE()	▪ Returns the most frequently occurring value in a range	A B C D E [5] [4] [3] [4] [1] =MODE(A1:E1)	=4
MIN()	▪ Returns the smallest value in a range	A B C D E [5] [4] [3] [2] [1] =MIN(A1:E1)	=1
MAX()	▪ Returns the largest value in a range	A B C D E [5] [4] [3] [2] [1] =MAX(A1:E1)	=5
COUNT()	▪ Counts the number of cells that contain numbers	A B C D E [5] [S] [3] [A] [1] =COUNT(A1:E1)	=3
COUNTA()	▪ Counts the number of non-empty cells in a range	A B C D E [5] [A] [3] [2] [X] =COUNTA(A1:E1)	=5
COUNTBLANK()	▪ Counts the number of empty cells in a range	A B C D E [ ] [4] [3] [2] [ ] =COUNTBLANK(A1:E1)	=2
COUNTIF()	▪ Counts the number of cells that meet a specific condition	A B C D E [5] [4] [3] [2] [1] =COUNTIF(A1:E1, ">4")	=1

Logical Functions

Function	Description	Example	Result
AND()	▪ Returns TRUE if all arguments are TRUE, otherwise FALSE	=AND(A1>10, B1<20)	TRUE, if both conditions are true
OR()	▪ Returns TRUE if any argument is TRUE, otherwise FALSE	=OR(A1>10, B1<20)	TRUE, if any condition is true
NOT()	▪ Reverses the logical value (TRUE becomes FALSE, FALSE becomes TRUE)	=NOT(A1>10)	TRUE, if A1 is not greater than 10
IF()	▪ Checks whether a condition is met and returns one value if TRUE, another if FALSE,	=IF(A1>10, "YES", "NO")	YES if A1 > 10, else NO

Operators in MS Excel

- Operators are used to perform mathematical and logical operations.
- These are classified as

Arithmetic Operators

Operator	Use
+ (Addition)	▪ Adds two or more numbers.
- (Subtraction)	▪ Subtracts one number from another.
* (Astrik)	▪ Multiplies two or more numbers.
/ (Forward Slash)	▪ Divides one number by another.
^(Exponentiation)	▪ For calculating power

Comparison Operators

Operator	Use
= (Equal to)	▪ Compares if two values are equal.
<> (Not Equal to)	▪ Compares if two values are not equal.
> (Greater than)	▪ Compares if the value is greater than another.
< (Less than)	▪ Compares if the value is less than another.
>= (Greater than or equal to)	▪ Compares if the value is greater than or equal to another.
<= (Less than or equal to)	▪ Compares if the value is less than or equal to another.

Reference Operator

Operator	Use
: (Colon)	▪ Defines a range of cells between two references.
, (Comma)	▪ Combines multiple ranges of cells.
(Space)	▪ Returns the intersection of two ranges.

Charts in MS Excel

- Charts in Excel are graphical tools used to represent data visually, making it easier to analyze and interpret information.
- They help identify trends, compare values and reveal patterns in data.

Types of Charts in MS Excel

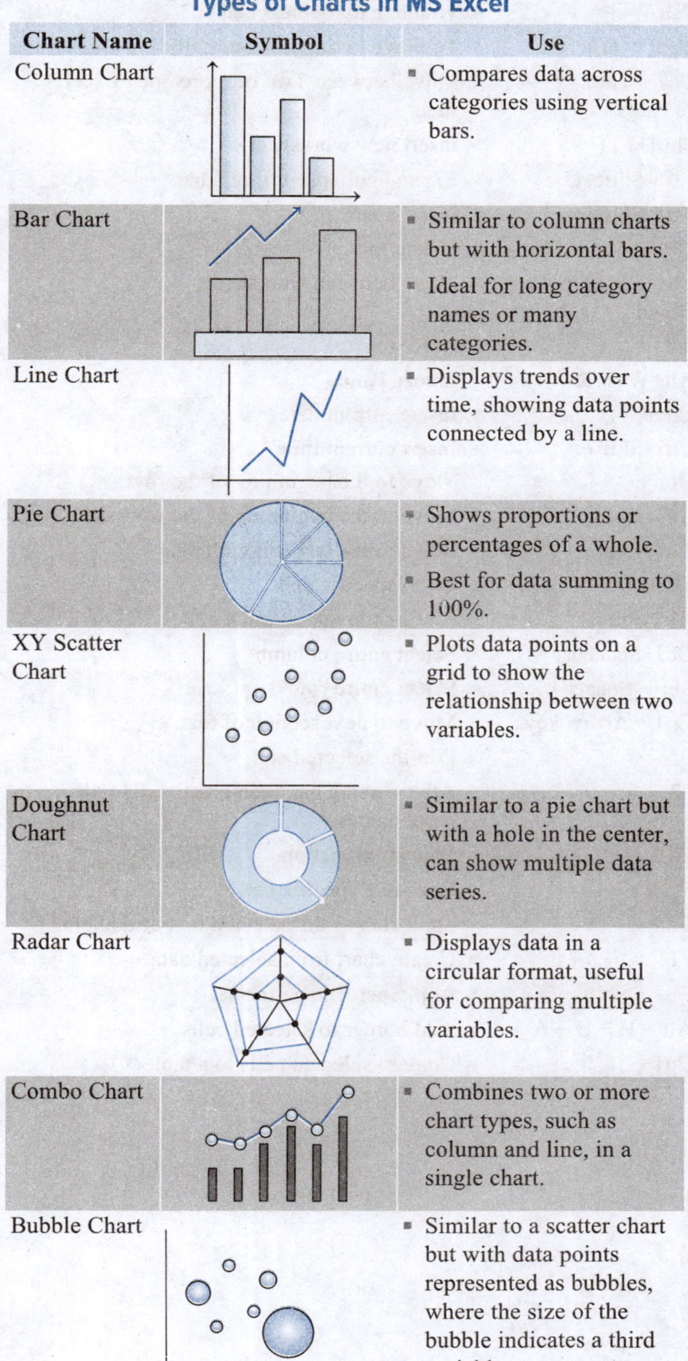

Chart Name	Symbol	Use
Column Chart		▪ Compares data across categories using vertical bars.
Bar Chart		▪ Similar to column charts but with horizontal bars. ▪ Ideal for long category names or many categories.
Line Chart		▪ Displays trends over time, showing data points connected by a line.
Pie Chart		▪ Shows proportions or percentages of a whole. ▪ Best for data summing to 100%.
XY Scatter Chart		▪ Plots data points on a grid to show the relationship between two variables.
Doughnut Chart		▪ Similar to a pie chart but with a hole in the center, can show multiple data series.
Radar Chart		▪ Displays data in a circular format, useful for comparing multiple variables.
Combo Chart		▪ Combines two or more chart types, such as column and line, in a single chart.
Bubble Chart		▪ Similar to a scatter chart but with data points represented as bubbles, where the size of the bubble indicates a third variable.

Shortcut Keys in Excel

Shortcut Key	Action
Ctrl+O	▪ Open existing workbook
Ctrl+N	▪ Open new workbook
Ctrl+S	▪ Save workbook
Ctrl+W/ Ctrl+F4	▪ Close workbook
Ctrl+1	▪ Open format cells dialog box
Tab	▪ To move to the next cell
Shift + Tab	▪ To move to the previous cell
Ctrl + Tab	▪ Move between Two or more open Excel files.
Shift+F11	▪ Insert new worksheet
Ctrl+Shift+U	▪ Expand/collapse formula bar
Ctrl+Shift++	▪ Insert a new row
Ctrl+-	▪ Delete row
Ctrl+Page Up/ Page Down	▪ Move between worksheets
Alt+=	▪ AutoSum
Alt+W+F/R	▪ Freeze Panes
Ctrl+;	▪ Insert current date
Ctrl+Shift+:	▪ Insert current time
Home	▪ Move to the beginning of the row
Ctrl+Home	▪ Move to the beginning of the worksheet
Ctrl+End	▪ Move to the last cell with data
Ctrl+G/ F5	▪ Go to specific cell
Alt+Enter	▪ Add line break within a cell
Ctrl+Spacebar	▪ Select entire column
Shift+Spacebar	▪ Select entire row
Ctrl + Arrow key	▪ Move to next section of text.
F2	▪ Edit the selected cell.
F3	▪ After a name has been created, F3 will paste names.
F4	▪ Repeat last action.
F5	▪ Goes to a specific cell
F7	▪ Spell checks the selected text or document.
F11	▪ Create chart from selected data.
Ctrl + Shift + %	▪ Apply percentage format
Alt + H + B + A	▪ Add border to selected cells
Ctrl + T	▪ Convert selected cells to a table

Facts Drive

- **$ sign** locks the cells location to a fixed position.
- Latest version of excel have 16384 **columns** (labeled as A to XFD) and 1048576 **rows**.
- **Freeze Panes** feature in MS Excel allows you to lock specific rows and columns in place so that they remain visible while you scroll.
- **Pivot Tables** are used to summarize, analyze and explore large sets of data, making it easier to generate reports.
- **Macros** in Excel allow users to automate repetitive tasks by recording a sequence of actions, saving time and reducing errors.
- The **VLOOKUP** (Vertical Lookup) function in MS Excel searches for a value in the first column of a table or range and returns a value from a specified column in the same row.

PYQs Oneliner

1. **255** is the maximum length of characters that can be accommodated in a column in MS Excel 2003. ***SSC CGL (T-II) 18.01.2025***
2. **TODAY()** function is used for today's date in MS-Excel 2019. ***CPCT 2024***
3. Rows in MS-Excel are identified by **numbers**. ***SSC CHSL 2024***
4. In MS-Excel 2019, an entire worksheet can be selected by pressing the keyboard shortcut **Ctrl + A**. ***CPCT 2024***
5. **NOW()** function returns the serial number of the current date and time in MS-Excel. ***CPCT 2024***
6. Each cell in the worksheet of MS-Excel is identified by a cell **reference**. ***SSC CGL 2023***
7. Microsoft Excel file is saved with the **.xlsx** file extension. ***CPCT 2023***
8. **3** will be the result of MS Excel formula =FLOOR(5, 3). ***Delhi Police Constable 2020***

Practice Exercise

Introduction to Microsoft Excel

1. Microsoft Excel file is saved with the .... file extension. *CPCT 2023*
(a) .xlsx (b) .bmp
(c) .doc (d) .pptx

2. What happens when a user inserts a new row into an MS Excel worksheet? *SSC CGL (T-II) 20.01.2025*
(a) The existing rows are shifted to the right.
(b) The existing data in the row is overwritten.
(c) The existing rows are shifted down.
(d) The new row is added at the bottom of the worksheet.

3. There are three types of data found in a spreadsheet *CPCT 2024*
(a) Number, text and logical
(b) Data, words and object
(c) Data, numbers and labels
(d) Equation, data and object

4. An MS-Excel macro-enabled workbook has the filename extension .... *CPCT 2024*
(a) .xls (b) .xlsm
(c) .xlss (d) .xlsx

5. What is the maximum length of characters that can be accommodated in a column in MS Excel 2003? *SSC CGL (T-II) 18.01.2025*
(a) 512 characters (b) 65536 characters
(c) 1064 characters (d) 255 characters

6. What is the default alignment of numbers in an Excel cell? *IBPS Clerk 2020*
(a) Left (b) Right (c) Center (d) Justify

7. The default width of a column in MS Excel is
(a) 7 characters (b) 9 characters *SSC CHSL 2024*
(c) 8 characters (d) 6 characters

8. What will happen when you select the cell contents of a particular row in MS-Excel and then click the Delete button? *SSC CHSL 2024*
(a) Entries in all the selected cells will be deleted.
(b) Only first three cells will be deleted.
(c) Entire row will be deleted.
(d) First five cell entries will be deleteed.

9. Which of the following is not an alignment option for text in a cell? *SSC CGL 2024*
(a) Center (b) Right
(c) Justified (d) Left

10. Rows in MS-Excel are identified by *SSC CHSL 2024*
(a) letters (b) numbers with letters
(c) numbers (d) timings

Terms Related to MS Excel

11. Which of the following is a predesigned spreadsheet in MS-Excel, that can be used to create a new workbook quickly? *CPCT 2024*
(a) Pivot table (b) Template
(c) Microsoft Account (d) Ribbon

12. In Microsoft Excel, a pivot table is used to .... *CPCT 2024*
(a) record a sequence of steps
(b) repeat a sequence of steps
(c) summarise data in a table
(d) test data in a table

13. What is the intersection of a row and a column in Excel called? *SSC CGL 2020*
(a) Chart (b) Cell (c) Table (d) Range

Main Components of MS Excel Window

14. Which component of the Excel window is used to enter or edit the data in a selected cell?
(a) Formula Bar (b) Status Bar
(c) Ribbon (d) Title Bar

15. Where can you find options like Home, Insert and View in Excel?
(a) Formula Bar (b) Ribbon
(c) Status Bar (d) Task Pane

16. What is the area called where you can see the current cell address (like A1)?
(a) Status Bar (b) Formula Bar
(c) Name Box (d) Title Bar

17. What is the name of the bar that shows the file name and the application name?
(a) Formula Bar (b) Title Bar
(c) Ribbon (d) Scroll Bar

18. What are the rectangular boxes in an Excel worksheet called?
(a) Columns (b) Rows (c) Cells (d) Sheets

19. What is the default name of a new worksheet in Excel?
(a) Sheet1 (b) Workbook1
(c) Excel1 (d) NewSheet

Open, Insert, Rename, Move Excel Workbook

20. How can you rename an Excel worksheet?
(a) Double-click on the worksheet tab
(b) Right-click on the tab and select "Rename"
(c) Use the Name Box
(d) Both (a) and (b)

21. To move a worksheet within the same workbook, what is the easiest way to do it?
(a) Copy and paste the data
(b) Drag the worksheet tab to the desired location
(c) Use the Cut command
(d) Use the Name Box

22. When you insert a new worksheet, where does it appear by default?
(a) To the left of all existing sheets
(b) To the right of the currently active sheet
(c) As the first sheet in the workbook
(d) In a new workbook

23. Which of the following can you do in the Move or Copy dialog box?
(a) Delete a worksheet
(b) Protect a worksheet
(c) Move a worksheet to a new workbook
(d) Change the worksheet tab color

24. How can you insert a blank row at the top of a worksheet? ***SSC CHSL 2024***
(a) Right click on the row number and select Insert.
(b) Drag the mouse on the row border to select the row and click Insert in the cells group on the Home tab.
(c) Click on the row number and press the Insert key on the keyboard.
(d) Click on the row number and press the Delete key on the keyboard.

Main Functions Used in MS Excel

25. The correct syntax for the SUM function in Microsoft Excel is .... ***CPCT 2024***
(a) =SUM(C1.C2.C3) (b) SUM(C1,C2,C3)
(c) SUM(C1+C2+C3) (d) =SUM(C1+C2+C3)

26. What is the purpose of sorting data in Microsoft Excel 365? ***Delhi Police Constable 2023***
(a) Arranging data in a specific order based on values
(b) Creating charts and graphs
(c) Calculating the average of data
(d) Applying formatting only to cells

27. What will be the result of the following MS Excel formula?
=FLOOR(5, 3) ***Delhi Police Constable 2020***
(a) 4 (b) 0
(c) 5 (d) 3

28. In Microsoft Excel, which of the following is not a valid function? ***RSMSSB LDC 2025***
(a) Count Numbers (b) Average
(c) Merge (d) Sum

29. Suppose there is a table in MS-Excel 2019 containing marks of students of a class. If we want to filter the data in the table to display only the details of students who scored more than 70 marks, the .... option is used.
(a) sort (b) custom sort
(c) filter (d) custom select

30. Which among the following MS-Excel function converts a serial number to a minute? ***CPCT 2023***
(a) MIN (b) MINUTE
(c) MINA (d) MINVERSE

31. Which MS-Excel 2019 function is used to return the seconds of a time value? ***CPCT 2024***
(a) SECOND() (b) VLOOKUP()
(c) FIXED() (d) FIND()

32. In MS-Excel, to change the reference from relative to absolute, you need to add the .... sign before the column notation and the row number. ***CPCT 2024***
(a) $ (b) @ (c) # (d) *

33. In MS-Excel, the .... function removes the duplicate spaces and spaces at the start and end of a text string. ***CPCT 2024***
(a) MID (b) ROUND
(c) TRIM (d) TRUNC

34. Which function returns the serial number of the current date and time in MS-Excel? ***CPCT 2024***
(a) DATE function (b) NOW function
(c) TODAY function (d) CURDATE function

35. In an MS-Excel formula, the range of cells from E2 to E10 are denoted by .... ***CPCT 2024***
(a) E2.E10 (b) E2..E10
(c) E2:E10 (d) E2_E10

36. Which of the following Excel formula will find out the minimum value from the range D1 to D6? ***CPCT 2024***
(a) =MIN(D1:D6) (b) MIN(D1:D6)
(c) =MINIMUM(D1:D6) (d) MINIMUM(D1:D6)

37. In Microsoft Excel, a formula should always be preceded by a/an .... sign. ***CPCT 2024***
(a) $ (b) =
(c) * (d) #

38. Which among the following is the function for today's date in MS-Excel 2019? ***CPCT 2024***
(a) DAY() (b) DAYS()
(c) TODAY() (d) WEEKDAY()

39. Which function returns the most frequently occurring or repetitive, value in an array or range of data in MS-Excel 2019? ***CPCT 2024***
(a) MCM function (b) MODE function
(c) MCV function (d) MCOM function

40. In Excel, which function is used to round off numbers to a specified number of decimal places? ***RRB NTPC 2019***
(a) ROUND() (b) TRUNCATE()
(c) FLOOR() (d) CEILING()

41. What is the value of expression '=8*(5+3)-8/2' using the order in which MS Excel 2019 performs operations in formulas? ***CPCT 2024***
(a) 8 (b) 60
(c) 28 (d) 58

42. In Microsoft Excel 2019, to add all numbers greater than 7 in a range, we may use .... ***CPCT 2024***
(a) =SUM(range, >7) (b) =SUM(range, ">7")
(c) =SUMIF(range, ">7") (d) =SUMIF(range, "7")

43. The .... function returns the smallest value in a set of values in MS-Excel 2019. ***CPCT 2024***
(a) MAX (b) MIN
(c) AVG (d) LEAST

44. The Product function in Microsoft Excel 2019 .... ***CPCT 2024***
(a) accepts exactly two arguments
(b) multiplies the first two numbers given as arguments
(c) expects three arguments
(d) multiplies all the numbers given as arguments

45. Which formula is used to find the average of a range of cells in Excel? ***SSC CPO 2020***
(a) =AVERAGE(A1) (b) =SUM(A1)
(c) =COUNT(A1) (d) =MAX(A1)

46. In Excel, which function is used to count the number of non-empty cells in a range? ***SSC MTS 2021***
(a) COUNTIF() (b) COUNTA()
(c) COUNTBLANK() (d) COUNT()

47. In Excel, what is the purpose of the Freeze Panes option? ***SSC Stenographer 2022***
(a) To hide a worksheet
(b) To lock rows or columns in place while scrolling
(c) To split the worksheet into two parts
(d) To merge cells

48. What does the function COUNT() do in MS Excel 2010? ***SSC CGL (T-II) 20.01.2025***
(a) Prints the number of cells
(b) Counts the number of cells
(c) Duplicates the number of cells
(d) Stores the number of cells

49. Which of the following functions can be used to round a number down to the nearest integer? ***IBPS PO 2020***
(a) ROUNDUP() (b) ROUNDDOWN()
(c) INT() (d) CEILING()

50. Which MS Excel function can be used to sum up the numbers entered in a group of cells? ***SSC CHSL 2024***
(a) COUNT (b) AVERAGE
(c) MAX (d) SUM

51. Which function is used to calculate the maximum value in a selected column in MS Excel? ***SSC CHSL 2024***
(a) Auto max (b) High
(c) Max (d) Auto high

Charts in MS Excel

52. .... chart in Microsoft Excel plots two groups of numbers as one series of XY coordinates. ***CPCT 2023***
(a) An area (b) A pie
(c) A scatter (d) A stock

53. Which of the following is used to create a chart in Excel? ***FCI Assistant Grade III 2020***
(a) Insert > Table
(b) Insert > Chart
(c) Data > Sort
(d) File > New

54. Which of the following chart types is best suited for displaying trends over time in Excel? ***UPSC EPFO 2019***
(a) Bar Chart
(b) Line Chart
(c) Pie Chart
(d) Scatter Plot

55. In Microsoft Excel, which chart type is best suited for comparing proportions or percentages of a whole? ***SSC CHSL (T-I) 2024***
(a) Pie chart (b) Bar chart
(c) Scatter chart (d) Line chart

Shortcut Keys in Excel

56. The keyboard shortcut to undo the previous action in MS-Excel is .... ***CPCT 2024***
(a) Ctrl + D (b) Ctrl + U
(c) Ctrl + X (d) Ctrl + Z

57. In MS-Excel 2019, an entire worksheet can be selected by pressing the keyboard shortcut .... ***CPCT 2024***
(a) Ctrl + A (b) Ctrl + Enter
(c) Ctrl + F1 (d) Ctrl + F8

58. What is the shortcut key to insert a new worksheet in Excel? ***SSC CHSL 2019***
(a) Ctrl + W (b) Ctrl + N
(c) Shift + F11 (d) Alt + Insert

59. In MS Excel 365, which of the following keyboard shortcuts is used to manually auto fit row height in MS Excel? *Delhi Police Constable 2023*
(a) Alt + O + C + W
(b) Alt + H + O + A
(c) Alt + O + C + N
(d) Alt + H + O + H

60. Which of the following shortcut is used to close an open workbook in MS-Excel 365? *SSC CHSL 2023*
(a) Ctrl + X
(b) Ctrl + W
(c) Ctrl + L
(d) Ctrl + C

61. What does the shortcut key Ctrl + D do in Excel? *RBI Assistant 2022*
(a) Deletes the selected cells
(b) Fills down the content of the selected cells to other cells
(c) Duplicates the workbook
(d) Opens the Format Cells dialog box

62. In MS Excel 365, which of the following shortcut key is correct to open a spreadsheet in MS-Excel? *Delhi Police Constable 2023*
(a) Press Ctrl + N
(b) Press Alternate + O
(c) Press Ctrl + O
(d) Press Alternate + N

63. Which is the correct keyboard shortcut for adjusting the column width in MS Excel? *SSC CGL (T-II) 18.01.2025*
(a) Shift + H + O + W (b) Alt + H + O + W
(c) Ctrl + O + W + H (d) Ctrl + H + O + W

64. Which of the following keyboard shortcut in MS-Excel 2019 display the Create Table dialog box? *CPCT 2024*
(a) Ctrl + L (b) Alt + T
(c) Ctrl + Shift + T (d) Ctrl + Alt + L

65. In MS-Excel 365 which of the following shortcut is used to copy the contents and format of the topmost cell of a selected range into the cells below? *SSC CHSL 2021*
(a) Alt + D (b) Ctrl + D
(c) Alt + C (d) Ctrl + C

66. A key is used to edit current cell?
(a) F1 (b) F2
(c) F5 (d) F6

67. Shortcut key to underline a text in MS Excel.
(a) Ctrl + P (b) Ctrl + B
(c) Ctrl +U (d) None of these

68. Which shortcut key is used to apply outline borders?
(a) Ctrl + Shift + 7
(b) Shift + F1
(c) Ctrl + F5
(d) Shift + 7

Answers

1.	(a)	2.	(c)	3.	(a)	4.	(b)	5.	(d)	6.	(b)	7.	(c)	8.	(a)	9.	(c)	10.	(c)
11.	(b)	12.	(c)	13.	(b)	14.	(a)	15.	(b)	16.	(c)	17.	(b)	18.	(c)	19.	(a)	20.	(d)
21.	(b)	22.	(b)	23.	(c)	24.	(a)	25.	(d)	26.	(a)	27.	(d)	28.	(c)	29.	(c)	30.	(b)
31.	(a)	32.	(a)	33.	(c)	34.	(b)	35.	(c)	36.	(a)	37.	(b)	38.	(c)	39.	(b)	40.	(a)
41.	(b)	42.	(c)	43.	(b)	44.	(d)	45.	(a)	46.	(b)	47.	(b)	48.	(b)	49.	(c)	50.	(d)
51.	(c)	52.	(c)	53.	(b)	54.	(b)	55.	(a)	56.	(d)	57.	(a)	58.	(c)	59.	(b)	60.	(b)
61.	(b)	62.	(c)	63.	(b)	64.	(a)	65.	(b)	66.	(b)	67.	(c)	68.	(a)				

Microsoft PowerPoint

- PowerPoint is a **presentation software** developed by **Microsoft**.
- Its first version was released in 1990.
- It is the part of **microsoft office suite**.
- It is widely used for creating engaging and interactive presentations for educational, business and personal purposes.
- With PowerPoint, users can easily create slideshow presentation.
- It is also called **slide presentation software**.
- The file extension for MS PowerPoint slides is .pptx (newer versions) and .ppt (older versions).

In this Chapter

- Terms Related to PowerPoint
- Main Components of PowerPoint Window
- PowerPoint Views

How to start MS PowerPoint?

- Click on Start button → All Programs → MS Office → MS PowerPoint.

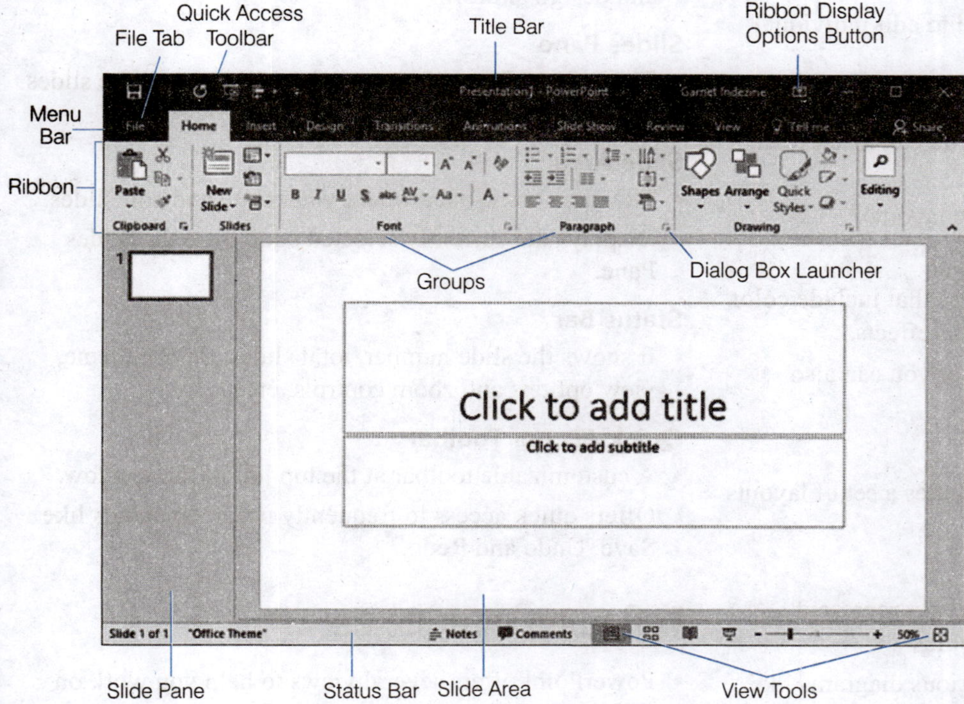

"Vision isn't a template in PowerPoint."

~ Roger McNamee

Terms Related to PowerPoint

Slide

- It is a **single page** or **screen** in a presentation.
- It can contain text, images, graphics, charts and videos.

Slide Layout

- Slide Layout refers to the arrangement of elements like text boxes, images, charts, tables and other content on a slide.
- PowerPoint offers several pre-defined slide layouts, such as Title Slide, Title and Content, Two Content and more.

Transition

- Visual effects that occur when moving from one slide to another is called transition.
- It adds a professional touch to presentations and keeps the audience engaged.

Animation

- Visual effect applied to text, images and objects within a slide.
- It allows content to appear, move and disappear in a controlled manner.

Slide Master

- It is a powerful feature that controls the overall design of slides in a presentation.
- It saves time by eliminating the need to edit individual slides repeatedly.

Placeholder

- A predefined area on a slide where you can insert text, images or videos.
- It is used to maintain consistent slide layouts.

Theme

- A theme is a set of pre-designed styles that include color schemes, fonts, background styles and effects.
- PowerPoint offers built-in themes, but you can also customize them.

Template

- A pre designed presentation that includes a set of layouts themes and placeholder content.

SmartArt

- SmartArt is a tool that helps you visually represent information using pre-designed graphics.
- It allows you to convert text into various diagrams like lists, flowcharts, hierarchies, cycles and more.

Slide Show

- A slide show is a visual presentation mode where slides are displayed one after another on the full screen.
- It is used to showcase your content in a sequential and engaging way.

Speaker Notes

- It is a section at the bottom of each slide for adding extra information for the presenter.
- Only visible to the presenter in Presenter View, keeping the audience focused on the main content.

Main Components of PowerPoint Window

Title Bar

- It is located at the top of the window.
- It displays the name of the current presentation, followed by the name of the program.
- Also includes buttons to minimize, maximize and close the window.

Ribbon

- A toolbar with multiple tabs like Home, Insert, Design, etc.
- Commands on the Ribbon allow you to insert, format and design slides.

Slides Pane

- This area of Power Point window displays all the slides that are added in the presentation.

Slide Area

- The main workspace where you create and edit slides.
- Displays the currently selected slide from the Slides Pane.

Status Bar

- It shows the slide number, total slides, design theme, view options and zoom controls, etc.

Quick Access Toolbar

- A customizable toolbar at the top left of the window.
- Offers quick access to frequently used commands like Save, Undo and Redo.

PowerPoint Views

- PowerPoint offers several views to help you work on different aspects of your presentation.

Main PowerPoint Views

View	Description
Normal View	▪ This is the default view and the main workspace for editing slides.
Slide Sorter View	▪ Displays all slides in a thumbnail view, making it easy to rearrange and organize them.
Reading View	▪ A presentation view that allows you to preview your slides without entering the slideshow. ▪ Shows the slides in full-screen mode.
Slide Show View	▪ It is used to display presentation on full-screen.
Notes Page View	▪ Shows each slide with its associated speaker notes beneath it. ▪ Allows you to edit or add notes for the presenter.
Master Views (Slide Master, Notes Master, Handout Master)	▪ **Slide Master View** Used for setting the overall design and layout of the slides. Changes made here apply to all slides in the presentation. ▪ **Notes Master View** Lets you customize the appearance of notes pages. ▪ **Handout Master View** Customizes the layout of handouts that will be printed for the audience.

Shortcut Keys in PowerPoint

Shortcut	Function
Ctrl + N	▪ Create a new presentation document
Ctrl + O	▪ Open a previously saved presentation
Ctrl + S	▪ Save a presentation
Ctrl + M	▪ Insert new slide
Alt + F2 or F12	▪ Open the Save As dialog box
Ctrl + W or Ctrl + F4	▪ Close a presentation
Ctrl + Q	▪ Save and close a presentation
Ctrl + F2	▪ Print preview view
Alt or F10	▪ Turn the key tips ON or OFF
Alt + F	▪ Access the file tab menu
Alt + H	▪ Go to the home tab
Alt + N	▪ Go to the insert tab
Alt + G	▪ Go to the Design tab
Alt + K	▪ Go to the Transitions tab
Alt + A	▪ Go to the Animations tab
Alt + S	▪ Go to the Slide Show tab
Alt + R	▪ Go to the Review tab
Alt + W	▪ Go to the View tab
Alt + X	▪ Go to the Add-ins tab
F5	▪ Start presentation from the First slide
Shift + F5	▪ Start presentation from the Current slide
Alt + N, X	▪ Insert a text box
Ctrl + Home	▪ Go to the first slide
Ctrl + End	▪ Go to the last slide
Ctrl + D	▪ Duplicate the current slide
Shift + F9	▪ Show/Hide gridlines
Ctrl + K	▪ Insert hyperlink
Ctrl + Shift + N	▪ Apply the normal slide layout

Facts Drive

- In PowerPoint, the minimum zoom percentage is **10%** and the maximum zoom percentage is **400%.**
- Printed version of slides provided to the audience for reference is called **handouts**.
- PowerPoint's default orientation is **landscape**.
- **Greyscale** is a variety of shades of grey without apparent colors.
- **Trigger** is defined as an object or item that performs an action on the slide when we click the mouse.
- In MS-PowerPoint we can add many types of image and sound format such as .gif, .bmp, .png, .jpg, .giv, .wav, .mid etc
- **Slide timing** is the time period that a slide appears on the screen.
- **Window group** is used to work on more than one presentation at a time.

PYQs Oneliner

1. You can exit a slide show and return to editing mode by pressing **Escape Key** in MS PowerPoint. ***SSC CGL (T-II) 20.01.2025***
2. **Normal View** is useful for editing or formatting a single slide at a time. ***SS CHSL 2024***
3. **Title Slide** is the default layout of the first slide in a new PowerPoint Presentation. ***SSC CHSL 2020***
4. **Slide Sorter** feature in PowerPoint allows you to rearrange slides in a presentation. ***RRB PO 2020***
5. **Normal View** allows you to create, edit and view the layout of slides at the same time. ***SBI Clerk 2020***
6. **F5** keyboard shortcut is used to start a slide show from the first slide in MS PowerPoint. ***IBPS PO 2019***
7. **Themes** in MS PowerPoint allows you to create a presentation based on pre-designed templates. ***SSC CHSL 2019***
8. In PowerPoint **Slide Master** feature allows you to apply a consistent style to text across all slides. ***SBI PO Prelims 2019***

Practice Exercise

Introduction to Microsoft PowerPoint

1. The presentation in Microsoft PowerPoint is saved with ……… extension. *CPCT 2024*
   (a) .ptpx (b) .pptx (c) .pttx (d) .tppx

2. What we have to type in the Run dialog box to open Powerpoint?
   (a) Powerpoint (b) PowerPoint
   (c) Pwrpoint (d) Powerpnt

3. We can create a new presentation in powerpoint from-
   (a) Blank presentation
   (b) From existing presentation
   (c) Both (a) and (b)
   (d) Neither (a) nor (b)

4. What is the primary advantage of being able to insert and delete slides in an MS PowerPoint presentation? *SSC CGL (T-II) 18.01.2025*
   (a) To enable the addition of multimedia content
   (b) To allow for dynamic content adjustment and organisation
   (c) To enhance slide transitions
   (d) To apply different templates to individual slides

5. Which of the following is a valid way to create a new slide in PowerPoint? *RRB Office Assistant Prelims 2019*
   (a) Right-click the slide sorter and select new slide
   (b) Press Ctrl + M
   (c) Click on Insert > New Slide
   (d) All of the above

6. In PPT, what method can be used to move among slides if your hands are already on the keyboard? *SSC CHSL 2024*
   (a) Pressing the escape key to exit the presentation
   (b) Using the keyboard direction key
   (c) Scrolling with the mouse wheel
   (d) Clicking on the slide thumbnail in the slides tab

7. The slide number can be added to each slide of the MS PowerPoint presentation from which of the following? *SSC CHSL 2024*
   (a) Page formatting (b) View
   (c) Footer (d) Table design

8. What are the correct steps for creating a blank presentation in MS PowerPoint? *SSC CGL (T-II) 20.01.2025*
   (a) File -> New -> Blank Presentation
   (b) File -> Blank Presentation -> New
   (c) New -> Blank Presentation -> File
   (d) Blank Presentation -> New -> File

9. Which of the following is the by default page orientation of slides in PowerPoint?
   (a) Portrait (b) Landscape
   (c) Vertical (d) A4

Terms Related to PowerPoint

10. Which of the following is not a valid slide layout in MS-PowerPoint 2019? *CPCT 2024*
    (a) Title Slide (b) Title and Content
    (c) Section Header (d) Paragraph Header

11. Which of the following is called as page to create a presentation in PowerPoint?
    (a) Sheet (b) Slide
    (c) Paper (d) None of these

12. In PowerPoint, the objects on the slide used to hold different objects are called as
    (a) placeholders (b) textbox
    (c) text holders (d) None of these

13. The special effects in a PowerPoint presentation used to introduce slides are called as
    (a) effect (b) transitions
    (c) slide animation (d) custom animation

14. What is the main purpose of using a template when creating a presentation in MS PowerPoint? *SSC CGL (T-II) 18.01.2025*
    (a) To ensure consistency and professionalism
    (b) To automatically insert multimedia content
    (c) To add complex animations easily
    (d) To create interactive quizzes within slides

15. Which of the following is the collection of design choices, including special effects, colors and fonts?
    (a) Data (b) Theme
    (c) Slide (d) None of these

16. In PowerPoint, which of the following is used to apply a transition effect between slides? *IBPS PO 2020*
    (a) Slide Master (b) Animation Pane
    (c) Design Tab (d) Transitions Tab

17. Which of the following is a valid method to start a PowerPoint presentation as a slideshow? *SSC CGL 2018*
    (a) Press F5
    (b) Right-click on the first slide and Select Show
    (c) Click the Slide Show tab and select From Beginning
    (d) All of the above

18. Which of the following is used to apply a visual effect to text or objects in PowerPoint? ***RRB Assistant 2020***
(a) Animations (b) Transitions
(c) Slide Master (d) Slide Show

19. How can we add text to a slide in MS PowerPoint?
(a) Note box (b) Dialogue box ***SSC CHSL 2024***
(c) Notes pages (d) Textbox

20. Which feature in PowerPoint is used to apply motion effects to text and objects?
(a) Transition (b) Animation
(c) Slide layout (d) Slide design

21. Which of the following is not a slide layout option?
(a) Title slide (b) Content slide
(c) Blank slide (d) Page layout

22. The file which consists of readymade styles that we can easily use for our presentations is known as
(a) Template (b) Wizard
(c) Auto style (d) Pre-formatting

23. Object on the slide that hold text are known as
(a) Object holders (b) Text holders
(c) Place holders (d) Auto layouts

Main Components of PowerPoint Window

24. In Microsoft-PowerPoint, if you choose...... a new presentation is displayed using the design selected by the user, consisting of a single slide. ***HSSC 2021***
(a) Tool bar (b) Design template
(c) Menu bar (d) Status bar

25. Which of the following is the default standard layout in PowerPoint?
(a) Blank slide (b) Title and content slide
(c) Title slide (d) None of these

PowerPoint Views

26. Which of the following is used to see all slides at once?
(a) Using slide sorter view (b) Using slide view
(c) Using normal view (d) None of these

27. Which of the following is not a type of view in PowerPoint?
(a) Slide show (b) Slide sorter
(c) Normal (d) None of these

28. In which of the following menu, the slide sorter view is available in PowerPoint?
(a) Insert (b) View
(c) Design (d) Animations

29. Which of the following view in PowerPoint is used to add comments?
(a) Slide sorter view (b) Notes page view
(c) Normal view (d) None of these

30. Which view in PowerPoint displays a small thumbnail of each slide for easy navigation? ***RRB PO 2018***
(a) Slide Show (b) Normal View
(c) Slide Sorter View (d) Outline View

31. What feature in MS PowerPoint allows you to apply a consistent style to text across all slides? ***SBI PO Prelims 2019***
(a) Slide Master (b) Format Painter
(c) PowerPoint Wizard (d) Animation Pane

32. Which view in MS PowerPoint is useful for editing or formatting a single slide at a time? ***SSC CHSL 2024***
(a) Reading view (b) Slide sorter view
(c) Outline view (d) Normal view

33. Which option is used to view PowerPoint slides with notes?
(a) Outline view (b) Slide master
(c) Notes page (d) Handout

34. Which of the following view in PowerPoint is used to deliver a presentation?
(a) Normal view
(b) Slide sorter view
(c) Slide show view
(d) Outline view

35. What is the purpose of the outline view in PowerPoint?
(a) To edit slide titles and main text quickly
(b) To see all slides thumbnails
(c) To apply transitions between slides
(d) To rehearse slide timings

36. Which of the following is not a view option available in Microsoft Power Point? ***RSMSSB LDC 2025***
(a) Normal (b) Outline View
(c) Print Preview (d) Reading View

Shortcut Keys in PowerPoint

37. Which of the following keyboard combination is used to insert a text box in a PowerPoint presentation? ***DSSSB Patwari 2022***
(a) Alt+N,X (b) Alt+N,J
(c) Alt+O,B (d) Alt+O,S

38. Which of the following keyboard combination is used to add a new slide in an existing PowerPoint 2019 presentation? ***DSSSB Patwari 2022***
(a) CTRL+M (b) CTRL+X
(c) CTRL+N (d) CTRL+B

39. Which of the following shortcut key is used to start the slideshow?
(a) F5 key (b) F3 key
(c) F1 key (d) F6 key

40. Which of the following is the shortcut key to insert a new slide between the current presentation?
(a) Ctrl + N (b) Ctrl + K
(c) Ctrl + M (d) Ctrl + O

41. Which of the following shortcut key is used to stop the slide show?
(a) Esc key (b) Ctrl + O
(c) Ctrl + N (d) Ctrl + K

42. How can you exit a slide show and return to editing mode in MS PowerPoint? *SSC CGL (T-II) 20.01.2025*
(a) Press Ctrl + S
(b) Press Esc
(c) Press Spacebar
(d) Press Alt + Tab

43. What happens when you select first and second slide and then try to insert the new slide?
(a) New slide will be inserted as first slide
(b) New slide will be inserted as last slide
(c) New slide will be inserted as third slide
(d) None of these

44. What is the shortcut key to insert a hyperlink in the slide?
(a) Ctrl + H
(b) Ctrl + K
(c) Ctrl + A
(d) Not possible to insert hyperlinks

45. Which of the following is the shortcut key used to start the presentation from the current slide?
(a) F5 (b) Shift + F5
(c) Ctrl + F5 (d) None of these

46. Which of the following shortcut key is used for help in PowerPoint?
(a) F1 (b) F2 (c) F3 (d) F4

47. Which of the following shortcut key is used to add a new blank slide to an existing presentation of MS-PowerPoint? *SSC CHSL 2023*
(a) Ctrl + N (b) Ctrl + Alt + M
(c) Ctrl + M (d) Ctrl + Alt + N

48. Which of the following shortcut key is used to show or hide the grid in PowerPoint?
(a) Shift + F9 (b) Shift + F1
(c) Shift + F2 (d) None of these

49. In PowerPoint, what is the shortcut to duplicate a slide?
(a) Ctrl+D (b) Ctrl+N (c) Ctrl+M (d) Ctrl+C

50. Which shortcut key is used to close PowerPoint?
(a) Ctrl+W (b) Alt+F4
(c) Ctrl+Q (d) All of these

51. What is the shortcut key to add a new text box in PowerPoint?
(a) Ctrl+N (b) Ctrl+X
(c) Ctrl+Shift+T (d) Alt+N,X

Answers

1.	(b)	2.	(d)	3.	(c)	4.	(b)	5.	(d)	6.	(b)	7.	(c)	8.	(a)	9.	(b)	10.	(d)
11.	(b)	12.	(a)	13.	(b)	14.	(a)	15.	(b)	16.	(d)	17.	(d)	18.	(a)	19.	(d)	20.	(b)
21.	(d)	22.	(a)	23.	(c)	24.	(b)	25.	(c)	26.	(a)	27.	(d)	28.	(b)	29.	(b)	30.	(c)
31.	(a)	32.	(d)	33.	(c)	34.	(c)	35.	(a)	36.	(c)	37.	(a)	38.	(a)	39.	(a)	40.	(c)
41.	(a)	42.	(b)	43.	(c)	44.	(b)	45.	(b)	46.	(a)	47.	(c)	48.	(a)	49.	(a)	50.	(d)
51.	(d)																		

Database Concepts

- Data is a collection of a distinct small units of information.
- A database is an organized collection of data, designed to store, manage and access information.

Database Management System (DBMS)

- Database management system is a software which is used to manage the database.
- In DBMS, data is stored in tables, which consist of **rows** and **columns**.
- The first-ever DBMS, called **IDS** (Integrated Data Store), was developed in the 1960s by **Charles Bachman**.
- The world's first **relational DBMS** was invented by **Edgar F. Codd** in 1970.
- **Example** MySQL, Oracle, MongoDB, Microsoft Access, Fox Pro, MariaDB, Postgre SQL, Redis, Neo4j, Couchbase etc.

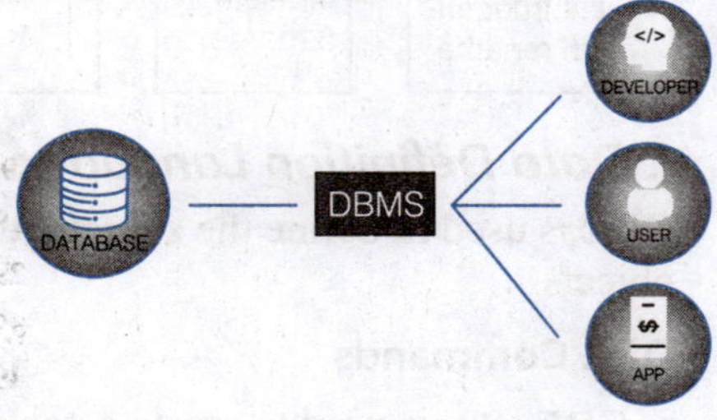

Functions of DBMS

- It provides data independence.
- It provides concurrency control.
- It provides recovery services and utility services.
- It provides a clear and logical view of the process that manipulates data.
- It provides data integrity management.

Uses of DBMS

- Airlines and Railways
- Education
- Human resources
- Banking
- Telecommunication
- Online retailers

Advantages of DBMS

- Minimal data redundancy
- User friendly
- Data security
- Fast data sharing

In this Chapter

- Database Management System (DBMS)
- Terms Related to DBMS
- DBMS Languages and their Commands
- Database Models
- Keys in DBMS
- Database Schema
- Database Storage Hierarchy

"In the 21st century, the database is the market place."

~ Stan Rapp

- Reduced development time and maintain need
- Easy retrieval of data
- Helps in decision making

Disadvantages of DBMS

- Performance issues
- Large in size
- Complexity
- Expensive
- Dependence of technology

Components of DBMS

The components of a Database Management System (DBMS) are as follows –

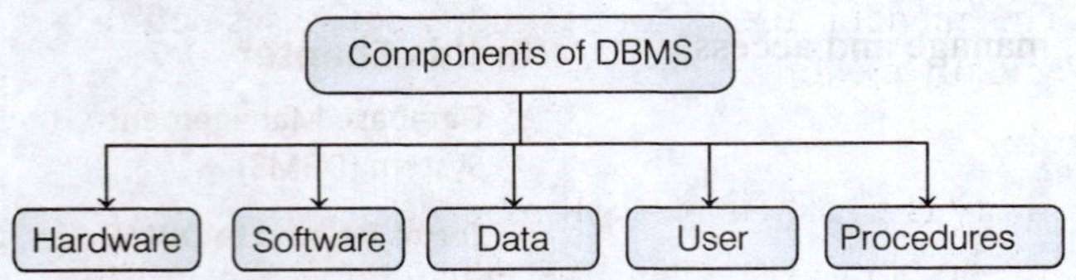

1. **Hardware** includes the **physical devices** used to store and access the database, such as servers, storage devices and network infrastructure.
2. **Software** refers to the DBMS software itself, which manages database operations and interacts with users and applications.
3. **Data** is the core component, including the actual data stored in the database and metadata (data about data).
4. **Users**
   (i) **End Users** People who interact with the database to query or update data.
   (ii) **Database Administrators (DBAs)** Person who manages the database and ensures performance and security.
   (iii) **Application Programmers** People who develop software to access and manipulate the database.
5. **Procedures** are guidelines or instructions for users on how to operate and manage the database efficiently.

Terms Related to DBMS

Term	Description
Field	▪ It is a single piece of data, also called a column in a table.
Record	▪ It is a complete set of related data, often referred to as a **row** in a table.
Attribute	▪ It is a property of an entity, represented as a **column** in a table.
Tuple	▪ A single row or record in a table, which contains values for each attribute.
Relation	▪ A table in a database, consisting of tuples (rows) and attributes (columns).
Degree	▪ The number of attributes (columns) in a relation (table).
Cardinality	▪ It refers to the number of tuples (rows) in a relation (table).
Meta Data	▪ Data about the data is called meta data.
Normalization	▪ The process of reducing redundancy is called normalisation.
Aggregation	▪ The process of combining two or more entities into single result.
Primary Key	▪ It is a unique identifier for each record in a table.

DBMS Languages and their Commands

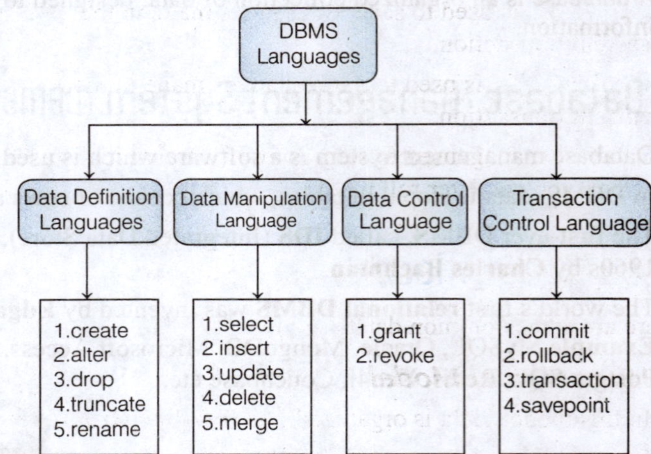

1. Data Definition Language (DDL)

DDL is used to define the **structure** of the database objects.

DDL Commands

- **CREATE** is used to create a new database object.
- **ALTER** is used to modify an existing database object.
- **DROP** is used to delete a database object.
- **TRUNCATE** is used to delete all rows from a table without deleting the table itself.
- **RENAME** is used to rename the objects in database.

2. Data Manipulation Language (DML)

DML is used for **managing data** within the tables.

Common DML Commands

- **SELECT** is used to retrieve data from one or more tables.
- **INSERT** is used to add new data into an existing table.
- **UPDATE** is used to modify existing data in a table.

- **DELETE** is used to remove data from a table.
- **MERGE** is used to join a source table object with target table.

3. Data Control Language (DCL)

DCL is used to **control access** data in the database.

Common DCL Commands

- **GRANT** is used to give user access to the database.
- **REVOKE** is used to remove previously granted permissions.

4. Transaction Control Language (TCL)

TCL is used to manage **transactions** in a database.

Common TCL Commands

- **COMMIT** is used to save all changes made in the current transaction.
- **ROLLBACK** is used to undo changes made in the current transaction.
- **SAVEPOINT** is used to set a point in a transaction to which you can later roll back.

Database Models

Here are some common database models.

1. Hierarchical Model

- In this model, data is organized in a **tree-like structure.**
- It uses one to many or parent-child relationship.
- It has single root to which all the other data is linked.
- This model uses **DML**.

2. Network Model

- It is an extension of the hierarchical model.
- This allows to have more than one parent nodes.
- It supports **many-to-many** relationships.
- This model uses both DDL as well as DML.

3. Relational Model

- This model stores data in tables (relations) with rows (tuples) and columns (attributes).
- It uses **primary keys** to uniquely identify rows in a table.

4. Object-Oriented Model

- The object-oriented model represents data as **objects**.
- This model has overcome the limitations of hierarchical, network and relational data model.

5. ER Model

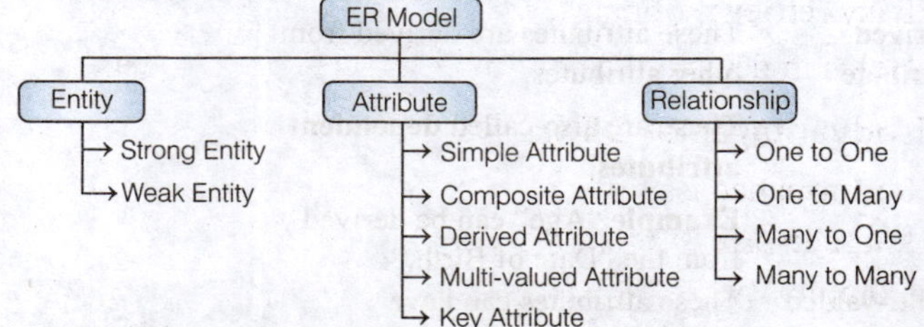

- The ER(Entity-Relationship) model is the logical representation of data as objects and relationships among them.
- These objects are known as **entities**.
- It follows the **top-down** approach.
- This model is useful for designing databases before actually creating them.

Entity

- Entity is a basic unit of ER model.
- It is an object that has its existence in the real world.
- Entity is represented as **rectangles** in ER diagrams.
- It is basically a group of attributes.

  Examples Student, Course, Employee.

  There are two types of entities

1. Strong Entity

- An entity that have a primary key is called **strong entity**.
- It is represented by a rectangle in ER diagrams.

2. Weak Entity

- An entity that does not have a primary key is called **weak entity**.
- It is represented by a double rectangle in ER diagrams.

Attributes

Attributes are the properties that define the entity type.

Attribute	Description	Representation Symbol
Simple Attribute	▪ Attributes that cannot be further divide into subparts. **Example** A student's "Age" or an employee's "Salary."	
Composite Attribute	▪ An attribute composed by many other attributes. **Example** A "Full Name" attribute can be divided into "First Name" and "Last Name."	Full Name, F. Name, L.Name

Attribute	Description	Representation Symbol
Derived Attribute	▪ These attributes are derived from other attributes. ▪ These are also called **dependent attributes.** **Example** "Age" can be derived from the "Date of Birth."	Age
Multi-valued Attribute	▪ These attributes can have multiple values for a single entity. **Example** A "Phone Number" attribute for a person, which can have multiple phone numbers.	Phone–No
Key Attribute	▪ These are attributes that uniquely identify an entity. **Example** A "Roll No" that uniquely identifies a student.	Roll–No

Relationship

- A relationship represents how two or more entities are related to each other.
- Relationships are represented by diamond in ER model.

Types of Relationship

One-to-One

- A single record in one entity is associated with a single record in another entity.

Example One person has one passport.

One-to-Many

- A single record in one entity is associated with multiple records in another entity.

Example A teacher can teach many students.

Many-to-One

- Multiple records in one entity are associated with a single record in another entity.
- Essentially the reverse of a one-to-many relationship.

Example Many employees work in one department.

Many-to-Many

- Multiple records in one entity are associated with multiple records in another entity.

Example Students can enroll in multiple courses and each course can have multiple students.

Keys in DBMS

The key is an **attribute** or **group of attributes** whose values can be used to uniquely identify an individual entity in a data set.

Types of keys

There are following types of keys-

Primary Key

- The primary key uniquely identifies each record in a table.
- It must contain **unique values.**
- It cannot contain **null values.**
- One table has only one primary key.

STUDENT_DETAILS

Roll-no	Name	Marks
101	X	34
102	Y	46
103	Z	94

Primary Key (Roll-no)

Secondary Key

- A secondary key is simply any index that is not the primary key of a table.
- It is also called **alternate key.**
- It doesn't always contain unique data.

STUDENT_DETAILS

Roll-no	Name	Marks
101	X	34
102	Y	46
103	Z	94

Primary Key (Roll-no); Secondary Key (Name, Marks)

Foreign Key

- It is a field in one table that refers to the primary key in another table.
- The table with foreign key is called the **child table.**
- It can have null values and may not be unique.

- It is also called **reference key.**

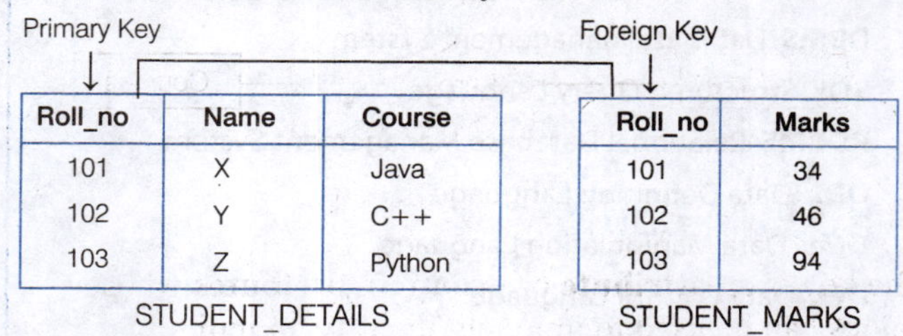

Roll_no	Name	Course
101	X	Java
102	Y	C++
103	Z	Python

STUDENT_DETAILS

Roll_no	Marks
101	34
102	46
103	94

STUDENT_MARKS

Candidate Key

- It can uniquely identify records in a table.
- A table can have multiple candidate keys, but one is selected as the primary key.
- Every candidate key is a **super key.**

STUDENT_DETAILS

Roll_no	Name	Registration_no
101	X	895
102	Y	564
103	Z	567

Candidate Key (Roll_no) — Candidate Key (Registration_no)

Alternate Key

- A candidate key that is not selected as the primary key is called alternate key.
- It provides a unique identifier for a record in a table as an alternative.

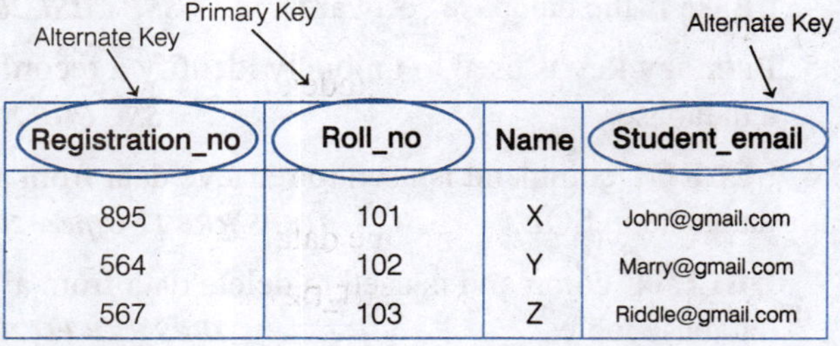

Registration_no	Roll_no	Name	Student_email
895	101	X	John@gmail.com
564	102	Y	Marry@gmail.com
567	103	Z	Riddle@gmail.com

Super Key

- It is a set of one or more attributes that can uniquely identify each record in a table.
- It contains multiple values.

Example Employee ID and Employee Aadhar Number together can form a Super Key, though Employee ID alone is sufficient.

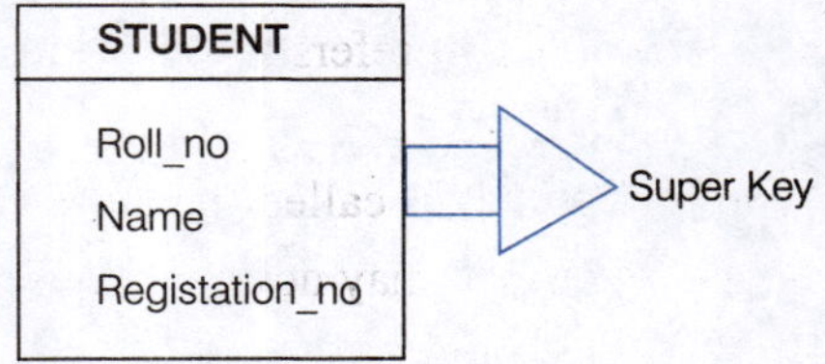

Composite Key

A key that uses two or more attributes to uniquely identify a record in a table.

Composite Key (Roll_no, Name)

Roll_no	Name	Age	City
101	X	24	Noida
102	Y	21	Delhi
103	Z	25	Kanpur

Database Schema

- A database schema is a **logical representation** of database that shows how the data in a database should be stored logically.
- There are three layers in database schema.

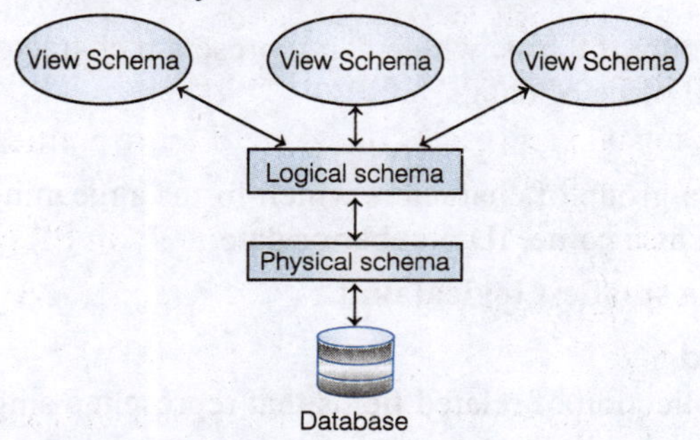

Physical Schema

- It describes how data is physically stored in the system.
- It is also called the **internal schema.**
- It deals with storage details like file systems, indexing and data retrieval methods.

Logical Schema

- It is also called **conceptual schema.**
- It defines the structure and relationships of data in a database.
- It focuses on how data is logically organized without considering the physical storage.

View Schema

- It is also called the **external schema.**
- It represents how the data is presented to different users or applications.
- It focuses on access control and user-specific views of the database.

Database Storage Hierarchy

- The database storage hierarchy refers to the arrangement of data storage in a database system, from the lowest to the highest level.

- It shows how data is organized in a structured manner to optimize storage and retrieval.

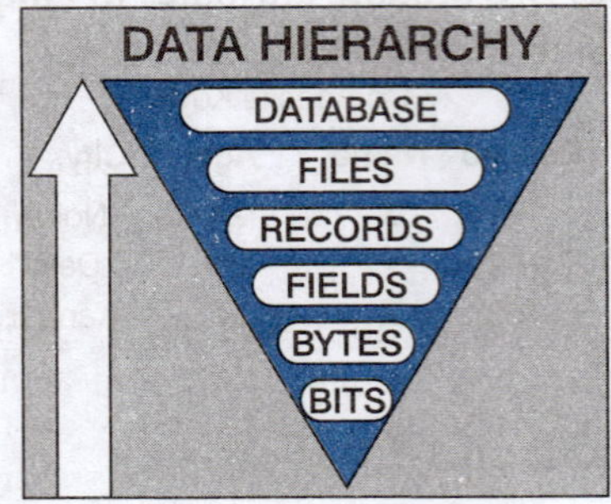

Bit
- The smallest unit of data, represented by a binary value (0 or 1).

Byte
- A group of 8 bits, which can represent a character or a small piece of data.

Field
- It is a group of characters which forms a meaningful data such as a name, ID number or date.
- It is a **smallest logical unit**.

Record
- A collection of related fields that represent a single entity is called a record or row.

File
- A collection of related records is called a file or table.

Database
- A collection of related files is called a database.

Facts Drive

- **SQL** is a computer language used to interact with relational database systems.
- SQL is also known as **fourth generation** language.
- In DBMS, **views** are virtual tables that display data from one or more actual tables without storing it.
- A **RDBMS** is a type of database that stores data in tables.
- **Null** is a special symbol that does not mean zero. It means the data is missing or unknown.

Important Abbreviations

DBMS Database Management System
SQL Structured Query Language
RDBMS Relational Database Management System
DDL Data Definition Language
DML Data Manipulation Language
DCL Data Control Language
TCL Transaction Control Language
ERD Entity-Relationship Diagram
PK Primary Key
FK Foreign Key
DBA Database Administrator

PYQs Oneliner

1. In database management system, **Data Manipulation Language (DML)** is a query language for accessing and manipulating data. ***SSC Selection Post 2023***
2. **Network database model** is represented using data graph. ***SSC Selection Post 2023***
3. **CREATE** is a command for Data Definition Language in SQL. ***SSC Selection Post 2023***
4. **dBase** is the database software. ***SSC CHSL 2023***
5. **Primary key** is used to uniquely identify a record in a database. ***SSC CGL 2020***
6. **SELECT** command is used to retrieve data from a database in SQL. ***IBPS RRB IT Officer 2020***
7. **DELETE** command is used to delete data from a database table. ***IBPS RRB PO 2020***
8. **TURNCATE** command is used to delete all rows in a table in SQL. ***IBPS Clerk 2019***
9. The full form of DBMS is **Database Management System.** ***IBPS RRB PO 2019***

Practice Exercise

Introduction to Database Management System

1. Which of the following is not a feature of DBMS? *IBPS RRB 2019*
(a) Data redundancy (b) Data integrity
(c) Data security (d) Data consistency

2. Which of the following is an example of a DBMS?
(a) Microsoft Excel (b) Oracle *UPSC CDS 2020*
(c) Notepad (d) PowerPoint

3. Which of the following is not a function of DBMS? *SSC CGL 2018*
(a) Data storage (b) Data retrieval
(c) Data manipulation (d) Data reporting

4. What is the primary function of a DBMS? *UPSC CDS 2018*
(a) Store and manage data (b) Create new applications
(c) Design user interfaces (d) Generate reports

5. Which of the following is an advantage of using DBMS? *IBPS PO 2020*
(a) Increased data redundancy
(b) Increased data inconsistency
(c) Enhanced data security
(d) Increased data duplication

6. A collection of interrelated files and a set of programs that allows users to access and modify these files is known as *RRB NTPC 2021*
(a) data analytic system
(b) database management systems
(c) data files
(d) system management

7. Which of the following is the organised collection of large amount of interrelated data stored in a meaningful way used for manipulation and updating?
(a) Database (b) File
(c) Folder (d) Data-mining

8. Which of the following objects is/are contained in database?
(a) Table (b) Query
(c) Form (d) All of these

9. Which of the following operations can a DBMS perform?
(a) Create a database
(b) Update a database
(c) Retrieve data from a database
(d) All of the above

10. Which of the following is the function of database administrator in an organization?
(a) To be responsible for the technical aspects of managing the information contained in organizational databases
(b) To be responsible for the executive level aspects of decision regarding the information management
(c) To show the relationship among entity classes in a data warehouse
(d) To define which data mining tools must be used to extract data

11. Periodically adding, changing and deleting file records is called .... file.
(a) updating (b) upgrading
(c) restructuring (d) renewing

12. .... means that the data contained in a database is accurate and reliable.
(a) Data redundancy
(b) Data integrity
(c) Data reliability
(d) Data consistency

13. An advantage of the database management approach is
(a) data is dependent on programs
(b) data redundancy increases
(c) data is integrated and can be accessed by multiple programs
(d) All of the above

14. Which of the following is the drawback of DBMS?
(a) Improvement in data
(b) Backup and recovery
(c) Complexity
(d) Maintenance of data integrity

15. In which of the following, database is used?
(a) Banking (b) Finance (c) Sales (d) All of these

16. What is the primary purpose of a database file?
(a) To store multiple unrelated databases
(b) To organize related records into a cohesive structure
(c) To represent a single attribute
(d) To serve as a container for bits and bytes

Terms Related to DBMS

17. What does normalization refer to in DBMS?
(a) Organizing data to reduce redundancy *IBPS RRB 2018*
(b) Creating a backup of the data
(c) Adding more data to the database
(d) Retrieving data from the database

18. What is a Tuple in DBMS?
(a) A table in a database
(b) A single column of data
(c) A single row in a database table
(d) A data field in a database

19. In a database, a record is made up of
(a) multiple fields (b) multiple databases
(c) multiple files (d) multiple tables

20. The smallest unit of information about a record in a database is called a
(a) cell (b) field
(c) record (d) query

21. Rows of a relation are called
(a) relation (b) tuples
(c) data structure (d) an entity

22. A collection of related files is called a ....
(a) character (b) field
(c) database (d) record

23. Which of the following contains information about a single entity in the database like a person, place, event or thing?
(a) Query (b) Form
(c) Record (d) Table

24. DBMS is comprised of tables that made up of rows called .... and columns called ....
(a) fields, records (b) records, fields
(c) address, fields (d) ranges, sheet

25. A set of possible data values is called
(a) attribute (b) degree
(c) tuple (d) domain

DBMS Languages and their Commands

26. Which SQL command is used to remove a table from a database? *SSC CGL 2020*
(a) REMOVE (b) DELETE
(c) DROP (d) ERASE

27. Which of the following is used to change the data in an existing record? *IBPS PO 2018*
(a) UPDATE (b) MODIFY
(c) CHANGE (d) REPLACE

28. Which command is used to insert data into a table in SQL? *SSC CHSL 2019*
(a) INSERT (b) ADD
(c) PUT (d) ENTER

29. Which of the following is not an SQL command? *UPSC CDS 2019*
(a) SELECT (b) DELETE
(c) REMOVE (d) UPDATE

30. Which of the following SQL commands is used to modify data in a table? *IBPS Clerk 2020*
(a) UPDATE (b) MODIFY
(c) CHANGE (d) EDIT

31. Which of the following is used to define the structure of a database? *SSC CGL 2020*
(a) Data Definition Language (DDL)
(b) Data Manipulation Language (DML)
(c) Data Query Language (DQL)
(d) Data Control Language (DCL)

32. Which of the following is an example of a database constraint? *SSC CGL 2019*
(a) SELECT (b) UNIQUE
(c) JOIN (d) UPDATE

33. Which of the following SQL commands is used to modify a table's structure? *IBPS Clerk 2020*
(a) UPDATE (b) ALTER
(c) MODIFY (d) CHANGE

34. Which of the following is used to perform all SQL operations in DBMS? *IBPS Clerk 2020*
(a) Data Manipulation Language
(b) Data Definition Language
(c) Data Control Language
(d) Transaction Control Language

35. In database management system ... is a query language for accessing and manipulating data. *SSC Selection Post 2023*
(a) Data Manipulation Language (DML)
(b) Data Transaction Language (DTL)
(c) Data Definition Language (DDL)
(d) Data Control Language (DCL)

36. Which of the following is a command for Data Definition Language in Structured Query Language? *SSC Selection Post 2023*
(a) CREATE (b) SELECT
(c) DELETE (d) MAKE

Database Models

37. Which of the following database models is represented using data graph? *SSC Selection Post 2023*
(a) Object-oriented database model
(b) Network database model
(c) Hierarchical database model
(d) Relational database model

38. Which of the following is a feature of a Relational DBMS? *SSC CGL 2019*
(a) It uses a table-based structure.
(b) It uses a hierarchical model.
(c) It stores data in files.
(d) It uses a network model.

39. Which of the following is not a type of DBMS model? *UPSC CDS 2020*
(a) Hierarchical (b) Relational
(c) Object-oriented (d) Microsoft

40. In which of the following models does the DBMS store data in the form of rows and columns? *SSC CGL 2018*
(a) Network model (b) Hierarchical model
(c) Relational model (d) Object-oriented model

41. Which of the following is not a type of database? *UPSC CDS 2020*
(a) Relational (b) Object-oriented
(c) Object-relational (d) Object-SQL

42. Which of the following is the most commonly used DBMS model? *UPSC CDS 2019*
(a) Hierarchical model (b) Network model
(c) Relational model (d) Object-oriented model

43. Which of the following is not a type of relationship in a relational database? *SSC CHSL 2018*
(a) One-to-one (b) One-to-many
(c) Many-to-many (d) None-to-one

44. Which of the following is not a DBMS type? *UPSC CDS 2019*
(a) Hierarchical (b) Relational
(c) Object-Oriented (d) Linear

45. Which type of relationship exists when a single record in one table is related to multiple records in another table? *SSC CHSL 2019*
(a) One-to-one (b) One-to-many
(c) Many-to-many (d) Many-to-one

46. Which of the following is not a property of a relational database? *IBPS PO 2020*
(a) Data is stored in tables
(b) Data can be accessed using SQL
(c) Data can be retrieved using simple queries
(d) Data is stored in an unstructured manner

47. Which of the following is a disadvantage of the hierarchical database model? *IBPS RRB PO 2020*
(a) Complex relationships between data
(b) Redundancy of data
(c) Scalability issues
(d) High performance

48. In Entity Relationship diagram of database management system, when attribute is single valued then … is used in diagram. *SSC Selection Post 2023*
(a) double dotted lines
(b) dotted single line
(c) dotted line
(d) single line

49. In Entity Relationship model of database, … describe the components of an entity. *SSS Selection Post 2023*
(a) attributes (b) cardinality
(c) degree (d) relationship

50. In ER diagram, relationship type is represented by
(a) ellipse (b) dashed ellipse
(c) rectangle (d) diamond

51. Relationship can be divided into
(a) One-to-one (b) Many-to-one
(c) One-to-many (d) All of these

Keys in DBMS

52. What is a foreign key in a relational database? *SSC CHSL 2019*
(a) Key used to create a table
(b) Key that links one table to another
(c) A unique identifier
(d) None of the above

53. What is a primary key? *SSC CHSL 2019*
(a) A key used to connect two tables
(b) A key that uniquely identifies a record
(c) A key that stores primary data
(d) A key used to select data from a table

54. What is a composite key in DBMS? *IBPS Clerk 2019*
(a) A primary key formed by a combination of more than one column
(b) A key formed by joining multiple tables
(c) A key used in a foreign table
(d) A key that stores composite data

55. What is a NULL value in SQL? *IBPS Clerk 2020*
(a) A value that has been explicitly set to zero
(b) A value that is missing or undefined
(c) A value that is empty but exists in the database
(d) A default value assigned to a column

56. In files, there is a key associated with each record which is used to differentiate among different records. For every file, there is at least one set of keys that is unique. Such a key is called
(a) unique key (b) prime attribute
(c) index key (d) primary key

57. Which of the following types of keys will prevent the entry of duplicate rows?
(a) Primary key (b) Unique
(c) Null (d) Foreign key

58. In Relational Data Structure of database management system, the remaining candidate keys other than primary key are called …… key. *SSC Selection Post 2023*
(a) composite (b) foreign
(c) attribute (d) alternate

Database Schema

59. In DBMS, what is a schema? *SSC CGL 2020*

(a) A temporary table
(b) A type of query
(c) A blueprint of the database structure
(d) None of the above

60. Which of the following is true about a schema in DBMS?

(a) It defines how data is stored in a database.
(b) It contains data about the physical storage.
(c) It represents the structure of database objects like tables and views.
(d) It is the actual data stored in the database.

61. Which of the following types of schema represents the conceptual design of a database?

(a) Physical schema (b) External schema
(c) Logical schema (d) Internal schema

62. A schema in DBMS can be divided into which of the following levels?

(a) Internal, conceptual and external
(b) Conceptual, physical and user
(c) External, internal and external
(d) Internal, logical and physical

63. A logical schema is …………

(a) the entire database
(b) a standard way of organising information into accessable part
(c) describes how data is actually stored on disk
(d) All of the above

Database Storage Hierarchy

64. What is the correct order of data storage hierarchy in a database?

(a) File < Database < Record < Field
(b) Field < Record < File < Database
(c) Database < File < Record < Field
(d) Record < Field < File < Database

65. What is a field in a database?

(a) A collection of related records
(b) A column that stores data
(c) A collection of related tables
(d) A specific set of instructions for data management

66. Which of the following represents the highest level in the database storage hierarchy?

(a) Table (b) Field
(c) Database (d) Record

67. Which of the following is the smallest unit of data in the database storage hierarchy?

(a) Field (b) Bit
(c) Record (d) Byte

68. In a storage hierarchy, a file consists of

(a) a group of related records
(b) bits and bytes only
(c) fields without any specific order
(d) several unrelated database

69. Which of the following is not a part of the database storage hierarchy?

(a) Table (b) File
(c) Bit (d) Folder

Answers

1.	(a)	2.	(b)	3.	(d)	4.	(a)	5.	(c)	6.	(b)	7.	(a)	8.	(d)	9.	(d)	10.	(a)
11.	(a)	12.	(d)	13.	(c)	14.	(c)	15.	(d)	16.	(b)	17.	(a)	18.	(c)	19.	(a)	20.	(b)
21.	(b)	22.	(c)	23.	(c)	24.	(b)	25.	(b)	26.	(c)	27.	(a)	28.	(a)	29.	(c)	30.	(a)
31.	(a)	32.	(b)	33.	(b)	34.	(a)	35.	(a)	36.	(a)	37.	(b)	38.	(a)	39.	(d)	40.	(c)
41.	(d)	42.	(c)	43.	(d)	44.	(d)	45.	(b)	46.	(d)	47.	(c)	48.	(d)	49.	(a)	50.	(d)
51.	(d)	52.	(b)	53.	(b)	54.	(a)	55.	(b)	56.	(d)	57.	(a)	58.	(d)	59.	(c)	60.	(c)
61.	(c)	62.	(a)	63.	(a)	64.	(b)	65.	(b)	66.	(c)	67.	(b)	68.	(a)	69.	(d)		

Data Communication

- The term **communication** means sending and receiving information.
- Data communication is the process of sending and receiving data from one device to another.
- In data communication, data is transferred from one place to another in the form of signals.
- Data is transmitted through mediums like cables, wireless signals or fiber optics.

In this Chapter

- Characteristics of Data Communication
- Components of Data Communication
- Modes of Data Communication
- Signals
- Medium of Communication
- Network Protocols
- Internet Service Provider (ISP)
- Wireless Technologies
- Generations of Mobile Communication

"Errors using in adequate data are much less than those using no data at all.

~ Charles Babage"

Characteristics of Data Communication

1. **Delivery** The data should be delivered to the correct destination or correct user.
2. **Accuracy** The communication system should deliver the data accurately, without any errors.
3. **Timeliness** Audio and video data has to be delivered in a timely manner without any delay.
4. **Jitter** It refers to the variation in the packets arrival time.

Components of Data Communication

- **Sender** The device that sends the data.
- **Message** The actual information being transmitted, like text, audio or images.
- **Receiver** The device that receives the data.
- **Transmission Medium** The channel through which the message is carried from sender to receiver.
- **Protocol** A set of rules that governs how data is sent and received.

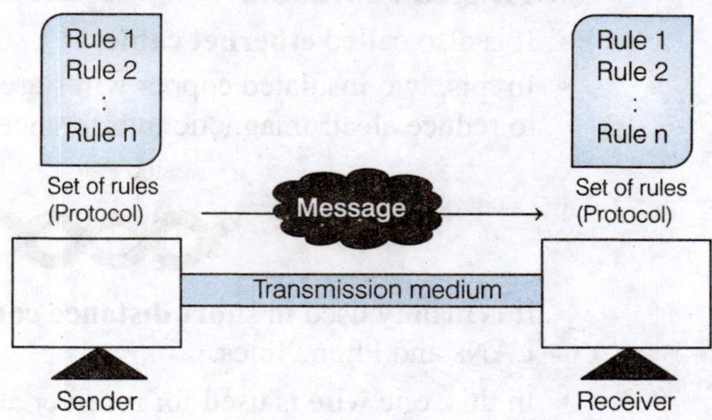

Modes of Data Communication

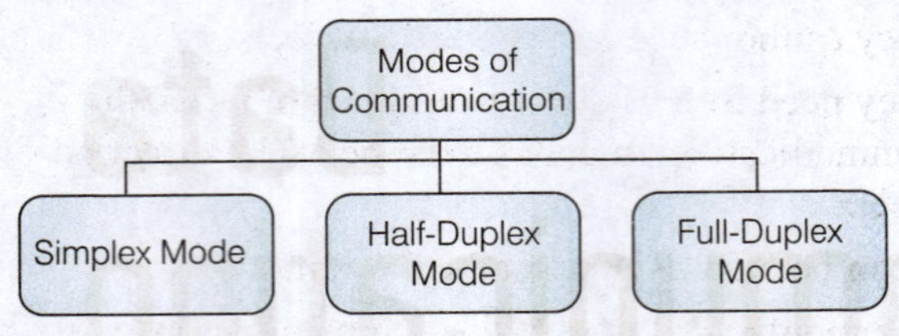

Simplex Mode

- In this, the communication is **unidirectional**, it means data flows in one direction only.
- The receiver cannot send data back to the sender.

Example Radio, remote, TV broadcasting.

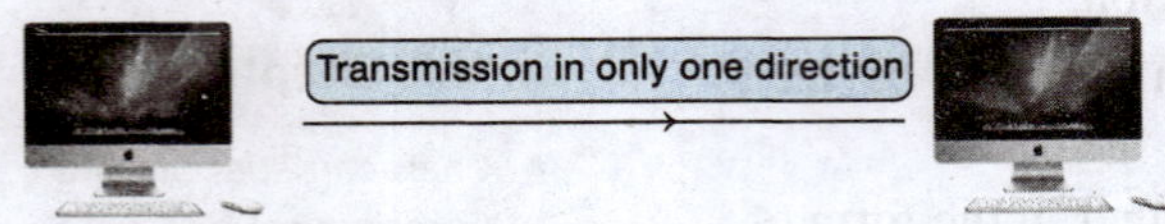

Half-Duplex Mode

- Data can flow in both directions, but not at the same time.
- A device can either send the data or receive it at a time.

Example Walkie-talkies, two-way radios.

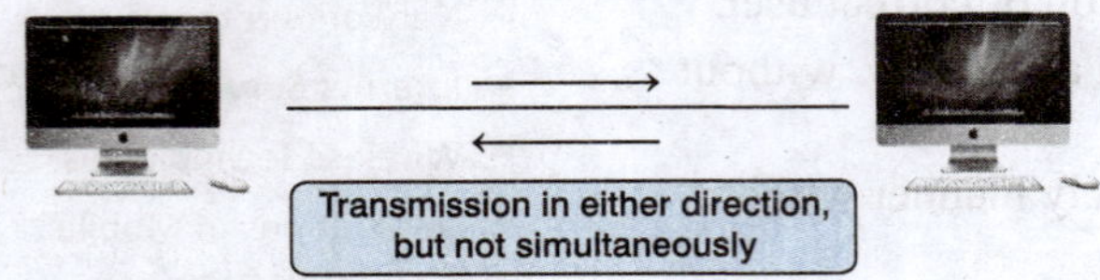

Full-Duplex Mode

- It is a **bidirectional** communication.
- In this, data flows in both directions simultaneously.

Example Video conferencing, mobile phone chatting.

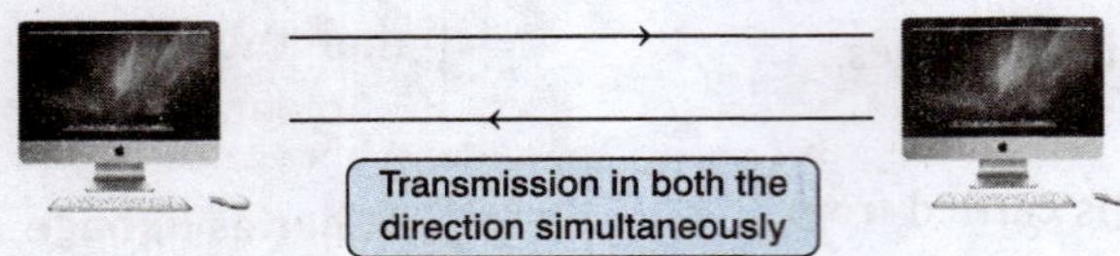

Signals

- A signal is a function of one or more variables that includes some phenomenon.

Types of Data Signal

There are two types of signals

Analog Signal

- These signals are transmitted in the form of **radio waves**.
- These are represented by the **sine wave**.

Example Telephone line, television waves.

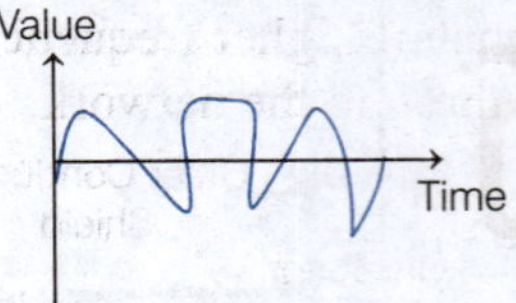

Digital Signal

- In this signal, data is transmitted in **electronic form**, i.e. binary digits (0 or 1).

Example digital clocks.

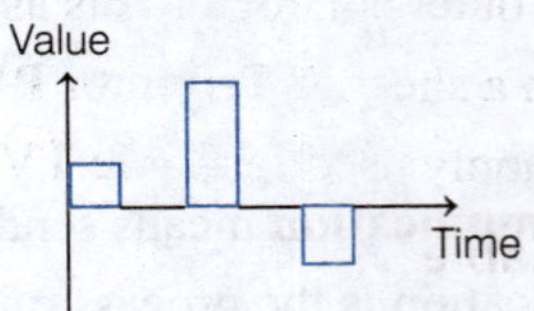

Medium of Communication

- The channel through which data is transmitted from one device to another is called **medium of communication**.
- It is divided into following categories

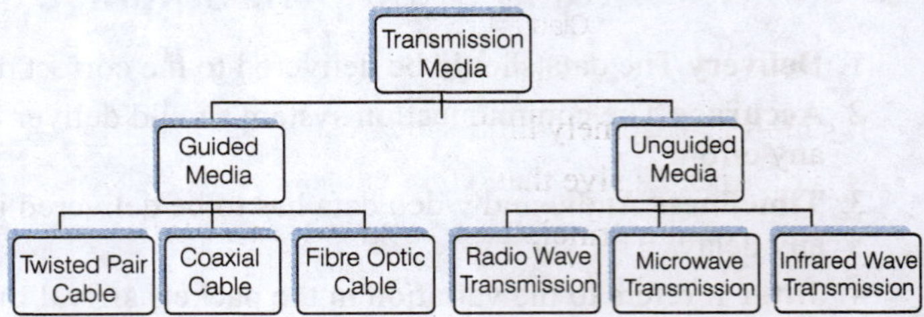

Guided Medium/ Wired Communication

- The medium in which data is transmitted with the help of **cables** is called **guided medium**.
- It is also called **bounded media**.

Example Ethernet cables, fiber-optic cables, co-axial cables.

- These are classified into three categories

1. Twisted Pair Cable

- It is also called **ethernet cable**.
- In this, two insulated copper wires are twisted together to reduce electromagnetic interference.

- It is mainly used in **short distance communication** like LANs and Phone lines.
- In this, one wire is used for receiver and other is used for earthing.

2. Coaxial Cable

- It carries the signal of higher frequency data communication through the network.

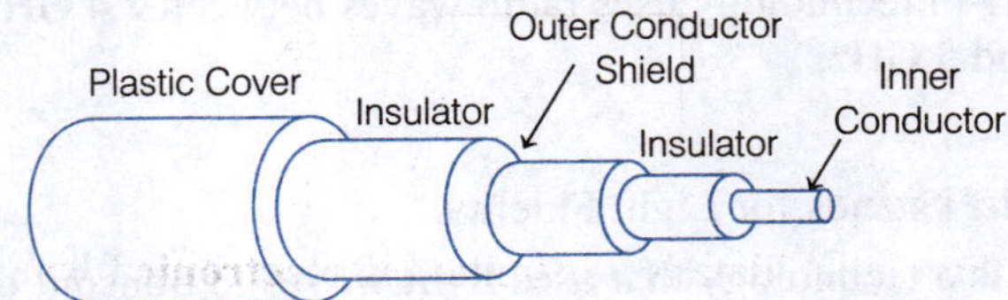

- It has a single inner conductor that transmits electric signals and the outer conductor acts as a ground.
- It is wrapped in a sheet of **Teflon** or **PVC**.
- They are commonly used for cable TV network.

3. Fiber Optic Cable

- It uses thin strands of glass or plastic fibers to transmit data as light signals.

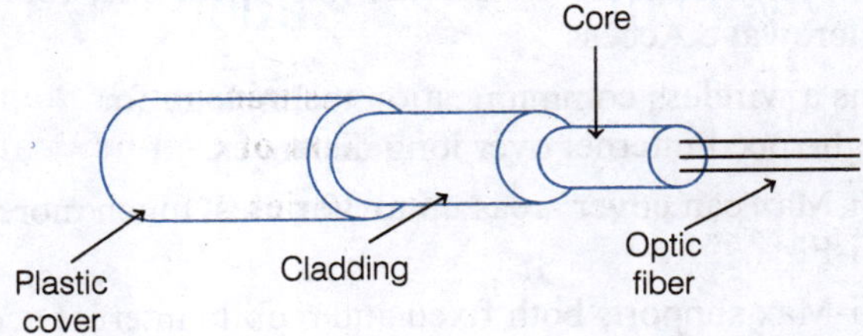

- It supports extremely high-speed data transmission.
- It is more expensive than other cables.
- It works on the principle of **Total Internal Reflection** (TIR).

Unguided Medium/ Wireless Communication

- Unguided media refers to communication channels, where data is transmitted **wirelessly**.
- It uses **electromagnetic waves** to transmit data through the air or space.

  Example Wi-Fi, bluetooth, radio waves, satellite communication.

These are classified into following categories

1. Radiowave Transmission

- In this, data is communicated through radio frequencies.
- Used for long-distance communication like FM radio.
- It can pass through solid objects.
- Radio waves are **omnidirectional**, i.e., the signals are transmitted in all the directions.

2. Microwave Transmission

- These are **electromagnetic waves** of frequency range 1GHz - 300GHz.
- These are **unidirectional**, i.e., can move in only one direction.
- They cannot pass through solid objects.
- They need **line-of-sight propagation** i.e. both communicating antennas must be in the direction of each other.
- It can be affected by weather conditions.
- Commonly used in satellite communication.

3. Infrared wave Transmission

- These are high frequency waves that enable fast data transfer for short distances.
- Commonly used in TV remote controls, wireless keyboards etc.
- They also cannot pass through solid objects.

Network Protocols

- Network protocols are a set of rules that determine how data is transmitted and received over a network.
- They ensure devices on a network can communicate with each other efficiently and securely.
- There are many types of network protocols, that are given below

1.TCP/IP

- It is the foundational protocol for the internet.
- It is responsible for breaking data into packets and ensures that it reaches its destination.

2.HTTP (Hypertext Transfer Protocol)

- It establishes connection between client and server.
- Used for transferring web pages and resources on the internet.

3.FTP (File Transfer Protocol)

- It is used to transfer files between client and server.
- It allows users to upload and download files from remote servers.

4.SMTP (Simple Mail Transfer Protocol)

- It is used for sending and receiving email messages.

5.Gopher Protocol

- It is a communication protocol used for searching, distributing and retrieving documents.
- It provides a simple, hierarchical interface to access text-based documents.

6. Telnet Protocol

- A network protocol used to access and control remote device using **CLI** (Command Line Interface).

Some other Network protocols are

- Post Office Protocol (POP)
- Media Access Control Protocol (MAC)
- Address Resolution Protocol (ARP)
- Domain Name System (DNS)
- Internet Message Access Protocol (IMAR)

Internet Service Provider (ISP)

- An ISP is a company or organization that provides access to the internet for individuals or businesses.
- The Internet service is provided through a variety of channels, including DSL, fiber optics, dial-up and satellite etc.

Example Google Fiber, Verizon, AT&T, Airtel etc.

Some main ISPs in India are

VSNL

- VSNL was a government-owned telecommunications company focused on international and national long-distance services.
- It was established in 1986.
- Presently, it is known as Tata Communication.

BSNL

- It was established in the year 2000.
- Headquarter of BSNL is located in Delhi.

MTNL

- It was established in the year 1986.
- Its headquarter is located in New Delhi.

Wireless Technologies

1. Bluetooth

- Bluetooth is a short-range wireless communication technology.
- It is used in many devices like headphones, keyboard, mouse, printer etc.
- Bluetooth technology uses radio waves between 2.4 to 2.8 GHz.
- It was invented by **Dr. Jaap Haartsen** in 1994.
- Up to 7 devices can be connected *via* Bluetooth network.
- It is used in **Personal Area Network** (PAN).

2. Wi-Fi

- Wi-Fi stands for Wireless Fidelity.
- It is a wireless technology that enables devices to connect to the internet and communicate with each other in a Local Area Network (LAN).
- It was created by John O'Sullivan.
- It typically ranges up to 100 meters indoors and about 300 meters outdoors.
- Wi-Fi technology uses radio waves between 2.4 GHz and 5 GHz.

3. Li-Fi

- Li-Fi stands for Light Fidelity.
- It is a technology that uses **light waves** to transmit data wirelessly.
- It was invented by **Harald Hass** in 2011.
- Li-Fi offers very high-speed data transfer, faster than Wi-Fi.
- It uses **LED** for sending data and **photo diode** for receiving data.

4. Wi-Max

- Wi-Max stands for Worldwide Interoperability for Microwave Access.
- It is a wireless communication technology for high-speed internet over long distances.
- Wi-Max can cover areas up to 30 miles, much more than Wi-Fi.
- Wi-Max supports both fixed and mobile internet access.

5. Hotspot

- A hotspot is a location or device that provides internet access through Wi-Fi.
- It is created using a router or a mobile device with internet-sharing capability.
- They allow multiple devices to connect to the internet wirelessly.
- It is also called Wireless Access Point Technology.

6. GSM

- GSM stands for Global System for Mobile Communications.
- GSM divides the area into small cells, allowing efficient communication.
- GSM uses SIM cards to identify and authenticate users on the network.
- In this, **EDGE** (Enhanced Data rates for GSM Evolution) is used to transfer data.

7. CDMA

- CDMA stands for Code Division Multiple Access.
- It is a mobile communication technology that uses unique codes to allow multiple users to share the same frequency.
- It uses **EVDO** (Evolution Data Optimised) for data transfer.

Generations of Mobile Communication

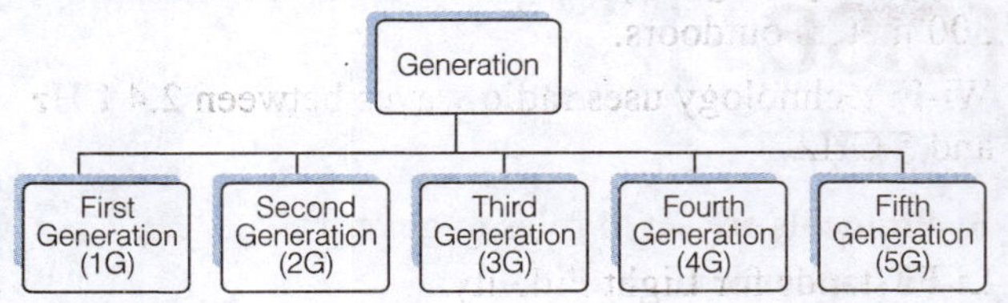

1G (First Generation)

- **Introduced in** 1979, Japan
- **Technology** Analog
- **Data Transfer Rate** Up to 2.4 Kbps (kilobits per second)
- **Use** Voice calls only, no data services.

2G (Second Generation)

- **Introduced in** 1990s, Finland
- **Technology** Digital (TDMA, CDMA)
- **Data Transfer Rate** 50 Kbps to 100 Kbps
- **Use** Voice calls, SMS, basic mobile data (like WAP browsing).

3G (Third Generation)

- **Introduced in** 2000s, Japan
- **Technology** UMTS, CDMA2000
- **Data Transfer Rate** 384 Kbps to 14.4 Mbps.
- **Use** Mobile internet, video calls, mobile TV, better multimedia.

4G (Fourth Generation)

- **Introduced in** 2010s, Sweden
- **Technology** LTE, Wi-MAX
- **Data Transfer Rate** 100 Mbps (mobile), up to 1 Gbps (stationary)
- **Use** High-speed internet, HD video streaming, online gaming, real-time services.

5G (Fifth Generation)

- **Introduced in** 2020s, South Korea
- **Technology** NR (New Radio)
- **Data Transfer Rate** 10 Gbps (theoretical peak), real-world speeds of 1-3 Gbps
- **Use** Ultra-fast internet, augmented reality, IoT, autonomous vehicles, real-time applications.

Note 5G was launched in India by Prime Minister Narendra Modi on October 1, 2022 at Pragati Maidan in Delhi.

Facts Drive

- The world's longest cable is **submarine fibre-optic cable.**
- **Secure Socket Layer** is used to protect sensitive information during data transmission.
- The **first mobile call** in India was made on 31 July 1995 between the Chief Minister of West Bengal Jyoti Basu and Union Telecom Minister Sukh Ram.
- The **wireless phone call** made over a cellular network happened in 1973.
- **Multiplexing** technology allows multiple signals to be sent over a single communication channel, improving efficiency.

Important Abbreviations

HTTP Hyper Text Transfer Protocol
FTP File Transfer Protocol
IP Internet Protocol
TCP Transmission Control Protocol
Wi-Fi Wireless Fidelity
Li-Fi Light Fidelity
Wi-Max Worldwide Interoperability for Microwave Access
GSM Global System for Mobile Communications
CDMA Code Division Multiple Access
VPN Virtual Private Network
BPS Bits Per Second
SMTP Simple Mail Transfer Protocol
VSNL Videsh Sanchar Nigam Limited
BSNL Bharat Sanchar Nigam Limited
MTNL Mahanagar Telephone Nigam Limited

PYQs Oneliner

1. **Secure Socket Layer** is used to protect sensitive information during data transmission. *SSC CGL (T-II) 18.01.2025*
2. **Fiber optic cable** is commonly used for WAN communication. *SSC CGL (T-II) 20.01.2025*
3. **LTE** is associated with providing high-speed wireless data transmission for mobile devices. *SSC CHSL 2024*
4. **SMTP** is commonly used for sending and receiving emails. *SSC CHSL 2024*
5. **Infrared** method is used in unguided transmission media. *Delhi Police 2023*
6. **Simplex** mode does not support bidirectional data transmission. *RRB NTPC 2022*
7. **Fiber optic cables** provide the highest data transfer rate in a wired network. *SSC CHSL 2021*

Practice Exercise

Introduction to Data Communication

1. What is data communication?
(a) Transmission of data over long distances without a medium
(b) Transfer of data between devices using a communication medium
(c) Storage of data in a database
(d) Processing of data into meaningful information

2. Which method is used to protect sensitive information during data transmission? *SSC CGL (T-II) 18.01.2025*
(a) Decryption
(b) Secure Socket Layer (SSL)
(c) Compression
(d) Hashing

3. The term latency in data communication refers to
(a) the speed of data transmission
(b) the delay between data being sent and received
(c) the amount of data lost during transmission
(d) the capacity of the communication channel

4. .... is the bit-rate of available or consumed information capacity expressed typically in metric multiple of bits per second. *SSC CGL 2023*
(a) Frequency (b) Protocol
(c) Speed (d) Bandwidth

5. What is delay in a communication over a network called? *CPCT 2024*
(a) Latency (b) Throughput
(c) Frequency (d) Turnaround time

6. Bandwidth refers to
(a) the cost of the cable required to implement a WAN
(b) the cost of the cable required to implement a LAN
(c) the amount of information a peer-to-peer network can store
(d) the amount of information a communication medium can transfer in a given amount of time

Components of Data Communication

7. In computer networks, a process of recovering signal containing multiple analog or digital signal streams back into the original separate and unrelated signals is called .... *DSSSB Patwari 2022*
(a) decoding
(b) multiplexing
(c) encoding
(d) demultiplexing

8. Protocols are set of rules to govern ....
(a) communication
(b) standard
(c) metropolitan communication
(d) bandwidth

9. Which of the following is not a component of a data communication system?
(a) Sender (b) Receiver
(c) Transmission medium (d) Operating system

10. What is the role of the sender in data communication?
(a) To receive data from the source
(b) To transmit data to the receiver
(c) To store data temporarily
(d) To convert data into binary form

11. In a data communication system, the receiver is responsible for
(a) storing transmitted data
(b) converting the data into signals
(c) accepting and interpreting the transmitted message
(d) sending acknowledgment to the sender

12. Which of the following can act as a transmission medium in data communication?
(a) Copper wire
(b) Fiber optic cable
(c) Radio waves
(d) All of the above

Mode of Data Communication

13. In which of the following modes of data transmission can the data flow in both directions but in only one direction at a time? *SSC CHSL 2023*
(a) Half duplex (b) Simplex
(c) Full duplex (d) Quarter duplex

14. In which one of the following, the early FM push to talk telephone system, was used?
(a) Half duplex (b) Full duplex
(c) Simple duplex (d) None of these

15. Which of the following is a key feature of 'Full-Duplex Communication System'? *RSMSSB LDC 2025*
(a) Receives information in one direction only
(b) Both parties can communicate with each other but not simultaneously
(c) Sends information in one direction only
(d) Both parties can communicate with each other simultaneously

16. In which of the following modes of data transmission, can the data flow in both directions simultaneously? *SSC CHSL 2023*
(a) Simplex (b) Quarter duplex
(c) Half duplex (d) Full duplex

17. Which of the following does not support bidirectional data transmission? *RRB NTPC CBT 2022*
(a) Half duplex
(b) Simplex
(c) Full duplex
(d) Both, half duplex and full duplex

18. Communication between a computer and a keyboard involves .... transmission.
(a) automatic (b) half duplex
(c) full duplex (d) simplex

19. Mobile phone is an example of which type of communication channel?
(a) Simplex (b) Half duplex
(c) Full duplex (d) None of these

Signals

20. What is the main difference between analog and digital signals?
(a) Analog signals are continuous, while digital signals are discrete.
(b) Digital signals are continuous, while analog signals are discrete.
(c) Both signals are continuous.
(d) Both signals are discrete.

21. Which of the following is an example of an analog signal?
(a) Morse code (b) AM radio waves
(c) Binary code (d) MP3 file

22. Which signal type is commonly used in modern computers?
(a) Analog
(b) Digital
(c) Both analog and digital equally
(d) Neither analog nor digital

23. Digital signals are measured in
(a) Decibels (dB) (b) Bits
(c) Hertz (Hz) (d) Amperes (A)

Medium of Communication

24. Which is the following methods is used in unguided transmission media? *Delhi Police 2023*
(a) Infrared
(b) Coaxial cable
(c) Twisted pair cable
(d) Optical fibre cable

25. What is wireless communication?
(a) Sending data from one location to another with the use of physical medium
(b) Sending data from one location to another without the use of physical medium
(c) Sending data from one location to another without the use of virtual medium
(d) None of the mentioned

26. Which of the following is not an example of wireless communication?
(a) Wi-Fi (b) Mobiles
(c) Landline (d) Wireless computer parts

27. What type of media is commonly used for WAN communication? *SSC CGL (T-II) 20.01.2025*
(a) HDMI Cable
(b) Twisted Pair Cable
(c) Fiber Optic Cable
(d) Coaxial Cable

28. In twisted pair, wires are twisted together, which are surrounded by an insulating material and an outer layer called
(a) frame (b) box
(c) disk (d) jacket

29. Which of the following is the greatest advantage of coaxial cabling?
(a) High security (b) Physical dimensions
(c) Long distances (d) Easily tapped

30. Which of the following cables can transmit data at high speeds?
(a) Flat cable (b) Coaxial cable
(c) Optic fibre cable (d) Twisted pair cable

31. Which of the following is an advantage for using fibre optics data transmission?
(a) Resistance to data theft
(b) Fast data transmission rate
(c) Low noise level
(d) All of the above

32. Networking using fibre optic cable is done as
(a) it has high bandwidth.
(b) it is thin and light.
(c) it is not affected by electro magnetic interference/power surges etc.
(d) All of the above

33. Which of the following is not a property of fibre optic cabling?
(a) Transmits at faster speeds than copper cabling
(b) Easier to capture a signal from the copper cabling
(c) Very resistant to interference
(d) Carries signals as light waves

34. A device that connects to a network without the use of cables is said to be
(a) distributed (b) cabled
(c) centralised (d) wireless

35. Which of the following is the fastest communication channel?
(a) Radio wave
(b) Microwave
(c) Optical fibre
(d) All are operating at nearly the same propagation speed.

Network Protocols

36. What protocol is commonly used for sending and receiving emails? *SSC CHSL 2024*
(a) SSH (Secure Shell Protocol)
(b) SMTP (Simpe Mail Transfer Protocol)
(c) FTP (File Transfer protocol)
(d) HTTP (Hypertext transfer Protocol)

37. ...... is a way to download, upload and transfer files from one location to another on the Internet and between computer systems. *SSC Selection Post 2023*
(a) DNS (b) HTTP
(c) FTP (d) VoIP

38. How many types of HTTP (Hypertext Transfer Protocol) messages are there? *SSC Selection Post 2023*
(a) 1 (b) 2 (c) 3 (d) 4

39. Which protocol allows users to make real-time voice and video calls over the internet? *Delhi Police 2023*
(a) FTP (b) VoIP (c) Email (d) DNS

40. What facilitates remote login on a computer? *RRB NTPC 2021*
(a) HTTP (b) Telnet
(c) TP (d) RTP

41. The rules governing the sending, travelling and receiving of information within the internet are called *Delhi Police 2022*
(a) protocols (b) algorithms
(c) programs (d) procedure

Internet Service Provider (ISP)

42. What does ISP stand for?
(a) Internet Speed Provider
(b) International Service Protocol
(c) Internet Service Provider
(d) Internal Server Protocol

43. Which of the following is a primary role of an ISP?
(a) Selling computers
(b) Providing internet connectivity
(c) Developing operating systems
(d) Designing web browsers

44. Which of the following is not an ISP?
(a) Google Chrome (b) Comcast
(c) AT&T (d) Vodafone

45. Which of the following is a popular ISP in India?
(a) Verizon
(b) Airtel
(c) T-Mobile
(d) Charter Spectrum

Wireless Technologies

46. What does Wi-Fi stand for?
(a) Wireless Fidelity
(b) Wide Frequency
(c) Wireless Frame
(d) Wave Frequency

47. Which of the following is a common wireless communication technology?
(a) Bluetooth (b) Ethernet
(c) HDMI (d) USB

48. Which wireless technology is used for short-range communication, such as connecting headphones to smartphones?
(a) Bluetooth (b) Wi-Fi
(c) Infrared (d) NFC

49. Which wireless communication standard is widely used in mobile networks?
(a) GSM (b) DSL
(c) HDMI (d) Fiber optics

50. What is the main advantage of wireless technology over wired technology?
(a) Lower cost
(b) Higher speed
(c) Portability and flexibility
(d) Unlimited range

51. What does Wi-Max stand for?
(a) Wireless Maximum
(b) Worldwide Interoperability for Microwave Access
(c) Wide Internet and Mobile Access
(d) Wireless Internet for Maximum Users

52. Which of the following is a key feature of Wi-Max?
(a) High-speed data transmission
(b) Low-cost deployment
(c) Support for both fixed and mobile connectivity
(d) All of the above

53. Wi-Max is commonly used for
(a) Mobile payments
(b) Long-distance broadband internet access
(c) Local file sharing
(d) Short-range data transfer

Generations of Mobile Communication

54. Which of the following is supported data rates of 4G networks?
(a) 1024 kbps (b) 100 mbps
(c) 200 mbps (d) None of these

55. When was the 2G communication introduced in the market?
(a) 1982 (b) 1984
(c) 1986 (d) 1990

56. Mobile communication network is also called as ……… network.
(a) cellular network (b) mobile network
(c) 2G network (d) Both (a) and (b)

57. ……… technology has grouped different mobile telephony and data type technologies to over 3G.
(a) 3.2G (b) 3.5G
(c) 3.6G (d) 4G

58. Which of the following are the features of mobile communication?
(a) High load balancing capacity
(b) Highly scalable
(c) Good network management system
(d) All of the above

59. Which of the following are the technologies used in mobile communications?
(a) 1G (b) 2G
(c) 3G (d) All of these

60. Mobile communication technology used in 2021 is ………. .
(a) 4G (b) 3G
(c) 5G (d) Both (a) and (c)

61. 1G uses ……….. type of signals to communicate data.
(a) digital (b) analog
(c) discrete (d) None of the above

62. 1G was introduced by ……….. country.
(a) India (b) Japan
(c) Germany (d) China

63. 2G technology uses ……….. signals.
(a) analog (b) digital
(c) continuous (d) None of these

64. 2G technology was released by ……….. country.
(a) Germany (b) Finland
(c) French (d) China

65. Third-generation mobile communication technology is represented as ……….. .
(a) 3G (b) 3.4 G
(c) 4G (d) 2G

66. What is the data speed range of 3G mobile communication?
(a) 384 kbps to 2 mbps
(b) 100 kbps to 2 mbps
(c) 200 kbps to 2 mbps
(d) 300 kbps to 345 kbps

67. Which technology is associated with providing high speed wireless data transmission for mobile devices? *SSC CHSL 2024*
(a) GRPS (b) GPS
(c) Wi-Max (d) LTE

68. LTE technology is used in which of the following generations of wireless technologies? *SSC CHSL 2023*
(a) 3G (b) 2G (c) 4G (d) 1G

Answers

1.	(b)	2.	(b)	3.	(b)	4.	(d)	5.	(a)	6.	(d)	7.	(d)	8.	(a)	9.	(d)	10.	(b)
11.	(c)	12.	(d)	13.	(a)	14.	(a)	15.	(d)	16.	(d)	17.	(b)	18.	(d)	19.	(c)	20.	(a)
21.	(b)	22.	(b)	23.	(b)	24.	(a)	25.	(b)	26.	(c)	27.	(c)	28.	(d)	29.	(c)	30.	(c)
31.	(d)	32.	(c)	33.	(b)	34.	(d)	35.	(c)	36.	(b)	37.	(c)	38.	(b)	39.	(b)	40.	(b)
41.	(a)	42.	(c)	43.	(b)	44.	(a)	45.	(b)	46.	(a)	47.	(a)	48.	(a)	49.	(a)	50.	(c)
51.	(b)	52.	(d)	53.	(b)	54.	(b)	55.	(d)	56.	(d)	57.	(b)	58.	(d)	59.	(d)	60.	(d)
61.	(b)	62.	(b)	63.	(b)	64.	(b)	65.	(a)	66.	(a)	67.	(d)	68.	(c)				

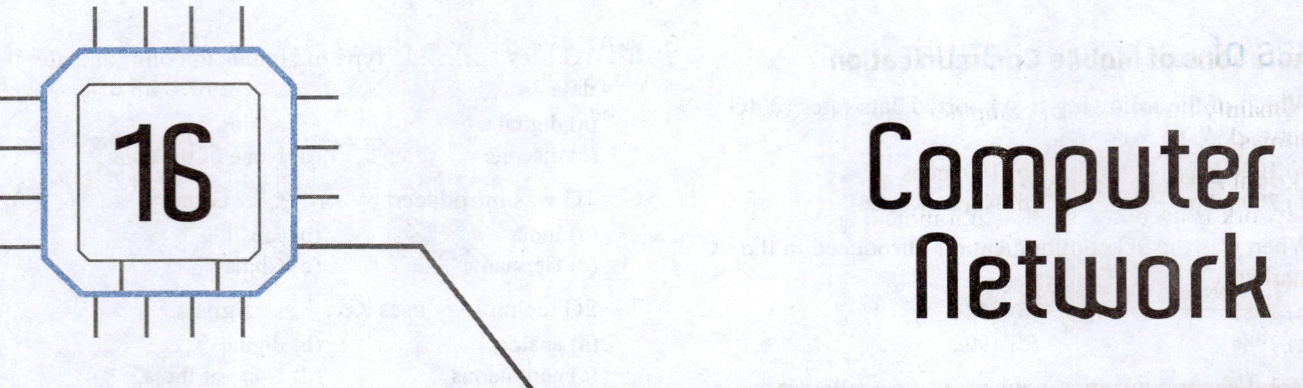

16 Computer Network

- A computer network is a system that connects two or more computing devices to share information.
- These devices are linked using wired (like cables) or wireless (like Wi-Fi) connections.
- **Analog** and **digital** signals are used for data communication in computer network.
- Networks enable activities like file sharing, internet access and collaborative work.

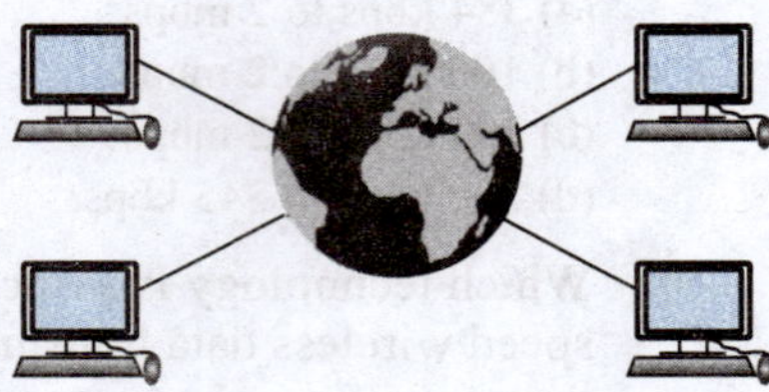

In this Chapter

- Components of Computer Network
- Types of Computer Network
- Networking Devices
- Network Topology
- OSI Model
- TCP/IP Model

"Computer Science empowers Students to create the world of tomorrow

~ Satya Nadella"

Components of Computer Network

Servers

- Servers are powerful computers that provide services like file storage, email or hosting applications.

Example Web server, application server

Clients

- Devices that request and use resources or services from servers are called **clients**.

Network Interface Cards (NICs)

- It is a hardware installed on devices that allows them to connect to a network.
- NIC is also called the ethernet card, network adapter, LAN card or external network card.

Transmission Media

- It is the physical or wireless medium through which data is transmitted.

Example Cables (Ethernet, fiber optics), wireless signals (Wi-Fi, radio waves)

Protocols

- These are the rules that govern data exchange over the network.

Example TCP/IP, HTTP or FTP

Types of Computer Network

There are mainly three types of computer networks which are as follows

1. LAN (Local Area Network)

- This network is used in a small geographical area.

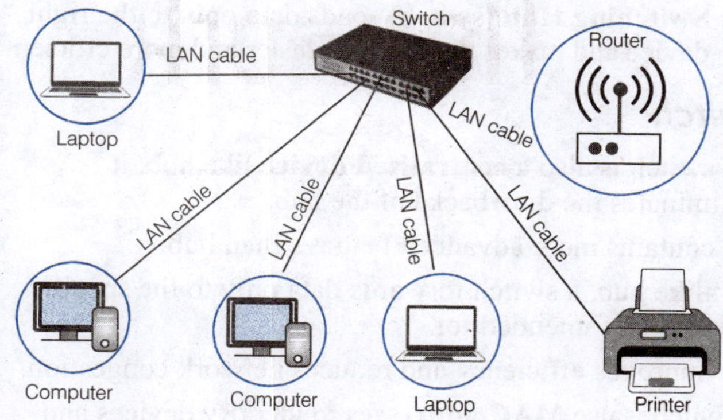

- They are usually private networks and can be easily set up and managed by individuals.
- The range of this network is approximately 0 to 1 kilometer.
- The speed of data communication is fast.
- This is also known as **ethernet technology**.

Example Home network, Wi-Fi

2. MAN (Metropolitan Area Network)

- MAN covers a larger area than a LAN but is smaller than a WAN.
- It connects multiple LANs within a city or region.

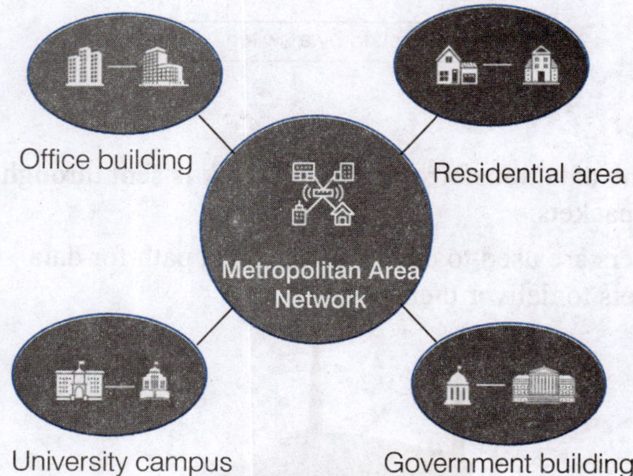

- It enables communication between different offices, schools or businesses in that area.
- The range of this network is approximately 1 to 100 kilometer.

Example Cable, TV networks

3. WAN (Wide Area Network)

- WAN is the world's largest network spread all across the globe.

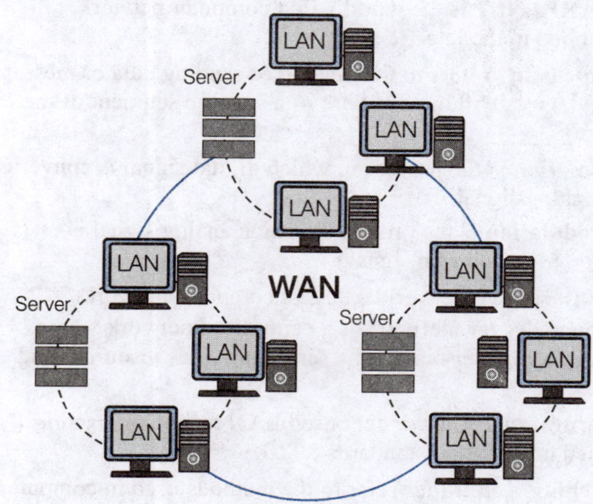

- The **internet** is the largest example of a WAN, connecting networks worldwide.
- The range of this network is more than 100 kilometers.
- It offers slower speeds compared to other networks.

Some Other Types of Computer Networks

PAN (Personal Area Network)

- It is a very small network, typically within a range of 10 meters.
- Used to connect personal devices like smartphones, laptops and tablets.

VPN (Virtual Private Network)

- It is a network that creates a secure, encrypted connection over the internet.
- It allows users to access a private network remotely from any location.
- It is commonly used by remote workers to access company resources securely from home or while travelling.

CAN (Campus Area Network)

- It is a network that connects multiple LANs within a campus, like a university or business campus.
- Covers a larger area than a LAN but smaller than a MAN.

SAN (Storage Area Network)

- It is a specialised network designed to provide high-speed, reliable access to storage devices.
- Used by large organisations for centralised data storage and backup.

- The **ARPANET** is the world's first computer network, developed in the late 1960.
- **Broadcasting** refers to the method of sending data or messages to all devices within a network or a specific segment of the network.
- **Modulation** is the process in which digital signal is converted into analog signal.
- **Demodulation** is the process in which analog signal is converted into digital signal.
- The **internet** is the world's largest computer network.
- **A Client-Server Network** is a centralised network where clients request services and a server provides resources and services.
- **Ethernet** is the most widely used LAN technology and is defined under IEEE standards 802.3.
- **Switching techniques** refer to the methods used in computer networks to direct data packets between devices. These techniques define how data is transmitted across the network.
- **Ethernet** is the most widely used LAN technology.

Networking Devices

- Networking devices are hardware components used to connect devices within a network.
- They allow devices to connect to the network efficiently and securely.
- They improve network speed and manage data flow better.

Some popular networking devices are –

Hub

- A hub is a **centralised device** used to connect multiple devices in a Local Area Network (LAN).
- Hub transmits data to all connected devices, regardless of the intended recipient.
- It cannot filter or manage data traffic.
- Hub is also called **dumb device** or **non-intelligent device**.

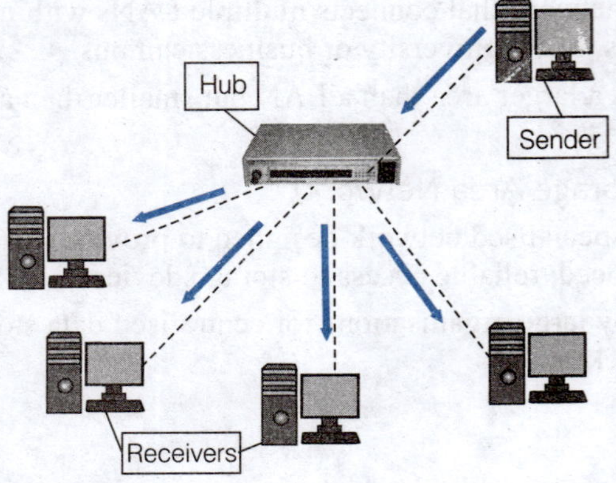

Types of Hub

1. **Passive Hub** connects devices but does not change or boost signals.
2. **Active Hub** boosts signals to help them travel further.
3. **Intelligent Hub** can manage traffic and provide remote control.
4. **Switching Hub** (switch) sends data only to the right device and makes the network faster and more efficient.

Switch

- A switch is also a **centralised device** like hub, it eliminates the drawbacks of the hub.
- It contains more advanced features than hub.
- Unlike hub, a switch forwards data only to the specific device it is intended for.
- It improves efficiency and reduces network congestion.
- Switches use **MAC addresses** to identify devices and manage data transmission.
- It is also called the **intelligent device**.

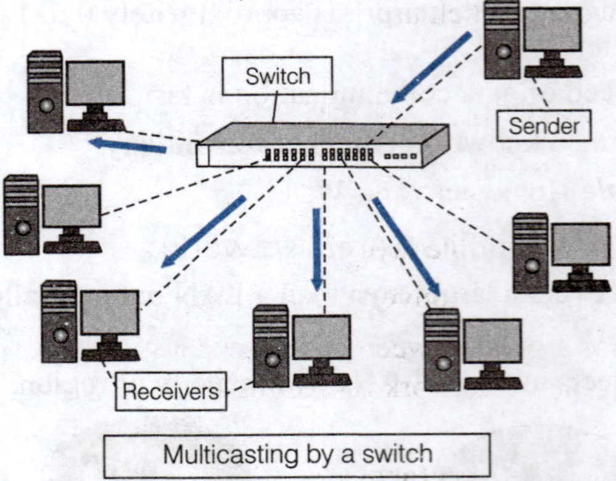

Multicasting by a switch

Router

- All the data transferred in the network is sent through data packets.
- Routers are used to determine the best path for data packets to deliver them faster.

- They help information to reach its correct destination.
- They operate at the **network layer** (layer 3) of the OSI model.
- Routers use **IP addresses** to determine the path for forwarding packets.

Bridge

- A bridge is a networking device used to connect two or more similar types of network segments, helping them work as one.

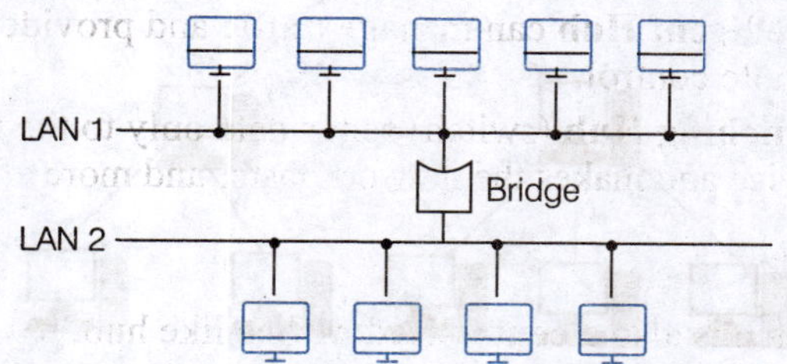

- It operates at the **data link layer** (layer 2) of the OSI model.
- They help in reducing network congestion by dividing large networks into smaller and more manageable segments.

Gateway

- A gateway is a device that connects two different types of networks, which uses different protocols.

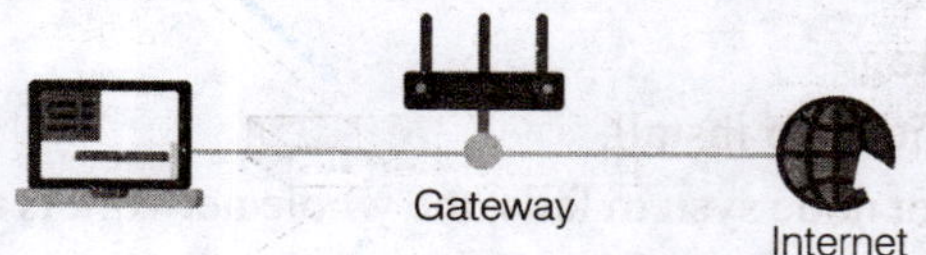

- It works at multiple layers of the OSI model.
- It is also used to convert one protocol to another.
- It acts as a **gate** between networks and allows, data to pass from one network to another, even if they use different protocols.
- It is also called **protocol converter**.

Repeater

- A repeater converts a weak signal into strong signal between two computer networks.

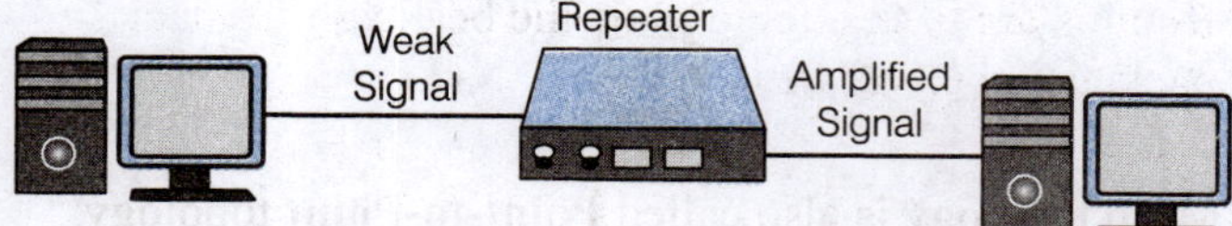

- It works at the **physical layer** (layer 1) of the OSI model.
- It regenerates a signal before transmitting data.
- It allows signals to travel longer distances.

Modem

- Modem stands for **modulation** and **demodulation**.
- A modem is a device that connects a computer or network to the internet.
- It changes the digital data into analog signals and *vice-versa*.

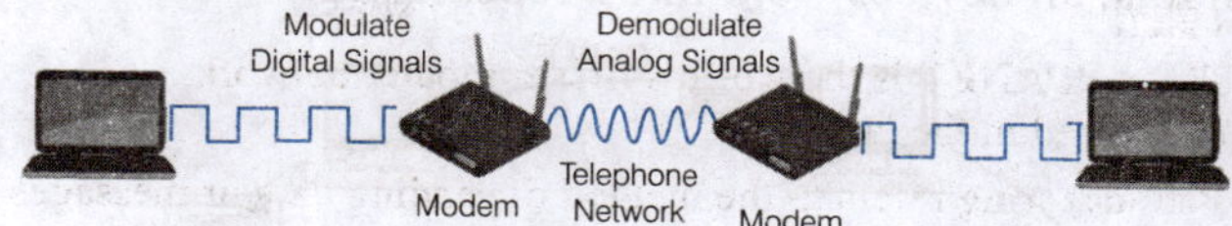

Network Topology

- Network topology refers to the arrangement of different elements (such as devices, links and nodes) in a computer network.
- It defines how the devices are connected and how data flows between them.

Types of Network Topology

Network topology is classified into following types

1. Bus Topology

- In bus topology, all the devices of the network are connected to a single cable.
- In this, information is sent on the basis of device destination address.
- The cable used in this topology is called the **back bone cable**.
- If the destination address does not match, then the rest of the data is terminated.
- It is also called the **linear** or **multi-point topology**.
- This topology is used in **Local Area Network** (LAN).

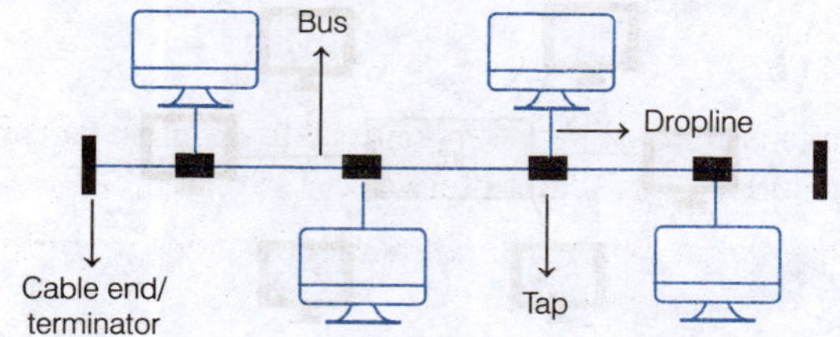

Advantages

- It is easy to add and remove computers (nodes) in it.
- Its cost is not very high.
- If a computer fails, the entire network is not affected.

Disadvantages

- If the main cable fails, the entire network shuts down.
- The system becomes slow as more nodes are added.
- It is difficult to locate a damaged node.

2. Ring Topology

- In this topology, devices are connected in a **closed loop** (ring).
- All devices remain connected to their nearest two devices.

- It works on **token passing** technology.
- In this, all devices work like a repeater.

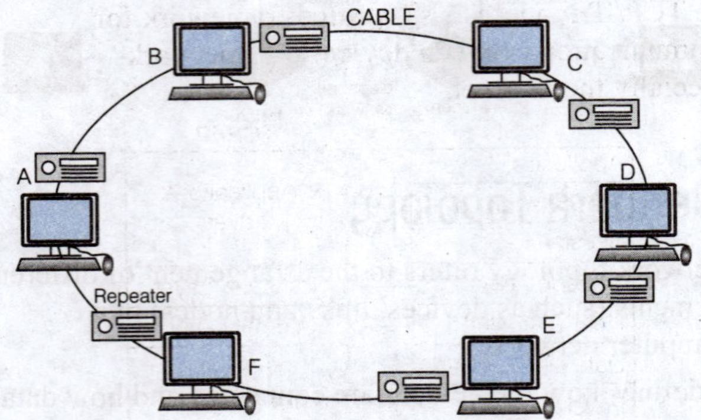

- In this, the data flow is in one direction only.
- It is also called the **circular topology**.

Advantages

- Easy to manage due to its orderly structure.
- It is cost-effective to install and expand.
- Features minimum collision and enhances data flow efficiency.
- Speed for data transfer is notably high in this setup.

Disadvantages

- If one device or cable fails, the whole network gets affected.
- Troubleshooting can be difficult.

3. Star Topology

- All computers are connected to a **central device** (hub or switch).

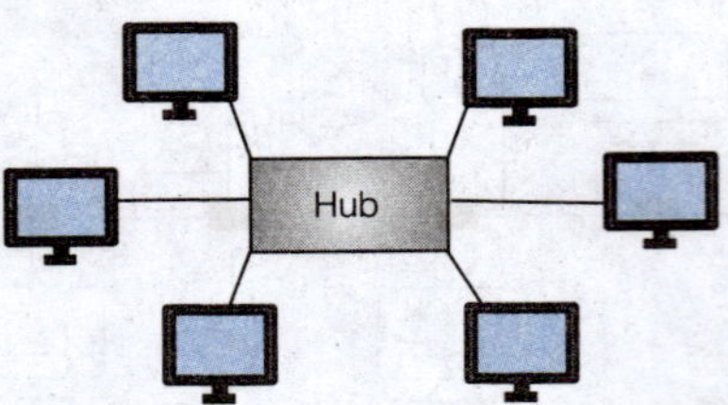

- This is the most commonly used network topology today.
- The speed of the network is not affected by increasing the number of local computers.
- The number of computers can be increased or decreased easily.

Advantages

- Avoids point-to-point connections.
- Failure of one device doesn't affect others.
- Low chances of data collision.

Disadvantages

- It is expensive to install as this type of network requires more cables.
- If the central device fails, the entire network is affected.

4. Tree Topology

- It is a combination of **bus** and **star** topologies.

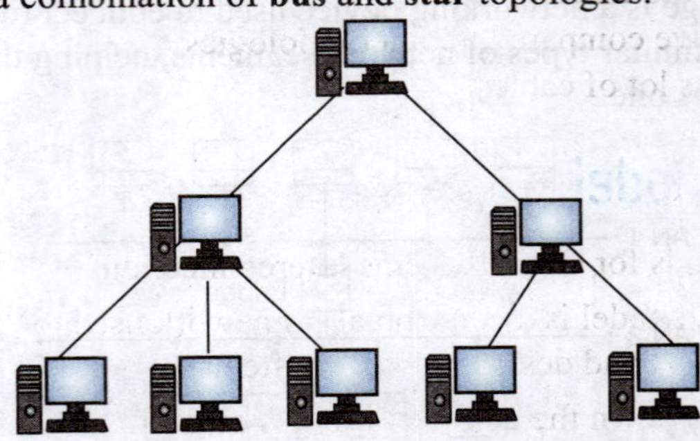

- Devices are connected in a **hierarchical tree structure**.
- Generally, twisted pair cables are used in this topology.
- It is difficult to connect nodes, so this topology is used less.
- In this, many switches are connected to a single cable.

Advantages

- Scalable and flexible for large networks.
- Easy to manage and expand.
- Issues in one branch do not impact the entire network.

Disadvantages

- It is difficult to install.
- If the root node system fails, the whole network is affected.
- Expensive compared to other topologies.

5. Mesh topology

- Mesh topology is used in places, where the network breaks frequently.

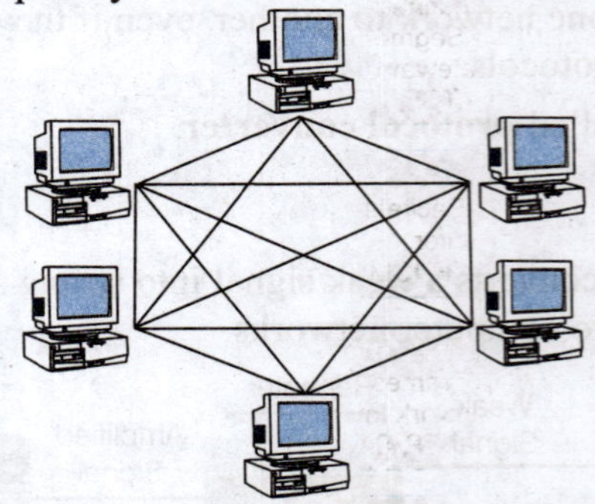

- Mesh topology is also called **Point-to-Point** topology.
- In this, data flow can happen in any direction.
- It is the most suitable topology for long distance networks.
- In this topology, all the devices are connected to each other.

Advantages

- High security and privacy.
- Highly reliable and fault-tolerant.
- Provides multiple paths for data transmission.

Disadvantages

- Difficult to install.
- Expensive compared to other topologies.
- Requires lot of cables.

OSI Model

- OSI stands for Open Systems Interconnection.
- The OSI model is a conceptual framework used to understand and design network systems.
- It breaks down the complex process of data communication into **7 distinct layers**.
- Each layer is responsible for specific tasks in the transmission of data from one device to another.
- The OSI model was developed by the International Organisation for Standardisation (ISO) in 1980.

Layers of OSI Model

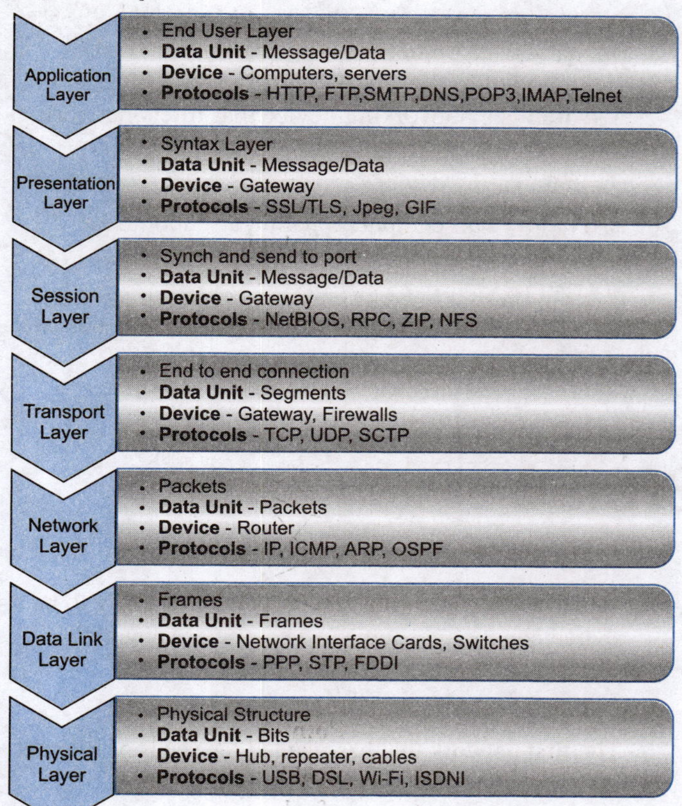

Note
- Transport layer is also called the **heart of OSI model**.
- Application layer is also called the **user interface layer**.
- The session, presentation and application layers are collectively called the **software** or **host layers** of OSI Model.
- The physical, data link and network layers are collectively called the **hardware** or **media layers** of OSI Model.

TCP/IP Model

- The TCP/IP model is a simplified framework for communication between devices on a network, especially the internet.

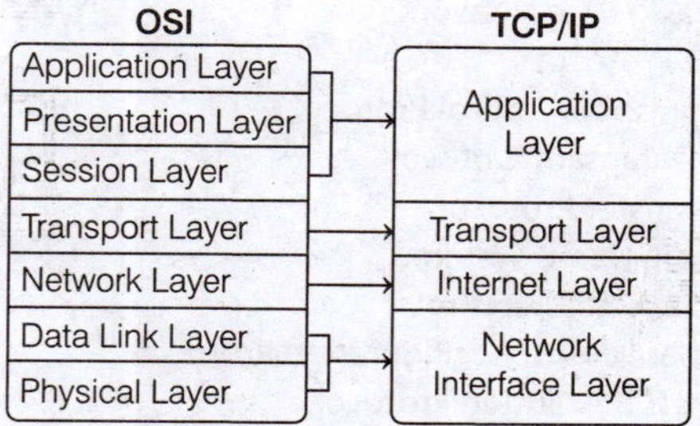

- It is also called the **protocol suite**.
- It is the foundation of modern networking.
- It was developed by the U.S. Department of Defense in the 1970s.
- This model consists of **4 layers.**

1. Network Interface Layer

- It is the lowest layer of TCP/IP model.
- It handles the physical transmission of data between devices over a network medium.
- It is also called **link layer** and **network access layer**.

2. Internet Layer (Network Layer)

- This layer works similar as the network layer of OSI model.
- It transmits **data packets** between devices and manages logical addressing.

3. Transport Layer

- It ensures that data packets are delivered accurately and reliably between a sender and receiver.
- It is also called the **Host-to-Host** layer.
- The two protocol that works in transport layer are **UDP** and **TCP**.

4. Application Layer

- This is the topmost layer of the TCP/IP Model.
- It provides network services directly to applications or users, such as web browsing or file transfers

HTTP Error Codes

Error	Reason
400 Bad File Request	▪ Invalid request due to incorrect syntax.
401 Unauthorised	▪ Authentication is required.
403 Forbidden	▪ Server refuses to fulfill the request.
404 File Not Found	▪ Resource cannot be found on the server.
500 Internal Server Error	▪ Generic server-side error.
502 Bad Gateway	▪ Server received an invalid response from an upstream server.

Important Abbreviations

LAN Local Area Network
WAN Wide Area Network
MAN Metropolitan Area Network
VPN Virtual Private Network
IP Internet Protocol
TCP Transmission Control Protocol
UDP User Datagram Protocol
FTP File Transfer Protocol
DNS Domain Name System
MAC Media Access Control
DHCP Dynamic Host Configuration Protocol
ARP Address Resolution Protocol
NAT Network Address Translation
ICMP Internet Control Message Protocol

Facts Drive

- The **internet** is the world's largest computer network, connecting billions of devices worldwide.
- A **Peer-to-Peer (P2P)** network is a decentralised network, where devices (peers) share resources directly without relying on a central server.
- A **Client-Server** network is a centralised network where clients (user devices) request services and a server (central device) provides resources and services.
- The OSI model is only a **theoretical model** and not used directly in real-world communication.
- Every device connected to a network has a unique **MAC address**, like a fingerprint for devices.

PYQs Oneliner

1. **Switch** is commonly used to connect computers within a LAN. *SSC CGL (T-II) 18.01.2025*
2. ISO/OSI reference model has **7 layers.** *CPCT 2024*
3. Terminators are used in **bus topology.** *CPCT 2024*
4. **Modulator-Demodulator** is the full form of MODEM. *CPCT 2024*
5. NIC stands for **Network Interface Card**. *CPCT 2024*
6. **Layer 5** of open system interconnection model lies between presentation layer and transport layer in computer system. *SSC Selection Post 2023*
7. **Gateway** is a passage to connect two networks that may work on different networking models. *SSC CGL 2023*
8. Router is used on **network layer** of OSI model. *DSSSB Patwari 2023*
9. A **switch** is a networking device that filters network traffic while connecting multiple computers or communicating devices. *SSC CGL 2023*
10. **LAN** allows all computers within a school to be connected. *DSSSB Patwari 2022*
11. **Bus topology** is used as local area network topology. *DSSSB Patwari 2022*

Practice Exercise

Introduction to Computer Network

1. Which of the following is a composed of several computers connected together to share resources and data?
(a) Internet (b) Network
(c) Backbone (d) Hyperlink

2. Which of the following is the component of coaxial cables used in the computer networking?
(a) Copper conductor (b) Core *SSC Selection Post 2023*
(c) Plastic jacket (d) Cladding

3. Which of the following is a terms associated with networks?
(a) MS-Excel (b) Mouse
(c) Word (d) Connectivity

4. Which of the following resources is most likely to be a shared common resource in a computer network?
(a) Printers (b) Speakers
(c) Floppy disk drives (d) Keyboards

5. The first network that has planted the seeds of Internet was
(a) ARPANET (b) NSFnet
(c) V-net (d) I-net

6. The process of connecting computer on a communication system is known as *SSC CGL 2018*
(a) processing
(b) compiling
(c) networking
(d) hosting

7. What do you mean by broadcasting in networking? *CPCT 2024*
(a) It means addressing a packet to all machines.
(b) It means addressing a packet to some machines.
(c) It means addressing a packet to a particular machine.
(d) It means addressing a packet to all machines, except a particular machine.

Components of Computer Network

8. .... is the most important/powerful computer in a typical network.
(a) Desktop (b) Network client
(c) Network server (d) Network station

9. A protocol is a set of rules governing a time sequence of events that must take place
(a) between peers (b) between an interface
(c) between modems (d) across an interface

10. ......is the hardware device most essential to establishing communication between computers.
(a) Net Interface Card
(b) Network Interface Card
(c) Network Information Card
(d) Both (a) and (b)

Types of Computer Network

11. WAN stands for *CPCT 2024*
(a) Web Area Network (b) World Area Network
(c) Wide Area Network (d) Worst Area Network

12. WAN in the context of computers and networking stands for *RRB NTPC 2021*
(a) WiFi Amended Network
(b) World Access Network
(c) Wide Access Network
(d) Wide Area Network

13. LAN can use .... architecture.
(a) peer-to-peer (b) client and server
(c) Both (a) and (b) (d) Neither (a) nor (b)

14. Which of the following type of computer network uses 'satellite links to connect with other devices? *SSC Selection Post 2023*
(a) Personal Area Network
(b) Wide Area Network
(c) Corporate Area Network
(d) Local Area Network

15. Which of the following is an advantage of LAN?
(a) Sharing peripherals (b) Backing up your data
(c) Saving all your data (d) Accessing the web

16. Which of the following network types is also termed a long haul network? *RRB NTPC 2021*
(a) WAN (b) LAN (c) PAN (d) TAN

17. The Internet is a group of interconnected computers across the globe. The Internet itself is a type of...... . *Delhi Police 2022*
(a) WAN (b) MAN (c) LAN (d) VPN

18. A network of computers and other devices that are confined to a relatively small space is called *RRB NTPC 2021*
(a) Local Area Network (b) Wide Area Network
(c) Peer-to-Peer Network (d) Global Network

19. Which of the following network types covers the largest geographical area? *RRB NTPC 2021*
(a) LAN (b) WAN (c) MAN (d) PAN

20. .... is a network located entirely on one site such as an office, school or within a group of buildings that are in close area, that are connected together. *CPCT 2024*
(a) LAN (b) PAN (c) MAN (d) WAN

21. .... is a computer network organised by an individual for personal use. *CPCT 2024*
(a) Local Area Network (LAN)
(b) Metropolitan Area Network (MAN)
(c) Personal Area Network (PAN)
(d) Wide Area Network (WAN)

Networking Devices

22. What is the use of bridge in network?
(a) To connect LANs (b) To separate LANs
(c) To control network speed (d) All of the above

23. A device operating at the physical layer is called a
(a) bridge (b) router (c) repeater (d) All of these

24. Which of the following device is used to regenerate and amplify signals?
(a) Switch (b) Hub (c) Repeater (d) Bridge

25. In networking device MODEM, the process of converting digital data into analog data is called.... *SSC Selection Post 2023*
(a) demodulation (b) modulation
(c) transmission (d) iteration

26. In a Local Area Network (LAN), which of the following is most commonly used to ensure that data packets are efficiently forwarded to the correct device, based on its MAC address? *SSC CGL (T-II) 20.01.2025*
(a) Router (b) Bridge
(c) Hub (d) Layer 3 Switch

27. What is the primary function of a router in a network? *SSC Selection Post 2023*
(a) Forwarding data packets between different networks.
(b) Providing wireless connectivity to devices.
(c) Filtering and blocking incoming network traffic.
(d) Managing user authentication and access control.

28. A …… is an electronic device that receives a weak signal and regenerates it. ***SSC CHSL 2023***
(a) hub (b) router (c) repeater (d) switch

29. The network device that converts digital signals into analog signals and can be connected through a telephone is called ……… . ***UPSC 2021***
(a) modem (b) hotspot (c) router (d) bridge

30. Which device is commonly used to connect computers within a LAN? ***SSC CGL (T-II) 18.01.2025***
(a) Modem (b) Router (c) Switch (d) Repeater

31. Which device is used to connect a computer to a network? ***SSC CGL 2019***
(a) Modem (b) Router (c) NIC (d) All of these

32. ……. serves as the entry and exit point of a network, as all data coming in or going out of a network must first pass through it in order to use routing paths. ***SSC CHSL 2023***
(a) Gateway (b) Bridge (c) Repeater (d) Router

33. ……. is also known as a protocol converter. ***SSC CGL 2023***
(a) Hub (b) Bridge (c) Switch (d) Gateway

34. …….. is a passage to connect two networks that may work on different networking models. ***SSC CGL 2023***
(a) Router (b) Switch (c) Gateway (d) Hub

35. A network device for controlling network security is called ***RSMSSB LDC 2025***
(a) bridge (b) firewall
(c) hub (d) router

Network Topology

36. In a … topology, all nodes are connected to a single communication line and share it for all their communication needs. ***SSC CHSL 2023***
(a) ring (b) completely connected
(c) star (d) multi access bus

37. In a star network, how many lines are required for connecting N nodes to the host node? ***SSC CHSL 2023***
(a) N+1 (b) N/2
(c) (N/2)-1 (d) N-1

38. In which topology of computer networks, for n-nodes, n × (n-1)/2 physical links are required for connection? ***SSC Selection Post 2023***
(a) Ring topology (b) Mesh topology
(c) Star topology (d) Hybrid topology

39. Which of the following refers to the layout arrangement of various devices in a network? ***SSC CHSL 2023***
(a) Closed system (b) Transmission mode
(c) Network topology (d) Open system

40. In a completely connected network, how many lines are required for connecting 6 nodes? ***SSC CHSL 2023***
(a) 12 (b) 15 (c) 30 (d) 24

41. In which of the following network topologies do the connected components makes a closed loop? ***RRB NTPC (CBT II) 2022***
(a) Tree topology (b) Ring topology
(c) Star topology (d) Bus topology

42. Ethernet uses
(a) bus topology (b) ring topology
(c) mesh topology (d) All of these

43. A small message in network used to pass between one station to another is known as
(a) token (b) byte
(c) word (d) ring

44. Which of the following is the most common type of network topology used in LANs? ***SSC CHSL 2019***
(a) Star (b) Ring
(c) Bus (d) Mesh

45. In star topology, all devices connected to a central device by ………… . ***CPCT 2024***
(a) hub only (b) switch only
(c) router (d) hub or switch

46. In which topology, every node is connected to two other nodes? ***IBPS RRB PO Mains 2018***
(a) Bus topology (b) Ring topology
(c) Star topology (d) Mesh topology

47. Which of the following is the network topology in which there are bi-directional links between each possible node?
(a) ring (b) star
(c) tree (d) mesh

48. ……… is an alternate name for the completely interconnected network topology.
(a) Mesh (b) Star
(c) Tree (d) Ring

49. Which is the highest reliable topology? ***IBPS RRB PO Mains 2018***
(a) Mesh topology (b) Tree topology
(c) Bus topology (d) Star topology

50. Which of the following network topologies is most suitable for large-scale networks? ***UGC NET, 2018***
(a) Star (b) Ring
(c) Mesh (d) Bus

51. Which topology provides the highest fault tolerance? ***UGC NET 2020***
(a) Star (b) Mesh
(c) Bus (d) Ring

52. Which of the following best describes a hybrid topology? *UGC NET, 2018*
(a) A combination of two or more topologies
(b) A single-point network topology
(c) A network with only bus topology
(d) A ring topology network

OSI Model

53. Find out the OSI layer, which performs token management.
(a) Transport layer (b) Network layer
(c) Presentation layer (d) Session layer

54. In Open System Interconnection(OSI) model of computer networks, switches work at....layer and consider data as....not as signals. *SSC Selection Post 2023*
(a) application, protocol (b) physical, bits
(c) data link, frames (d) network, data packets

55. Encryption and decryption are the functions of
(a) transport layer (b) session layer
(c) presentation layer (d) All of these

56. Which of the following is the fourth layer of OSI model
(a) Application layer (b) Data link layer
(c) Transport layer (d) Session layer

57. In OSI network architecture, the routing is performed by which of the following layers?
(a) Network layer (b) Data link layer
(c) Transport layer (d) Session layer

58. Which of the following protocols working on the transport layer provides a connectionless service between hosts? *CPCT 2024*
(a) IP (b) ARP (c) TCP (d) UDP

59. In the following list of devices which of the following device is used at the network layer?
(a) Repeaters (b) Router
(c) Application gateway (d) Switch

60. Switches work on which OSI layer?
(a) Data link layer (b) Physical layer
(c) Transport layer (d) Network layer

61. Which of the following layer of open-system interconnection model lies between presentation layer and transport layer in computer system? *SSC Selection Post 2023*
(a) Layer 7 (b) Layer 5 (c) Layer 3 (d) Layer 2

62. Which networking device operates at layer 2 of the OSI model and forwards data based on MAC addresses? *SSC CGL 2023*
(a) Switch (b) Hub
(c) TCP/IP Model (d) Router

63. In IT networking, which of the following devices is used in the physical layer?
(a) Repeater (b) Router
(c) Transport gateway (d) Bridge

64. Which of the following is the main function of the data link layer? *UGC NET 2018*
(a) Routing of packets
(b) Error detection and correction
(c) Encryption and decryption
(d) Segmentation of data

TCP/IP Model

65. TCP/IP ....layer corresponds to the three layers of OSI model.
(a) application (b) presentation
(c) session (d) transport

66. The standard suit of protocols used by the Internet, Intranets, extranets and some other networks.
(a) TCP/IP (b) Protocol
(c) Open system (d) Internet work processor

67. What does TCP stand for with respect to computer networks?
(a) Transmission Control Protocol
(b) Transfer Call Plan
(c) Transfer Control Process
(d) Transmission Call Protocol

68. How many layers are there in the TCP/IP model of computer network?
(a) 4 (b) 7
(c) 6 (d) 9

Answers

1.	(b)	2.	(a)	3.	(d)	4.	(a)	5.	(a)	6.	(c)	7.	(a)	8.	(c)	9.	(a)	10.	(b)
11.	(c)	12.	(d)	13.	(c)	14.	(b)	15.	(a)	16.	(a)	17.	(a)	18.	(a)	19.	(b)	20.	(a)
21.	(c)	22.	(a)	23.	(c)	24.	(c)	25.	(b)	26.	(d)	27.	(a)	28.	(c)	29.	(a)	30.	(c)
31.	(d)	32.	(a)	33.	(d)	34.	(c)	35.	(b)	36.	(d)	37.	(d)	38.	(b)	39.	(c)	40.	(b)
41.	(b)	42.	(a)	43.	(a)	44.	(a)	45.	(d)	46.	(b)	47.	(d)	48.	(a)	49.	(a)	50.	(a)
51.	(b)	52.	(a)	53.	(d)	54.	(c)	55.	(c)	56.	(c)	57.	(a)	58.	(d)	59.	(b)	60.	(a)
61.	(b)	62.	(a)	63.	(a)	64.	(b)	65.	(a)	66.	(a)	67.	(a)	68.	(a)				

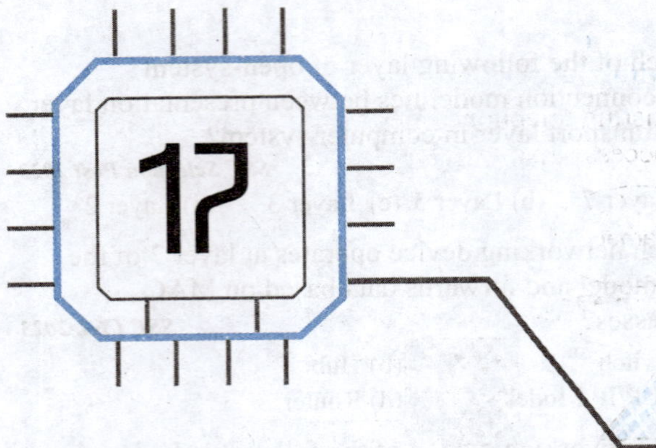

Internet and Its Services

- Internet stands for **Interconnected Network**.
- It is a network of networks that connects billions of computers across the world with each other.
- It allows computers to communicate and share data using standardised communication protocols.
- The Internet enables various services such as the WWW, email, file sharing and social media.
- This era is called **era of communication revolution** due to the utility of Internet.

In this Chapter

- History of Internet
- Internet Connections
- Internet Terms and Definitions
- Applications/Services of Internet

> "We are all now connected by the Internet, like neurons in a giant brain."
>
> **~ Stephen Hawking**

History of Internet

- **1969** ARPANET was created by the U.S. Department of Defense's ARPA (Advanced Research Project Agency). It was the world's first computer network and the precursor to the Internet.
- **1970s** TCP/IP (Transmission Control Protocol/Internet Protocol) was developed by **Vint Cerf** and **Bob Kahn**, forming the standard for data transmission on the Internet.
- **1983** ARPANET adopted TCP/IP and the Internet was officially born.
- **1989** Tim Berners-Lee developed the **World Wide Web** (WWW), a system of hyperlinked documents that could be accessed through Internet.

Internet in India

- The first public Internet service in India was introduced by **VSNL** in 1995.
- National Information Center, New Delhi was one of the first agencies to connect to the Internet, contributing to the national efforts to bring Internet services to the public.

Internet Connections

- Internet connections refer to the methods or technologies that allow a device to access the Internet.
- These connections are provided by **ISP** (Internet Service Provider) companies.

Here are the main types of Internet connections provided by ISPs

1. Dial Up Connection

- It is an older method of accessing the Internet using a **telephone line**.
- It uses a **modem** to convert digital data into an analog signal that can travel over the phone line.
- Dial Up connections are very slow, with speeds typically up to **56 kbps**.
- It is also called the **analog connection** or **switch line connection**.

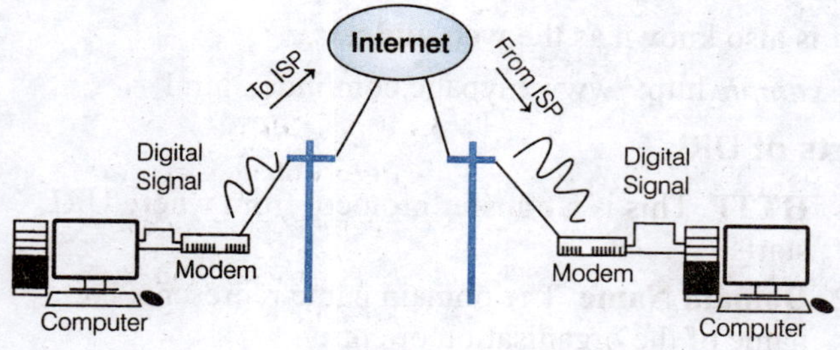

2. Leased Line Connection

- It is a dedicated, **private connection** between customer and service provider.
- It is used by businesses for reliable and high-speed Internet access.
- Leased lines offer high-speed transmission, with speeds ranging from 1 Mbps to several Gbps.

3. Broadband Connection

- It is widely used for both home and business purposes due to its reliability and speed.

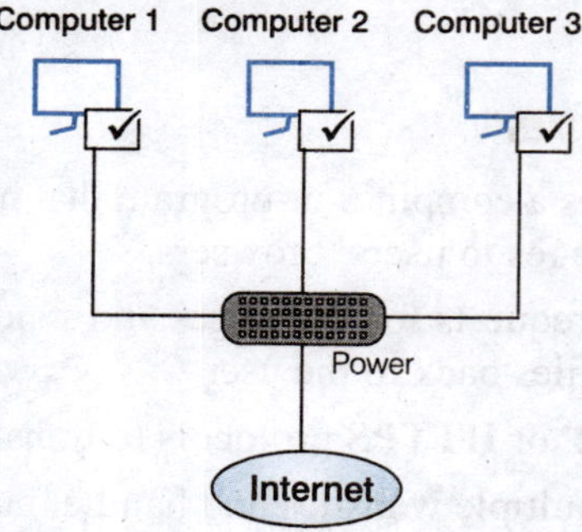

- Broadband offers much faster speeds compared to dial-up, typically ranging from 1 Mbps to 1 Gbps or more.

Types of Broadband Connections

Broadband connections are classified into following categories

(i) DSL (Digital Subscriber Line)

- It uses existing telephone lines to deliver high-speed Internet access.

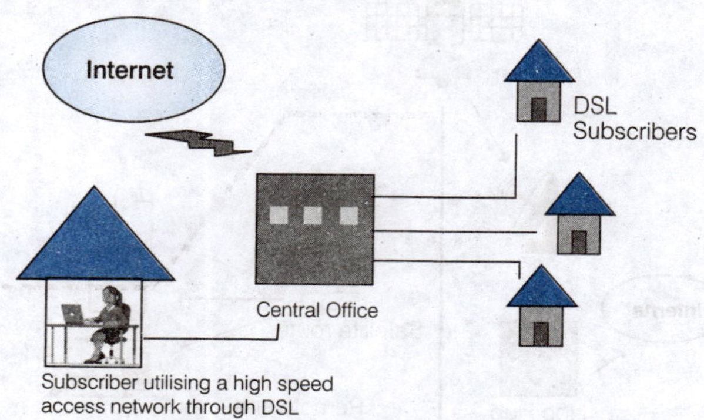

- It separates voice and data signals, which allows simultaneous use of the phone line for voice calls and Internet access.
- DSL speeds range from 256 Kbps to 100 Mbps, depending on the specific type of DSL.

(ii) Cable Broadband

- It uses **coaxial cables** to deliver high speed Internet access, typically ranging from 10 mbps to 1 Gbps.

(iii) BPL (Broadband over Power Line)

- It is a **wired** broadband connection that uses the existing electrical power lines to deliver high-speed Internet access.
- BPL is good for areas, where there are no other broadband connections, but power infrastructure exists.

4. ISDN (Integrated Services Digital Network)

- ISDN is a digital communication technology that allows the transmission of voice, data and video over traditional telephone lines.
- It provides a faster and more reliable Internet connection compared to traditional dial-up.

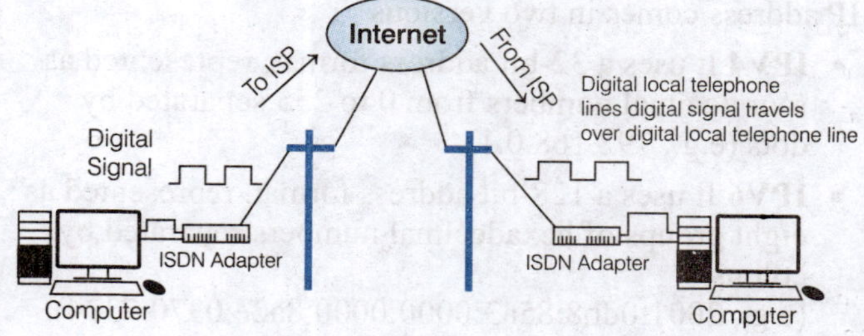

5. Satellite Connection

- It is a **wireless** communication technology that provides Internet access *via* satellites orbiting the Earth.

- It is particularly useful in remote or rural areas, where traditional wired connections like DSL are unavailable.

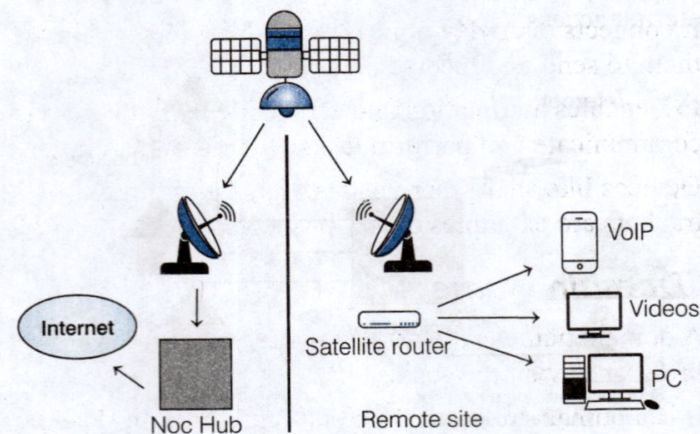

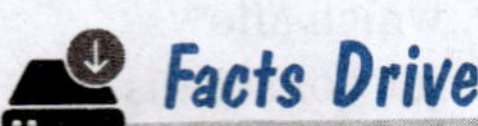

- Vint Cerf is known as the Father of the Internet.
- The process of transmitting data or signals from a ground station to a satellite in space is called **uplink**.
- The process of transmitting data or signals from a satellite to ground station is called **downlink**.
- India's first Internet cafe was opened in Mumbai in 1996.
- The first website domain registered in India was Rediff. com.
- Sabeer Bhatia is considered as the father of Hotmail, the first free e-mail service in India.

Internet Terms and Definitions

1. IP Address

- Every computer connected to the Internet has a special numerical address for its unique identification, which is called **IP Address** (Internet Protocol Address).
- IP address is given by **ISP** (Internet Service Provider).
- If a computer is given a new IP Address every time, it is called **dynamic** IP Address.
- If a computer is given a permanent IP Address, it is called **static** IP Address.
- IP address comes in two versions
  - **IPV4** It uses a 32-bit address format, represented as four decimal numbers from 0 to 255 separated by dots (e.g., 192.168.0.1).
  - **IPV6** It uses a 128-bit address format, represented as eight groups of hexadecimal numbers separated by colons (e.g., 2001:0db8:85a3:0000:0000:8a2e:0370:7334).

2. World Wide Web (WWW)

- WWW is also known as **The Web, Information Superhighway** or **W3**.
- Millions of web pages are available on it in the form of documents which are connected to each other through hyperlinks.
- It was developed by **Tim Berners-Lee** in 1989 at Physics Research Lab (CERN) in Geneva.
- It provides the facility to view all the information posted on the Internet.
- Major parts of the World Wide Web are Website, Web Page, Browser, Search Engine, URL, etc.

3. URL (Uniform Resource Locator)

- A URL is a **unique address** used to locate and access specific resources on the Internet.
- It is also known as the **web address**.

Example http://www.mypage.com/index.html

Parts of URL

1. **HTTP** This is a transfer protocol from where URL starts.
2. **Domain Name** The domain name represents the name of the organisation or entity.
3. **Absolute Path** Specifies the exact location or page on the server.

4. Web Page

- A web page is what you see in a web browser when you're on the Internet.
- It is often written using **HTML** (Hypertext Markup Language).
- It is of two types - **static web page** and **dynamic web page**.
- Static webpages have fixed content, while dynamic webpages update based on user interaction or real-time data.

5. Web Server

- Web Server is a computer or program that hosts and serves webpages to users' browsers.
- It processes requests for webpages and sends the appropriate files back to the user.
- It uses **HTTP** or **HTTPS** protocols to transfer data.
- It can host multiple websites and handle multiple requests simultaneously.

6. Website

- A collection of related webpages is called a **website**.
- All websites are available on the web server.
- The first page of every website is called the **home page**.

7. MAC (Media Access Control) Address

- A MAC address is a unique identifier assigned to a Network Interface Card (NIC) for communication on a physical network.
- It is unique and different for every system.
- It is usually of **48 bits**.
- It is also called **physical** and **hardware address**.
- The device is identified in the network on the basis of Mac Address.

8. Cloud Computing

- Connecting to the Internet and using the facilities available on the Internet is called **cloud computing**.

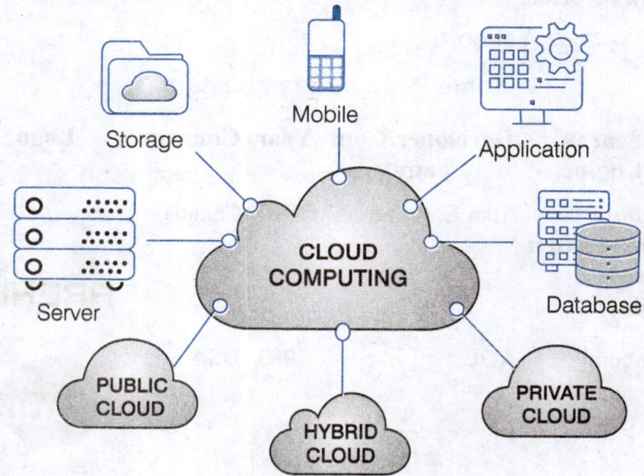

- It is also called **cloud storage**.
- In this, various types of services are provided in the form of software through the Internet.

Example Google Drive, Google Photos etc.

Advantages of Cloud Computing

- **Cost Efficiency** No need for expensive hardware.
- **Scalability** Easily adjusts to demand.
- **Accessibility** Access from anywhere with Internet.
- **Data Backup** Easy data storage and recovery.

9. Cookies

- Cookies are small pieces of data stored on a user's device by a web browser.
- They are used by websites to remember information about the user, such as login details, preferences and browsing history.
- It enhances user experience by personalising content, keeping users logged in and tracking website activity.

10. Internet of Things

- It is also called IoT.
- It connects everyday objects to the Internet and allows them to send and receive data.
- IoT enables automation and efficiency by letting devices communicate and perform tasks without human input.
- Devices like smart thermostats, lights and fitness trackers are examples of IoT products.

11. Domain Name

- A domain name is the **address** you type in the web browser to visit a website.
- It is a human-friendly name that represents an IP address, makes it easier for user to find websites online.

Example In the web address www.example.com "example.com" is the domain name, with '.com' domain extension.

Types of Domain Name

(i) Geographical Domain

- A domain name that is based on a specific geographic location or country.

Example Country-code top-level domains (ccTLDs) like .uk (United Kingdom), .in (India), .ca (Canada).

(ii) Organisational Domain

- A domain name that is linked to a specific organisation, business or entity.

Example Generic top-level domains (gTLDs) like .com (Commercial Groups), .gov (Government Organisation), .edu (Educational Institutes) or .mil (Military Organisations).

Note DNS (Domain Name System) is a protocol used to translate domain name into IP address and *vice-versa*.

12. Web Browser

- A web browser is a **software program** that helps in connecting a computer to the Internet.
- Through this, the World Wide Web can be accessed.

Some Popular Web Browsers

Web Browser	Logo	Developer/Company	Key Feature
Mosaic (1993)		Marc Andreessen	▪ First graphical web browser
Netscape Navigator (1994)		Netscape Communications	▪ Early leader in the browser market

Web Browser	Logo	Developer/Company	Key Feature
Internet Explorer (1995)		Microsoft	▪ It was the default browser on Windows computers, discontinued on 15 June 2022.
Opera (1995)		Opera Software	▪ Known for its built-in VPN and blocker features
Mozilla Firefox (2002)		Mozilla Foundation	▪ Privacy-focused and customisable browser
Safari (2003)		Apple	▪ Optimized for Apple devices
UC Browser (2004)	UCBrowser	UCWeb	▪ Popular browser for mobile browsing, data compression
Google Chrome (2008)		Google	▪ It is one of the most widely used web browsers globally
Epic Browser (2010)		Hidden Reflex	▪ India's first web browser
Microsoft Edge (2015)		Microsoft	▪ It is the successor to Internet Explorer

13. Search Engine

- A search engine is a software system that allows users to search for information on the Internet.
- It indexes billions of web pages and retrieves relevant results based on user queries.
- There are several types of search engines, each serving different purposes.

Here are the main types

1. Crawler Based Search Engine

- A crawler-based search engine works like a robot that explores the Internet.
- It is also called **web spider**.

Example Google, Bing

2. Human Powered Directories

- These directories rely on people to manually submit and categorize websites into different topics or categories.

Example DMOZ, Yahoo, Directory

3. Meta Search Engines

- This is a type of search engine that doesn't search the web directly.
- It sends your search query to multiple other search engines, then combines the results into one list.

Example DuckDuckGo, Dogpile

4. Hybrid Search Engines

- A hybrid search engine combines features of both crawler-based search engines and human-powered directories.

Example Yahoo

Some Popular Search Engines

Search Engine	Developer/Company	Year	Country	Logo
Archie **(World's first search engine)**	Alan E. Reiter	1990	Canada	ARCHIE
Aol.com	AOL	1983	USA	Aol.
Google	Google	1998	USA	
Bing	Microsoft	2009	USA	
Yahoo	Yahoo	1994	USA	Y!
DuckDuckGo	DuckDuckGo Inc.	2008	USA	
Baidu	Baidu Inc.	2000	China	Bai百度
Yandex	Yandex N.V.	1997	Russia	Yandex

Search Engine	Developer/Company	Year	Country	Logo
Ask.com	Ask Media Group	1996	USA	
Netscape Search	Netscape Communications	1994	USA	
Guruji **(India's first search engine)**	Guruji.com	2006	India	

14. Bookmark

- A bookmark is a saved shortcut in a web browser that lets you quickly access your favorite websites.
- Instead of typing the website's address every time, you can just click on the bookmark to visit the site instantly.

Steps to bookmark a website

- Open the website you want to bookmark.
- Press **Ctrl+D** or click the **star icon** in the browser's address bar.
- Choose the folder where you want to save the bookmark.
- Click Done to save the bookmark.

Applications/Services of Internet

1. E-Mail (Electronic Mail)

- Email is a method of sending digital messages over the Internet.
- It allows users to send and receive messages, documents and files to others using email addresses.
- Email was developed by **Ray Tomlinson** in 1971.
- Some popular free email services are Gmail, Yahoo mail, Rediff mail, Outlook.com, AOL mail, Zoho mail, Hotmail, Proton mail, iCloud mail etc.

An email address has 2 main parts

1. Local Part

- This is the first part of the email address, before the "@" symbol.
- It represents the username.

  Example In john@example.com, "john" is the local part (username).

2. Domain Part

- This is the part after the "@" symbol.
- It identifies the mail server that is responsible for receiving the email.

  Example In john@example.com, "example.com" is the domain part.

Parts of an email Message

1. **Subject** This is a brief summary of the email's content. It helps the recipient understand what the email is about.
2. **From** The email address of the person sending the mail is written in it.
3. **To** The email address of the person receiving the mail is written in it.
4. **CC (Carbon Copy)** Used to send the email to additional recipients. Everyone in the "To" and "CC" fields can see each other's email addresses.
5. **BCC (Blind Carbon Copy)** Used to send the email to additional recipients while keeping their email addresses hidden from others. Only the sender sees the BCC recipients.

Mail Box and Its Parts

1. **Inbox** The folder where you receive incoming emails.
2. **Sent** Stores copies of all the emails you've sent.
3. **Drafts** Holds emails that you have started but haven't finished or sent yet.
4. **Trash/Junk** Stores deleted emails temporarily, which can be recovered before they are permanently deleted.
5. **Outbox** Stores failed or unsent emails.
6. **Spam** Holds emails identified as unwanted or suspicious.

Steps to Send an email Message

1. Log in to your email account (e.g., Gmail, Outlook, Yahoo Mail).
2. Click on the "Compose" button to start a new message.
3. Enter the recipient's email address in the "To" field.
4. Type a subject for your email in the "Subject" line to summarise the content of the message.
5. Write the message in the main body section. This is where you add the content of your email.
6. Review your email to check for errors or missing information.
7. Click on "Send" button to send the email.

Note
- The username in the email address cab be maximum **64 characters** long.
- A maximum of **25 MB** file can be sent in email.
- Text, photo, audio, video files can be sent along with the email message, which is called **attachment**.

2. Social Networking

- Social networking services are online platforms that allow users to create profiles, interact with other users, share content and communicate in real-time.
- These platforms help people connect with friends, family, colleagues and even strangers with similar interests.
- Users can post updates, share photos, videos, links and articles, creating a personalised online presence.

Some Popular Social Networking Sites

Social Networking Site	Logo	Founded By	Launch Year	Country of Origin
LinkedIn		Reid Hoffman	2003	USA
Facebook		Mark Zuckerberg	2004	USA
Orkut		Orkut Buyukkokten	2004	Brazil
YouTube		Steve Chen, Chad Hurley, Jawed Karim	2005	USA
Reddit		Steve Huffman	2005	USA
Twitter		Jack Dorsey	2006	USA
WhatsApp		Jan Koum, Brian Acton	2009	USA
Pinterest		Ben Silbermann, Paul Sciarra	2010	USA
Instagram		Kevin Systrom, Mike Krieger	2010	USA
Snapchat		Evan Spiegel, Bobby Murphy	2011	USA

3. E-commerce (Electronic Commerce)

- It refers to the buying and selling of goods and services over the Internet.
- It allows consumers to shop from home 24/7, offering a wide variety of products.

Example Amazon, Flipkart, eBay etc.

4. E-banking (Electronic Banking)

- It is a service that allows customers to perform financial transactions *via* the Internet.

Example PhonePay, Google Pay.

5. Video Conferencing

- Video conferencing allows people to communicate in real-time through both audio and video over the Internet.

Example Zoom, Skype, Google Meet and Microsoft Teams.

6. E-news

- E-news is the delivery of news and updates through digital platforms, often involving websites or apps.

Example BBC News, The New York Times and The Times of India.

7. E-books (Electronic Books)

- E-books are digital versions of printed books that can be read on electronic devices like e-readers, tablets or smartphones.
- E-books allow readers to carry entire libraries in their pockets or bags.

8. E-reservation

- E-reservation refers to booking services like travel, accommodation, tickets and other reservations online through Internet-based platforms.

Example MakeMyTrip, Booking.com and IRCTC

9. Blogging

- It is a type of Internet service that allows individuals or organisations to create and publish content (called "blog posts") on the Internet.
- It enables users to share personal opinions, experiences, ideas or information on various topics.

Example Tumblr, WordPress and Medium.

Important Abbreviations

ISP Internet Service Provider
WWW World Wide Web
URL Uniform Resource Locater
IP Internet Protocol
MAC Media Access Control
DNS Domain Name System
IoT Internet of Things
SEO Search Engine Optimisation
TLD Top Level Domain

Facts Drive

- The first IoT device was a **Coca-Cola vending machine** at Carnegie Mellon University in 1982.
- The first domain name was **symbolics.com** registered on March 15, 1985 by Symbolics.
- **WWW** was the world's first web browser created by Tim Berners Lee.
- **Ray Tomlinson** is credited with sending the first email between two computers connected on the ARPANET network.
- The term **'social network'** was first coined by **J.A. Barnes** in 1950s.
- **Facebook** is the world's largest social networking site with over 2.9 billion active users as of 2024.
- **Twitter** is the most popular platform for microblogging.
- The first video ever uploaded on YouTube was titled **Me at the zoo**, uploaded by Jawed Karim on April 23, 2005.
- **Downloading** refers to transferring data from the Internet to your device.
- **Uploading** refers to sending data from your device to the Internet.
- **Incognito mode** (also known as private browsing) is a feature in web browsers that allows users to browse the Internet without saving history.
- **Usenet** is an early online discussion system, created in 1980, where users post messages and share files in newsgroups.

PYQs Oneliner

1. A global network of interconnected computers and devices is called **Internet.** *Delhi Police 2023*
2. **Outlook** is an example of an email client. *IBPS PO 2021*
3. Google Meet, Zoom, Skype technologies are commonly used for **video conferencing**. *RRB NTPC 2021*
4. **Mosaic** was the first graphical web browser. *SSC GD 2020*
5. "Private browsing without saving history" is the main feature of **Incognito Mode** in web browsers. *SSC CGL 2023*
6. **Lynx** is a text-based web browser. *RRB JE 2019*
7. URL stands for **Uniform Resource Locater**. *RRB NTPC 2021*
8. **Yahoo** is an example of a search engine. *SSC CHSL 2021*
9. **Hotmail** is considered the first email service. *SSC CHSL 2020*

Practice Exercise

Introduction to Internet

1. Which of the following is not a feature of the Internet? *SSC CGL 2020*
(a) E-mail
(b) File sharing
(c) Private network connectivity
(d) Video conferencing

2. A global network of interconnected computers and devices is called.... *Delhi Police 2023*
(a) Manet (b) Ethernet (c) Intranet (d) Internet

3. The Internet is a system of
(a) software bundles (b) web page
(c) website (d) interconnected networks

4. The Internet is
(a) a large network of networks
(b) an internal communication system for a business
(c) a communication system for the Indian government
(d) All of the above

5. The Internet allows you to
(a) send electronic mail
(b) view web pages
(c) connect to servers all around the world
(d) All of the above

6. Which of the following is an example of connectivity?
(a) Internet (b) Floppy disk
(c) Power cord (d) Data

7. Internet was developed in the
(a) 1950s (b) 1960s (c) 1970s (d) 1980s

8. .... is the standard protocol of the Internet.
(a) TCP/IP (b) Java (c) HTML (d) Flash

9. Which of the following is the major use of Internet?
(a) Browsing webpages
(b) Sharing data and information
(c) Social networking
(d) All of the above

Internet Connections

10. Which of the following is a type of Internet connection that uses a telephone line for data transmission? *Delhi Police 2022*
(a) Satellite (b) Broadband
(c) Dial up (d) Fibre optic

11. .... involves using a smartphone's data connection to provide Internet access to other devices such as laptops or tablets. *Delhi Polic 2023*
(a) Satellite (b) Dial up
(c) Wi-fi (d) Tethering

12. .... networks can be used for public Internet access at hotspot such as restaurants, coffee shops etc.
(a) Wi-Fi (b) Wi-Max
(c) DSL (d) BPL

13. Which of the following is not an Internet connection?
(a) Dial-Up (b) DSL
(c) WAN (d) Broadband

14. What is the full form of ISDN?
(a) Internet Service Digital Network
(b) Integrated Services Digital Network
(c) International Service Digital Network
(d) Integrated Short Digital Network

15. Which type of Internet connection uses telephone lines but provides faster speeds than dial-up? *SSC CGL 2021*
(a) Cable (b) DSL
(c) Fiber Optic (d) Satellite

16. Which type of Internet connection uses radio signals to provide broadband? *SSC CHSL 2021*
(a) Fiber Optic (b) Cable Broadband
(c) Satellite Internet (d) Wi-Fi

17. Which of the following best describes the primary difference between broadband and dial-up Internet connections? *SSC CHSL 2024*
(a) Broadband is only available in urban areas, while dial-up is available everywhere.
(b) Dial-up uses a telephone line, while broadband uses various technologies for higher speeds.
(c) Dial- up requires a cable connection, while broadband does not.
(d) Broadband is slower than dial-up.

Internet Terms and Definitions

18. What does 'www' stand for in a web address? *SSC CGL 2019*
(a) World Wide Web
(b) World Wide Word
(c) Web Wide World
(d) Wide Web World

19. The .... service allows a group of Internet users to exchange their views on some common topic.
(a) nicnet (b) milnet
(c) telnet (d) usenet

20. The web server on the Internet is also known as
(a) host (b) client
(c) hub (d) repeater

21. The term surfing on the Internet refers to which of the following? *SSC CHSL 2019*
(a) Sending an email
(b) Browsing web pages
(c) Downloading files
(d) Connecting to a server

22. Which among the following was first graphical web browser? *RRB NTPC 2019*
(a) Lynx (b) Mosaic
(c) Chrome (d) Internet Explorer

23. What is the main purpose of DNS in Internet communication? *IBPS PO 2018*
(a) Assigning IP addresses to websites
(b) Resolving domain names to IP addresses
(c) Monitoring Internet traffic
(d) Storing website data

24. What does the term 'microblogging' refer to? *SSC CGL 2019*
(a) Writing large blogs
(b) Short posts or messages online
(c) Sending mass emails
(d) Posting pictures online

25. What is the main purpose of cookies in web browsing? *IBPS Clerk 2020*
(a) To store user preferences
(b) To execute programs
(c) To clean cache memory
(d) To increase processing speed

26. What does DNS stand for in Internet terminology? *SSC CGL 2021, RRB NTPC 2021*
(a) Data Network Service (b) Domain Name System
(c) Direct Name Service (d) Digital Network System

27. Which technology is used to identify users on the Internet? *SSC CGL 2024*
(a) IP Address (b) URL
(c) HTML (d) DNS

28. An IP version 4 address is ...... long. *Delhi Police 2022*
(a) 16 bytes (b) 32 bytes
(c) 64 bits (d) 32 bits

29. Which of the following servers convert IP addresses to domain names? *RRB NTPC 2021*
(a) Cloud Services (b) Email
(c) P2P (d) DNS

30. .... is collection of web pages and .... is the very first page that we see on opening of website.
(a) Home page, web page
(b) Website, home page
(c) Web page, home page
(d) Web page, website

31. A web browser is a
(a) tool for creating a database
(b) software program to view web pages on the Internet
(c) printing device
(d) software program to delete a folder

32. Which of the following is an address on the world wide web that is used to access specific web resources and is the specific path to a resource? ***Delhi Police 2023***
(a) Hyperlink (b) Web server
(c) Web pages (d) Uniform resource locator

33. Which among the following is a part of the URL (Uniform Resource Locator)? ***SSC CHSL 2024***
(a) Server (b) Port number
(c) Error code (d) Multiplexer

34. Each webpage has a unique address, called.... which identifies its location on the Internet. ***SSC Selection Post 2023***
(a) Integrated Service Digital Network (ISDN)
(b) Internet Service Provider (ISP)
(c) Uniform Resource Locator (URL)
(d) Internet Protocol (IP)

35. The last three letters of the domain name describes the type of ***SSC FCI 2012***
(a) organisation (domain name)
(b) connectivity
(c) server
(d) protocol

36. which of the following parts of a given URL is a domain name?
http://www.india.in/tallybook/tallybook.xyz ***SSC CHSL 2023***
(a) https: (b)www.india.in
(c) tally book (d) tallybook.xyz

37. Which is not the feature of Internet?
(a) E-mail (b) Newsgroup
(c) Chat (d) Designing

38. Which of the following is most commonly used to identify return visitors to a website?
(a) Logged-in visitors
(b) Digital certificates
(c) Electronic time stamping
(d) Cookies

39. The transmission of a file to our computer from the Internet is called
(a) downloading (b) uploading
(c) saving (d) receiving

40. Every computer host on the Internet has
(a) unique 15 digit number
(b) unique IP address
(c) similar IP address
(d) None of the above

41. .... is a unique name used in the URLs to identify website.
(a) IP (b) TCP
(c) Domain name (d) Host

42. Which of the following statement is false about the webpage?
(a) Webpage is a document that is displayed in the web browser on WWW.
(b) Static webpage contains fixed information to visitors that are not frequently changed.
(c) In a dynamic webpage, information frequently changes.
(d) None of the above

43. .com, .edu, .gov and .net are the examples of
(a) protocol (b) tag
(c) top level domain (d) IP address

44. A computer that is used to store data or information for users on the Internet is called
(a) web server (b) web client
(c) web database (d) web application

45. What is the protocol in the given URL "http/www.mypage.com"?
(a) www (b) http
(c) mypage (d) .com

46. Which of the following is not an open-source, cross-platform web server software? ***IBPS Clerk 2020***
(a) Apache (b) Nginx
(c) IIS (d) Tomcat

47. Which of the following is the most commonly used web browser? ***IBPS Clerk 2021***
(a) Internet Explorer
(b) Mozilla Firefox
(c) Google Chrome
(d) Safari

48. Which of the following is used to assign unique identifiers to devices on a network? ***SSC CGL 2020***
(a) IP Address (b) MAC Address
(c) HTTP (d) DNS

49. What is the function of an IP Address? ***IBPS Clerk 2020***

(a) To store data on a network
(b) To provide security to network data
(c) To identify and locate a device on a network
(d) To transfer files between computers

50. What is the maximum character length for a domain name? ***SSC CHSL 2020***

(a) 60 characters (b) 100 characters
(c) 253 characters (d) 120 characters

51. Which of the following is the correct description of the World Wide Web (WWW)? ***RRB NTPC 2020***

(a) A network that connects all computers worldwide
(b) A protocol used to transfer files over the Internet
(c) A system of interlinked hypertext documents accessed *via* Internet
(d) A type of Internet security system

Applications/Services of Internet

52. Which of these is a popular blogging platform? ***UPSC Prelims 2019***

(a) WordPress (b) Blogger
(c) Tumblr (d) All of these

53. Which technology is commonly used for video conferencing? ***SSC CGL 2022***

(a) LAN (b) Skype
(c) FTP (d) Bluetooth

54. Which of the following is the maximum file size that can be attached to an email message in Gmail? ***SSC CHSL 2024***

(a) 100 MB (b) 200 MB
(c) 50 MB (d) 25 MB

55. Which among the following is an area of e-mail that is short description of the message?

(a) Subject (b) Cc
(c) Bcc (d) Attachment

56. Which of the following is always a part of e-mail address?

(a) Period (.) (b) At sign (@)
(c) Space () (d) Underscore (_)

57. An e-mail attachment is referred to as

(a) The body of the e-mail
(b) The address of the sender
(c) A document that is sent with an e-mail.
(d) Any document that can be attached and sent with an e-mail

58. Which of the following best describes Electronic Mail (E-mail)? ***SSC CGL (T-II) 18.01.2025***

(a) A method of sending messages electronically over a computer network
(b) A system for storing digital files on the cloud
(c) A type of secure online transaction system
(d) A service used to make phone calls over the Internet

59. Which of the following is a communication service provided by the Internet? ***Delhi Police 2020***

(a) Email (b) Gopher
(c) FTP (d) Utility computing

60. Which of the following fields of an e-mail hides the identity of the recipients?

(a) To (b) From
(c) Cc (d) Bcc

61. Sending an e-mail is similar to

(a) writing a letter (b) drawing a picture
(c) talking on the phone (d) sending a package

62. In a multipart email message, what does the boundary parameter in the Content-Type header signify? ***SSC CGL (T-II) 20.01.2025***

(a) It defines the length of the email message.
(b) It separates the email's body from the attachments.
(c) It marks the start and end of each part in a multipart message.
(d) It limits the file size of each attachment.

63. Which of the following actions can typically be performed in the Outbox? ***SSC CGL (T-II) 20.01.2025***

(a) Viewing archived emails
(b) Deleting received emails
(c) Editing emails that are yet to be sent
(d) Managing contact lists

64. Junk e-mail is also known as

(a) crap
(b) spoof
(c) sniffer script
(d) spam

65. If you receive an e-mail from someone you don't know, what should you do?

(a) Forward it to the police immediately
(b) Delete it without opening it
(c) Open it and respond to them saying you don't know them
(d) Reply and ask them for their personal information

66. Which action should be taken in Microsoft Outlook to send a received email to another person, while keeping the original message for your records? ***SSC CGL (T-II) 18.01.2025***

(a) Use the 'Archive' option and create a new email.
(b) Open the email, click on 'Forward' and enter the recipient's email address.
(c) Click on 'Reply' and add the new recipient's email address.
(d) Click on 'Reply All' and select 'Forward' from the options.

67. Which of the following cannot be part of an e-mail address?
(a) Period (.)
(b) At Sign (@)
(c) Space ()
(d) Underscore (_)

68. Gmail belongs to
(a) great mail (b) yahoo mail
(c) google mail (d) gopher mail

69. Which of the following is not a term related to e-mail?
(a) PowerPoint (b) Inbox
(c) Sender (d) Receiver

70. Which of the following technologies allows real-time communication over the Internet, such as voice and video calls, without requiring additional software or hardware beyond a web browser? ***SSC CGL (T-II) 18.01.2025***
(a) FTP (b) VoIP
(c) WebRTC (d) Email

71. Which one of the following is not an online chat software? ***Delhi Police 2020***
(a) AWS (b) Internet Relay Chat
(c) Google Talk (d) Slack

72. Online conversations in which you are immediately able to send messages back and forth to one another another is called…. ***Delhi Police 2022***
(a) VLOG
(b) EMAIL
(c) CHAT
(d) BLOG

73. A …… is a telecommunication technology, which permits two or more people in different locations to interact *via* mutual video or audio transmission simultaneously. ***Delhi Police 2022***
(a) payment gateway (b) Blog
(c) Email (d) Video conferencing

74. Who is the founder of Facebook.
(a) Orkut Buycukkokten
(b) Mark Zuckerberg
(c) Bill Gates
(d) Martin Cooper

75. Which social networking service have the biggest emphasis on professional networking? ***SSC CHSL 2024***
(a) Facebook (b) Google +
(c) LinkedIn (d) Twitter

Answers

1.	(c)	2.	(d)	3.	(d)	4.	(a)	5.	(d)	6.	(a)	7.	(d)	8.	(a)	9.	(d)	10.	(c)
11.	(d)	12.	(a)	13.	(c)	14.	(b)	15.	(b)	16.	(c)	17.	(b)	18.	(a)	19.	(d)	20.	(a)
21.	(b)	22.	(b)	23.	(b)	24.	(b)	25.	(a)	26.	(b)	27.	(a)	28.	(d)	29.	(d)	30.	(b)
31.	(b)	32.	(d)	33.	(b)	34.	(c)	35.	(a)	36.	(b)	37.	(d)	38.	(d)	39.	(a)	40.	(b)
41.	(c)	42.	(d)	43.	(c)	44.	(a)	45.	(b)	46.	(c)	47.	(c)	48.	(b)	49.	(c)	50.	(c)
51.	(c)	52.	(d)	53.	(b)	54.	(d)	55.	(a)	56.	(b)	57.	(d)	58.	(a)	59.	(a)	60.	(d)
61.	(a)	62.	(c)	63.	(c)	64.	(d)	65.	(b)	66.	(b)	67.	(c)	68.	(c)	69	(a)	70.	(c)
71.	(a)	72.	(c)	73.	(d)	74.	(b)	75.	(c)										

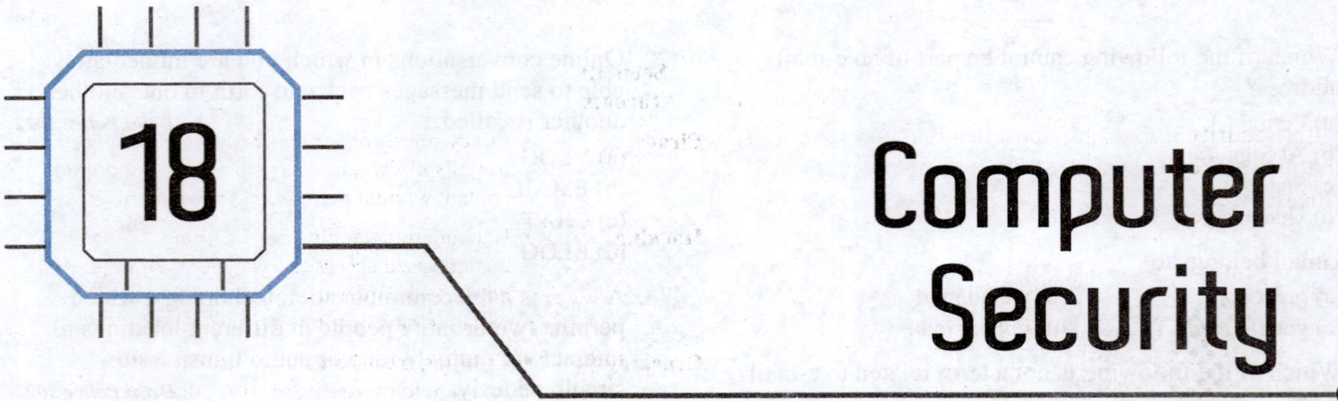

Computer Security

- Computer security refers to the **protection of computer systems**, networks and data from unauthorised access.
- It is required to protect against cyber-attacks, maintain smooth functioning and protect important data.
- With the growing dependence on digital technologies, computer security has become essential.
- It involves measures such as firewalls, encryption and antivirus programs, to defend against various security threats.
- It is also known as **network security**.

In this Chapter

- Components of Computer Security
- Threats to Computer Security
- Computer Virus
- Computer Security Measures
- Hackers

"At the end of the day the goals are simple safety and security."

~ **Jodi Rell**

Components of Computer Security

The main components of computer security are

1. Confidentiality

- It ensures that data is not accessed by any unauthorised person.

2. Integrity

- Integrity ensures that data has not been modified or accidentally altered by an unauthorised user.

3. Availability

- Availability ensures that data and resources are available or accessible by an authorised user whenever they are needed.

4. Authentication

- It is the process of verifying the identity of a user before granting access to resources.
- It ensures that users are the persons they claim to be.

5. Non-repudiation

- It ensures that originators of messages cannot deny that they are not sender of the message.
- It provides proof that the action really happened and who did it.

6. Access control

- It ensures that users access only those resources that they are allowed to access.

Threats to Computer Security

- Computer security threats are activities that can steal information, make the system stop working properly or harm the devices.

- These threats can cause damage to the system or make it unsafe by affecting the way it works.

Security threats	Description
Malware	▪ Malware is a **malicious software** that harm or exploit a computer system.
Phishing	▪ Phishing is a type of cyber-attack where attackers trick people into revealing sensitive information, such as usernames, passwords or credit card details.
Denial-of-Service Attack	▪ A DoS attack is when someone makes a website or online service stop working by flooding it with too much traffic. ▪ This causes the system to slow down or crash, making it impossible for people to use it.
Cyber Bullying	▪ When someone uses the internet, social media or other digital platforms to harass or threaten, another person is called cyberbullying. ▪ It can include sending mean messages, sharing hurtful posts or spreading rumors online.
Identity Theft	▪ When someone steals your personal information, like passwords or bank details, to pretend to be you and commit fraud is called identity theft.
Salami Attack	▪ Salami attack is a technique, where an attacker steals small amounts of money from many bank transactions. ▪ It is also known as **salami slicing**.
Cyber Stalking	▪ When someone uses the internet or digital platforms to monitor another person's activities is called cyber stalking. ▪ It has been declared a crime under section 354 C and 354 D of the Indian Penal Code.
Spoofing	▪ When someone pretends to be a trusted person or system to trick others is called spoofing. ▪ This can involve faking an email address, phone number or website to trick victims.
Piracy	▪ Piracy refers to the illegal copying, sharing or use of software, movies, music or other digital content without permission or paying for it.
Hacking	▪ Hacking refers to the act of gaining unauthorised access to computer systems or networks in order to steal or manipulate sensitive data or information.
Cracking	▪ Cracking means breaking into a system or software to bypass its security, like unlocking a password or removing protection from a program. ▪ It's usually done to access something without permission.
Data Diddling	▪ Data diddling means changing or tampering with data in a system to make it incorrect or fake.
SQL Injections	▪ It is a type of attack, where a hacker inserts harmful code into a website's database through things like search boxes or login forms. ▪ This can allow the hacker to steal, change or delete important data from the database.
Eavesdropping	▪ It refers to the act of secretly listening to or intercepting private communications, like emails, phone calls or data being sent over a network, without permission.
Cyber Pornography	▪ It refers to the distribution, viewing, sharing or downloading of pornographic content in electronic form, such as videos, images or text files.
Cyber Warfare	▪ It refers to the use of digital attacks by one country to damage or disrupt the computer systems of another country.

Malware

- Malware is short for **malicious software**, which refers to any software designed to harm, exploit or damage a computer or network.
- It can come in many forms, such as viruses, worms, trojans, ransomware and spyware.

Types	Description
Virus	▪ The full form of virus is **Vital Information Resource Under Siege**. ▪ It is a malicious program that can corrupt, delete or steal data.
Trojan Horse	▪ It is a malware that looks like a legitimate program but once you open it, it secretly gives hackers access to your computer. ▪ It is also called **hide malware program**.

Types	Description
Worm	▪ It is a **self-replicating** program that spreads across networks without needing to attach to files. ▪ It fills up the computer's memory and slows down its speed.
Spyware	▪ It is a malware program that is installed on a computer by hacker to monitor all activities of the user.
Ransomware	▪ It is a malware program that locks computer files and demands money or ransom in exchange for unlocking them.
KeyLogger	▪ It is a type of spyware program that records your keystrokes to steal your passwords or credit card numbers.
Adware	▪ It is a malware program that displays unwanted advertisements on your computer, often in the form of pop-ups, banners or videos.
Botnet	▪ A botnet is a network of computers that have been infected with malware and are controlled by a hacker. ▪ It is used to steal login IDs and passwords, to control computers and for DoS attacks.
Scare Ware	▪ It tricks users into downloading harmful software or visiting infected websites.
Backdoor	▪ It is a secret way for hackers to access your computer or network without your knowledge.
Rootkits	▪ It allows cyber criminals to access a computer without being detected.

Computer Virus

- A computer virus is a type of malware that can infect your computer and cause harm.
- It attaches itself to files or programs and spreads when you open or share those files.
- The term virus was first used by a computer scientist, **Fred Cohen** in 1983.

Note All viruses are malwares but not all malwares are viruses.

Types of Virus

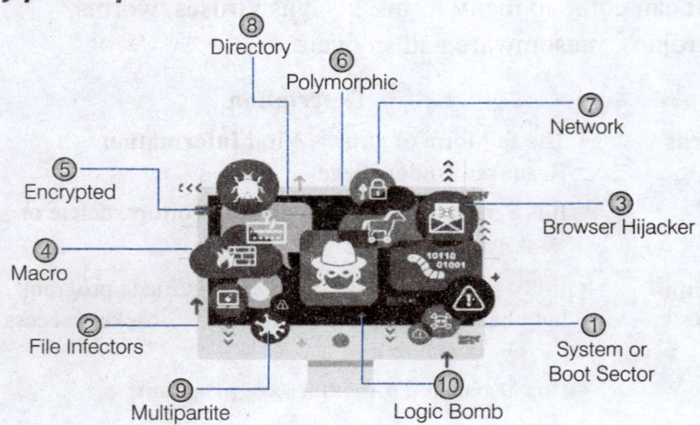

1. Boot Sector Virus

- It is a type of virus that infects the boot sector of a computer's hard drive.
- When the computer starts up, this virus can load itself into memory, allows itself to spread and infect other systems.
- This virus overwrites and changes the boot record program.

Example Brain, Disk Killer, Stoned Virus

2. File/Program Infector Virus

- This virus infects **executable program files** with extensions such as .exe, .bin, .txt etc.
- It makes its own copies and become active in memory by infecting the executable files.

Example Sunday, Cascade

3. Browser Hijacker

- This virus takes control of your web browser settings without your permission.
- It changes things like your homepage, search engine or new tab page and redirects you to unwanted websites.

Example Ask Tookbar, Sweet Page

4. Macro Virus

- This virus infects files created by software programs that use macros, like Microsoft Word or Excel.
- **Macros** are small programs used to automate tasks and a macro virus exploits these to spread and execute harmful commands.

Example DMW, Concept

5. Encrypted Virus

- This type of virus hides itself by encrypting its code.
- These viruses are harder to detect by antivirus programs.

6. Polymorphic Virus

- It is a type of virus that changes its code or structure each time it infects a new file or system.
- This makes it harder for antivirus programs to detect because it appears different every time.

Example Storm Worm, VirLock, Ursnif

7. Network Virus

- It is a type of virus that spread through computer networks.
- They are designed to move quickly between systems, causing disruptions and spreading infections across the network.

Example SQL Slammer, Nimda

8. Directory Virus

- This virus changes the path of the file.
- It tricks the system into running the virus instead of the intended program.

Example Dir-2 Virus

9. Multipartite Virus

- It is a type of virus that can infect both the boot sector and executable files.
- It can spread through storage devices, email attachments or file downloads.

Example Tequila

10. Logic Bomb/Time Bomb

- This type of viruses are programmed to activate under specific conditions, like a certain date or action.
- They remain hidden in the system until triggered.

Common reasons for the spread of viruses

- Opening infected email attachments.
- Downloading files from unsafe websites.
- Using infected USB drives or external media.
- Clicking on phishing links or fake ads.
- Sharing files over insecure networks.

Some common effects of viruses

- Data loss or corruption.
- Slows down system performance
- Causes crashes or freezes.
- Allows unauthorised access.
- Displays unwanted ads.
- Disables security features.

Famous viruses and their invention years

Virus	Year	Description
Creeper	1971	▪ The first computer virus, spreads on networks.
Brain	1986	▪ First boot sector virus. ▪ Designed as copy protection, made in Pakistan.
Jerusalem	1987	▪ A virus that activated on the Friday 13th, causing file corruption.
Melissa Virus	1999	▪ Spread through email and caused widespread email traffic.
I Love You	2000	▪ Spread *via* email attachments and cause damage worldwide.
Code Red	2001	▪ Targeted Microsoft IIS servers and caused website crashes.
My Doom	2004	▪ Affected email systems and caused denial-of-service attacks.
Conficker	2008	▪ A worm that spread across Windows systems and created a botnet.
Petya Ransomware	2016	▪ A ransomware virus that encrypted files and demanded payment to restore access.
Stuxnet	2010	▪ Targeted industrial systems, specifically Iranian nuclear plants.

Computer Security Measures

1. Antivirus

- Antivirus is a type of **utility software**.
- It is designed to detect, prevent and remove viruses on computers or networks.
- It blocks viruses from entering your system.

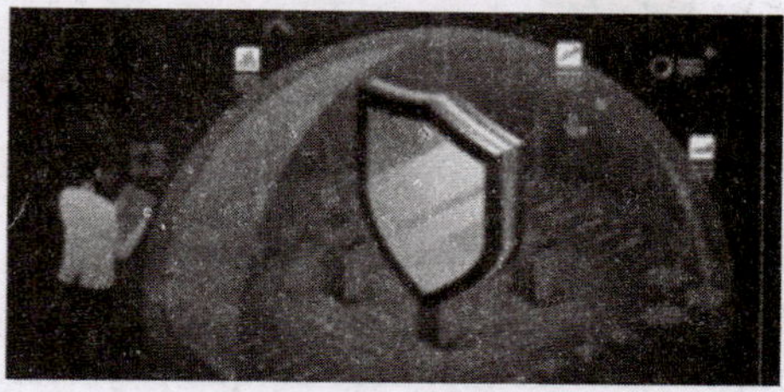

Examples of some popular antivirus softwares

(i) Norton (ii) McAfee
(iii) Kaspersky (iv) Avast
(v) Bitdefender (vi) AVG
(vii) Windows Defender (built into Windows)
(viii) PANDA (ix) Quick Heal
(x) Trend Micro

2. Password

- Passwords are used to secure a computer and network.
- It is basically a secret word or phrase used to authenticate a user's identity and grant access to a system.
- Passwords are of two types – weak and strong passwords.
- Strong passwords are long, complex and unique, they include combination of alphabets, numbers or special characters.

- Weak passwords are more vulnerable to attacks.

3. Firewall

- It is a security system that monitors and controls incoming and outgoing network traffic based on predefined security rules.
- It acts as a barrier between a trusted internal network and untrusted external networks.
- It can be both hardware and software.
- It prevents unauthorised access to the computer system.

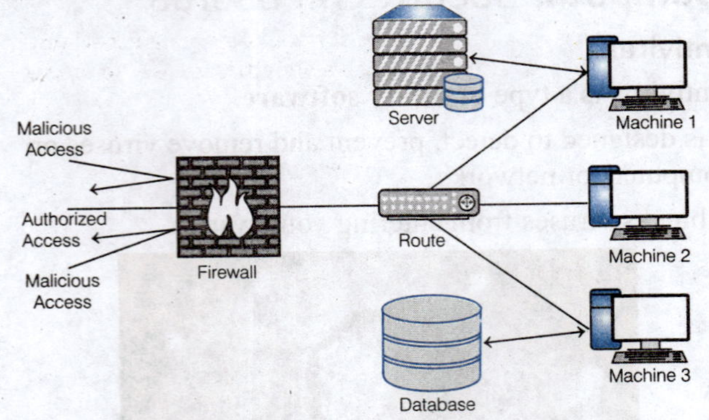

4. Biometric

- It is a security measure that uses unique physical characteristics (like fingerprints, face recognition or iris scans) to verify identity.

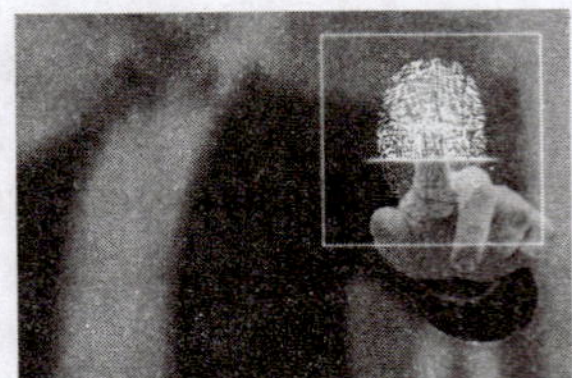

5. CAPTCHA

- It stands for Completely Automated Public Turing Test to Tell Computers and Humans Apart.
- It is used to protect website from spammers.
- It is a challenge-response test used to determine, if the user is human or a robot.

6. Encryption

- It is the process of converting original message into a secret code to prevent unauthorised access.

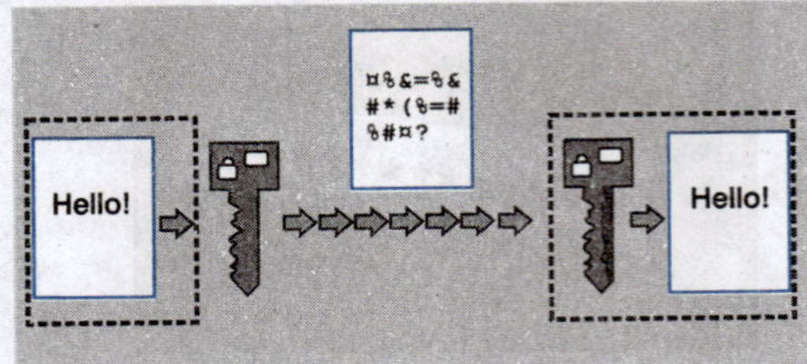

- The original message is called **normal text** and the secret code is called **cipher text**.
- Encryption happens on the sender's side.

7. Decryption

- The process of converting encrypted code back into its original form is called **decryption**.
- This happens on the receiver's side.

8. Cryptography

- Cryptography is the process of securing communication and information by converting it into a secret code.
- It uses algorithms and keys to protect data from unauthorised access.

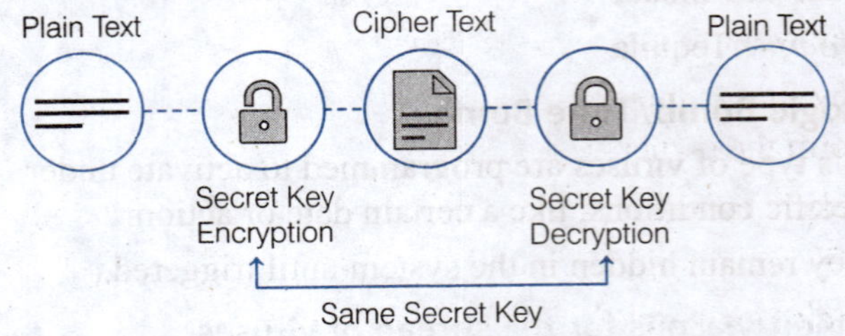

- Encryption and decryption both are used together in cryptography.

9. Patch

- It refers to the small software updates, released time to time by software companies to fix bugs, vulnerabilities or security issues in a software.
- Regular patching ensures systems are protected from known threats.

10. Digital Signature

- It is a cryptographic technique used to verify the authenticity and integrity of digital documents.
- It is similar to hand signature but it is digital.
- This ensures that the document is original.

Hackers

- The act of gaining unauthorised access to computer systems, networks or data is called **hacking**.

- The person or professional who does hacking is called a **hacker**.
- They gain access to systems by detecting security vulnerabilities in computer and network systems.
- Hackers are mostly programmers.

Types of Hackers

Hackers are classified into following categories

1. White Hat Hacker

- They are also known as **ethical hackers**.
- They work to improve security.
- They find vulnerabilities in systems or networks and inform the owners to fix them.
- Hackers falling into this category do hacking for good work.

2. Black Hat Hacker

- These are also called **crackers**.
- They perform illegal activities.
- They exploit security weaknesses for personal gain, such as stealing data, spreading malware or causing damage.

3. Grey Hat Hacker

- Hackers of this category are a mixture of black and white hat hackers.
- They may break into systems without permission but usually don't cause harm.
- They might report the vulnerabilities they find, often without authorisation.

4. Blue Hat Hacker

- Hackers who expose and correct the flaws of the software before it is launched are called blue hat hackers.

5. Green Hat Hacker

- Hackers who are still learning hacking come under this category.
- They are eager to learn and develop their skills.
- These are also known as **pre-hacker**.

6. Red Hat Hacker

- Their objective is same as that of white hat hackers.
- They go after black hat hackers with the intention to destroy or block their activities.

Facts Drive

- **'Steganography'** is an art of hiding the existence of a message.
- The legal right to use software based on specific restrictions is granted *via* **software license**.
- A **proxy server** also called application gateway, acts as an intermediary between user's device and the internet.
- **SSL** (Secure Sockets Layer) and **TLS** (Transport Layer Security) both are cryptographic protocols used to secure communication over the internet.
- **Masquerading** in computer security refers to an attack where an unauthorized entity impersonates a legitimate user or system to gain access to sensitive data.
- A **hacktivist** is a person who uses hacking techniques to promote political, social or environmental causes.

Important Abbreviations

DDoS Distributed Denial of Service

OTP One-Time Password

CAPTCHA Completely Automated Public Turing Test to Tell Computers and Humans Apart

CIA Confidentiality, Integrity and Availability

PYQs Oneliner

1. The **hashing** method is commonly used to verify the integrity of data. *SSC CGL (T-II) 20.01.2025*
2. The process of verifying a user's identity is called **authentication**. *DSSSB TGT 2023*
3. The information transformed during encryption is **plain text**. *DSSSB TGT 2023*
4. **Trojans** appear to perform one function but in fact perform another malicious function. *DSSSB Patwari 2022*
5. **Resident viruses** are embedded in a system's memory so it can be reactivated if the original virus is deleted. *SSC CGL 2023*
6. **Keyloggers** can be either hardware or software to record the keys pressed by a user on the keyboard. *SSC CGL 2023*
7. **Worm** is a type of malware that appear useful but in reality, damages the files. *CPCT 2024*
8. **Macro virus** spreads through application software. *IBPS RRB 2022*

Practice Exercise

Introduction to Computer Security

1. ……… is a branch of information technology known as information security.
(a) Computer security (b) Cyber security
(c) IT security (d) All of these

Components of Computer Security

2. Which of the following is not a component of computer security? *SSC CGL 2020*
(a) Confidentiality (b) Integrity
(c) Availability (d) Popularity

3. What does the process of encryption ensure in computer security? *SSC CGL 2021*
(a) Protection of hardware
(b) Protection of software
(c) Protection of data during transmission
(d) Protection of system files

4. If you are allowing a person on the network, based on his/her credentials to maintain the security of your network, then this act refers to the process of
(a) authentication (b) automation
(c) firewall (d) encryption

5. The ………… method is commonly used to verify the integrity of data. *SSC CGL (T-II) 20.01.2025*
(a) Hashing (b) Caching
(c) Duplication (d) Compression

6. Which of the following is a method of securing a computer system by encrypting data and limiting access to authorised users only? *SSC CGL 2018*
(a) Authentication
(b) Authorisation
(c) Encryption
(d) Firewall

7. Which one of the following is a method of verifying the identity of a user or system? *SSC CGL 2023*
(a) Encryption (b) Authentication
(c) Authorisation (d) Audit trail

8. Which of the following ensures that data is accurate and not tampered?
(a) Availability
(b) Confidentiality
(c) Integrity
(d) Authentication

9. What does the term integrity in computer security refer to?
(a) Preventing unauthorised access to resources
(b) Ensuring data is accurate and not tampered with
(c) Providing access to resources when needed
(d) Encrypting sensitive data

10. The process of ensuring that authorised users have reliable access to information is known as
(a) authentication (b) confidentiality
(c) integrity (d) availability

Threats to Computer Security

11. A malware is a
(a) program (b) hardware
(c) person (d) None of these

12. Softwares such as viruses, worms and trojan horses that have a malicious content, are known as
(a) malicious software (malware)
(b) adware
(c) scareware
(d) spyware

13. Which of the following is a well-known security threat in computer networks that involves sending unsolicited messages to a large number of users?
(a) Phishing (b) Spamming *SSC CHSL 2021*
(c) Hacking (d) Scamming

14. A worm
(a) can automatically move in network
(b) can only be transferred with human intervention
(c) worms are harmless
(d) None of the above

15. A …… replicates on its own and can spread to other computers through the network. It incurs unexpected or damaging behaviour on an infected computer system. *SSC Selection Post 2023*
(a) trojan (b) keylogger
(c) worm (d) rootkit

16. In the context of cyber security, what does phishing refer to? *SSC CGL 2021*
(a) A method of securing web traffic
(b) A type of virus that spreads via email
(c) A fraudulent attempt to obtain sensitive information by pretending to be a trustworthy entity
(d) A method of encrypting data for storage

17. It is a software program designed to record (log) every keystroke on the machine on which it runs.
(a) Keylogger (b) Worm
(c) Virus (d) Cracker

18. What kind of program spreads across a computer network, replicating itself, unlike a virus? *IBPS RRB 2022*
(a) Keylogger (b) Cracker
(c) Worm (d) All of these

19. What is the term used for software that sends popups for advertisements? *IBPS PO 2021*
(a) Spyware (b) Malware
(c) Adware (d) Rootkit

20. Hackers often gain entry to a network by pretending to be at a legitimate computer, it is called
(a) spoofing (b) forging
(c) IP spoofing (d) All of these

21. An act of sending e-mails or creating webpages that are designed to collect an individual's online bank, credit card or other login information?
(a) Phishing (b) Spam
(c) Hacking (d) Cracking

22. Which of the following is a criminal activity attempting to acquire sensitive information such as passwords, credit cards, debits by masquerading as a trustworthy person or business in an electronic communication?
(a) Spoofing (b) Phishing
(c) Stalking (d) Hacking

23. All of the following are examples of real-security and privacy risks except
(a) hackers (b) spam
(c) viruses (d) None of these

24. It is a toolkit for hiding the fact that a computer's security has been compromised, is a general description of a set of programs which work to subvert control of an operating system from its legitimate (in accordance with established rules) operators.
(a) Rootkit (b) Keylogger
(c) Worm (d) Cracker

25. It hides the true network addresses and used to intercept all messages entering and leaving the network.
(a) Logic bomb (b) Firewall
(c) Patches (d) Proxy server

26. Illegal copying and distribution of software is
(a) Hacking (b) Software piracy
(c) Software literacy (d) Cracking

27. Which of the following is the most common form of computer malware? *SSC CGL 2021*
(a) Virus (b) Worm
(c) Trojan horse (d) Antivirus

28. What does phishing aim to do in terms of computer security? *SSC CHSL 2023*
(a) Gain unauthorized access to networks
(b) Steal sensitive information by pretending to be a trustworthy entity
(c) Block access to websites
(d) Encrypt data to demand ransom

29. Which of the following is an example of a computer security threat? *SSC CHSL 2023*
(a) Antivirus (b) Worm
(c) Firewall (d) Encryption

30. Which of the following is not a type of malware? *SSC CHSL 2023*
(a) Virus (b) Trojan horse
(c) Adware (d) Wi-Fi

31. What is a common feature of a Ransomware attack? *SSC CHSL 2023*
(a) Data loss due to accidental deletion
(b) Encryption of files demanding payment
(c) Eavesdropping on network traffic
(d) Unauthorised modification of files

32. What type of attack involves collecting small amounts of money from many different transactions? *SSC CGL 2019*
(a) Salami attack (b) Phishing
(c) Data diddling (d) Identity spoofing

33. Repeated acts of harassment or threats using electronic means is referred to as *SSC CHSL 2021*
(a) cyber stalking (b) cyber bullying
(c) phishing (d) salami attack

34. Which of the following cyber security threats involves altering or manipulating data in a system without authorisation? *SSC CGL 2019*
(a) Data diddling (b) Identity spoofing
(c) Phishing (d) Salami attack

Computer Virus

35. Which one of the following is a computer virus? *SSC CHSL 2021*
(a) Penguin (b) Panda
(c) Spider (d) Creeper

36. Which of the of following computer viruses damages the formatting of a document and does not allow it to edit? *RRB NTPC 2021*
(a) File virus (b) Macro virus
(c) Worm (d) Boost sector virus

37. What is a common sign that a computer might be infected with a virus? *SSC CGL (T-II) 20.01.2025*
(a) Improved system security
(b) Unusual system slowdowns and unexpected errors
(c) Faster system boot times
(d) Increased hard drive space

38. Which type of virus infects the boot sector of floppy disks or the Master Boot Record (MBR) of hard disks? *SSC CGL (T-II) 18.01.2025*
(a) Direct Action Virus (b) Resident Virus
(c) Macro Virus (d) Boot Sector Virus

39. What is the term for a virus that triggers a payload at a specific time? *IBPS RRB 2022*
(a) Time bomb (b) Worm
(c) Trojan horse (d) Keylogger

40. Which virus fools a user into downloading and executing it by pretending to be a useful application? *IBPS RRB 2022*
(a) Cracker (b) Worm
(c) Trojan horse (d) Keylogger

41. Which of the following viruses infects the master boot record? *SSC CGL 2023*
(a) Trojan (b) Boot sector virus
(c) Worm (d) Polymorphic virus

42. Which type of virus modifies itself to avoid detection? *SSC CHSL 2022*
(a) Multipartite virus (b) Polymorphic virus
(c) Trojan (d) Worm

43. Which was the first PC boot sector virus?
(a) Creeper (b) Payload
(c) Bomb (d) Brain

Computer Security Measures

44. What is 'Trend Micro'? *IBPS RRB 2022*
(a) It is an antivirus software
(b) It is just a program
(c) It is a virus program
(d) None of the above

45. What is the primary purpose of antivirus software? *IBPS RRB 2022*
(a) To clean files
(b) To prevent malware infections
(c) To speed up the computer
(d) To increase disk space

46. Which of the following is not a security measure to prevent unauthorised access to a network? *SSC CGL 2021*
(a) Firewalls (b) Antivirus software
(c) Encryption (d) Virtual Private Network

47. What is a digital signature?
(a) Scanned signature (b) Signature in binary form
(c) Encrypting information (d) Handwritten signature

48. .....acts as network filter and based on the predefined security rules, it controls the incoming and outgoing traffic. *SSC Selection Post 2023*
(a) Trojan (b) Keyloggers
(c) Cookies (d) Firewall

49. Which of the following cyber security measures involves verifying the identity of users before granting access to a system or network? *SSC JE 2023*
(a) Multifactor authentication
(b) Regular software updates
(c) Firewall configuration
(d) Network encryption

50. Coded entries which are used to gain access to a computer system are called
(a) entry codes (b) passwords
(c) security commands (d) code words

51. Which of the following is an example of multifactor authentication for PC security? *SSC CHSL 2024*
(a) Antivirus software (b) Fingerprint scan
(c) OS protection (d) Firewall protection

52. What security mechanism ensures that system updates are installed without user intervention? *SSC CGL (T-II) 18.01.2025*
(a) Patch management software
(b) Firewall
(c) Secure Boot
(d) Intrusion Detection System

53. .... refers to privileges that allow a user to read, write or execute a file.
(a) Authentication (b) File access permission
(c) Password (d) Firewall

54. What is the primary function of a firewall in a computer network? *SSC CGL 2020*
(a) To store data
(b) To prevent unauthorised access
(c) To monitor network speed
(d) To manage network devices

55. What is a firewall in the context of network security? *SSC CGL 2023*
(a) A software application for managing files. and folders.
(b) A type of malware that spreads through email attachments.
(c) A security mechanism that filters and controls network traffic.
(d) A hardware device used to boost network performance.

56. Which of the following is an antivirus software? *RRB NTPC 2021*
(a) Google (b) XML
(c) Norton (d) Microsoft

57. What is the purpose of enabling passwords on a PC? *SSC CGL (T-II) 20.01.2025*
(a) For improving the data signal strength
(b) For providing an additional layer of security
(c) For reducing the installed applications
(d) For printing of the data in the PC

Hackers

58. Hackers
(a) all have the same motive
(b) are another name of users
(c) many legally break into computer as long as they do not do any damage
(d) break into other people's computer

59. Which of the following types of hackers, also known as crakers, hack to gain unauthorised access to a system and harm its operations or steal sensitive information. *SSC CGSL 2023*
(a) White hat (b) Black hat
(c) Red hat (d) Grey hat

60. The person who uses a computer to cause harm to people or destroy critical systems is called
(a) cyber terrorist
(b) Black hat hacker
(c) cyber cracker
(d) hacktivist

61. Which of the following types of hackers is also known as a 'cracker'? *SSC CGL 2020*
(a) White hat (b) Black hat
(c) Grey hat (d) Hacktivist

62. Which hacker is known for ethical hacking and works to improve system security? *SSC CHSL 2021*
(a) Black hat (b) White hat
(c) Script kiddie (d) Hacktivist

63. Which of the following is the primary objective of a 'Black Hat' hacker? *SSC CGL 2019*
(a) To help organisations improve their security
(b) To gain unauthorised access for malicious purposes
(c) To promote social justice
(d) To work with organisations to test security

64. A hacker who compromises systems for political or social causes is referred to as a *SSC CHSL 2020*
(a) Script kiddie (b) Black hat
(c) Hacktivist (d) White hat

65. What is a White Hat hacker also known as? *SSC CGL 2022*
(a) Black hat hacker (b) Ethical hacker
(c) Cracker (d) None of these

66. Which of the following is a characteristic of a black hat hacker? *SSC CHSL 2021*
(a) Works with government authorities to fix security loopholes
(b) Cracks system security for malicious purposes
(c) Uses hacking skills to secure websites
(d) Works for corporations to protect their systems

67. A grey hat hacker does the following. *SSC CGL 2020*
(a) Only hacks with the permission of the target system owner
(b) Always hacks for malicious purposes
(c) Sometimes hacks systems and reports flaws, sometimes exploits them
(d) Never engages in hacking activities

Answers

1.	(d)	2.	(d)	3.	(c)	4.	(a)	5.	(a)	6.	(c)	7.	(b)	8.	(c)	9.	(b)	10.	(d)
11.	(a)	12.	(a)	13.	(b)	14.	(a)	15.	(c)	16.	(c)	17.	(a)	18.	(c)	19.	(c)	20.	(c)
21.	(a)	22.	(b)	23.	(d)	24.	(a)	25.	(d)	26.	(b)	27.	(a)	28.	(b)	29.	(b)	30.	(d)
31.	(b)	32.	(a)	33.	(b)	34.	(a)	35.	(d)	36.	(b)	37.	(b)	38.	(d)	39.	(a)	40.	(c)
41.	(b)	42.	(b)	43.	(d)	44.	(a)	45.	(b)	46.	(d)	47.	(c)	48.	(d)	49.	(a)	50.	(b)
51.	(b)	52.	(a)	53.	(b)	54.	(b)	55.	(c)	56.	(c)	57.	(b)	58.	(d)	59.	(b)	60.	(a)
61.	(b)	62.	(b)	63.	(b)	64.	(c)	65	(b)	66.	(b)	67.	(c)						

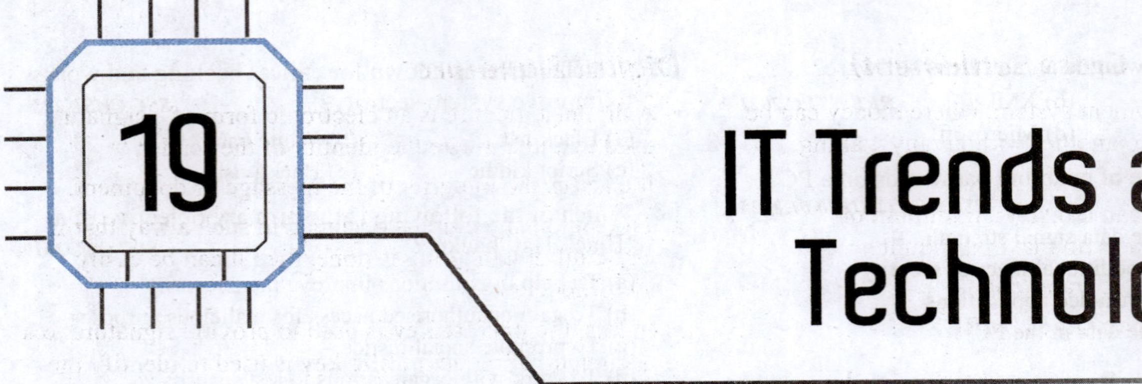

19 IT Trends and Technology

- IT trends refer to the evolving patterns and directions in the field of Information Technology that reflect changes in technology practices and business needs.
- These trends often drive how technology is developed, implemented and used in various industries.

In this Chapter
- UPI
- Electronic Payment System
- NEFT
- RTGS
- IMPS
- Cloud Computing
- Digital Signature
- OTP
- Biometric Sensor
- Mobile Wallet/E-Wallet
- QR Code
- Cryptocurrency

" Predicting the future is not magic, it is artificial intelligence.

~ **Dave Waters** "

UPI

- UPI stands for **Unified Payments Interface**.
- It is a real-time payment system technology introduced by the **NPCI** (National Payments Corporation of India) in 2016.
- It allows users to transfer money, pay bills and make online purchases directly from their bank accounts using their mobile phones.
- **MPIN** is used while making UPI Payment.
- MPIN is a 4 or 6-digit personal identification number used to authenticate transactions in the UPI system.
- The full form of MPIN is Mobile Banking Personal Identification Number.

Electronic Payment System

- An Electronic Payment System (E-Payment) is defined as a mode of payment over an electronic network, such as the internet.
- It is a type of financial exchange, which is established online between the seller and the customer.
- E-payment systems are safe, speedy and cost-effective alternatives to cash-based payment systems.

NEFT (National Electronics Fund Transfer)

- NEFT is an electronic payment system in India that facilitates the transfer of funds between banks on a one-to-one basis.
- It is operated by the **Reserve Bank of India (RBI)** and is widely used for secure online transactions.
- NEFT was established in November 2005 by the Institute for Development and Research in Banking Technology (IDRBT).

RTGS (Real Time Gross Settlement)

- This is an online payment system, where money can be sent from one bank to another without any waiting period.
- Through RTGS you can transfer a minimum of Rs 2,00,000 and there is no maximum limit.
- It is ideal for high-value transactions.
- This system is also maintained by **RBI**.

IMPS (Immediate Payment Service)

- IMPS is an instant interbank electronic fund transfer system in India.
- It enables real-time transfers 24x7.
- It is managed by the NPCI (National Payments Corporation of India).
- It is popular for its speed and convenience.
- IMPS was started in 2010.

Cloud Computing

- Cloud computing is the delivery of computing services such as storage, servers, databases, networking, software and analytics over the internet.
- In this, various types of services are provided in the form of software through the Internet.
- It is also called **cloud storage**.
- In this, only internet is required to access the data.

  Example Google Drive, AWS, Microsoft Azure, OneDrive (Microsoft), iCloud (Apple) etc.

Types of Cloud Computing Services

1. IaaS (Infrastructure as a Service)

- It provides virtualized computing resources over the internet, including virtual machines, storage and networking.

  Example Amazon Web Services (AWS), Microsoft Azure.

2. PaaS (Platform as a Service)

- It offers a platform that allows customers to develop, run and manage applications without worrying about the underlying hardware and software layers.

  Example Google App Engine, Heroku.

3. SaaS (Software as a Service)

- It delivers software applications over the internet on a subscription basis.
- Users don't need to install or maintain software, they can access it *via* a web browser.

  Example Google Workspace (Docs, Gmail), Microsoft 365, Dropbox.

Digital Signature

- A digital signature is an electronic form of a signature used to authenticate the identity of the sender.
- It ensures the integrity of the message or document.
- The digital signature is designed in such a way that if any kind of tampering is done, then it can be easily identified.
- In this, the **private key** is used to provide signature to a document while the **public key** is used to identify the document.

OTP (One Time Password)

- OTP is a unique, temporary code used to verify a user's identity during digital transactions or logins.
- It is valid for a single session or transaction and adds an extra layer of security.
- Each OTP is unique and usually expires within a few minutes.
- It is usually a **6-digit** code.
- OTP is used to protect digital accounts.

Biometric Sensor

- A biometric sensor is a device that captures biological or physical characteristics of a person, such as fingerprints, facial features or iris patterns, to verify their identity.
- These sensors are commonly used in authentication systems for security purposes.
- In biometric devices, fingerprints are mostly used to collect biometric data of a person.

Mobile Wallet/E-Wallet

- A mobile wallet or e-wallet is a digital application that allows users to store payment information securely and perform transactions electronically using a smartphone or other devices.
- It enables quick payments for shopping, bills and online purchases.
- It eliminates the need for carrying physical cash or cards.
- It is also known as **mobile money**.

Some Popular Mobile Wallets

E-Wallet	Launching Year	Logo	Inventor
PayPal	1998	PayPal	Max Levchin, Peter Thiel, Luke Nosek
Google Pay	2011 (as Google Wallet), rebranded in 2018	G Pay	Google

E-Wallet	Launching Year	Logo	Inventor
Apple Pay	2014	Pay	Apple Inc.
Paytm	2010	paytm	Vijay Shekhar Sharma (One97 Communications)
PhonePe	2015		Sameer Nigam, Rahul Chari
Amazon Pay	2007	amazon pay	Amazon Inc.
Oxigen Wallet	2004		Pramod Saxena and Blue Label Telecom
BHIM Pay	2016	BHIM UNIFIED PAYMENTS INTERFACE	National Payments Corporation of India (NPCI)
Bharat Pay	2018		Ashneer Grover, Shashvat Nakrani

Digital Library

- A digital library is an organized collection where information and resources are stored in digital form and made accessible through computer networks.
- Unlike traditional libraries that have physical books, digital libraries contain e-books, journals, images, audio, and video files in electronic formats.

  Example Project Gutenberg, Internet Archive.

QR Code (Quick Response Code)

- A QR code is a type of **two-dimensional barcode** that can store a significant amount of information, such as URLs, text or payment details.
- It is designed for quick scanning and decoding using a smartphone or QR code scanner.
- It is used during digital payments.

Cryptocurrency

- Cryptocurrency is a type of **digital** or **virtual currency** that uses cryptography techniques for secure transactions.
- Cryptocurrency started with Bitcoin.
- Cryptocurrencies are not controlled by any central authority, such as a government or bank. Instead, they are powered by blockchain networks.
- There are more than 1,000 cryptocurrencies around the world.
- It is used to buy goods and services online.

  Example Bitcoin, Ethereum, Ripple, Dogecoin, Solana and Libra.

Bitcoin

- Bitcoin (BTC) is the first and most widely recognized cryptocurrency.
- It was created by an anonymous person or group of people using the pseudonym **Satoshi Nakamoto**.
- It was introduced in 2008 through a whitepaper titled Bitcoin, a Peer-to-Peer Electronic Cash System and officially launched in 2009.
- The smallest unit of Bitcoin is **Satoshi**.
- No country, government, bank or company has control over Bitcoin.

Blockchain

- Blockchain is a **decentralised digital ledger** that records transactions across multiple computers in a way that makes it secure, transparent and immutable.
- Once data is added to the blockchain, it cannot be altered.
- It is most commonly used in cryptocurrencies like Bitcoin, but also has applications in areas such as supply chain management, smart contracts and voting systems.

OTT (Over-The-Top)

- OTT refers to the delivery of media content, such as movies, TV shows and streaming services, directly over the internet without the need for traditional cable or satellite television subscriptions.
- OTT services bypass traditional distribution channels and are accessible on a variety of devices, including smartphones, tablets, smart TVs and computers.
- **Reliance Entertainment** launched the OTT platform for the first time in India in the year 2008.
- Some popular OTT platforms are Netflix, Amazon Prime, Voot, MX player, Hotstar etc.

Digital Locker

- A Digital Locker (also known as **DigiLocker**) is an online service which allows citizens to store and access their important documents and certificates in a secure digital format.
- It is part of the Digital India initiative to promote **paperless governance** and reduce the dependency on physical documents.
- It was launched by the Government of India on 1 July 2015.
- All important documents such as PAN card, driving license, voter ID card, Aadhaar card etc. can be saved in it.
- To create an account in it, it is mandatory for you to have an Aadhaar card.

E-Commerce

- E-commerce (Electronic Commerce) refers to the buying and selling of goods and services over the internet.
- E-commerce allows businesses to sell products and services to customers worldwide, breaking geographical barriers.
- It includes advertising of products, selling, buying of goods and services etc.

Types of e-commerce

E-commerce is classified into following types

B2C (Business to Consumer)

- This is the most common form of e-commerce, where businesses sell products or services directly to consumers.

Example Amazon, Flipkart, Myntra, Ajio

B2B (Business to Business)

- In this model, businesses sell products or services to other businesses.

Example India Mart, Alibaba, ThomasNet

C2C (Consumer to Consumer)

- In this model, consumers sell directly to other consumers.

Example Quikr, OLX, eBay

C2B (Consumer to Business)

- In this model, individual consumers sell their products or services to businesses.

Example Shutterstock, Google AdSense, Freelancer

C2G (Consumer to Government)

- In this model, consumers provide services, feedback or goods to the government.

Example MP Online, E-Challan

B2G (Business to Government)

- In this model, businesses provide goods and services to government entities.

Example GoWin, FedBid, Trip Advisor

Some Popular E-Commerce Market Place

Company	Year	Logo	Founder	Headquarters
Amazon	1994		Jeff Bezos	Seattle, Washington, USA
Flipkart	2007		Sachin Bansal, Binny Bansal	Bangalore, Karnataka, India
eBay	1995		Pierre Omidyar	San Jose, California, USA
Alibaba	1999		Jack Ma, Peng Lei	Hangzhou, Zhejiang, China
Snapdeal	2010		Kunal Bahl, Rohit Bansal	Gurgaon, Haryana, India
Myntra	2007		Mukesh Bansal, Vineet Saxena, Ashutosh Lawania	Bangalore, Karnataka, India
IndiaMart	1996		Dinesh Agarwal, Brijesh Agrawal	Noida, Uttar Pradesh, India
Jabong	2012		Arun Chandra Mohan, Praveen Sinha	Gurgaon, Haryana, India
Meesho	2015		Vidit Aatrey, Sanjeev Barnwal	Bangalore, Karnataka, India

E-Governance

- Providing all government services to the citizens of the country online through the Internet is called e-governance (Electronic Governance).
- It involves the digitalisation of government functions, services and interactions with the public to make them more efficient, transparent and accessible.
- It reduces administrative costs by cutting down on paper-based processes.
- The e-Governance initiative in India was formally launched in 2006 through the National e-Governance Plan (NeGP).

Pillars of E-Governance

1. People 2. Process 3. Resources 4. Technology

Types of E-Governance

Types	Examples
G2C (Government to Citizen)	e-District (India)
G2B (Government to Business)	GST Portal (India)
G2G (Government to Government)	e-Office (India)
G2E (Government to Employee)	National e-Governance Services Portal

Some Popular E-Governance Portals and their related Areas and Objectives

E-Governance Portal	Description
DigiLocker	▪ Provides a secure cloud platform for storing and sharing important documents and certificates.

E-Governance Portal	Description
e-District	▪ Offers access to district-level services such as certificates, licenses and public grievances.
UMANG	▪ Provides a single platform for multiple government services.
e-Procurement System	▪ Facilitates online tendering and procurement services for government departments and businesses.
Bhoomi Portal	▪ Karnataka government's land records management system allowing citizens to access land details.
National Scholarship Portal	▪ Single-window access for students to apply for various government scholarships.
GeM (Government e-Marketplace)	▪ Provides an online platform for public procurement of goods and services by government bodies.
MCA21	▪ E-governance initiative by the Ministry of Corporate Affairs for company registration and compliance.
Passport Seva	▪ Facilitates online application and processing of passport-related services in India.
Income Tax e-Filing	▪ Portal for taxpayers to file income tax returns and other tax- related services online.
RTI Online	▪ Allows citizens to file Right to Information (RTI) requests with various public authorities.
EPFO Portal	▪ Online platform for Employees, Provident Fund services including balance checks and withdrawals.
Aadhaar	▪ Provides services related to the unique identification system (Aadhaar) including updates and verifications.
Saral Haryana	▪ Single service delivery portal for citizens in Haryana to access government schemes and services.

Robotics

- Robotics is the branch of technology that deals with the design, construction, operation and use of robots.
- Robots are machines or devices that can carry out tasks autonomously, often with the ability to be controlled or programmed by humans.
- The field combines elements of engineering, computer science and artificial intelligence (AI) to create machines that can assist or replace human labor in various industries.
- The word robot originates from the Czech word **robota**, which means **forced labor** or **drudgery**.
- **Joseph Engelberg** is known as the father of robotics.

Some Popular Robots

Robot Name	Description	Category
Unimate	▪ The first industrial robot, developed by George Devol and Joseph Engelberger in the 1960s	Industrial Robot
ASIMO	▪ A humanoid robot developed by Honda, designed to walk, talk and perform tasks like delivering objects and interacting with humans.	Humanoid Robot
Roomba	▪ A robotic vacuum cleaner developed by iRobot.	Service Robot
Curiosity Rover	▪ A robot used by NASA for the exploration of Mars.	Exploration Robot
Sophia	▪ A humanoid social robot developed by Hanson Robotics. It got the citizenship by Saudi Arabia in October 2017	Humanoid Robot
Khamosh Prahari	▪ A robot developed by the Indian Army for surveillance and patrolling in military areas.	Military Robot
Brabo	▪ Developed by the helper company of Tata Motors TAL Manufacturing Solutions.	Industrial Robot
Manav	▪ A humanoid robot developed in the laboratory of A-SET Training and Research Institutes by Dewakar Vaish.	Humanoid Robot
Vyom Mitra	▪ A humanoid robot developed by ISRO (Indian Space Research Organisation) designed for space missions.	Space Exploration Robot
Daksh	▪ A bomb disposal robot developed by DRDO (Defence Research and Development Organisation) in India.	Military Robot
Drone Bhim	▪ A robot drone developed in India for delivering medical supplies, food and other essential items in remote and disaster-stricken areas.	Delivery Robot/Drone

Artificial Intelligence

- Artificial Intelligence (AI) refers to the field of computer science focused on creating machines or software that can perform tasks that typically require human intelligence.
- These tasks include reasoning, learning, problem-solving, perception, language understanding and decision-making.
- **John McCarthy** is known as the father of artificial intelligence.
- Programming languages like LISP, Java, Python are used in artificial intelligence.

Types of Artificial Intelligence

1. Narrow AI (Weak AI)

- AI systems designed to perform a specific task or set of tasks.
- They are highly specialised and can't perform tasks outside their programmed scope.

  Example Siri, recommendation algorithms, self-driving cars (limited to specific environments).

2. General AI (Strong AI)

- AI with the ability to understand, learn and apply intelligence across a broad range of tasks, just like a human.
- It is capable of performing multiple tasks simultaneously.

Example Deep Blue - Computer manufactured by IBM Company which defeated the famous chess player Garry Kasparov.

Applications of AI

1. **Healthcare** Diagnostic tools, personalised medicine, drug discovery, medical imaging analysis.
2. **Finance** Fraud detection, algorithmic trading, risk management, customer service automation.
3. **Retail** Personalised recommendations, inventory management, chatbots, sales forecasting.
4. **Transportation** Autonomous vehicles, route optimisation, traffic management, predictive maintenance.
5. **Education** Adaptive learning platforms, virtual tutors, administrative automation.
6. **Manufacturing** Predictive maintenance, quality control, supply chain optimisation, robotic automation.
7. **Entertainment** Content recommendation systems, video game AI, interactive storytelling.
8. **Agriculture** Crop monitoring, precision farming, yield prediction, pest control.

Some Popular AI Tools

AI Tools	Logo	Launch year	Company
Siri		2011	Apple
Alexa	alexa	2014	Amazon
Google Assistant		2016	Google
Cortana		2014	Microsoft
IBM Watson Assistant		2018	IBM
Bixby		2017	Samsung
Chat GPT		2022	Microsoft
Gemini	Gemini	2023	Google Deepmind
Copilot		2023	Microsoft
DeepSeek AI Chatbot	deepseek	2025	DeepSeek
Qwen 2.5-Max	Qwen2.5	2025	Alibaba
Ryan	تكامل Takamol	2025	Takamol

Important Abbreviations

AI Artificial Intelligence
AR Augmented Reality
VR Virtual Reality
IoT Internet of Things
ML Machine Learning
SaaS Software as a Service
PaaS Platform as a Service
IaaS Infrastructure as a Service
RPA Robotic Process Automation
UAV Unmanned Aerial Vehicle (Drone)
BHIM Bharat Interface for Money

Facts Drive

- **QR codes** were invented by Denso Wave, a subsdiary of Toyota in 1994.
- The world's first robot restaurant opened in **Beijing** in 2015.
- School of artificial intelligence was established in Delhi in 2020.
- **Madhya Pradesh** is the first state in India to teach Artifical Intelligence in school education.
- **CAIR** (Central for Artificial Intelligence), Bangalore, is India's leading AI institute established in 1986.
- The Government of India has launched the Artificial Intelligence Portal in September 2020, whose website is indiaai.gov.in
- **CogX** is one of the world's leading conferences organised on AI, which is organised every year in London.

PYQs Oneliner

1. "Ensuring digital literacy for all" is a major feature of the **Digital India Program**. ***SSC CGL 2023***
2. **Japan** is leading the world in implementing AI to robots in manufacturing. ***UPSC 2023***
3. **BharatNet** is a government initiative that aims to enhance internet access in rural areas through the development of affordable broadband and mobile services. ***SSC CGL 2022***
4. The term **machine learning** is used for a machine's ability to learn and improve from experience without being explicitly programmed. ***UPSC 2022***

Practice Exercise

1. Which of the following is not a feature of UPI?
(a) Peer-to-peer money transfer
(b) Direct debit from a credit card
(c) Bill payments
(d) Linking multiple bank accounts in one app

2. Which organisation developed and manages the UPI system in India?
(a) Reserve Bank of India (RBI)
(b) National Payments Corporation of India (NPCI)
(c) Securities and Exchange Board of India (SEBI)
(d) Indian Banks' Association (IBA)

3. What does the term VPA stand for in the context of UPI transactions?
(a) Virtual Payment Account
(b) Verified Payment Address
(c) Virtual Private Account
(d) Virtual Payment Address

4. Which of the following actions cannot be performed using UPI?
(a) Requesting money from another user
(b) Paying utility bills
(c) Applying for a loan directly through UPI
(d) Making online purchases

5. What is the primary advantage of internet banking?
(a) Lower transaction fees
(b) Physical access to a bank branch
(c) Convenience of 24/7 access to services
(d) Limited number of transactions

6. Net banking is also known as *SSC CHSL 2023*
(a) e-commerce (b) e-banking
(c) e-process (d) e-transfer

7. Which of the following is a common feature of internet banking?
(a) Applying for a new passport
(b) Managing multiple bank accounts online
(c) Performing physical cash withdrawals
(d) Verifying identity documents in person

8. What is the most secure method of logging into an internet banking portal?
(a) Using a username and password
(b) Using two-factor authentication (2FA)
(c) Using only your email ID
(d) Using a PIN number only

9. What is the full form of NEFT with reference to e-banking services? *Delhi Police 2020*
(a) Native Electronic Funds Transfer
(b) National Electronic Funds Transformation
(c) National Electronic Funds Transfer
(d) National Elementary Funds Transfer

10. Which of the following statements about internet banking is false?
(a) You can transfer funds to other accounts *via* NEFT or RTGS.
(b) You can pay utility bills through internet banking.
(c) Internet banking requires a physical token for every transaction.
(d) Internet banking allows online fixed deposit creation.

11. Which of the following is a risk associated with internet banking?
(a) High transaction fees
(b) Lack of customer support
(c) Exposure to phishing attacks
(d) Limited banking services

12. Which banking service cannot be performed using internet banking?
(a) Fund transfer
(b) Cash deposit
(c) Checking account balance
(d) Bill payments

13. Which of the following is required to access internet banking?
(a) A bank account in a foreign country
(b) Internet connection and login credentials
(c) Physical access to a bank branch
(d) Paper checks

14. Which of the following is commonly used for secure online transactions in internet banking?
(a) CAPTCHA
(b) OTP (One-Time Password)
(c) CAPTCHA only
(d) Username only

15. What is the typical role of an IFSC code in internet banking?
(a) It identifies an individual's mobile number.
(b) It identifies a specific bank branch for electronic fund transfers.
(c) It verifies the identity of the account holder.
(d) It is used for email communications between banks.

16. Which type of banking transaction can you typically not perform through internet banking?
(a) Opening a savings account
(b) Downloading account statements
(c) Opening a recurring deposit
(d) Applying for a debit card replacement in person

17. What is the full form of IMPS with reference to e-banking services? *Delhi Police 2020*
(a) Immediate Paid Service
(b) Immediate Payment Service
(c) Immediate Payment Solution
(d) Instant Payment Service

18. What is an e-wallet?
(a) A physical wallet with digital features
(b) A digital system that stores users payment information for transactions
(c) A mobile app for social media networking
(d) A software for online banking

19. Which of the following is a popular e-wallet service?
(a) Google Drive (b) PayPal
(c) Microsoft Word (d) Skype

20. What is the primary benefit of using an e-wallet?
(a) Ability to withdraw cash from ATMs
(b) Secure, quick and convenient online payments
(c) Higher interest rates on savings
(d) Free access to premium content

21. Which of the following is typically not a feature of an e-wallet?
(a) Storing multiple payment methods
(b) Transferring funds to a bank account
(c) Applying for a loan
(d) Paying bills and making online purchases

22. What kind of information does an e-wallet usually store?
(a) Personal identification documents
(b) Bank account numbers, credit/debit card details and digital currency
(c) Social media account passwords
(d) Personal notes and memos

23. Which of the following is an example of a mobile e-wallet?
(a) Amazon Kindle (b) Google Pay
(c) Microsoft Excel (d) Adobe Reader

24. How can users ensure the security of their e-wallets?
(a) Sharing their e-wallet password with friends
(b) Regularly updating the app and using two-factor authentication (2FA)
(c) Storing their e-wallet credentials on a public computer
(d) Ignoring software updates

25. Which of the following can be used to load money into an e-wallet?
(a) International wire transfer only
(b) Debit card, credit card or linked bank account
(c) Cash only
(d) None of the above

26. Which of the following is a limitation of using an e-wallet?
(a) Inability to access cash directly
(b) Limited global reach
(c) Requirement to always be connected to the internet
(d) Higher transaction fees for every payment

27. 'Project Gutenberg' is primarily a digital library of ....
(a) E-reports
(b) E-periodicals
(c) E-books
(d) E-theses

28. What does QR in 'QR' code stand For? *SSC CHSL 2024*
(a) Quantum Read (b) Quick Resolution
(c) Query Response (d) Quick Response

29. What is the primary purpose of a QR code?
(a) To encrypt data
(b) To store digital signatures
(c) To provide a quick way to access information using a smartphone or scanner
(d) To create a digital identity

30. Which of the following is not a typical use of a QR code?
(a) Accessing websites (b) Storing contact information
(c) Storing phone numbers (d) Storing large files

31. How many types of data can a QR code encode?
(a) Numeric only
(b) Alphanumeric only
(c) Binary only
(d) Numeric, alphanumeric, binary and kanji

32. What is the first and most well-known cryptocurrency?
(a) Ethereum (b) Ripple
(c) Bitcoin (d) Litecoin

33. Which of the following best describes 'A method of storing and transmitting data in a particular coded form so that only those can read and process it for whom it is intended. It includes encoding and decoding of data? *RRB NTPC 2021*
(a) Block chain (b) Programming
(c) Cryptography (d) Cloud computing

34. Which of the following is a key feature of Bitcoin?
(a) Centralised control (b) Anonymous transactions
(c) Unlimited supply (d) Regularly issued new coins

35. What technology underpins most cryptocurrencies, including Bitcoin and Ethereum?
(a) Blockchain (b) Cloud computing
(c) Quantum computing (d) Internet of Things (IoT)

36. Which of the following is not a type of cloud computing service model?
(a) Infrastructure as a Service (IaaS)
(b) Platform as a Service (PaaS)
(c) Software as a Service (SaaS)
(d) Hardware as a Service (HaaS)

37. Windows 10 allows you to sync the files between your computer and the cloud, so that you can access the files from anywhere. *SSC Selection Post 2023*
(a) Google Drive (b) My Drive
(c) OneDrive (d) Class Drive

38. Which of the following is a primary benefit of using cloud computing?
(a) Increased hardware maintenance
(b) Fixed costs
(c) On-demand self-service
(d) Limited accessibility

39. Which cloud computing model provides the most control over the underlying infrastructure?
(a) Software as a Service (SaaS)
(b) Platform as a Service (PaaS)
(c) Infrastructure as a Service (IaaS)
(d) Function as a Service (FaaS)

40. Google Drive, SkyDrive and Dropbox are perfect examples of *RRB NTPC 2021*
(a) internet computing (b) virtual drives
(c) virtual reality (d) cloud storage services

41. Which of the following cloud services is commonly used for software development and testing?
(a) IaaS (b) SaaS
(c) PaaS (d) DaaS (Desktop as a Service)

42. What does e-commerce primarily refer to?
(a) Trading physical goods exclusively through traditional stores
(b) Conducting business transactions over the internet
(c) Using email to communicate with customers
(d) Managing customer relationships through in-person meetings

43. Which of the following is an example of Business-to-Consumer (B2C) e-commerce?
(a) A wholesaler selling goods to a retailer
(b) A company providing software development services to another business
(c) An online retailer like Amazon selling products to individual customers
(d) A customer purchasing products from a local farmer market

44. What is the primary difference between Business-to-Business (B2B) and Consumer-to-Consumer (C2C) e-commerce?
(a) B2B involves transactions between businesses, while C2C involves transactions between consumers
(b) B2B is focused on physical goods, while C2C is focused on digital goods
(c) B2B involves consumer feedback, while C2C does not
(d) B2B transactions are always conducted in-person, while C2C transactions are online

45. Which e-commerce model involves selling goods and services through online auctions?
(a) Business-to-Business (B2B)
(b) Consumer-to-Consumer (C2C)
(c) Business-to-Consumer (B2C)
(d) Consumer-to-Business (C2B)

46. What type of e-commerce platform typically allows businesses to list their products for sale on an online marketplace?
(a) Business-to-Consumer (B2C)
(b) Consumer-to-Consumer (C2C)
(c) Business-to-Business (B2B)
(d) Consumer-to-Business (C2B)

47. Which platform type is Amazon an example of?
(a) B2B (Business-to-Business)
(b) C2C (Consumer-to-Consumer)
(c) B2C (Business-to-Consumer)
(d) C2B (Consumer-to-Business)

48. What is the key characteristic of a Consumer-to-Business (C2B) e-commerce model?
(a) Consumers sell products to businesses
(b) Businesses sell products to other businesses
(c) Businesses buy products from other businesses
(d) Consumers exchange goods directly with each other

49. Which e-commerce platform type would an online auction site like eBay best represent?
(a) B2B (b) C2C (c) B2C (d) C2B

50. What is the primary goal of e-governance?
(a) To replace traditional government employees with technology
(b) To use technology to improve government processes and services
(c) To create more government regulations
(d) To privatise all government services

51. Which of the following is a key benefit of e-governance?
(a) Increased bureaucracy
(b) Enhanced transparency and accountability
(c) Higher administrative costs
(d) Reduced public participation

52. What is an example of a service provided through e-governance?
(a) Physical tax filing at government offices
(b) Online citizen complaint portals
(c) In-person voter registration
(d) Traditional paper-based government communications

53. What role does a Citizen Portal play in e-governance?
(a) It is used to conduct offline surveys
(b) It provides a platform for citizens to access government services and information online
(c) It handles all in-person government transactions
(d) It is a form of traditional media outreach

54. Which technology is commonly used to ensure the security and integrity of online government transactions?
(a) Blockchain (b) Cloud computing
(c) Artificial intelligence (d) Augmented reality

55. What does AI stand for?
(a) Automated Intelligence (b) Artificial Integration
(c) Artificial Intelligence (d) Advanced Information

56. Which of the following is a subfield of AI focused on building systems that can make decisions based on data?
(a) Robotics (b) Machine Learning
(c) Computer Vision (d) NLP

57. What is the primary function of a voice assistant?
(a) To perform physical tasks and actions
(b) To assist with voice-based interactions and provide information
(c) To manage financial transactions exclusively
(d) To replace traditional user interfaces such as keyboards and mice

58. Which of the following is a popular voice assistant developed by Amazon?
(a) Siri (b) Google Assistant
(c) Cortana (d) Alexa

59. Which company developed the voice assistant named Siri?
(a) Microsoft (b) Apple
(c) Google (d) Amazon

60. Which of the following is a common application of voice assistants in smart homes?
(a) Managing temperature settings through voice commands
(b) Diagnosing hardware issues
(c) Performing advanced data analysis
(d) Building software applications

61. What is the primary purpose of a robot in industrial settings?
(a) To entertain
(b) To perform repetitive and precise tasks
(c) To conduct scientific research
(d) To provide medical diagnostics

62. What is the main difference between Virtual Reality (VR) and Augmented Reality (AR)?
(a) VR creates a fully immersive digital environment, while AR overlays digital information onto the real world
(b) VR uses physical objects, while AR relies on virtual objects
(c) VR is used for training, while AR is used for entertainment
(d) VR requires a smartphone, while AR requires a specialized headset

63. What is the full form of BHIM? *CPCT 2024*
(a) Balanced Interface for Money
(b) Bharat Internet for Money
(c) Bharat Interface for Multiuse
(d) Bharat Interface for Money

64. What kind of technology is the most frequently used to manage and digitise e-land records? *SSC CHSL 2024*
(a) Blockchain
(b) Augumented Reality (AR)
(c) Geographical Information System (GIS)
(d) Virtual Reality (VR)

65. What is the main sense organ that Virtual Reality displays are aiming for? *SSC CHSL 2024*
(a) Smell (b) Taste
(c) Vision (d) Touch

Answers

1.	(b)	2.	(b)	3.	(d)	4.	(c)	5.	(c)	6.	(b)	7.	(b)	8.	(b)	9.	(c)	10.	(c)
11.	(c)	12.	(b)	13.	(b)	14.	(b)	15.	(b)	16.	(d)	17.	(b)	18.	(b)	19.	(b)	20.	(b)
21.	(c)	22.	(b)	23.	(b)	24.	(b)	25.	(b)	26.	(a)	27.	(c)	28.	(d)	29.	(c)	30.	(d)
31.	(d)	32.	(c)	33.	(c)	34.	(b)	35.	(a)	36.	(d)	37.	(c)	38.	(c)	39.	(c)	40.	(d)
41.	(c)	42.	(b)	43.	(c)	44.	(a)	45.	(b)	46.	(a)	47.	(c)	48.	(a)	49.	(b)	50.	(b)
51.	(b)	52.	(b)	53.	(b)	54.	(a)	55.	(c)	56.	(b)	57.	(b)	58.	(d)	59.	(b)	60.	(a)
61.	(b)	62.	(a)	63.	(d)	64.	(c)	65.	(c)										

Appendices

- Computer Personalities
- Filename Extensions
- Computer Glossary

Computer Personalities

1. Charles Babbage

- Charles Babbage was born in 1791 in London.
- He was a British mathematician, inventor, and mechanical engineer.
- He is known as the **Father of Computer** for designing the first mechanical computer, the Analytical Engine.
- He conceptualized the Difference Engine, a device to automate mathematical calculations.
- His designs laid the groundwork for modern computing.

2. Ada Lovelace

- Ada Lovelace born in 1815, was an English mathematician and writer.
- She collaborated with Charles Babbage on the Analytical Engine.
- She wrote the first algorithm intended for machine execution, making her the world's **first computer programmer**.

3. Alan Turing

- Alan Turing was a British mathematician and computer scientist.
- Widely regarded as the **father of modern computing** and **artificial intelligence**.
- He developed the concept of the Turing machine, a theoretical framework for modern computing.

4. John von Neumann

- John von Neumann was a Hungarian-American mathematician, physicist, and computer scientist.He proposed the **von Neumann architecture**, the basis for most computers today.
- He played a vital role in the development of early computers, like the EDVAC.

5. Howard Aiken

- Howard Aiken was an American mathematician and computer scientist.
- He designed the Harvard Mark I, one of the earliest automatic digital computers.
- Pioneered advancements in large-scale computing and mechanical calculation.

6. Bill Gates

- Bill Gates, born in 1955 Seattle, Washington is an American business man, software developer, and philanthropist.
- Known as the **co-founder of Microsoft Corporation**, the world's largest software company.
- Microsoft revolutionized personal computing with Windows OS.
- Played a key role in making software accessible and user-friendly for businesses and households.

7. Steve Jobs

- Steve Jobs was born in 1955 in San Francisco, USA.
- He was an American entrepreneur, inventor, and **co-founder of Apple Inc.**
- Known for pioneering products like the iPhone, iPod, and Mac computers.
- Revolutionized the design and functionality of personal electronics.

8. Tim Berners-Lee

- Tim Berners-Lee is a British computer scientist born in 1955 in London.
- He is best known for inventing the **World Wide Web** in 1989.
- He also created the first web browser and the HTML and HTTP protocols.
- He is the director of World Wide Web Consortium (W3C).

9. Linus Torvalds

- Linus Torvalds is a Finnish-American software engineer best known for creating the **linux operating system**, an open-source software platform.
- His contributions are foundational for servers, mobile devices, and supercomputers.
- Promoted collaboration in the tech community through open-source development.

10. Mark Zuckerberg

- Mark Zuckerberg, born in 1984 in New York City, USA, is an American entrepreneur and software developer.
- He best known as the **founder of Facebook**, one of the world's largest social media platforms.
- Innovated how people connect, communicate, and share content online.
- Facebook (now known as Meta Platforms Inc.) acquired Instagram in 2012 and WhatsApp in 2014.

11. Seymour Cray

- Seymour Cray was born in 1925 in the USA.
- He was an American electrical engineer and computer scientist who revolutionized the field of high-performance computing.
- He is known as the **father of Supercomputing** for developing high-speed computers.
- He founded Cray Research and designed the Cray-1, one of the fastest computers of its time.

12. Douglas Engelbart

- Douglas Engelbart born in 1925 in Portland, was an American engineer and inventor.
- He invented the first computer mouse and pioneered Graphical User Interfaces (GUIs).
- His ideas revolutionized human-computer interaction.

13. Christopher Latham Sholes

- Christopher Latham Sholes was an American inventor, engineer, and journalist, best known as the creator of the **QWERTY keyboard layout** and one of the inventors of the modern typewriter.
- He is also known as the "Father of Typewriter".

14. Dennis Ritchie

- Dennis Ritchie was a pioneering computer scientist best known as the **creator of the C programming language**.
- He also played a pivotal role in developing the **UNIX** operating system.
- His contributions influenced countless programming languages and systems.

15. Bjarne Stroustrup

- Bjarne Stroustrup is a renowned computer scientist.
- He is best known as the creator of the C++ programming language, which introduced object-oriented programming.
- Enhanced the capabilities of C for more complex applications.
- C++ remains widely used in software development, gaming, and system programming.

16. Anita Borg

- Anita Borg was a visionary computer scientist and advocate for women in technology.
- She is best known for her work in promoting diversity and gender equality in the field of computing.
- She founded the Institute for Women and Technology (now AnitaB.org) in 1997.

17. Larry Page & Sergey Brin

- Larry Page and Sergey Brin are the co-founders of Google, one of the world's most influential technology companies.
- They created the PageRank algorithm that powers Google Search.
- Expanded Google into diverse areas like AI, cloud computing, and Android.
- The parent organization of Google Company is now Alphabet Inc.

18. Sabeer Bhatia

- Sabeer Bhatia is an Indian-American entrepreneur, born in 1968 in Chandigarh city, India.
- He is best known as the **co-founder of Hotmail**, one of the world's first web-based email services.
- He pioneered the concept of free email services accessible globally.
- He sold Hotmail to Microsoft in 1997.

19. Azim Premji

- Azim Premji is an Indian business man, philanthropist, and the former chairman of Wipro Limited, one of India's largest IT and software companies.
- His father Hashim Premji founded the Wipro Company in 1945.
- He transformed Wipro into a global IT services leader.
- He is also known as the "Czar of the Indian IT Industry."

20. N.R. Narayana Murthy

- N.R. Narayana Murthy, is an Indian entrepreneur and the **co-founder of Infosys**, a leading IT services company in India.
- He played a key role in India's emergence as a global IT hub.
- Currently the headquarters of Infosys Company is located in Bangalore.

21. Vijay Bhatkar

- Dr. Vijay Bhatkar is a well-known Indian computer scientist, technologist, and educationist.
- He is best known as the architect of India's first supercomputer, the PARAM series.
- He played a crucial role in advancing India's computational research capabilities.
- He is also known as the **father of indian supercomputers.**

22. Michael Dell

- Michael Dell is an American entrepreneur, philanthropist, and the founder of Dell Technologies, one of the world's largest technology companies.
- Dell Company is the leading sellers of personal computers and laptops in the world.
- Focused on customizable computers tailored to customer needs.

23. Sundar Pichai

- Sundar Pichai, born on June 10, 1972, in Madurai, Tamil Nadu, India, is the **CEO of Alphabet Inc. (Google).**
- He played a major role in the success of Chrome, Android, and Google AI initiatives.

24. Satya Nadella

- Satya Nadella was born in 1967 in Hyderabad city of India.
- He is an Indian-American business executive and the Chairman and **CEO of Microsoft.**

Filename Extensions

Filename Extensions in Windows

aac, adt, adts	Windows audio file
accdb	Microsoft Access database file
aif, aifc, aiff	Audio Interchange File format file
bin	Binary compressed file
bmp	Bitmap file
dll	Dynamic Link Library file
docm	Microsoft Word macro-enabled document
docx	Microsoft Word document
dotx	Microsoft Word template
exe	Executable program file
flv	Flash-compatible video file
gif	Graphics Interchange Format file
jpeg	Joint Photographic Experts Group photo file
mpeg	Moving Picture Experts Group movie file
mp3	MPEG layer 3 audio file
mp4	MPEG 4 video
m4a	MPEG-4 audio file
msi	Microsoft installer file
mui	Multilingual User Interface file
mdb	Microsoft Access database
mid, midi	Musical Instrument Digital Interface file
mpeg	Moving Picture Experts Group movie file
mui	Multilingual User Interface file
mac	MacPaint
map	Web page image map
mov or.QT	QuickTime Audio/Video
mtb or.mtw	MiniTab
pdf	Portable Document Format file
png	Portable Network Graphics file
potx	Microsoft Power Point template
ppsx	Microsoft PowerPoint slideshow
ppt	Microsoft PowerPoint format
pptx	Microsoft PowerPoint presentation
psd	Adobe Photoshop file
pub	Microsoft Publisher file
rar	Roshal Archive compressed file
rtf	Rich Text Format file
sldx	Microsoft PowerPoint slide
swf	Shockwave Flash file,
tif, tiff	Tagged Image Format file
tmp	Temporary Data file
txt	Unformatted Text file
vob	Video Object file
vsdx	Microsoft Visio Drawing file
vstx	Microsoft Visio template
wav	Wave audio file
wpd, wp5	WordPerfect document
wbk	Microsoft Word backup document
wks	Microsoft Works file
wma	Windows Media Audio file
wmd	Windows Media Download file
wmv	Windows Media Video file
xlsx	Microsoft Excel workbook
xltx	Microsoft Excel template
xps	XML-based document
zip	Compressed file

Some more file Extensions

Audio File Formats

cda	CD audio track file
wpl	Windows Media Player playlist

Compressed File Extensions

7z-7-Zip	Compressed file
pkg	Package file
rpm	Red Hat Package Manager
tar.gz	Tarball compressed file
zZ	Compressed file

Disc and Media File Extensions

dmg	macOS X disk image
iso	ISO disc image
toast	Toast disc image
vcd	Virtual CD

Data and Database File Extensions

csv	Comma Separated Value file
dat	Data file
db or dbf	Database file
log	Log file
sav	Save file
sql	SQL database file
tar	Linux / Unix tarball file archive
xml	XML file

Executable File Extensions

apk	Android package file
bat	Batch file
cgi or pl	Perlscript file
com	MS-DOS command file
gadget	Windows gadget
jar	Java Archive file
msi	Windows Installer package
wsf	Windows Script File

Font File Extensions

otf	Open type font file
ttf	True type font file
fnt	Windows font file
fon	Generic font file

Image File Formats by File Extension

ai	Adobe Illustrator file
ico	Icon file
ps	PostScript file
psd	PSD image
svg	Scalable Vector Graphics file

Internet-Related File Extensions

jsp	Java Server Page file
part	Partially downloaded file
php	PHP file
py	Python file
rss	RSS file
xhtml	XHTML file
asp and aspx	Active Server Page file
cer	Internet security certificate
cfm	ColdFusion Markup file
css	Cascading Style Sheet file
js	JavaScript file

System Related File Formats and File Extensions

drv	Device driver file
ico	Icon file
ini	Initialization file
ink	Windows shortcut the
sys	Windows system file
tmp	Temporary file
bak	Backup file
cab	Windows Cabinet file
cfg	Configuration file
cpl	Windows Control panel file
cur	Windows cursor file
dmp	Dump file

File Extension in Domains

Generic Top-level Domains (gTLD)

.com	It is for commercial sites.
.net	It is for networks.
.info	It is for information platforms.
.biz	It is for businesses.
.org	It is for organizations.

Sponsored Top-level Domains (sTLD)

.edu	It is for higher educational institutions.
.gov	It is for United States governmental agencies.
.cat	It is for Catalan linguistic and cultural community.
.travel	It is for travel industry businesses.
.museum	It is for museum organizations.

Country Code Top-level Domains (ccTLD)

.In	The .in domain name extension is for the country of India.
.Us	.us is the Internet country code top-level domain for the United States.
.De	The .de domain name extension is for the country of Germany.
.Uk	The .uk domain name extension is for the United Kindom.
.Cn	The .cn domain name extension is for the country of China.

Computer Glossary

A

Active Cell Currently selected cell in a spreadsheet, which can be identified by a bold outline that surrounds the cells.

Active Window Currently focused window in the current window manager.

Alignment An arrangement or a position of text in a straight line or in parallel lines.

Algorithm Procedure for accomplishing some tasks which given an initial state, will terminate in a defined end-state.

Alphanumeric A character set that contains letters, digits and other special characters such as @, $, +, *, %, etc.

Analog Computer A computer that operates on data which is in the form of continuous variable physical quantities.

Android LINUX based operating system designed primarily for touchscreen mobile devices such as smartphones and tablet computers.

Antivirus Software Consists of computer programs that attempt to identify threats and eliminate computer viruses and other malicious softwares (malware).

Application Software Employs the capabilities of a computer directly to a task that the user wishes to perform.

Arithmetic Logic Unit (ALU) Capable of calculating the results of a wide variety of basic arithmetical and logical computations.

Artificial Intelligence Enables computers and machines to simulate human intelligence and problem solving capabilities.

Assembler Translates mnemonic statement into executable instruction.

Authentication Any process by which a system varifies the identity of the user who wishes to access it.

Auxiliary Memory Non-volatile memory which is not directly accessible by CPU.

B

Backup A copy of a file or other item of data made, in case the original is lost and damaged.

Bandwidth The maximum amount of data that can travel in a communication path in a given time, measured in bits per second (bps).

Bar Code Machine-readable representation of information in a visual format on a surface.

Basic Input Output System (BIOS) Provides an abstraction layer for the hardware, i.e. a consistent way for application programs and operating system to interact with input/output devices.

Batch Processing Operating system, that process previously collected jobs in a single batch.

Biometric Device A device that identifies persons seeking access to a computing system by determining their physical characteristics through fingerprints, voice recognition, retina pattern, etc.

Bit Most basic information unit used in computing and information theory.

Blog A discussion or informational site published on the World Wide Web.

Bluetooth Permits a wireless exchange of information between computers, cell phones and other electronic devices.

Browser A special software that enables users to read/view Web pages and jump from one Web page to another.

Bug An error, flaw, failure or fault in a computer program or system that produces an incorrect or unexpected result.

Bus A circuit that provides a communication path between two or more devices of a digital computer system.

Byte Commonly used as a unit of storage measurement in computers, regardless the type of data being stored.

C

Cache Memory Very high speed memory that is placed between the CPU and main memory.

CD-R A blank compact disc which can be recorded at once only.

CD-RW A blank compact disc that can be recorded, erased and written many times.

Cell A box in a spreadsheet, in which you can enter a single piece of data.

Central Processing Unit (CPU) Performs the actual processing of data and also known as the brain of computer.

Channel A medium for transferring information which is also called a line or circuit.

Chart Graphical and pictorial representation of worksheet data.

Chip A tiny wafer of silicon containing small electric circuits that can store millions of bits of information.

Client Computer A computer that retrieves information or uses resources provided by the server or main computer.

Client-Server Network architecture which separates the client from the server.

Clipboard A temporary storage area where material out or copied from a file is kept for pasting into another file.

ClipArt Simple pictures and symbols made available for computer users to add to their documents.

Command Line Interface (CLI) A method of interacting with a computer by giving it lines of textual commands (i.e., a sequence of characters) from the keyboard.

Communication The transmission of data from one computer to another or from one device to another.

Compiler A computer program that translates a series of instructions from high level language to machine language.

Computer Aided Design (CAD) A computer software used by architects, engineers, artists and others to create precision drawings or technical illustrations.

Computer Graphics Visual presentations on a computer screen.

Computer Network A system for communication among two or more computers.

Computer Worm A self-replicating computer program, similar to a computer virus.

Cookie A packet of information that travels between a browser and the Web server.

Control Unit The part of a CPU that directs its operation.

Cursor A movable indicator on a computer screen identifying the point that will be affected by input from the user.

Cut To remove an object from a document.

D

Data A collection of facts and figures which are not in directly usable form.

Database A collection of data files integrated and organised into a single comprehensive file system which is arranged to minimise duplication of data.

DBMS A collection of programs that enable you to store, modify and extract information from a database.

Debugging A methodical process of finding and reducing the number of bugs, or defects, in a computer program or a piece of electronic hardware, thus making it behave as expected.

Demodulation The process is used at the receivers end to recover the original signal coming from the sender end in modulating form.

Desktop The area of a display screen where images, windows, icons and other graphical items appear.

Device Driver (often called a driver) Enables another program, typically, an operating system to interact with a hardware device.

Digital Computer A computer that operates with numbers expressed directly as digits.

Direct Access The capability of the computer equipment to obtain data from a storage device, or to enter data into a storage device.

Directory An entity in a file system which contains a group of files and other directories.

Disk Drive A device which allows a computer to read from and write on to computer disks.

Disk Operating System (DOS) An operating system which contains the disk oriented commands and uses disk devices for permanent storage.

Display Unit A device with a screen that displays characters or graphics representing data.

Domain Name A unique name that identifies a particular website and represents the name of the server where the Web pages reside.

Dot Pitch A measurement that indicates the diagonal distance between like-colored phosphor dots on a display screen.

Dots Per Inch (DPI) The number of dots in one inch line.

Download Act of transmitting data from a remote computer on the Internet or other network to one's own computer.

E

E-Commerce Where buying and selling of product or services is conducted over electronic systems such as the Internet.

Editing The process of changing information by inserting, deleting, replacing, rearranging and reformation.

EPROM A type of computer memory chip that retains its data when its power supply is switched OFF.

EEPROM Can be erased by exposing it to an electrical charge.

E-mail A method of composing, sending, storing and receiving messages over electronic communication systems.

Ethernet A modern technique which is used to connect local computers in LAN.

Exe (.exe) Filename extension denoting an executable file (a program) in the DOS, MS-Windows.

Execution Time Total time taken by computer to process some program or instruction.

Extranet A technology that permits the users of one organisation's intranet to enter portions of another organisation's intranet in order to conduct business transactions.

F

Fiber Optics Made up of glass or fiber through which data can be transferred from one place to another.

File A collection of information stored electronically and treated as a unit by a computer.

File Extension A suffix to the name of a computer file applied to indicate the encoding of its contents or usage.

File Manager An operating system utility that provides a user interface to work with file systems.

File Server A computer on a network that stores the programs and data files shared by the users of the network.

Firewall A security system usually consisting of hardware and software that prevents unauthorised persons from accessing certain parts of a program database or network.

Flash Memory Non-volatile computer storage chip that can be electrically erased and reprogrammed.

Font A fixed typeface of a particular size and style.

Formula An expression which calculates the value of a cell.

Format To set margins, tabs, font or line spacing in layout of a document.

Freeware A form of software distribution where the author retains copyright of the software but makes the program available to others at no cost.

FTP Used to transfer files from one place to another on Internet.

Function Predefined formula that performs calculations using specific values in a particular order.

G

Gadget A device that has a specific function in addition usually has small dimensions.

Gigabyte A unit of information or computer storage equal to approximately one billion bytes.

GigaHertz (GHz) A measurement used to identify the speed of the central processing unit.

Gopher A protocol used for locating and transferring information on the Internet.

Graphic Interchange Format (GIF) A simple file format for pictures and photographs, that are compressed so they can be sent quickly.

Graphic Tablet An input device which is used to create images, etc.

Graphical User Interface (GUI) A method of interacting with a computer through a metaphor of direct manipulating of graphical images and widgets in addition to text.

H

Hard Copy Permanent output provided by computer.

Hard Disk Non-volatile data storage device that stores data on a magnetic surface layered onto disk platters.

Hardware The mechanical, magnetic, electronic and electrical components that comprise a computer system such as CPU, monitor, keyboard, mouse, etc.

Home Page Refers to the Web page that identifies a website and contains the hyperlink to other Web page in the website.

Hyperlink An image or portion of text on a Web page that is linked to another Web page.

Hybrid Computer These computers are made by taking the best features of the analog computer and digital computer.

HyperText Markup Language (HTML) Used to write Web page and for designing.

HyperText Transfer Protocol (HTTP) Used on the world wide web for moving hypertext files across the Internet.

I

Icon A symbol (such as picture or a folder) that represents a certain function on your computer.

Impact Printers These printers transfer the image onto paper through a printing mechanism that strikes the paper called ribbon.

Information The summarization of data according to a certain pre-defined purpose.

Input Device These devices are used to put data and instructions in computer.

Instruction A command or order given to a computer to perform a task.

Integrated Circuits Multiple electronic components combined on a silicon chip.

Interface A device or program that helps a user to communicate with a computer.

Interpreter A program that converts and executes the source code into machine code line by line.

Internet Worldwide, publicly accessible system of interconnected computer networks that transmit data by packet switching using the standard Internet protocol.

Internet Surfing To search something on Internet.

Internet Protocol (IP) **Address** These addresses are assigned to each and every computer on a TCP/IP network.

Internet Service Provider (ISP) A business organisation that offers users to access the Internet and related services.

Joint Photographic Experts Group (JPEG) Commonly used method of lossy compression for digital images particularly produced by digital photography.

Joystick A computer peripheral or general control device consisting of a handheld stick that pivots about one end and transmits its angle in two or three dimensions to a computer.

Kernel The fundamental part of an operating system, that resides in memory at all times.

Keyboard Standard input device attached to all computers for input text.

Key-Stroke To press a button in keyboard.

Kilobyte A unit of information or computer storage equal to 1024 bytes.

Landscape A printer feature, generally controlled by software, which rotates the output image by 90° to print across the length rather than the width of the paper.

Laptop A small, lightweight and portable battery-powered computer that can fit onto your lap.

Laser Printer A computer-driven photocopier that creates an original image of the text or graphics from the output of the computer onto a paper.

Light Pen A light sensitive style for forming graphics by touching coordinates on a display screen, thereby seeming to draw directly on the screen.

Link A communication path between two nodes or channels.

LINUX An open source operating system, meaning that the source code of the operating system is freely available to the public.

Local Area Network (LAN) In LAN, the connected computers are geographically in the same building or within a smaller area.

MAC Address Hardware identification number that uniquely identifies each device on a network.

Main Memory A volatile and speedy memory that is divided into two parts RAM and ROM.

Malware A software that disrupts normal computer functions or sends a users personal data without the users authorisation.

Mass Storage Referred to storage where large volumes of backup/data is stored.

Memory Temporary storage for information, including applications and documents.

Menu The option list in some program or in software.

Menu Bar The horizontal strip across the top of an application's window.

Merge Combining two or more files into a single file.

Microcomputer A microprocessor-based computer, consisting of a CPU, internal semiconductor memory, input and output sections.

Microprocessor A complete Central Processing Unit (CPU) contained on a single silicon chip.

MIDI (Music Instrument Digital Interface) Allows a computer to store and replay a musical instrument's output.

Minimize Refers to reducing a window to an icon, or a label at the bottom of the screen, allowing another window to be viewed.

Mobile Apps Software programs designed specifically for mobile devices such as smartphones and tablets.

Mobile Wallet A way to carry your credit card or debit card information in a digital form on your mobile device.

Modem (Modulator-Demodulator) Refers to specific equipment that provides a means of communication between two computer systems over conventional telephone lines.

Modulation The conversion of digital signals into analog signals.

Monitor The visual readout device of a computer system.

Motherboard Main circuit board of a micro computer that contains the CPU, BIOS, memory, mass storage interfaces, serial and parallel ports, expansion slots and all the controllers.

Mouse A manually operated input device for moving or entering positional information and other data or commands by accessing (pointing to) images on a monitor.

Multimedia Software programs that combine text and graphics with sound, video and animation.

Multitasking Simultaneously work with several programs or interrelated tasks that share memories, codes, buffers and files.

Multithreading An operating system that allows multiple functions from the same application packages.

Multiuser The term describing the capability of a computer system to be operated at more than one terminal at the same time.

Network A group of two or more computers linked together in a way that they can share data and resources.

Network Interface Card (NIC) Part of the computer that allows it to talk to other computers a network protocol like TCP/IP.

Netiquette As a set of rules for acceptable online behaviour.

Node The endpoint of a network branch or the junction of two or more branches.

Non-Impact Printer In this printer, chemical and inkjet technique is used.

Non-Volatile Memory A memory where stored data remains undisturbed by the removal of electrical power.

Notebook A portable computer, that can fit into a briefcase.

Offline Refers to the state in which a computer is temporarily or permanently unable to communicate with another computer.

Online Refers to the state of being connected to the networked computer system or the Internet.

Operating System A set of instructions that tell a computer how to operate when it is turned ON.

Open Source Software Any computer software that is distributed with its source code available for modification.

Output Data that come out of a computer device.

Peripheral Refers to the hardware devices external to a computer.

Personal Computer (PC) A single-user computer containing a Central Processing Unit (CPU) and one or more memory circuits.

Pixels The smallest element (a dot) on a display screen.

Port Interconnects the computer's input and/or output terminals to an appropriate source and/or destination.

Portrait A term that designates the position of conventional printing across the width of a page.

Printer A mechanical device for printing a computer's output on paper.

Processor A logic circuitry that responds to and process the basic instructions that drive a computer.

Proprietary Software Owned by an individual or a company.

Program A set of instructions to perform a specific task.

Protocol A set of rules that defines exactly how information is to be exchanged between two systems over Internet.

QWERTY Standard computer keyboard, with the character Q, W, E, R, T and Y on the top row of letters.

Random Access Memory (RAM) A volatile, semiconductor storage structure that accesses temporary data with a random or direct accessing method.

Read Only Memory (ROM) A semiconductor memory whose data cannot be erased, or overwritten.

Register A temporary storage unit for quick, direct accessibility of a small amount of data for processing.

Scanner An electronic device that uses light-sensing equipment to scan paper images such as text, photos.

Search Engine Software that makes it possible to look for and retrieve information on the Internet, particularly the Web.

Secondary Memory Permanent and non-volatile memory that remains undisturbed by the removal of electrical signals.

Sector A section of a recording track on a magnetic disk.

Sequential Access To read some data in sequential manner.

Server A computer that shares its resources and information with other computers on a network.

Shareware A software that is not free but is available for a free trial period.

Simplex Transmission of data in one direction only.

Software The set of computer programs, procedures and associated documentation related to the effective operation.

Social network A way of making internet based connections.

Spam Irrelevant or unsolicited messages sent over Internet, typically to large number of users, for the purpose of advertising, phishing, spreading malwares, etc.

Spreadsheet Software that allows one to calculate numbers in a format that is similar to pages in a conventional ledger.

Static RAM A type of RAM, that contains its contents only whenever current supply is ON.

System Software A software that supervises, sequences and coordinates programs.

TCP/IP A large grouping of programs and standards that govern how information moves around the Internet.

Template A pre-established format for a document, stored in a computer.

Text Group of words, numbers and symbols.

Time Sharing Refers to the allocation of computer resources in a time dependent fashion to run several programs simultaneously.

Topology The structure of the network including physical connection such as wiring schemes and logical interactions between network devices.

Ubuntu An open source operating system based on the Debian GNU/Linux distribution.

Undo A feature of a computer program that allows a user to cancel or reverse the last command executed.

Uniform Resource Locator (URL) The specific Internet address for a resource such as an individual or an organization.

UNIX An operating system developed by AT & T that it allows one server to serve many different end users at one time.

Upload The processes of transferring information from a computer to a website (or other remote location on a network).

UPS An electrical power supply that includes a battery to provide enough power to a computer during an outage to back-up data and properly shut down.

User-Friendly Refers to anything that makes it easier for novices to use a computer.

Video Disc A disc on which movies, television programs, etc. are recorded in order to be watched on a computer or television screen.

Video Display Terminal A device for displaying input signals as characters on a screen, typically a monitor.

Video Teleconferencing A remote 'face-to-face chat,' when two or more people using a webcam and an Internet telephone connection chat online.

Virus Malicious act to spread from one computer to another by attaching itself to other programs.

Volatile Memory A memory whose contents are irretrievably lost when power is removed.

WAN A network of a large number of computers that cover a large area like a city, state or even a whole country.

Webcam A video camera/computer setup that takes live images and sends them to a Web browser.

Web Browser An application or a program which is used to view and interact with Web pages and to navigate between them.

Website A collection of Web pages or hyperlinked Web page, which owned by an individual, company or organization.

Window A portion of a computer display used in a graphical interface that enables users to select commands by pointing to illustrations or symbols with a mouse.

Word Processing A program that enables to compose a document within computer system with edit, store, format and print the specific document or insert, delete, copy and include text/graphics from other files.

World Wide Web (WWW) A network of servers on the Internet that use hypertext-linked databases and files.

Workstation The work area and/or equipment used for computer operations, including Computer Aided Design (CAD).

X-Y Plotter A computer-driven printing mechanism that draws coordinate points in graph form.

Zoom The enlarging or reducing an image displayed on a computer process of proportionately monitor.

V

W

Webcam: A video camera connected to a computer, that captures live images and sends them to a Web browser.

X

Z

Social Network: [illegible] Internet-based communities.

T

U

